FROM ᴛʜᴇ ASHES

FROM THE ASHES

A SPIRITUAL RESPONSE
TO THE ATTACK ON AMERICA

EXPERIENCE, STRENGTH, AND HOPE

FROM SPIRITUAL LEADERS

AND EXTRAORDINARY CITIZENS

Collected by the Editors of Beliefnet

RODALE

Cover Designer: Joanna Williams
Interior Designer: Richard Kershner
Cover Photographer: Matthew McDermott/Corbis Sygma

Distributed to the book trade by St. Martin's Press

2   4   6   8   10   9   7   5   3   hardcover

Visit us on the Web at www.rodalestore.com, or call us toll-free at (800) 848-4735.
Visit Beliefnet on the Web at www.beliefnet.com.

RODALE

WE **INSPIRE** AND **ENABLE** PEOPLE TO IMPROVE
THEIR LIVES AND THE WORLD AROUND THEM

CONTENTS

INTRODUCTION

By Steven Waldman

A few days after the attack, I came home from my son's 5th birthday party at a zoo in Brooklyn. The kids watched sea lions, fed cows, and petted rabbits while the parents talked about who they knew who had died that week.

We've moved ahead with the mundane parts of life— birthday parties, laundry, homework—as we try to make sense of the rest.

And we're better at some parts of this than others. Though the terrorists destroyed three magnificent buildings, we do at least know how to construct new ones. Though we are presented with enormous military challenges, we're actually pretty good at finding and punishing criminals. Though the economy is battered, we can regenerate financially.

The spiritual challenges seem more daunting. No retired-general-turned-TV commentator will be able to explain to families why their loved ones died or, to survivors, why they didn't. No NATO alliance will help us balance our determination to be pious with our desire for revenge. And no cabinet-level security czar will figure out why God allowed his children to be slaughtered.

For these questions, we turn—with some desperation—to spiritual leaders. We are in as much need of great clergy as great statesmen and great generals. And at times like this, we can all benefit from hearing a wide variety of voices. That is why we at Beliefnet, the leading multifaith Web site on religion and spirituality, teamed up with Rodale Inc. to collect the most eloquent and wise voices across the faith spectrum.

We were also awed by the wisdom of ordinary Americans. At the bottom of each page, you'll find the breathtaking reactions from the Beliefnet users who flooded the site during the minutes and days after September 11. By the hundreds of thousands, they gathered—friends and strangers, of every conceivable spiritual tradition—to pray, ask frustrated questions, lash out, search for online friends who lived in New York City, and just to be with each other.

Each message board post is time stamped, so reading them in sequence gives a gripping sense of how this event was being processed around the world. One can palpably feel each person's struggle to restrain their fury and summon their better angels. Their messages show not only the power of the online community but the power of community, period.

As a group, these essays and Beliefnet user contributions confront at least four massive spiritual challenges.

First, inside every belief system—and every human personality—are conflicting impulses. Right now, these impulses are at war. Do Christians focus on Jesus' radical pacifism or his fire for justice? Do Jews embrace *tikkun olam* (repairing the world) or seek an eye for an eye? How do Buddhists balance their desire for detachment with their duty to be compassionate? And how do Muslims focus on Islam's message of peace at a time that some Muslims are invoking Allah to massacre thousands? And for those who are spiritually minded but not closely affiliated with a religion or house of worship, how do they square their general sense that "things happen for a reason" with their conviction that this was utterly senseless? In other words, religion does not provide an answer to the difficult questions—it provides *many* answers, some contradictory.

Second, we face the challenge of understanding Islam, the world's second largest religion. America has long been a pluralistic society, a fact especially evident in New York. Muslims, Buddhists, and Hindus died in the World Trade Center alongside Christians and Jews. But most people who aren't Muslim (and even some who are) are ignorant about Islam. And let's be honest: If you don't know any better, blaming this religion is not a completely irrational reaction. If all you've heard about Islam is that the terrorists destroyed the World Trade Center as part of a jihad (holy war), that another Muslim terrorist group is called "Army of God," and that most repressive dictators in the Middle East are Muslim, it makes some sense that you'd point fingers at Islam.

That is, *if* you don't know about the true teachings of Islam. Right now, understanding Islam has moved from being the province of comparative religion scholars to a requirement for every American. Muslims have an obligation to separate themselves from extremists, but we non-Muslims have a moral obligation to eliminate our own ignorance. The backlash against innocent American Muslims began within hours after the attacks. Even on Beliefnet, a Web site that prides itself for hosting breathtakingly tolerant discussions, there was grotesque anti-Muslim sentiment. Talk about "killing all Muslims," "burning down Mosques," and other Hitlerian rhetoric came from some quarters.

When we look back at World War II, proud of how our country responded, and ask if there were any regrets, we seldom point to any gruesome battlefield tactics. We point to the internment of Japanese-Americans. Forty years from now, will we praise our soldiers but have to apologize for how we treated Muslims and Arabs?

The third spiritual challenge is figuring out how to make something good come of this. We have already seen so much courageous behavior—incredible heroism, patriotism, and generosity. Kindnesses proliferate. We have a new type of hero and celebrity. And those of us who are safe spend more time counting our blessings.

But, not to be too cynical, this reaction always happens after disasters—whether it's a flood or a relative suddenly dying of a heart attack. The real challenge is to make it last.

Could this lead to a sort of Gratitude Revolution? Could this be an event so jarring that it permanently changes the way we approach our lives and each other? Could this make us more empathetic and generous or enable us to keep our focus on the truly important matters of life instead of the trivial?

Many parents have wrestled with this question as they've talked to their children about what happened. My wife and I listened carefully to all the child psychologists telling us how to keep our children, ages 5 and 7, from being traumatized. And we followed those directions, answering their questions honestly but shielding them as much as possible from what happened. We kept the TV off when they were around or awake, made it clear that they were perfectly safe and that the bad guys would be captured.

But there came a moment when I wondered if my kids weren't *too* detached. We were walking to the local fire station, which lost 11 of its 20 firefighters. We were going to give them some drawings the kids had made and light a candle. The candle my wife selected was one that one of the boys had made some time earlier, embellished with red heart shapes. When my son saw that we had chosen his candle, he started complaining. "Why are you giving *that* away? Don't give away such a precious thing!" As we approached the fire station, now a sacred shrine, his whining grew, as did my rage.

Finally, I yanked him by the arm, reversed course, pulled him to a nearby park bench, and proceeded to disobey all the advice I'd heard from the child psychologists. "You think *this* is a precious thing to give away? How would you feel if you had lost a parent instead of a candle? You think this is a sacrifice? Think about the firefighters who gave their lives. There are children who have lost their parents, parents who'll never get to see their kids grow up."

I could see him trying to reconcile my sudden demand for gratitude with all my previous statements minimizing the scariness of all this. Timidly, hopefully, sweetly, he said, "But if they're in heaven, they'll still be able to watch their kids grow up, won't they?" I nodded, now ashamed at my outburst and confused about whether I had just scarred him unnecessarily.

I know that this is the way little kids are. They are inherently self-centered, and I probably should have just accepted that. But part of me wanted this moment to be memorable. I *want* my sons to be shaped by this event—if the impact is to make them more empathetic, tolerant, and grateful for what they have, not more afraid and insecure. That is a challenge.

Finally, there is the biggest challenge of all—figuring out what God was trying to tell us. Many people have been forced to reassess their own relationship with the Almighty. What are we to make of a God who allows this to happen? Is he trying to signal that Armageddon is coming soon, as some of our Beliefnet users believe? Is he trying to say that he has withdrawn his protection, as Jerry Falwell and Pat Robertson (and some other Beliefnet contributors) believed? Or is he weeping, like the rest of us, at how his creation has misused his gift of free will?

Does our behavior on Earth really relate to our fate at all? Clearly, among the World Trade Center victims were saints and sinners of all faiths. What, if anything, did they do to deserve this? And what can we learn about how we are supposed to lead our lives?

We won't pretend that the extraordinary men and women who contributed to this book have answered all these questions, but they have, at least, faced them. We humbly hope that the words between these covers will bring some comfort, understanding, and light, even as it raises more unanswerable questions.

Thank you for buying this book. In doing so, you are helping the victims of this disaster, as profits will go to relief-related charities.

STEVEN WALDMAN is cofounder and editor-in-chief of Beliefnet (www.beliefnet.com), the leading multifaith Internet site and media company for religion, spirituality, and inspiration.

Chapter 1
A CALL TO ACTION—
THE SPIRITUAL
CHALLENGE

Therefore we will not fear though the earth should change,
though the mountains shake in the heart of the sea; . . .
God is in the midst of her, she shall not be moved; . . .
The nations rage, the kingdoms totter;
he utters his voice, the earth melts. . . .
Come, behold the works of the LORD,
how he has wrought desolations in the earth.
He makes wars cease to the end of the earth;
he breaks the bow, and shatters the spear,
he burns the chariots with fire!
"Be still, and know that I am God. I am exalted among
the nations, I am exalted in the earth!"
—Psalm 46

Awake from Your Slumber
A Sermon by Bishop T. D. Jakes

I'm going to be talking to you about the gathering of America. I hasten to tell you that these are perhaps the most serious days I have ever witnessed in the 44 years of my life, and I hope that you don't take it lightly or merely think that it's just some tragedy, some unfortunate dilemma that has come against us that will be dismissed and replaced with other headlines.

We have certainly had our share of tragedies—the Columbine shootings and the Oklahoma City bombing and all the other things that have riddled us and shaken us and challenged us. We have had aircraft fall out of the sky or explode in the middle of the air, and we have been devastated by these tragedies. We have fought our share of skirmishes and even wars, but all of them dim in comparison to what is confronting this nation today.

If there ever was a need for prayer, if there ever was a need to grab the horns of the altar and begin to bombard heaven with prayers from every denomination, from every culture of every kind, it is today. It is my prayer that in every mosque, in every synagogue, and in every church around this country—regardless of our religiosities and our ecclesiastical entanglements—that men and women would lift up holy hands everywhere, calling on God to do exceedingly and abundantly all that we may ask of him.

Can you say amen?

Well, my brothers and sisters, we are deeply concerned and devastated for the tremendous loss, for the lives that have been broken, homes that have been fragmented, policemen who have lost their lives valiantly fighting to salvage others, firemen who have been trapped in buildings trying to get people out of them.

And it is certainly a dark and tragic day. I don't see how you

BELIEFNET MESSAGE BOARD: 9/11/01 8:58 A.M. Nallia: Television pictures showed a huge gash in one of the World Trade Center towers after a plane crashed into the building. This happened here about ten minutes ago. *...sigh...* I shudder to think how many

can be a human being and see the families wandering up and down the streets of Manhattan with pictures of their loved ones and tears streaming down their faces and not be touched, not be broken, not be sensitive, not be concerned.

Before I go deeper into this, I want to encourage, plead, solicit, beg, implore with all long-suffering that Americans and our friends around the world everywhere begin to pray for our president, that the hand of the Lord might be upon President Bush as never before, never before. It absolutely makes no difference whether you voted for him or did not vote for him. It means absolutely nothing. Absolutely nothing. He is the man at the helm. He is not contending for the presidency. He is the President of the United States of America, and I believe we are to give him our utmost support.

He literally will make the decisions over the next few weeks that will affect this country perhaps years after he's gone out of office, and we need to bombard the heavens that God might grant unto him the spirit of wisdom and revelation and knowledge. Amen.

I spoke with my daughters this morning. I said, I want you to pay keen attention to the message that I'm going to share this morning, because what is happening in this country is not something for young people to ignore. It's not a time to glance at the television set and continue to listen to rock music. And I don't say that as a criticism against the music. I'm criticizing that which would cause them to not focus on the magnitude of this event.

And right now God has brought this country to its knees. But you must understand when I say that God has brought this country to its knees, do not think that to be on our knees is a posture of defeat. I dare say to you, my brothers and sisters, that to be on our knees is a posture of warfare. It is the best position

people were hurt or killed. Please pray for everyone involved.
9/11/01 9:00 A.M. Nallia: And this wasn't an accident. Not two minutes ago, another plane hit the other tower.
9/11/01 9:11 A.M. Nallia: At least one of the planes was hi- »

that this country can ever take. And let Osama bin Laden and whosoever shall rise against this nation understand that we have not dropped to our knees because we are defeated, but we have dropped to our knees because we are armed and dangerous and ready to fight the good fight of faith. Glory to God.

And while our country strategizes and contemplates and prepares now for war, we who know the name of the Lord understand spiritual warfare, and we're praying to our God that if it should come down to a fight and if we should get the signal from our commander-in-chief to go fight, that while our boys and, yea, daughters are fighting on the front lines, that we will grab the horns of the altar and fight, because God's grace will give us the victory. I don't know about you, but I'm ready to go into warfare and to pray for a tremendous movement of God on behalf of this country and this world.

Let me hasten—let me hasten and say that this is not about revenge. This is about defense. This is not about retaliation. I don't think that we should advocate retaliation. This is about justice. We cannot afford to sit back passively and not react to the issues at hand and think naïvely that if we are silent and bury our heads up under the pillow that the enemy will go away because we are quiet. We are not dealing with that kind of enemy. We are not dealing with that kind of threat. We are dealing with a ruthless, reckless, evil, wicked debauchery such as this nation has not seen before, and if we proceed passively, we will not be prepared to guard what is rightfully ours.

We have been asleep, but we're awake this morning. Oh, yes. I want to say to you that we've been asleep for a long time. In the absence of war, we have used the term "war" as a cliché. We have got a war on crime, and a war on drugs, and a war on this, and a war on that. We have got video war games. We have spent millions of dollars on movies about playing war, entertaining our-

jacked and purposely crashed into one of the buildings.
9/11/01 9:14 A.M. kyriaki: Please pray for the victims and their families! I will be keeping them in my prayers. I cannot imagine such devastation, Nallia. I am shaking as I am typing this, I don't

selves with war. Oh, yes, we have been stuck in a state of sleep that has allowed us to become entertained by arguing and bickering amongst ourselves, between Democrats and Republicans.

While we were asleep, we have argued about racism and racial profiling and who was going to live in what neighborhood and pay scales in employment. While we were sleeping, we have argued about gender and Zionism and where we stood on foreign policy. While we were asleep, we have dealt with the issues, but they pale in comparison to the challenge that is before us now.

And suddenly, I don't hear anybody talking about women's rights or black and white or brown issues. I don't hear any policy jockeying between Democrats or Republicans, because with one swoop of the enemy, God bound America together, and suddenly you recognized that this is a wonderful country. And before we give it up, we will fight.

Still, we have been asleep, my brothers and sisters. And while we were asleep with nothing to write about and with nothing to do, we began to entertain ourselves with talk shows and Jerry Springer. While we were asleep, we started coming up with new types of television ideas and real-life television because we didn't have anything else to do. And in our boredom we have become voyeurs peeking in the windows of our leadership, discussing their sexualities and their weaknesses because we didn't have anything else to do and we didn't have anything else to fight about.

But now God is showing us an issue that is more significant than any of these other issues. While we were sleeping, the enemy was strategizing and moving and structuring and setting ambushes and getting ready for attack.

If we end up in the war that seems to be before us, it will not be a particular country that we will fight. We will not just be dispatching troops in one direction. This is more diabolical than that. It is more dangerous than that. There is no point of reference for this kind of war. It is an unprecedented attack. President Bush cannot look back in the annals of American history and find anything in a textbook that relates to the kind of war and challenges that are before him now.

America has been asleep, relaxing, taking it easy. But I want to serve notice on every evil, demonic force attacking us: We are awake now. Somebody shout, "Wake up, America!" I certainly agree that we need to repent, and I certainly agree that we need to pray, and I certainly agree that we need to seek the face of God as never before, but I do not suggest that God has gotten angry at us and decided to allow the enemy to destroy us. I do not believe that this is the work of God. And I am upset that anyone would suggest that the God whom I serve would do such a thing. This is not the God whom I serve. The God whom I serve wouldn't have killed those mothers and children and babies. The God whom I serve would not have used this wickedness and debauchery to execute wrath on people who are praying.

Even if America has its immoralities—and it does—might I remind you that God said, I would save Sodom and Gomorrah if I could find 10 righteous people. Somebody in America is praying. Somebody is praying while somebody is drinking and stealing and lying and discriminating. So if you have been sleeping and taking comfort in the lust of your flesh, it is time for you to wake up, my brothers and sisters, out of your sleep. You are not coming to church because your mother has been begging you to come. You're not coming to church because your wife has been after you. You're not coming to church because your son or your daughter has been trying to get you to come.

No, you are here because it is high time for you to wake out of your sleep and get ready for the battle. It is time for you to call on the name of the Lord like you have never called on him before—

people were just killed when that building fell, not to mention those already killed by the crashes. I only hope they got everyone around the buildings evacuated far enough away before it came down

and to commit your way unto the Lord and to rededicate your life back to God and to discipline yourself and prepare yourself that our faith is being tried. You are going to need the word now more than you ever needed it before, so faith cometh by hearing and hearing by the word of God. Revival must come in America.

I was on CNN the other day, and right in the middle of the interview, the interviewer said, "Will you just stop right where you are and pray for America?" I thought for a moment: I was on CNN, and nobody is arguing about separation of church and state now. America is coming home. Nobody is talking about praying in school. Nobody is talking about whether you should pray at a football game. My brothers and sisters, simply stated, we're praying for the nation. We're praying for the nations of the world to line up on the side of right. Hear me good. My trust is in God.

I'm not going to try to talk you into Jesus. But I tell you what: In the days to come you're going to need him. You have needed him before, but you were asleep. We have always needed prayer and worship and coming together, and we've always needed blacks and white and browns to melt down to just being Americans. We have always needed it, but we were asleep, playing political games, arguing about words, fighting over semantics, missing the greater issues.

I believe in a Jesus that can snatch a soul before a plane explodes; I believe in a Jesus who can snatch a fireman out of his suit before the fire burns his flesh. I just believe some crazy stuff about God. Quickly, I want to tell you this is the strategy. The nation is coming together. God is gathering America. Churches are coming together. He's gathering churches. This is what I want you to do with your family: Squeeze that hand you're holding. Bring your family together. Bring your kids together. Support one another. Embrace one another. Start family devotions. Start teaching and talking to your kids. You keep your eyes

9/11/01 10:27 A.M. Teine_Sith: I saw the news...this is crazy.... This is.... I propose we all do some kind of ritual, something, to stop this. Anything. Are you with me? All of us together, we can do something. So so sad.   >>

open. Keep your head up. Squeeze that hand. Don't be afraid.
Don't be intimidated.

If you're stuck out in the foreign country of sin, I'm waiting
for you. Come on, wayward brother. Come on, wayward girl.
Come on, America! Let's be one nation under God, one nation
under God, one nation under God, indivisible, with liberty and
justice for all.

BISHOP T. D. JAKES is the pastor of one of the fastest-growing churches in
the nation, the Potter's House in Dallas. A renowned speaker to audiences
of hundreds of thousands each year, he is also the best-selling author of
Maximize the Moment and *The Great Investment.*

NO FUTURE WITHOUT FORGIVENESS
By Archbishop Desmond M. Tutu (Interviewed by Anne Simpkinson)

Our hearts go out to all the people of the United States at this
time of grieving and much anguish and loss, praying that God
will fill you all with God's grace, comfort, and strength. We condemn unequivocally these and all other acts of terrorism.

*Does justice need to precede reconciliation efforts? Or, can one
begin a process of reconciliation and forgiveness even as events unfold? Is it too early to forgive the terrorists who attacked the U.S.?*
Forgiveness and reconciliation are not cheap. They are costly.
After all, they cost God the death of God's Son.

Forgiveness is not to condone or minimize the awfulness of
an atrocity or wrong. It is to recognize its ghastliness, but to
choose to acknowledge the essential humanity of the perpetrator
and to give that perpetrator the possibility of making a new beginning. It is an act of much hope and not despair. It is to hope

9/11/01 10:30 A.M. **rmatth:** I can't stop crying. I hope Tantris is
safe. God help us.
9/11/01 10:33 A.M. **erica_c:** I just left the TV in the secretary's office, unable to watch any more. Dear God. I pray that everyone

in the essential goodness of people and to have faith in their potential to change. It is to bet on that possibility. Forgiveness is not opposed to justice, especially if it is not punitive justice but restorative justice, justice that does not seek primarily to punish the perpetrator, to hit out, but looks to heal a breach, to restore a social equilibrium that the atrocity or misdeed has disturbed.

In our case in South Africa, the process of reconciliation began long before the perpetrators were brought to book; it began when the victims were able to say, "We don't want to nurse grudges; we do not want to be embittered. We are ready to forgive." So spectacularly embodied in former South African president Nelson Mandela was the magnanimity, that the generosity of spirit helped us to walk the path of reconciliation rather than that of retribution and revenge.

What are you in the U.S. willing to do? Are you willing to consider the possibility of forgiving even when you say that the perpetrators should be brought to justice? Are you willing to believe that even though they are guilty of a diabolical act, they still continue to be children of God—not monsters, not demons, but those with the capacity to change?

How does one reconcile the need for justice and the Christian message to love our enemies?

I hope so much that when the cry is for justice to be done that you in the U.S. will be ready to accept your own standards and values: that someone is presumed to be innocent until they are proven guilty; that there will be sufficient evidence, not just suspicions and hunches; that those who are accused must be found guilty in an open court of law because it has been proven beyond reasonable doubt. It will be salutary to recall Oklahoma when initial suspicions pointed fingers at Arab terrorists as likely perpetrators. It is too serious a matter and there is too much at stake

who could get out, got out. I pray for those who were killed. I pray for the families of those who were killed. I pray for the people who had to witness this horror firsthand. I pray for everyone whose sense of security and safety has been shaken >>

for the U.S. not to be able to produce hard, credible evidence that can pass muster. The terrorists will have won an important battle if they cause you to jettison your own high standards. Let the law then take its course.

The love that Jesus enjoins on his followers is not namby-pamby. It is realistic. What Jesus is asking his followers who may have been grievously wounded by the enemy is not that they should like—not that they should have warm feelings for—this enemy but that they should love him or her; should believe, despite all the evidence to the contrary, that the person guilty of this heinous deed is still a human being (and terms such as "terrorist" tend to depersonalize, to demonize the other); that this hated one is indeed a child of God; and should wish the best for them. It is not something we can accomplish on our own. Remember, Jesus did not demand that we should be merely good. No, he challenged us to be perfect, to seek to emulate the perfection of God, who makes the sun shine on good and bad alike. We are exhorted to forgive one another even as God in Christ forgave us; we are in the forgiving business, whether we like it or not. And we can do this only through God's grace. It is ultimately God at work in us to make us to be like God. Yes, it is a tall order, but that is the love that changes the world, that believes an enemy is a friend waiting to be made.

Is there such a thing as a "just" war?

The just-war theory was a recognition that we live in a less-than-perfect world. In an ideal world, there ought to be no war, for war is evil—but it might be the lesser of two evils. It might be better to go to war against Hitler than to allow him to throw babies into gas ovens.

There are criteria to be satisfied before the serious and ugly business is undertaken: Have you exhausted all possible peaceful

or shattered by this act.
9/11/01 10:38 A.M. NanKizziah: Lord have mercy... I too hope Tantris is okay. Who else is in NY?
9/11/01 10:47 A.M. WayneLu: I have seen the face of pure evil.

alternatives? Will you, if war is declared, abide by the conventions governing conflict—namely, that you target only the military?

There is no such thing as "collateral damage." The terrorist attacks were particularly reprehensible because they targeted innocent civilians. Collateral damage is a horrible euphemism for killing ordinary mothers and children and fathers and uncles and brothers.

Are you reasonably certain of success, and will things be better after the war than before the war? Had these questions been asked, then the Gulf War would not have been waged, for it failed to satisfy the conditions of a just war. But can any war ever be just again when we have such devastating weapons?

You've said that you believe that human beings were made for goodness, made for love. How then are some people capable of unspeakable evil? How do you accept the existence of evil, and yet still believe in the core goodness of human beings?

God does not give up on anyone, for God looks on each of us as a masterpiece in the making. But God took an incredible risk in creating us not to be automatons but to be decision-making creatures with the freedom to choose to obey or not to obey God, to love or not to love God.

God is impotent because God cannot and will not stop us from exercising the freedom God has given us; God will not, cannot, stop us from choosing evil without nullifying the gift of freedom God has given us. They say hell is the greatest compliment God has paid us. God, who alone has the perfect right to be a totalitarian, has such a deep reverence for our freedom that God had much rather we went freely to hell than to compel us to go to heaven. Some of us will choose wrongly, but that does not mean we are all flawed. Anything but.

That is why we admire not the macho, the aggressively suc-

I was on a train on the Manhattan Bridge this morning when someone pointed out that one of the World Trade Towers was burning. As I watched, I saw a large, dark gray jetliner, flying low, smash into the other building. Eventually I got to my of- >>

cessful. No, we revere a small, frail woman, Mother Teresa, because she was good. The world admires an old man because he is magnanimous, he is forgiving, he is good. We have an instinct for goodness; our hearts thrill in the presence of goodness, for God has made us for himself, and our hearts are restless until they find their rest in him. We are a glorious paradox, the finite made for the infinite. And you in the U.S. are some of God's best advertisements, so generous, so caring, so compassionate.

Is forgiveness possible at a national level? And if so, how can political leaders support that process?

A nation is made up of individual persons, but it also has an ethos, a culture, a tradition, a corporate memory and identity, distinct from those individuals. A nation can do good, can triumph, can fail. A nation can be held accountable for a holocaust, and so a nation must remember national achievements of which it is proud.

It must recall the things that make it hang its head in shame and perhaps be a little less arrogant as it recalls its own anguish, bewilderment, and impotence after September 11. It might then perhaps be led to think how others might have felt in Nagasaki and Hiroshima; how little girls running naked from napalm bombs were feeling; how those whose lands were devastated by smart bombs in Iraq felt. Or those in Nicaragua and the contras; or Chile after their President Allende was assassinated through the machinations of the CIA; or Angola and its civil war with a U.S.-backed Savimbi; and Congo still reeling from the U.S.-sponsored assassination of its first prime minister, Patrice Lumumba. And when it contemplates all of this, it will want to cry out to be forgiven and, in its turn, to want to forgive.

We were blessed that God gave us Nelson Mandela to lead us at a crucial time in our young history, and all those other leaders

fice, which is less than a mile away, and now I've heard that both buildings have crumbled to the ground.
9/11/01 10:57 A.M. mithrandeer: I am so sorry. I don't have words to express...

who said "no" to blanket amnesty and to Nuremberg-type trials and "yes" to reconciliation and forgiveness. For they realized that revenge and retribution merely unleash an inexorable cycle of reprisal provoking counter-reprisal, so much so that Gandhi once noted that an eye for an eye leaves the world blind.

Leaders can influence the mood of their people; they can make them vengeful or conciliatory; they can pander to their baser instincts, or they can hold out a vision of the sublime, of the noble, of the idealistic.

Violence provokes more violence and really solves nothing, as they seem to be finding in the Middle East, in Northern Ireland, in Sri Lanka, and in Bosnia. As you have experienced, real security does not come from the barrel of a gun. Despite your massive defense spending, you were vulnerable from within.

What would you personally want to say to Osama bin Laden? To President Bush?

I would say to Osama bin Laden: "Remember you are a child of God, and behave like one." I would like to say to President Bush: "Remember you are a child of God, and behave like one."

Last, from your perspective of someone living outside the U.S., why do you think Americans are so hated?

People don't hate the U.S. Too many have suffered from the effects of U.S. foreign policy; that is what they resent.

Dear friends, please remember that ultimately there is no future without forgiveness.

God bless you richly.

DESMOND M. TUTU is Archbishop Emeritus of the Diocese of Cape Town and the recipient of many honors and degrees, including the 1984 Nobel Peace Prize. He chaired South Africa's Truth and Reconciliation Commission, which made its final report in fall 1998.

9/11/01 11:00 A.M. WayneLu: I am trying to keep calm, hold myself together, and figure out what I should do to get home safe to my wife today. I think I will have to walk home. That will take 2 hours...if the bridges are even open...I am con-   >>

Twin Towers Viewed
from a Western Minaret
By Michael Wolfe

Today, you might say, I feel like three people.

As an American, I am filled with horror by what has occurred. My shock derives from the violence of the actions and
coldness of their execution. It isn't hard to feel the agony of
having loved ones ripped from your side so that a handful of
fools can make a point. Like most other Americans, I am angry
too. For one thing, we live in an open society; and now, in a
couple of hours, a handful of desperate people have jeopardized
the spirit of that society. I am also afraid that in the days ahead,
cooler heads will not prevail. Gandhi once said, "An eye for eye,
and soon everyone will be blind."

It is complicated enough to feel these things. Yet as a Muslim,
I have other, different feelings. As a Muslim, I'm appalled by the
actions of the extremists who, very likely, will claim to have been
acting, at least in part, in Islam's name when they committed
these atrocities. This is a flagrant case of political desperadoes
wrapping themselves in a religious flag. Islam teaches that when
a person takes another life unlawfully, it is as if he were killing
all humanity. There is no political rhetoric that can reverse this
moral law. The people who turned commercial airplanes into
flying bombs and murdered thousands of innocent people will,
in the imagery of the Koran, now burn in a spiritual hell. Their
families and remaining friends should confess their shame and
ask God's forgiveness, for starters. The actions of the perpetrators have nothing to do with Islam.

But some people in America obviously think otherwise.

As an American Muslim, I am, therefore, shamed by the lan-

cerned because they have evacuated the UN, which is two
blocks away from me. I don't know how safe it is here.
9/11/01 11:02 A.M. DanielTheImpendian: Pray for our country,
folks, for the people in New York and Washington, and for Is-

guage and attitudes I find some of my fellow Americans using about Islam.

In the immediate days after the attacks, we saw pigs' blood thrown at the door of a mosque in San Francisco, 300 marchers waving flags and shouting "U.S.A." as they tried to descend on a mosque in Chicago, a disturbed individual wearing what looked like a bomb in the parking lot of a Muslim school in Silicon Valley, gunshots in Texas, and mosques vandalized in Washington, D.C. Electronic hate mail has flooded the chat boards of ABC, NBC, CBS, and CNN. (Example: "It's time to eradicate Islam.")

It is no surprise that huge misunderstandings persist in this country concerning Islam, but there is greater ignorance afoot: the ignorance of assigning guilt by association, for instance, as though a political murderer's claim to your religion must automatically tar you with his convictions.

We also hear people making a lot of noise about "martyrdom" and Islam these days.

Concerning this confusion, try to remember that Christianity, America's mainstream religion, has in common with Islam a well-developed conception of religious sacrifice, that people of both faiths hope to be rewarded after death for good actions, that they believe they may reach a better place by being better human beings. It is a belief that has sustained billions of people over the centuries, guided their actions and illuminated their lives. It is also, as we know to our cost, a belief that is easily twisted: by rulers (beginning with the medieval Crusader kings); by millenarian, self-serving, misguided "leaders" (think of Jim Jones); and by desperate social revolutionaries (Nat Turner, John Brown). In terrible times, religion has been invoked for the greatest crimes, genocide (Nazism, the destruction of Bosnia)

rael, the Palestinians, and for all the young men who are about to face the fury this morning has unleashed. God's protection and care upon you WayneLu, may He keep you well and see you safely through this time.   »

and organized racism (the Ku Klux Klan). Yet Christians do not consider their religion tainted. And they are right.

If this is a time of mourning, it is also a time for acts of imagination.

If, for example, you are an "ordinary" American, try to imagine how it must feel right now for any of the 3.5 million Arab-Americans or the 6 million American Muslims, citizens all, simply to stroll down a crowded city street on the way to school or a bakery or a hospital. We have all just been reminded how fragile human life can be. Perhaps we can draw on that knowledge to bring some comfort to people who, in addition to their grief over what has occurred, must also walk in the shadow of guilt by association. Try to remember that there are Arab-Americans serving in the White House, six Arab-Americans in Congress, and that, side by side with all the others, approximately 200 Muslims were in the World Trade Center and the Pentagon when the airplanes struck on September 11.

Muslim Americans have the same job before them. If you're a Muslim, try to imagine how frightened a blonde, blue-eyed woman might be, this morning, as she stands in line at the airport about to board an airplane while a perfectly innocent Arab or Muslim couple stand in line in front of her. What can you do for her? Can you think of some way to erase the line that separates you and offer some human gesture that she may recognize?

A friend of mine writes: "Brutality (the use of power to degrade and to wound) is the essence of social misery. And increasing the acceptability of brutality, whether through self-indulgence, evasion, or outright lie, is criminal. I can think of no human reality that it is necessary to rise above other than brutality. I can think of no human misery—personal, political, economic—to which it is not central."

Let good sense prevail. Let Americans see this terrible action

9/11/01 11:06 A.M. hereinpa: Dear God, Please comfort those who can't get in touch with their loved ones right now. Please help us know what to say and do to comfort the bereaved as this terrible day continues.

for what it was—criminal terrorism perpetrated by extremists. The plotters and actors may call themselves Muslims, but they are religious failures. They have smeared the good name of a peaceful faith.

We should pray for protection when emotions run high. May God bring us sudden good and protect us from sudden evil.

MICHAEL WOLFE is an American Muslim and the author of *One Thousand Roads to Mecca*. He is currently at work on a documentary on the life and work of the Prophet Muhammad.

WHAT IS THE PROPER RESPONSE TO HATRED AND VIOLENCE?
By Neale Donald Walsch

The events of September 11 cause all thinking people to stop their daily lives, whatever is going on in them, and to ponder deeply the larger questions of life. We search again for not only the meaning of life but also the purpose of our individual and collective experience as we have created it—and we look earnestly for ways in which we might re-create ourselves anew as a human species, so that we may end at last the cycle of violence that has marred our history.

The hour has brought us much sorrow, yet behind the sorrow, if we look closely and long, we will see opportunity. It is the opportunity for us to take a new path, to show the world a new way, to demonstrate at the highest level our most extraordinary thought about who we really are—as a people, as a nation, and as a human family.

The whole human race is invited now to seek what it is we

9/11/01 11:06 A.M. Hatman: WayneLu- I am desolate. I do not know New York well enough to know any place that is safe for you, WayneLu. I am near DC, and heard the explosion at the Pentagon as I worked outside this morning. I have a friend   >>

truly wish to experience on this planet. Then we are invited to be the *source* of that for each other.

If we wish to experience peace, we are invited to provide peace for each other.

If we wish to know that we are safe, we are invited to create safety for each other.

If we wish to better understand seemingly incomprehensible things, we are invited to help each other to better understand.

If we wish to heal our own sadness or anger, we are invited to heal the sadness or anger in each other.

If we wish to have justice done, we are invited to act justly with each other.

The world is waiting now. It is anxiously awaiting the morrow, not knowing what may come. Its people are looking for guidance, for help, for courage, for strength, for understanding, and for assurance at this hour. Most of all, they are looking for love.

This is the moment of your ministry. This could be the time of your greatest teaching. What you teach at this time, through your every word and action, will remain as indelible lessons in the hearts and minds of those whose lives you touch, both now and for years to come.

We will set the course for tomorrow today. At this hour. In this moment.

There is much we can do, but there is one thing we cannot do. We cannot continue to cocreate our lives together on this planet as we have in the past. Yet we *will* continue to do so if we focus our energy on pinpointing where *blame falls*, rather than where *cause lies*, in the unhappiest of our experiences.

Unless we take this time to look at the cause of our wounds, we will never heal. Instead, we will forever live in fear of retribution from those within the human family who feel aggrieved—and, likewise, *we* will forever seek retribution from *them*.

that works there. I am praying for peace, and I suggest that we also stay alert...This is, IMHO, a direct result of the United States and United Nations failure to ensure fairness and justice, and evidence of the hardness of heart of many of mankind. Pray for

To me the cause is clear. The majority of the world's people have not learned the most basic human lessons. They have not remembered the most basic human truths. They have not understood the most basic spiritual wisdom. In short, most people have not been listening to God, and because they have not, they do ungodly things.

The message of God is clear. No matter what the religion, no matter what the culture, no matter what the spiritual or indigenous tradition, the bottom line is identical: We are all one.

The Bible, which is only one of humanity's many sources of spiritual teaching, carries this message throughout, in both the Old Testament and the New. (Have we not all one father? Has not one God created us? Why then are we faithless to one another, profaning the covenant of our fathers?—Malachi 2:10 . . . so we, though many, are one body in Christ, and individually members one of another.—Romans 12:5 . . . Because there is one bread, we who are many are one body . . . —1 Corinthians 10:17)

This is a message the human race has largely ignored.

Our religion, our politics, our economics, our education, our whole way of life are based on the idea that we are *not* one, that we are separate from each other. We are thus willing to inflict all manner of injury upon each other. We would never do this if we thought that we were actually inflicting injury upon ourselves, yet this injury inevitably *does* fall upon ourselves—for like begets like, and negativity only breeds negativity.

Our history has proven this. Still, there seems to be one thing for which many human beings will give up anything. They will give up peace, love, happiness, joy, prosperity, romance, excitement, serenity, *everything*—even their own health—for this one thing: Being right.

But even if we *are* right, what is spirituality's recommended course of action? What do the greatest spiritual teachers of all

Peace-
9/11/01 11:07 A.M. WayneLu: I'm concerned about looters and street thugs. I'm signing off now. Thanks for your prayers and thoughts.   >>

time, each in their own way, tell us at times such as these? It is
something that many of us cannot (or do not wish to) hear.

> . . . I say unto you, love your enemies, bless them that curse
> you, do good to them that hate you, and pray for them that
> despitefully use you and persecute you. (Matthew 5:44)

Can this be sound advice?

If we could love even those who have attacked us, and seek to
understand why they have done so, what would be the final result? Yet if we meet negativity with negativity, rage with rage, attack with attack, what then will be the outcome?

It is easy at times like this to fall into rage—and even to mistake
it for justice. Yet rage never produces authentic justice. Indeed, it
inevitably creates *injustice*—for someone. That is because rage is
anger that has been repressed, and, when released, it is always misdirected. *This is exactly what happened on September 11, 2001.*

Anger itself is not inappropriate. Anger is a natural human response and can even be a blessing if it leads to change. Yet as we feel
our anger and express it, there is one thing about which we should
make no mistake. The human race has the power to annihilate itself. We can end life as we know it on this planet in one afternoon.

In the early days of our civilization, we were able to inflict
hurt upon each other using sticks and rocks and primitive
weapons. Then, as our technology grew, we could destroy a village or a town or a major city or even an entire nation. Yet now
it is possible for us to destroy our whole world, and do it so fast
that nothing can stop the process once it has begun.

Is that the process we wish to begin? This is the question we
must answer.

In searching for our answer, I hope that each of us will have
our own conversation with God, for only the grandest wisdom
and the grandest truth can address the greatest problems, and

9/11/01 11:17 A.M. paulaedwina: Well so far I've heard - pardon
if I make any errors; World Trade Towers have collapsed. 2 of 5
hijacked planes are not yet accounted for... There's been a plane
crash in PA but whether it is connected has not yet been estab-

we are now facing the greatest problems and the greatest challenges in the history of our species.

It should be no surprise that we are doing so. It is not as if we have not seen this coming. Spiritual, political, and philosophical writers for the past 50 years have predicted it. So long as we continue to treat each other as we have in the past, they have said, the circumstance we face in the present will continue to present itself in the future.

We must change ourselves. We must change the beliefs upon which our behaviors are based. We must create a different reality, build a new society. And we must do so not with political truths or with economic truths, and not with cultural truths or even the remembered truths of our ancestors—for the sins of the fathers are being visited upon the sons. We must do so with new spiritual truths. We must preach a new gospel, its healing message summarized in two sentences:

We are all one.

Ours is not a better way, ours is merely another way.

This 15-word message, delivered from every lectern and pulpit, from every rostrum and platform, could change everything overnight. I challenge every priest, every minister, every rabbi and religious cleric to preach this. I challenge every political party spokesperson and the head of every national government to declare it.

And I challenge all of us, right now, to become spiritual activists. If we want the beauty of the world and not its ugliness to be experienced by our children and our children's children, *we must choose to be at cause in the matter.*

NEALE DONALD WALSCH is the author of the *Conversations with God* book series. His most recent book is *Moments of Grace: When God Touches Our Lives Unexpectedly.*

---

lished. I'm dazed. I don't know what people think this will accomplish - will they be treated with more respect? I don't think so....

9/11/01 11:24 A.M. AbrarAlsayed: I grieve for the families of ≫

What the Buddha Knew
By Christopher Largent

When we're dealing with evil, we confront—often shockingly—
these facts:

First, we cannot undo what happened. We can heal. We can
restore. But though we desire it with all our might, we cannot
make the event go away.

Second, we realize that evil, an abstract theological term, has
a face: inhuman destruction. In fact, we may gain nothing by
treating evil as an abstraction. We can, however, respond to a
lived reality.

And third, the fact that almost disturbs us: We learn from experiences of inhuman destruction. The learning is so intense, in
fact, that some earlier cultures—medieval Christian ones, for example—believed suffering to be the best way to learn about the
meaning of life. Thankfully, the history of culture shows this to
be debatable. But we nonetheless draw profound insights from
the horror we experience.

One of our most important insights is that the anxiety we feel
for undoing the tragedy—wishing it had never happened—can
be used to heal from the tragedy. And should be. Immediately.

Over 2,500 years ago in northern India, the Buddha asked
(I'm intentionally paraphrasing), if someone is shot with an
arrow, what should we do? Should we determine the caste of
the man who shot the arrow? The composition of the arrow?
The path of the arrow from the bow? Or should we first get the
arrow out?

The Buddha discovered an important truth about dealing
with evil: that an operational response should come first. Instead of reacting abstractly, we deal with specific suffering

the victims of this tragic and senseless loss, and I pray for the
future that we may come to a resolution without further
losses. A special prayer to the innocent American Muslims who
most assuredly will face many prejudices and hardships in the

here and now. We don't sit around philosophizing (and as a professional philosopher I have nothing against philosophizing). Rather, *we take constructive action: looking at the suffering that has been inflicted and doing something specific to alleviate it.*

What often surprises people who work with destruction is that compassionate action heals—and often is the only healing force needed. Human beings working together to end suffering can reestablish much of the harmony shattered by the tragedy. So our first response needs to be ongoing. And that, as the Buddha's example implies, is the highest imperative for dealing with evil: *Do something healing and keep doing it.*

But we also want a preventive strategy. We want to strike at the roots of evil to keep it from recurring, even if we feel the odds are against us. So we need to ask how *in practice* inhuman acts arise.

Of course, at the outset, we realize that any attempt to grasp the roots of inhumanity will miss something. We can't know everything about such a complex subject. But we can discover insights that help us focus our preventive efforts.

One practical point we realize, often painfully, is that though the immediate desire for revenge may relieve the anger pressure, it has no long-term healing effect. My own experience is an example. Thirty years ago, two of my family members were subjected to violence—which eventually led to the death of one of them—and I spent years wanting revenge. But true healing didn't come until I discovered the potential in the victim-offender mediation program—though by then the victimizers had slipped into an obscurity from which I could not extract them. I had to find an inner therapy. But only that inner cure—and not the years of anger—provided healing.

near future.
9/11/01 11:37 A.M. serenemama: DUE TO THIS TERRIBLE TRAGEDY, THERE IS A TRUE BLOOD SHORTAGE - ESPECIALLY IN NYC AND DC!! PLEASE CONSIDER VISITING YOUR LOCAL   >>

In the case of international evil, the demand to temper revenge becomes more imperative. As an individual, I may seek revenge. But I expect the nation of which I am a citizen to seek justice.

So, as we continue to work therapeutically in whatever way we can, we look around for preventive insights. And some of the most stunning come from a 20th-century classic, Viktor Frankl's book *Man's Search for Meaning*.

During his concentration camp imprisonment, psychologist Viktor Frankl came face-to-face with systematic dehumanization. He realized that, subjected to daily trauma, most human beings (though not all) suffer soul loss. But those who lack the internal resources to process trauma become vicious. Unable to deal with the inhumanity—much less express themselves creatively, a human need—these persons imitate their victimizers.

Frankl's descriptions matched what many other psychologists have written about, especially Alice Miller in her many works: that human beings subjected to systematic or chronic trauma eventually respond like their abusers. If we're traumatized long enough and often enough, the constant wounding makes us angry then depressed then destructive.

The operational insight here is that in dealing with evil, we're almost always dealing with traumas being acted out (and in *For Your Own Good*, Alice Miller offers this analysis for the actions of a drug addict, a serial killer, and Adolf Hitler). As psychiatrists treating trauma have discovered (see Sandra Bloom's *Creating Sanctuary*), most inhuman destruction is a theater of abuse from which we can learn.

Once upon a time, destructive action was a creative urge that had just been born. It was infant creativity growing toward ma-

BLOODBANK AND DONATING BLOOD!! BLESSINGS...
9/11/01 11:44 A.M. tangerine: I want to go home. I work in a customer service environment helping people with small appliances. I am having a hard time empathizing (sp) with their ma-

ture expression. But it got sidetracked, waylaid by wounding. Trauma turned Dr. Jekyll into Mr. Hyde.

This sidetracking happens to all of us to some degree. Traumatized, we have no access to our creativity. If the trauma deepens enough, we choose destruction rather than have no expression at all. We wish this weren't true, but in fact most of us have found ourselves lashing out when frustration overwhelms us.

Those of us who find ways to break free of the frustration heal. Those who don't sink more deeply into the trauma maelstrom—and may become high-profile victimizers.

I did work with street gangs in the last century, for instance, and witnessed what some sociologists had told me: that gang members precisely reverse the values of their culture. Frustrated by being shut out of the society and systematically traumatized at home and at school, gang members turn their creativity into destruction. They become upside-down versions of their original creative selves.

So for our ongoing healing work we need to add these preventive approaches: grasping how trauma distorts human character and expanding creative outlets.

On a national or international scale, trying to engender creativity seems an overwhelming challenge. But at the very least, we can expect our governments to investigate what trauma caused an inhuman response (that destructive persons are "fanatical" only begs the question) and then draw on the expertise of the many superb mediators we have.

On a local level, we can work with our own cultural institutions—families, schools, businesses, and the information and entertainment media. We can notice where they may wound to the point of causing destructive frustration. Where do some par-

chine issues...to me it's so trivial. Plus I am crying on and off. World Peace seems like a dream that's likely never to happen...but Christ defied the odds and rose from the dead so with that in mind I will storm the gates of Heaven with my >>

ents become abusive, teachers and bosses dictatorial, or media violent to the point of programming inhumanity?

Wherever we find these phenomena, we can call in the reserves—not the National Guard (though they may sometimes be a stopgap measure) but the community. The real roots of social order are *community members working together to reestablish their sense of normalcy, sanity, and harmony.* In fact, working in community gives us access to an immediate creativity: the positive energy and consciousness of humans collectively engaged in restorative work.

The effect here is, as the Buddha implied, to feel empowered even in the face of actions we cannot undo. By *doing.* The Buddha's implication is that philosophical or political abstractions may not help and may even hinder our healing efforts. Rather, as we support each other in tragedies—sometimes risking our lives—we realize that we experience some resolution. We are not at the mercy of faceless evil. We can apply our best strategies to each situation as it arises. We can work on trauma roots to correct what situations we can. We can stand against violence in our communities and seek more creative outlets for all our fellow citizens. And we can stretch our own creativity to maximize its healing impact.

In the face of the tragedy in New York on September 11, 2001, we felt the shock of inhuman destruction. We also felt the need to help. And we realized that we needed to understand something deeper about our lives in the world, something about meaning. But especially, we needed to see that the alternative to destruction, compassionate creativity, also has force. So we got to work helping others and creatively transforming our own lives.

According to the Buddha, we need to keep doing that. And keep doing it.

prayers.
9/11/01 11:47 A.M. psychocandy: Well, I was evacuated from work (in the AON building here in Chicago) about 2 hours ago so I've been sitting here watching the news. I am completely

We experienced the suffering. But we also experienced our lives changing and becoming deeper and more poignant.

Evil always feels like a wound that may never heal. But we can work toward healing, individually and collectively. A creative community in action can be an amazing balm.

CHRISTOPHER LARGENT, a professional philosopher, coauthored *The Soul of Economies, The Paradigm Conspiracy*, and *Love, Soul, and Freedom.* He cofounded the Wisdom-School in Delaware (Wisdom-School.net) and has an active life-coaching practice (YouAreAliveNow@aol.com).

To Pray for Peace
Is to Pray for War
By the Reverend Forrest Church

Wednesday, September 12, 2001

How precious life is and how fragile. We know this as we rarely have before, deep within our bones we do. I am not certain how much more we know right now. Our minds imprinted with templates of horror, our hearts bereft with truly unimaginable loss, we face a newly uncertain future. The signposts have all been blown away.

How profoundly we need one another, especially now, but more than just now. We are not human because we think. We are human because we care. All true meaning is shared meaning. The only thing that can never be taken from us is the love we give away.

So let me begin simply by saying, "I love you." I love your tears and the depths from which they spring. I love how much you want to do something, anything, to make this all better. We all feel helpless right now; I know that. How I ache for those of

sickened that human beings can commit these kinds of atrocities, and IN THE NAME OF "GOD" NO LESS!!!
9/11/01 11:48 A.M. dragons_fire: This will be how the world ends. We retaliate, others retaliate against us. before long we >>

you who have lost dear friends and loved ones to this senseless
and barbaric act of terror. How I ache for all of us, who awakened this morning to a new skyline, not only here in New York,
but all across America.

The future as we knew it is dead. Long after the smoke clears
from Lower Manhattan and the banks of the Potomac, our vision will be altered by the horror of September 11. No longer can
we measure human accomplishment by technological mastery
or by our standard of living. Henceforth, for years at least, we
shall be remembered by two things above all others, one conveniently ignored, the other too often forgotten over decades devoted to material progress. Unmistakably and forever inoculated
against innocence by this full-scale outbreak of terrorism's virus
on our own shores, as a nation we shall be known by the steadi-
ness of our resolve in leading the war against the perpetrators
and sponsors of terrorism all around the globe. And as individuals, truly now members of one embattled body, we shall be
known no longer by the symbols of abundance and prosperity,
but by how well we learn to recognize our own tears in one another's eyes. Hope will answer helplessness if, and only if, from
the sacrament of this shared sacrifice of innocence and the innocent, we become for one another channels through which our
faith may flow, and wells of love from which to draw much
needed comfort and new strength.

At first these visions of a future rebuilt upon yesterday's ashes
may seem to contradict each other. Justice and mercy. Retribution and compassion. War and love. Yet they will only be at
odds should we choose one vision in place of the other. On the
one hand, if hatred and vengeance spur our lust for retribution,
rather than the greater quest for peace, we will but add to the
world's terror even as we seek to end it. On the other, if we
pray only for peace, we shall surely abet the spread of terrorism.

are exchanging nukes. While you pray for the victims, pray for
those in power. Pray that sane heads prevail and this does not
end human life.
9/11/01 11:52 A.M. ping: all i can do is pray and hope for the

Our hands will end up far bloodier than those that lift up arms against it.

History supports each of these statements. In the first instance, we must recall history's most ironic lesson: Choose your enemies carefully, for you will become like them. Terrorism is powered by hatred. If we answer the hatred of others with hatred of our own, we and our enemies will soon be indistinguishable. It is hard, I know, to curb the passion for vengeance. When we see Palestinian children dancing in the street to celebrate the slaughter of our neighbors and loved ones, how can we help but feel a surge of disgust and anger, the very emotions that precipitate hatred? But the Palestinians are not our enemies. Nor are the Muslims. This is not, as some historians would have it, a war between civilizations. It is a war between civilization and anarchy, a war of God-demented nihilists against the very fabric of world order. I hope you will all go out of your way in the days ahead to practice the second great commandment and love your Arab neighbors as yourself. Few outside the circle of those who lost loved ones in yesterday's tragedy are more surely its victims than are the millions of innocent Muslims whose God's name has been taken so savagely in vain.

This said, to pray only for peace right now is unwittingly to pray for a war more unimaginable than awakening to the World Trade Center smoldering in ashes. After a day's worth of breathless repetition, we may be tiring of the Pearl Harbor metaphor, even finding it dangerous. Yet, if anything, the comparison is too comforting. After simmering for decades, World War III commenced in earnest yesterday, against an enemy more illusive and more dangerous than any we have ever known before. Good people here in America and around the world must join in a common crusade against a common enemy. From this day forward, any state that sequesters terrorists as a secret part of their

best. my brother is in manhattan for a meeting, he is ok, my daughter sent e mail. please pray for all. deep sadness overcomes me.
9/11/01 11:58 A.M. RobinCP: To all the Buddhas, please help >>

arsenal must be held directly accountable. The only way the world as we know it will not end in a chaos of nuclear terror is if, first, we take every appropriate measure to destroy the terrorist henchmen themselves; and then, if we make any cowardly nation state that finances and protects terrorists so manifestly answerable for this crime that they will never commit it again. Both challenges are daunting. I am not in the least confident that success in either or both will prove possible. And I know that the effort to curb terrorism will shed more innocent blood, claiming the precious and fragile lives of children and parents, lovers and friends, falling from windows, crushed under buildings. But the future as we knew it ended that Tuesday. Even as Churchill, not Chamberlain, answered the threat of Hitler, we must unite to respond to this new threat with force, not appeasement.

With the war to be fought between civilization and anarchy, our only hope lies in the balance we strike as we enter this uncertain and forbidding future. It rests in how well we balance justice and mercy, retribution and compassion, the might of weapons and the power of love. Our hope hinges on how effectively we unite a riven world against a common enemy. But it also requires that, singly and together, we answer to the challenge of maturity that will arise so quickly from the ashes of our shattered innocence. To do this, we must not only gird our minds, we must also prepare our hearts. Above all else, this is a spiritual challenge, one that each one of us must meet. If before we could seemingly afford the luxury of relegating our spiritual lives to the occasional Sunday, today, facing a transfigured future, we must redirect our energies and spirits. In times like these, measured against the preparation of our souls, all lesser priorities lose their urgency.

The Chinese ideogram for crisis juxtaposes two word-pic-

those who are suffering as either a direct or indirect result of these horrific attacks and may all the merit I have collected in this and past lives be used to that end. Om mani padme hum. **9/11/01 12:17 P.M. Acolyte1:** Do pray for Tantris' safety, but

tures: danger and opportunity. Even as our grief today can be measured by our love, the danger we now face suggests a commensurate opportunity. In the theater, a crisis is not something that happens, thenceforth driving the events of the play. In Greek the word "crisis" means decision. In the wake of this tragedy, it is the decisions we make that will shape our character and (to a degree) drive the plot our lives will follow.

The survivors in this city, every one of us, have been changed and will continue to be changed by the decisions we make. We can decide to be angry, vengeful, hateful, becoming like our enemies, and poisoning the one well. We can also decide that we can't do anything—that the world is hopeless—and go back to our trivial pursuits as if tomorrow were no different than the day before yesterday. Or we can rise to the challenge and pledge our hearts to a higher calling. We can answer to the better angels of our nature and join in a shared struggle, not only against our foes—who are the world's foes—but also on behalf of our friends and neighbors. We can listen more attentively for the voice of God within us than ever before. We can heed its urgings with acts of kindness and deeds of love.

This is already happening. It is happening here this evening. It has been happening on every street corner of this great and newly compassionate city, from sacraments of self-forgetting valor to the redemptive mingling of tears. Though our minds have been singed forever by imprints of horror, our hearts join in deep admiration for the ordinary courage and simple goodness of our neighbors, made one in shared suffering, reminding each other of how splendid we can truly be.

Never forget this. Never forget the e-mail sent by a doomed employee in the World Trade Center, who, just before his life was over, wrote, "Thank you for being such a great friend." Never

please remember that any phone lines that are still working in NYC are likely jammed and he may not be able to post anytime soon. I pray that God will keep him safe.
9/11/01 12:18 P.M. Johannes: i pray that You give the people >>

forget the man and woman holding hands as they leapt together to their death. Pay close attention to these and every other note of almost unbearable poignancy as it rings amidst the cacophony. Pay attention and then commit them to the memory of your heart. For though the future as we knew it is no longer, we now know that the very worst of which human beings are capable can bring out the very best. From this day forward, it becomes our common mission to be mindful of both aspects of our nature: to counter the former while aspiring to the latter; to face the darkness and yet redeem the day.

THE REVEREND FORREST CHURCH is senior minister at the Unitarian Church of All Souls in New York City. His most recent books are *Lifecraft* and *Life Lines*.

BREATHE AND REMEMBER GOD
By Kabir Helminski

Inscribed on the hilt of Muhammad's sword: "Forgive him who wrongs you; join him who cuts you off; do good to him who does evil to you, and speak the truth although it be against yourself."

Perhaps no single day in the history of humanity has focused our attention as has September 11. It is not that these events represent a greater suffering than many events happening year after year on this planet. After all, millions can die, and it may hardly be news. The events of September 11 are nothing less than a *sign*, a meaning to be grasped, a moment of truth that we have yet to understand. A pointless, yet hauntingly significant horror.

I will set myself in front of this horror, breathe, and remember God.

who are still trapped in the buildings & the rubble the courage & peace to face whatever they still have to. i pray for the poor people who have lost their friends or family in this tragedy. i pray that the people who lost their lives will find Peace in

America and the world were rudely awakened from a dream of invulnerability and security. Despite our spending 30 million dollars an hour to protect ourselves, a score of insanely committed angels of death offered their lives to attack a symbol of affluence and power and to wound the heart of the world.

I will wait at the threshold with a wounded heart, breathe, and remember God.

It will be a great tragedy if we fail to understand why, and a greater tragedy if the injured nation resorts to a similar evil in response. Affluence, privilege, and power numb the heart and soul. Much of humanity was in anguish before that fateful day. Now all of humanity feels that anguish.

This event itself is already the effect of a long chain of injustices. Perhaps the old religious imagery is not so far from the truth: The devil is searching for a crack to enter our hearts, and there are cracks of fear, self-righteousness, vengeance, and hatred.

I will take refuge from the evil within myself, breathe, and remember God.

If we acknowledge incarnate evil in the world, it is not to feel superior or self-righteous, not to apportion blame, but to accept responsibility for what we have all created. Humanity is one soul, one family, whether we admit it yet. Pitiless self-righteousness is perhaps the greatest evil of all, for it is the soil that breeds terror. Certainly we need to bring criminals to justice, but we do not need to fantasize war.

Evil manifested itself clearly in New York and Washington that day, but the unmanifested evil has been with us for a long time, wearing the cloak of respectability. If we as individuals were to enact what we allow our governments to enact for us, we would all be sentenced as perjurers, thieves, conspirators, and

other realms. i pray that the ignorami cheering on the streets in Palestine come to realize their folly. Forgive them Father, for they know not what they are doing.
9/11/01 12:10 P.M. AbrarAlsayed: Communications are down »

mass-murderers. The disastrous inequalities of wealth, the extreme poverty of 70 percent of the world's population, the perceived injustice of policies that we fail to question, all contribute
to a humanity in anguish.

*As a remedy for numbness, despair, and hatred, I will breathe
and remember God.*

And yet who can deny the beauty, generosity, and love that
human beings are capable of? Who can deny the heart-warming
contacts that we can meet on the streets, in the fields, and in the
homes of any people of this Earth? Yet something has gone
wrong. On the collective level, we lead lives of fear and denial.
We ignore our spiritual unity and we blame "the other." We attempt to control everything with our weapons and our wealth,
making a violent reaction inevitable.

As it is said in Deuteronomy from the very mouth of God, "I
have set before you life and I have set before you death, and I
have begged you to choose life for the sake of your children." Or
as it is said in the Koran, "Whoever kills one person without just
cause, it is as if he has killed all of humanity."

As Americans, we must change our own state of being from
a state of fear to a state of courage and compassionate sensitivity.
The only excuse for great power is great servanthood. We must
convince our leaders that we the people want them to lead the
way toward healing the human family. Love is the only solution
to any problem. We must solve our problems not with violence,
but with a generous, courageous, and faithful love.

*I will vow to apply love as the solution to any problem, breathe,
and remember God.*

Muslims must remember that they are not a victimized minority; they are a people, an *ummah* with transnational and

even here in Florida, and everyone is very tense, seeing as how
the last we knew the President himself was visiting Sarasota,
not very far away from where I am currently located. My whole
family is located in Pennsylvania and I pray for their safety, as I

transcendent concerns. They have a comprehensive and inclusive perspective, a vision that embraces all other sacred traditions and can find common cause with them all.

People have been gathering everywhere for prayer, but maybe prayer is not all that God wants. God is not waiting for us to beseech him to heal the world. God, who is "nearer than our jugular vein," is within the anguish of the human race, pleading with us to do the good that only our hands and hearts can do. Spirituality is not about easing fear, not about mere consolation; it is about facing truth.

I will begin the struggle for a unified and healed humanity, breathe, and remember God.

KABIR HELMINSKI is shaikh of the Mevlevi Order of Muslims (Sufi), which was founded by Rumi, and cofounder and codirector of the Threshold Society.

cannot call them through any land lines. My husband is also unable to contact his family in Saudi Arabia. May Allah watch over us all and protect us so there will be no more innocent victims.

Chapter 2

WHERE WAS GOD?

What is hidden from you will be disclosed to you.
For there is nothing hidden that will not be revealed.
Split a piece of wood; I am there.
Lift up the stone, and you will find me there.
—The Gospel of St. Thomas

DON'T TELL ME WE
SHOULD NOT BLAME GOD
By Rabbi David Wolpe

A few days after the attack, I was on a panel on CNN. There was a great deal of talk about love. The Muslim cleric spoke about love. The priest spoke about love. I too spoke about love. But I also spoke about anger.

"Islam," I have been counseled, means submission. "Yisrael" means wrestling with God. We are God wrestlers and must wrestle with this.

I am angry. I am angry at God and at human beings. I am angry at the manifold idiocies and indifference that have permitted such hatred to flourish.

Don't tell me we should not blame God since human beings did this, because even though God gave us free will and we are culpable, I also know that God fashioned our hearts and our world. Must we be angry with those who do evil? Absolutely. We must also be angry at God, for to be angry with God, as Elie Wiesel has taught us, means to be in relationship to God. I feel God in my fury and love God in my bewilderment.

I am trying to focus on my own sins, but it is hard. I know that the magnitude of others' sins does not wipe out my own, but it is hard.

The United States has wreaked a good deal of havoc in the world. In this time of repentance, we have much to repent for as a country, as individuals. We are not guiltless. We should not let the horror cut off our self-examination.

We are sinners, but we are not deserving of this cruelty. We are imperfect, but we are not evil. This is the face of radical evil.

And it must be fought.

Yes, it is obscene to see the plane go into the building again

9/11/01 12:41 P.M. Danae: I live in Canada, but when I saw the news this morning, I cried. I cried at the injustice, I cried for those who lost loved ones, for those who died. I cried that we all live in a time where such things can happen.

and again. America's obsession with the vivid image is not our best feature.

But it reminds us that we are called to mobilize our best efforts to unify ourselves over the petty divisions and foolish estrangements.

Why are we here? *L'ovdo Uleshomro.* To guard and tend the garden God has given. We have been given this remarkable corner of the cosmos. And the power to destroy it.

We know this enemy. He is the same one who blew up Sbarro's in Ben Yehuda street. He is the same one who blew up the Dolphinarium and ended the lives of scores of teenagers and bereaved their parents.

The name has changed, but we know him.

We know this ideology-driven fanatic. We have seen his face. We are the world's canary in the coal mine, and though we do not wish to be the first to know, we are.

We must be careful. We have great power. Power means moral choice.

We should feel gratitude that we have such choices. To be powerless is not moral, it is merely powerless. Jews remember too vividly the days we had no power. The millions who perished in Stalin's camps without a word, whisked away at night. The millions who died in concentration camps, and the world turned away because the Jews were expendable.

After the carnage of the 20th century, the Jew who is not grateful for power is unforgivably naïve. Do not lament our power. We know too much history. It is the only bulwark blocking the abyss. Powerlessness in the face of evil leads to Auschwitz.

Power requires great guarding of the soul, no doubt of it. But Edmund Burke told us long ago that evil thrives on the apathy of goodness. We dare not slide into indolence; our enemies will not make that mistake. Remember Yeats's pointed line that the

9/11/01 12:58 P.M. milled: My heart and spirit are grieved as I write this. I'm at work at a local hospital in Texarkana, TX, and have been going back and forth to the closest TV to keep track of the most recent reports. I grieve most for the passen- >>

worst are full of passionate intensity. We too must have that intensity.

You cannot tend the garden without effort. That effort should derive from what we cherish, not what we despise.

This is not a fight driven by enmity. G. K. Chesterton wrote: "The true soldier fights not because he hates what is in front of him, but because he loves what is behind him."

This way of life must be more than affluence and comfort. Let us summon what we love, what we cherish, and act in war consonant with the ideas we have fashioned as a free society.

I shall never forget seeing a tape of survivor testimony at the Holocaust museum. A man tells of watching another inmate in the camp praying. "Why are you praying?" he asks.

The man answers, "I am thanking God."

The first man is stunned. "For what could you be thanking God? What is there to thank God for in this hell?"

And the second man calmly responds: "I am thanking God that he did not make me like them."

We must be careful. It is our job to defend this country and keep it worth defending. The aim of this war is to fight them without becoming them.

The second point, to put beside our sadness, is our debt. Miraculously, we have been spared. We do not know what tomorrow will bring, but for now we are spared.

If you are sitting beside someone you love, take their hand. You are alive. Tonight, as your children sleep, kiss them. Because you are alive. Because we know again that life can be taken in an instant. Like you, I am overcome with sadness.

For me, the most indelible moment of this cataclysm was when I left home to go to work one morning, and I looked at my 4½-year-old daughter. As I left, I thought of all the mommies and daddies who are not coming home. Thousands of them. As

gers of those planes and cannot imagine the terror they felt as they saw the plane approaching their targets knowing that their lives were ending - God Bless their souls!
9/11/01 1:22 P.M. Finduilas: The world is shocked. - I am writing

I cried on the way to my car, I thanked God that I was not yet in their number, that I was alive.

In her Holocaust memoir, Etty Hillesum, a Dutch Jew, wrote:

"Give your sorrow all the space and shelter in yourself that is its due, for if everyone bears her grief honestly and courageously, the sorrow that now fills the world will abate. But if you do not clear a decent shelter for your sorrow, and instead reserve most of the space inside you for hatred and thoughts of revenge—from which new sorrows will be born for others—then sorrow will never cease."

We have to fight, but without filling our hearts with hatred. This is a time of memory. Let us remember Brian Sweeney, 38, who left a message for the wife he would never again see in this world, in which he said: "Hey Jules, it's Brian, I'm on a plane and it's hijacked and it doesn't look good. I just wanted you let you know that I love you and hope to see you again. If I don't, please have fun in life and live your life the best you can. Know that I love you and no matter what, I'll see you again."

Remember Jeremy Glick, 31, on the plane, who reached his wife. They said I love you over and over again, and he told her he needed her to be happy . . . and then he was gone.

In that moment, no words of revenge, or of hate. Only love endured.

We are together in this synagogue. This is why the synagogue is here. Maybe you come once a year, or twice, but here we stand. Here we have stood for over 2,000 years, and here we will continue to stand. To rejoice together, to grieve together, to be willing to fight together.

We are people of broken and yearning hearts. And of love.

I would like to close with a poem of Edna St. Vincent Millay that is both a poem and a prayer. It is called "Dirge without Music." The first and last stanzas read:

this in Europe. Nobody deserves acts like these. Nobody. But whoever did this hit two very symbolic places. However, those who are responsible for what happened today, need our prayers just as much as those who were made victims. >>

I am not resigned to the shutting away of loving hearts in the
hard ground. So it is, and so it will be, for so it has been, time out
of mind. Into the darkness they go, the wise and the lovely.
Crowned with lilies and laurel they go; but I am not resigned.

. . .

Down, down, down into the darkness of the grave. Gently
they go, the beautiful, the tender, the kind; Quietly they go, the
intelligent, the witty, the brave. I know. But I do not approve.
And I am not resigned.

We do not approve. We are not resigned. But we are people
of hope and children of God. So we pray.

DAVID WOLPE is the rabbi of Sinai Temple in Los Angeles.

WHERE WAS GOD?

By the Reverend Andrew M. Greeley

Many Americans are angry not only at all Muslims and all Arabs,
they are angry at God. Where was he when those planes were hijacked? How could he permit such terrible things to happen?

The questions miss the point. One could just as well ask
where God is when a premature baby, desperately fighting for
life, can't quite make it. Or when a drunken driver wipes out a
whole family. Or when each of us must die.

Why does God permit death? That's the proper question. A
number of theologians have asked how one can believe in God
after the Holocaust. The more fundamental question is how one
can believe in God after the death of a single child.

Where was God on September 11? He was somewhere (which
in his case is everywhere) grieving for his suffering children. Like

9/11/01 1:24 P.M. p060265: This should not catch people off
guard, what has just happened, but awaken us and make us
aware that we are living in the "last days" just like the Word
says. Let us all come together in this nation and return our focus

every good parent, God mourns for his children. We don't know enough about God to understand what his sadness is like or how it happens. But God is sad, so the Scriptures tell us repeatedly, even if theologians have a hard time explaining it. As a Russian mystic says, when a little baby cries, God weeps. What is God's weeping like? One can speak of the sadness of God only in metaphors, because one can speak of God only in metaphors.

Paul Murray, an Irish Dominican poet, puts it this way:

> *He who has no need of our gifts,*
> *Who gives us all that we bring,*
> *Still needs us so that if one of us should cease to exist*
> *He would die of sadness.*

For reasons that we do not and cannot understand fully, God cannot prevent death, though he can triumph over it, no matter how horrible it is. Like any good parent, he will eventually wipe away all his children's tears. That is all we have in this life and in the face of death.

Blame God for death if you want and if it makes you feel good. Demand to know why he stood silent at the "worst disaster in American history" (conveniently forgetting such incidents as the battles of Antietam or Cold Harbor). Make God the enemy just like the Arabs and Muslims we have to kill. You know what? That won't help you one minute.

Nor does it help to claim God as our ally in the "war" our leaders promise and plan. You may be able to create a God who will lead us into battle, the God who will bless America on demand. But when you put that God in an American uniform, you'll find out that you have created him in our own image and likeness and that this God is not God at all, but a blasphemous idol.

The real God is mysterious. If he weren't mystery, he wouldn't be God. We cannot fit him into our categories, our plans, our

to God Almighty
9/11/01 1:40 P.M. Nallia: I stood here today, and watched those buildings fall with my own eyes. I stood here today, and watched 10,000-50,000 people fall to the earth and be   »

programs, our ideologies, our wars of revenge. God is not the Roman god Mars. He is not a God of battle.

To make matters worse, he loves our enemies too. He weeps at their deaths as he weeps at ours. They are his beloved children just as we are. He dotes on their tiny tots just he dotes on ours. The rain of his mercy falls on the just and the unjust. Nor is it wise to claim that our cause always and every way is just. If we are to follow in the path of the God of Christians and Jews, we must probe tentatively and uncertainly, to make sure that we have not created the path in our own name instead of his. We must seek justice, we must prepare to defend ourselves. But we must not hate. We must not become like our enemies.

We must also be prepared to forgive. This may be what a correspondent tells me is "Jesus drivel." Okay, perhaps it is. But those who prate the Lord's Prayer trippingly on the tongue should reflect on its words. We forgive others because we are forgiven ourselves and thus manifest God's forgiveness in the world. That does not mean that we abandon the quest for justice and self-protection, but it does mean that we understand that hatred and revenge are not options.

That's Jesus drivel too perhaps, but for those of us who claim to be of Jesus must pray with him "Father, forgive them, they know not what they do." And if we don't, then we have repudiated the essence of Jesus.

THE REVEREND ANDREW M. GREELEY is a priest, sociologist, and best-selling author. He is a professor of social sciences at the University of Chicago and the University of Arizona and a research associate at the National Opinion Research Center at the University of Chicago.

crushed due to the fanatical convictions of a few. I stood here today, in NYC, and watched more lives torn apart in an instant than I thought I would ever see. I stood next to a 60-something-year-old woman, as she screamed when the first tower fell, be-

Is America Being Punished
for Its Sinfulness?

By Rabbi Shmuley Boteach

Recently, the United States witnessed two extreme acts of religious arrogance. The first was the catastrophic terror attack against New York, presumably carried out by religious extremists for whom the United States is the Great Satan. But the second was in some ways even more heinous, as it came from within. Two of this country's most respected religious leaders asserted that the attacks came about because "God had removed his protection from the United States" due to the sinfulness of its citizens. These ministers cited gay and abortion rights, as well as the denial of prayer in public schools and the American Civil Liberties Union, as being indirectly responsible for the terrorist atrocities by making America deserving of divine retribution like Sodom and Gomorrah.

The utter conceit of any person, be they cleric or laity, to know the mind of God is staggering, especially when God himself tells us that "the hidden things belong to God, but the revealed things are for us humans and our children to understand, now and forever." Furthermore, what magnitude of arrogance do these clerics have to condemn 6,000 victims, none of whom they knew, and affirm that they deserved to be punished? Had they ever met them? Did they know their hearts? But the over-roasted religious chestnut of man deserving the horrible things that befall him due to his sinfulness deserves greater examination.

Whereas "Islam" means submission to God, and Christianity advocates faith above all else, the word "Israel" translates as "he who wrestles with God." As human beings, it is not our role to concern ourselves with God's affairs and offer rationalizations for other peoples' suffering by saying that it carries an internal, al-

cause she had family in there. I watched coworkers run around, frantic, looking for wives, children, sisters, brothers, and friends...
9/11/01 2:23 P.M. HumanistDiva: I am so angry and upset. I   >>

beit latent, good. The moral imperative beholden upon us when witnessing the suffering of another individual is simply to cause it to cease, not to attempt to understand it. The reason that Judaism has traditionally had such weak theodicies is that we have always viewed it as immoral to try and rationalize suffering. Every rationalization is an attempt to make peace, to accept, to come to terms with. And there should be no coming to terms with human suffering. Man was created to challenge God, not to submit his head in blind obedience when innocent victims suffer.

The real question which should be posed to God upon witnessing a child with leukemia, or a staggering human tragedy like the destruction of the World Trade Center, is not, "Please God, explain to us why this happens and how it fits into your overall plan for creation," but rather, "Master of the Universe, how could you allow this to happen?! Was is not you who taught us in your Bible that life is sacred and must be preserved at all costs? So where is that life now?! Was it not you who also promised that the good deserve goodness, and not pain? Where is your promise now? By everything which is sacred to you, I demand that this cease, and that these people recover, now!"

Far from being an act of heresy, challenging God affirms God's plan for the preservation of life. It does not constitute a denial of God's providence. By wrestling with God, we are not denying God's higher plan. Less so are we asserting that no positive ends can result from suffering. Rather, we are simply saying it is not our job to justify life's horrors. Life is our business, not death. The last thing that religion needs today are Dr. Kevorkians in our midst who think that death and destruction can serve Godly purposes. Challenging God in the face of suffering is a powerful statement that goes something like this: We trust in you, O Lord, and believe that somehow these terrible things may be to our benefit and that you are a good and just

have a headache from crying. I have this awful pit in my stomach...just gnawing away.
I'm sorry to say this, but I feel it and I want to express it. This evil perpetuated on our nation today is in the name of religion.

Creator. But you are also all-powerful and would it not therefore be possible for you to bring about this desired end through a joyous means?

Judaism sees death, illness, and suffering as aberrations in creation that were brought about through the sin of Adam in Eden. Man's mission was never to make peace with suffering and death, but to abolish them from the face of the Earth for all eternity by joining God as junior partners in creation. By using physical tools such as studying medicine, giving charity, and being there in times of need, and by using spiritual means such as prayer and protest, we help usher in an era where only goodness will prevail over the Earth.

Rabbis and priests should be harbingers of redemption rather than prophets of doom. As long as we can explain how people can be gassed or die of incurable illness, the pain associated with these losses will be mitigated. And that is not meant to happen. *Our responsibility is to demand that they cease.*

For those who argue that challenging God is sacrilege, let them learn from the great biblical giants. What was their response upon witnessing human suffering? When God came to Abraham and informed him that he was about to crush Sodom and Gomorrah, cities which Abraham himself knew were deserving of punishment, did Abraham bow his head and accept divine judgment? No! He pounded with his fist and demanded, "You are the judge of the whole Earth. Shall you not practice justice?" (Genesis 18:25).

In the same vein, when informed by the Almighty that he intended to devour the Jewish nation for their sin of the golden calf, Moses responded, "If you do not forgive their sin . . . blot me out, I pray you, from the Torah which you have written" (Genesis 32:32). Where in the history of apocalyptic literature does a human admonish the Master of the Universe to remove

People all over the world are killing each other every single day over religion. Protestants and Catholics...who BELIEVE IN THE SAME THING are murdering each other's children with no remorse or shame. It makes me sick. >>

his name from a divine work, so that he will not be associated with the terrible deed of failing to save the victim?

My argument is not simply that this response is proper because it was practiced by Moses. Rather, it was the Almighty himself who demanded that Moses spar with him and defend human life. As God says, "And now [Moses] leave me so that I can devour [the Jewish people] immediately" (Exodus 32:10). Moses had not yet even begun to speak, yet the Almighty commanded him not to interfere! It seems God was summoning Moses to open his mouth and defend the people, not to accept the terrible fate that he had decreed for them.

Once, when I hosted Elie Wiesel at Oxford, a teary-eyed student asked him, "Mr. Wiesel, why did God allow the Holocaust?" Wiesel just looked at the student sympathetically and said, "I cannot—I dare not—answer your question. Because if I do, I fear that you will sleep easier tonight." And truth be told, I would rather stay awake being angry that God has allowed this devastation to happen, than to sleep easier believing that those who suffered deserved what they got.

RABBI SHMULEY BOTEACH is director of the L'Chaim Society (www.lchaim.com) and the author of numerous books, including *Kosher Sex* and *Why Can't I Fall in Love?*

GOD MADE US MORAL AGENTS
By Charles Colson

This weekend I received a call from a Christian friend who was deeply troubled. The husband of a woman to whom she had been witnessing had been killed in the World Trade Center attack. The woman called my friend and demanded bitterly:

9/11/01 2:27 P.M. just2facts: This was bound to happen people, we ARE living in the last days of this wicked system
9/11/01 2:28 P.M. Honor: ..The US is hated...but why? What is it really? What fires passions so great to call for the deaths

"Where was your God that you've been telling me about this week?"

Everywhere, people are raising the same question: How could a good God have allowed such massive evil? No question poses a greater stumbling block to Christian faith; no question is more difficult for Christians to answer. Yet the biblical worldview does give us a good answer.

The simple answer to why bad things happen to so-called good people is that God loved us so much that he made us free moral agents in his image. He designed creatures with the ability to make choices, to choose either good or evil. The original humans, Adam and Eve, exercised that choice—and chose to disobey God. In doing so, they rejected God's good, thus creating sin and opening the door to death and evil.

What happened last week was raw, naked evil—committed by men who made evil choices. But it was something else as well: It was merely a consequence of the fact that there is sin in the world. God could erase the consequences of sin immediately. But then we'd no longer be free moral agents; we would be robots. For without consequences, there is no real choice. God cannot simultaneously offer us free choice and then compel one choice over another—which is what would happen if he stopped all evil.

Jesus himself was asked why bad things happen to good people. In Luke 13, we read that people asked him if the Galileans who were killed while worshipping at the altar were worse sinners than anyone else. "No," Jesus answered. And then he added, "Unless you repent you will all likewise perish." Jesus then reinforced his point. Recently, a tower in a nearby city had fallen; 18 people had been crushed to death. Jesus said, "Do you think that they were worse offenders than all the others who dwelt in Jerusalem? I tell you, no; but unless you repent you will all likewise perish."

of thousands?

9/11/01 2:48 P.M. RichardB: Let each of us try to listen to what the Inner Teacher is telling us at this moment. His words may be hard to hear in the midst of our very human reactions. >>

This is one of the hard sayings of Jesus, but there's great truth in it. We are in no position to ask God why terrible things happen. We're only to seek forgiveness ourselves.

What happened last week was one of worst tragedies in American history. But God can bring good out of evil, and he often works through adversity. Since the terrorist attacks, we have seen the nation come together with greater unity than I've witnessed since Pearl Harbor. And this Sunday, my church was filled to capacity at all services—very unusual in Florida at this time of year. Churches all over the country were packed, and were in England as well. People may be angry at God, but they're also asking questions about the meaning of life and God's role in it.

Where was God last week? He was with us—just as he always is. He gave us everything we need to cope with this or any other evils: He gave us himself at the cross at Calvary.

CHARLES COLSON is the founder of Prison Fellowship Ministries, which, in collaboration with churches of all confessions and denominations, has become the world's largest outreach to prisoners, ex-prisoners, crime victims, and their families. From BreakPoint (www.breakpoint.org).

GOD WAS WHERE GOD CHOSE TO BE
By Kathleen Norris

The word "apocalypse" comes from the Greek for uncovering or revealing. It is a stripping away of the masks and illusions that normally help us function in the world. The apocalypse of September 11, 2001, has revealed to us that, contrary to what our consumer culture has complacently asserted as our birthright—"the good life at a great price," according to one department

---

Listen for that voice which is not your own.
9/11/01 3:10 P.M. thegraycat: My husband works for a computer firm. They have issued warnings to all of their Arab employees, even those employees who look Arab, to be very careful when

store chain—life is not ours to own or control. It is a precious gift, and a precarious one.

The fact that we take our lives into our hands whenever we get into a car or airplane, enter the elevator of an office building, or walk along a city street, is something we customarily set aside in the interest of conducting our daily business. We need some sense of security to live at all, and in mustering hope and confidence after any calamity, we generally find that it is helpful to return as soon as possible to our ordinary routines. But now, having had our sense of security so cruelly stripped away, I think we will be better off if we do not ignore the lessons of this particular apocalypse. What can we say about the world that has been revealed to us, and our place in it?

We can't undo the unspeakable death that has been placed before our eyes, or will away the gruesome television images that are indelibly burned into our minds. But as we move beyond the shock and horror, we can examine ourselves and our culture in a new light. I've winnowed four points of observation to share.

American culture glories in celebrity. People can be famous, it seems, simply for being famous, and the antics and opinions of celebrities have come to be considered legitimate news. But the events of September 11 exposed the shallowness of our preoccupation with fame. In a real crisis, people didn't want to hear from movie stars. They were more likely to turn to the neighborhood clergy. Suddenly, it was more important to have reporters give us information about the internal affairs of Pakistan than to fawn over the director and cast of the latest special-effects extravaganza set for next Friday's opening. This is a perspective we need to retain if we are to have any hope of understanding the world we live in.

American culture thrives on the promotion of material

walking to their cars after work.
9/11/01 3:19 P.M. SecondSonOfDavid: "Jesus wept" John 11:35
9/11/01 3:38 P.M. lovingangel1976: I will be SO very happy when the world will end and all suffering on this earth will be >>

things. But after September 11, the voices hawking current fashions, the latest prescription drugs, the top-of-the-line appliances and technological wonders—voices that normally drown us in their ubiquity—were silenced. With remarkable disregard for the bottom line, television networks shoved advertisements aside and kept the news coming. And corporate executives agreed, recognizing that commercials would seem callous under the circumstances. For a few days, the distraction of advertising was blessedly absent from our lives. We did not have to listen to anyone exult over a stain remover, a bathroom cleanser, or a new car, as if these products were of genuine importance in our lives. During the week of September 11, it was easy to remember that relationships with other people matter far more than things. Now that advertisements are back in full force, it will be more difficult to remember, but it is worth the effort.

American culture promotes the imagery of violence, even as it seeks to ignore the effects of real violence on people's lives. Action-film actors are cartoon figures, surviving gun battle, auto accidents, fires, falls, and explosions that would kill an ordinary mortal. Death is entertainment, especially when it's mostly the bad guys who die. But now that the death of so many innocent people has been forced into our consciousness, we will do well to recall our own mortality in a meaningful way. The suggestion St. Benedict made over 1,500 years ago, to "keep death daily before your eyes," can be a spiritual tool that helps us to value life and those we share it with. Let petty disagreements go, kiss your wife or husband good-bye, send your kids off to school with a word of encouragement rather than complaint. It may be an ordinary Tuesday morning, but it is also precious time, because life doesn't last forever.

Americans have a love-hate relationship with religion. Many people explain themselves as "spiritual" but not "religious," im-

no more. No more attacks and useless deaths. No more cowards and people willing to give their life to end so many more.
9/11/01 3:51 P.M. kc62301: ...bin Laden has shamed the Islamic faith by his murderous actions in the name of the Prophet and

plying that institutional religion has no place in their lives. But during the week of September 11, we turned on our televisions and saw Americans at prayer, in churches and cathedrals, in mosques, synagogues, and ashrams. The old religious traditions and sacred spaces had something to offer us after all in our hour of need. The truth is that these communities of faith were there all along, and will still be there after the present crisis has passed. But in the clutter of American life, the loud culture of argument, we simply could not see them, or hear their messages of good will.

In the world revealed to us during the week of September 11, religion has a legitimate place, and recognizing this is especially important in light of the appalling distortion of Islam that led to the terrorist attacks. We need not remain mired in bitterness, assuming that God somehow caused or allowed these horrible acts to take place. "Where was God?" is a question that naturally arises whenever we are faced with terrible loss. On the morning of September 11, I believe that God was where God has chosen to be, nailed to a cross, constructed by human beings.

For me, the belief that God suffers with us helps explain the fact that disaster so often brings out our strengths. As I wrote in my book, *Amazing Grace*, in a chapter on the word "apocalypse," "We human beings learn best how to love when we're a bit broken, when plans fall apart, when our myths of self-sufficiency and safety are shattered. Apocalypse is meant to bring us to our senses, allowing us a sober if painful glimpse of what is possible in the new life we build from the ashes of the old."

It is a difficult task that is set before us, but it helps to realize that in the world revealed by apocalypse, destruction does not have the last word. It is hope that emerges, inviting us to believe that, despite considerable evidence to the contrary, it is not evil

in the name of Allah. Muslims who do not lift a finger to stop the shame bin Laden is bringing to Islam will be held accountable by Allah on the day of judgment.
9/11/01 4:09 P.M. Johannes: The news in Hong Kong is now   »

that prevails, but the good. If this seems far-fetched, hopelessly pie-in-the-sky, we have only to recall the firemen, police officers, medical personnel, and chaplains of New York City, who, when confronted with unthinkable evil, chose the good. In the hope of bringing aid and comfort to people who were strangers to them, they gave up their lives. In the Christian tradition, there is no greater good than this.

KATHLEEN NORRIS is a best-selling novelist and the author of the spiritual trilogy *Dakota*, *The Cloister Walk*, and *Amazing Grace*.

THE THEISTIC GOD IS DEAD
By Bishop John Shelby Spong

Since September 11, the image of airplanes loaded with both human beings and fuel crashing into the World Trade Center has been etched on our consciousness. The willingness on the part of fanatics to die for beliefs deeply held is seen as powerful, but still unbelievable. Chance and the randomness of death are inescapable. We cry out for some purpose, some meaningful explanation, yet nothing makes sense.

This tragedy brought a wide variety of religious leaders to public attention, each seeking to provide comfort. Their pious rhetoric, however, was strangely stilted, unconvincing, and sentimental. A few were actually bigoted and evil. Jerry Falwell, in a televised interview, said that this tragedy was God's punishment on America for tolerating abortionists, feminists, homosexuals, and pagans. Pat Robertson smiled in agreement.

A desperate need seemed to exist among these religious leaders to demonstrate that God was still in charge. One suspects that this claim covers a deep suspicion, seldom spoken by

coming up with live feed. Now i can see & hear the screams, the cries, feel the chaos & panic. i can feel the terror, the hurt, the anguish. It frightens me now....gassho itashimasu.
9/11/01 4:25 P.M. jumbojava: First heard about the attacks

human lips, that no such God exists and that we are alone in this vast, chaotic, and frequently painful world. When tragedies occur and no divine protection is forthcoming, human hysteria forces us to struggle to restore our protective parent God to believability. That is what produced the pious words and religious clichés, which included the assurance that heaven is real and God can still be trusted.

Many people pretend that they still believe those things, but deep down they know they only believe in believing them. That statement is as true in the religious world as it is in the secular world—though not as often admitted.

We once conceived of God as external to life, supernatural in power, and able to intervene in human history to accomplish miraculous rescue. We know intellectually that such a God is but a phantom of human hope. The image of hijacked planes crashing into buildings killing thousands of people gives us no hiding place for theological pretending. The skies are empty of a protective deity ready to come to our aid. God defined theistically has died. That is the lingering conclusion created by last week's events.

Is atheism, then, our only option? Must we gird our loins, and with stoical faces stare our cold, godless reality down, while we get about the task of living courageously in a meaningless world? Or can we use a moment like this current crisis to seek a new God definition that might fit a new world? This is the primary modern faith task of this moment, and though it carries with it no guarantees of success, it also admits no illusions.

In the childhood of our humanity, when believing was easy, we assumed our Earth was the center of the universe. We believed God, understood theistically, directed the affairs of human history, controlling the weather, and keeping record books on us all. This God punished us and rewarded us ac-

when the phone rang, it was my brother who is in the air force. His base is on high alert. I am concerned he will be sent back to the mideast...... The phone rang again, a friend in Pittsburgh, whose cousin was at the pentagon when it was attacked....   >>

cording to our deserving. This was the primary view of God in
the Bible who split the Red Sea to allow the chosen ones to escape and then closed that sea to allow their enemies to drown.
But that is no longer our world. The idea that the Earth is the
center of the universe has disappeared.

We live today with the knowledge that the Earth rotates
around our sun—which is itself only one star in the galaxy called
the Milky Way that contains over 100 billion other stars. Our
single galaxy is so large that light, traveling at the approximate
speed of 186,000 miles per second, would take more than
100,000 years to go from one end of it to the other. Beyond that,
our galaxy is only one of at least 125 billion other galaxies in the
visible universe. A supernatural God—who lives above the sky
and is intimately involved in the affairs of human history, miraculously changing events to conform to some divine purpose—
is simply no longer believable.

If God is real, then we must look to a new definition that
opens up new religious possibilities. I find a doorway into this
experience in what I call the minority voices found in our sacred
writings. Among the people of the world there have always been
those who are willing to probe new arenas and to develop different perspectives. They do not confuse their God experiences
with the familiar God explanations of their times. So I probe
those minority voices in search of a new God concept or
metaphor, even a new pathway into the Holy.

The Jewish people seemed to know intuitively that God and
the popular definition of God could never be identical. That is
why they spoke so vehemently against idolatry. They understood that no human creation could finally capture the Holy:
not idols, not words, not scriptures, not creeds, not theological constructs.

Furthermore, while the popular voices of the Bible spoke of

He called again later and the cousin is okay.... Talked to another
friend in PA not too far from the crash of the plane in Somerset,
she's okay... I am in shock. I am sickened. The ugliness and
utter callousness of the human mind is so deep.... it makes

the external supernatural God who did miracles, the minority voices spoke of God in impersonal images. They saw God in the analogy of the wind, which, like God, was formless, mysterious, and unbounded. One experienced the wind—one did not define it. Its purpose was to animate, vitalize, and give life. This image of God is seen in the creation story where God creates Adam out of the dust of the earth, but Adam is brought to life only when God gives him mouth-to-mouth resuscitation, filling him with God's breath, thought to be the source of the wind. Life, says this biblical insight, is itself the medium through which the Holy lives. In this passage God is not a being, but the dynamic, emerging source of life itself.

This divine life force is found again in a story in the Book of Ezekiel. The Jewish nation has been conquered, and its people have been carried off into a Babylonian exile, ending its life. Ezekiel, in a dream, sees his now-deceased nation as a valley filled with dead dry bones. The question is asked, "Will these bones ever live again?" Then, in the dream, God blows the wind over the mountain and into that valley until it touches the dry bones. At that moment, the toe bone gets connected to the foot bone, the foot bone to the anklebone, the anklebone to the leg bone until all those bones stand up and come to life again. The life we possess, our vitality itself, reflects the vital life of God, this narrative says. God is the source of life.

God, as wind, is seen once more in the Book of Acts where the gathered Christian community waits in the upper room. Suddenly, that room is filled with a mighty rushing wind that calls these Christians into an inclusive vision not limited by tribal identity. This new humanity cannot be bounded. The God who is the source of life, this story says, does not stop at human security barriers. That wind, rather, creates a new God image, a life force flowing through the universe, embracing Parthians,

the soul sick...
9/11/01 4:37 P.M. xylina12: I'm tired of Christians acting like this has been foretold in the Bible. It hasn't. All it says in the Bible is that things will get worse....which is something all religions >>

Medes, Elamites, and dwellers in Mesopotamia. When human beings live fully, this God becomes visible and real.

The Epistle of John says that God is love, and whoever abides in love abides in God. Love comes to consciousness in the human experience. Love makes life possible. Love creates wholeness. When love is shared, life is enhanced, but when hatred replaces love, life is diminished. An even keener insight emerges when we reverse those biblical words. For if we can say that God is love, then surely we can say that love is God. This biblical insight proclaims that love is what God is. We thus make God visible, not by receiving an external revelation from on high, but by the human act of loving wastefully.

Once again, this minority voice is saying that God is not an external, supernatural being, ruling over human history. God is rather the power of love, which flows through each of us, calling us to life, inviting us to step beyond whatever binds our humanity, even if it is the old images of God.

In the rubble of the World Trade Center, we see the results when lives are lived in hatred—but we also see lives willing to sacrifice themselves for the sake of other people, opening to us the wonder and awe that comes when the love of God is seen in human form.

Finally, this minority voice in the Bible describes God as a cold, hard, lifeless, impersonal rock. "God is our rock," the psalmist says. "There is no rock like our God." In this image, once again, God is not a being, but the unwavering foundation under our feet. As the late Harvard theologian Paul Tillich would say, God is experienced as "the Ground of Being," when we "have the courage to be all that each of us can be."

I roam inside these minority voices in the biblical story, in order to see God in a new way. God is not an external, super-

believe- something has to change in our world, or we are doomed. Show me the verse in the Bible where it says that the US will have a terrorist attack of this magnitude take place.
9/11/01 4:38 P.M. kbstanton: I left work early because I couldn't

natural entity, ruling the world from above the sky. God is rather the Source of Life, the Source of Love, the Ground of Being. It is a nontheistic definition. Life has taught us that theism is dead. There is no supernatural God directing the affairs of history. Atheism, however, is not the only other viable conclusion. Supernatural theism is nothing but a human definition of God. We need not despair when our human definitions of God die. We use that death to force open our eyes to new possibilities, to see God as the wind that animates humanity; as the love that expands humanity, and as the rock that is the ground of humanity's being.

This is the God I confront when the theistic images of the past crumble and fall apart amid the irrationalities of life, with its violence and pain. Neither we nor the theistic God can control our fate or make secure our fragile world. All we or the God within us can do is to grasp our moment and commit ourselves to live fully and thus reveal the Source of Life, to love wastefully and thus reveal the Source of Love, and to be all that we can be and thus reveal the Ground of Being. In that way, we enter, experience, and reveal the reality of God. Here, we touch transcendence, welcome the emerging world, and by conscious act of our mature wills, we discover ourselves entering into the deepest mystery of both life and God.

The terrorist tragedy becomes an opportunity to step self-consciously beyond the God of yesterday that promised us a protection theism has never been able to deliver. It calls us away from pious delusions. That is a frightening conclusion, but that is where we live.

The worship of this God, who is life, love, and being, will never be a magic potion that exists to keep us safe. It will, however, call us to move toward universalism, to move beyond the

concentrate. I feel so sick. I can't believe this has happened and I am trying to put the pieces together. I am hooked to the news, which is only rehash at this point. I am scared that it is not over. I am so sad and feel so alone. »

need to find acts of revenge that only expand the cycle of violence. It will build in us the commitment to live our lives in such a way as to create a new world in which everyone has a better chance to experience God by living fully, loving wastefully, and being all that they are capable of being in the infinite variety of the human family.

That is, in my opinion, the only way religious people can finally and appropriately respond to the madness of human life that occurred on September 11.

BISHOP JOHN SHELBY SPONG, D.D., is the retired bishop of the Episcopal Diocese of Newark and the author of 14 books.

9/11/01 4:46 P.M. Johannes: This is the time of Mappo, when Dharma, the Law, degenerates.
It was foretold in Buddhist tradition LONG AGO

Chapter 3

SEEDS
OF GRACE

I rock with grief,
Fear and trembling overwhelm me;
For I see violence and strife in the city.
I say, "If only I had wings like a dove
That I might fly away and find rest."
—Psalm 55

REST IN PEACE
By Frederic and Mary Ann Brussat

How do we see this terrible event from a spiritual perspective? How do we respond to the complexity and magnitude and mystery of this day of death and destruction? From the news reports and interviews with public figures, we are already being barraged with outraged and angry rhetoric. The attacks are being called an act of war, the worst attack on America since Pearl Harbor, a day of infamy, the very worst of human nature. Some are demanding a swift and merciless retaliation, even before we know who was behind these terrible acts.

All the world's religions encourage us to forgive those who have hurt us, to do good to those who hate us, and to pray for those who abuse us. Christians recall Jesus' admonition to love our enemies. Jews cling to the practice of shalom. Muslims rely upon Allah, the most compassionate and the most merciful, to guide their relationships with others. In the aftermath of the tragedy, leaders from all spiritual traditions have condemned the violence, pointing out that no cause justifies such immoral acts.

After searching our souls, we have found ourselves drawn back to the spiritual practices of compassion, connections, and unity conveyed so beautifully in Thich Nhat Hanh's classic poem "Call Me by My True Names." This Vietnamese Buddhist monk and peace activist has seen the suffering of war firsthand and written often about the attitudes that lead to real peace. He refuses to divide the world into easily identifiable victims and villains. With powerful prose and vivid imagery, he reaches out to take into his heart all those who are suffering—the innocent and the violent, the powerful and the powerless, the oppressed and the oppressors. In "Call Me by My True Names," he practices radical empathy as he identifies with a frog and the snake that eats it, then with a

9/11/01 4:47 P.M. onmyownjourney: This is truly an awful blight on our short human record. But paradoxically, this type of event might serve a purpose in helping mankind to finally "wake up" and see the utter senselessness of such acts and to put a stop to

starving child in Uganda and the arms merchant who sells deadly weapons to Uganda. In a very poignant passage, he describes himself as a 12-year-old girl raped by a sea pirate and as the pirate whose "heart [is] not yet capable of seeing and loving."

No one can be excluded from our thoughts and prayers. Even elements of the natural world and things are to be cherished as recipients of our compassion. Even the perpetrators of horrible violence are part of the many names we call ourselves. "Please call me by my true names," he pleads, "so I can see that my joy and pain are one . . . and the door of my heart could be left open, the door of compassion."

We live in a city in shock and grief. We identify deeply with the pain of our neighbors. We share the joy at news of reunions taking place and rescues being accomplished. We are disquieted by the loss of life, the destruction of a section of the city we know and love, the disruption of so many lives, and the palpable fear and numbness gripping Americans and others around the world. Yet we are also disquieted by any hate that spreads across the land, by any rush to judgment, the need to immediately affix blame, and the very real possibility that an entire group of people will be demonized and stereotyped because of the acts of a few. How do we respond?

We pray for the victims and those who are trying to help them. We pray for the dead, may they rest in peace, and their families and friends, may they know peace. We pray for those seeking to learn who was behind these attacks, may they be clearheaded and thorough. We pray for our government leaders, may they have the wisdom to handle this crisis without contributing to further violence. We pray for the people of the world, may we learn what needs to be learned from these overwhelming events, and may we respond to them in the best way possible with the help of the One who sustains us all.

them forever. We have been lolling in spiritual unawareness for too long now. What else will it take to finally pull mankind together and make us realize that we are all an integral part of each other?   >>

We pray—and we offer this poem. Please call us by these names so that we may open the door of compassion.

REST IN PEACE

I am a World Trade Center tower, standing tall in the clear blue sky, feeling a violent blow in my side, and
I am a towering inferno of pain and suffering imploding upon myself and collapsing to the ground.
May I rest in peace.

I am a terrified passenger on a hijacked airplane not knowing where we are going or that I am riding on fuel tanks that will be instruments of death, and
I am a worker arriving at my office not knowing that in just a moment my future will be obliterated.
May I rest in peace.

I am a pigeon in the plaza between the two towers eating crumbs from someone's breakfast when fire rains down on me from the skies, and
I am a bed of flowers admired daily by thousands of tourists now buried under five stories of rubble.
May I rest in peace.

I am a firefighter sent into dark corridors of smoke and debris on a mission of mercy only to have it collapse around me, and
I am a rescue worker risking my life to save lives who is very aware that I may not make it out alive.
May I rest in peace.

I am a survivor who has fled down the stairs and out of the building to safety who knows that nothing will ever be the same in my soul again, and

9/11/01 6:05 P.M. Cerridwen: First of all, I am not a normally violent person, but even Jesus got pissed. It is not the time for inaction. It is the time to seek out the leaders of these groups no matter what it takes and remove the threat. I am not even into

*I am a doctor in a hospital treating patients burned from head
to toe who knows that these horrible images will remain in my
mind forever.*
May I know peace.

*I am a tourist in Times Square looking up at the giant TV
screens thinking I'm seeing a disaster movie as I watch the Twin
Towers crash to the ground, and*
*I am a New York woman sending e-mails to friends and
family letting them know that I am safe.*
May I know peace.

*I am a piece of paper that was on someone's desk this morning
and now I'm debris scattered by the wind across lower
Manhattan, and*
*I am a stone in the graveyard at Trinity Church covered with
soot from the buildings that once stood proudly above me, death
meeting death.*
May I rest in peace.

*I am a dog sniffing in the rubble for signs of life, doing my best
to be of service, and*
*I am a blood donor waiting in line to make a simple but very
needed contribution for the victims.*
May I know peace.

*I am a resident in an apartment in downtown New York who
has been forced to evacuate my home, and*
*I am a resident in an apartment uptown who has walked 100
blocks home in a stream of other refugees.*
May I know peace.

the "killing more innocents" argument. Sorry, when those
people were in the street cheering the deaths of my innocent
fellow countrymen, they ceased to be innocent.
9/11/01 6:23 P.M. noodlegirl: "How can you hold a whole reli- >>

I am a family member who has just learned that someone I love has died, and

I am a pastor who must comfort someone who has suffered a heartbreaking loss.

May I know peace.

I am a loyal American who feels violated and vows to stand behind any military action it takes to wipe terrorists off the face of the earth, and

I am a loyal American who feels violated and worries that people who look and sound like me are all going to be blamed for this tragedy.

May I know peace.

I am a frightened city dweller who wonders whether I'll ever feel safe in a skyscraper again, and

I am a pilot who wonders whether there will ever be a way to make the skies truly safe.

May I know peace.

I am the owner of a small store with five employees that has been put out of business by this tragedy, and

I am an executive in a multinational corporation who is concerned about the cost of doing business in a terrorized world.

May I know peace.

I am a visitor to New York City who purchases postcards of the World Trade Center Twin Towers that are no more, and

I am a television reporter trying to put into words the terrible things I have seen.

May I know peace.

---

gion responsible for the actions of a small group of fanatics? That is like blaming all of Christianity for the violent acts of white supremacists."
9/11/01 6:34 P.M. Patience1: The Jesuit who taught me logic

I am a boy in New Jersey waiting for a father who will never come home, and

I am a boy in a faraway country rejoicing in the streets of my village because someone has hurt the hated Americans.

May I know peace.

I am a general talking into the microphones about how we must stop the terrorist cowards who have perpetrated this heinous crime, and

I am an intelligence officer trying to discern how such a thing could have happened on American soil, and

I am a city official trying to find ways to alleviate the suffering of my people.

May I know peace.

I am a terrorist whose hatred for America knows no limit and I am willing to die to prove it, and

I am a terrorist sympathizer standing with all the enemies of American capitalism and imperialism, and

I am a master strategist for a terrorist group who planned this abomination.

My heart is not yet capable of openness, tolerance, and loving.

May I know peace.

I am a citizen of the world glued to my television set, fighting back my rage and despair at these horrible events, and

I am a person of faith struggling to forgive the unforgivable, praying for the consolation of those who have lost loved ones, calling upon the merciful beneficence of God/Lord/Allah/Spirit/ Higher Power.

May I know peace.

says that that which is universally asserted may be universally denied. I am a Muslim and I am not cheering. Many of my loved ones are - I am proud to say - Palestinians; and they are not cheering. »

I am a child of God who believes that we are all children of God and we are all part of each other.
May we all know peace.

FREDERIC AND MARY ANN BRUSSAT are media and Web editors at the magazine *Spirituality & Health* and the authors of *Spiritual Literacy*.

FATHER MIKE WENT AHEAD TO GREET THEM ALL
By Steven McDonald (Interviewed by Wendy Schuman)

One of the many crushing losses of the World Trade Center attack was the death of Father Mychal Judge, 68, a Franciscan friar and a chaplain of the New York City Fire Department, who was killed by falling debris on September 11 while giving last rites to a dying firefighter. Father Mike, as he was known, was a close friend and spiritual advisor of Police Detective Steven McDonald, who, in 1986, had been shot in Central Park by a 15-year-old he was questioning about a stolen bike. McDonald remained near death for months, unable to speak, and each day a priest came to his hospital room to say mass with the young detective and his wife, who was expecting a child. Often that priest was Father Mike. Paralyzed from the neck down and still on a ventilator, McDonald later reached out to his assailant and publicly forgave him. He has since made it his mission to speak for the healing power of forgiveness.

Father Mike's death was the first one officially recorded at the World Trade Center. Tell me about your relationship and what he meant to you.

9/11/01 6:41 P.M. peace_is_now: ...As a friend said in an e-mail today, times like these really make you reevaluate what's important. The mundane, ordinary nuances of daily life seem so much more precious when you realize how quickly things can change.

I'm sure there were people that died earlier when the plane exploded, but Father Mike's was the first death certificate recorded. That was significant, because he was already on the other side bringing in those people who died and suffered so terribly. Father Duffy, his good friend, said in his eulogy that Father Mike never could have dealt with the deaths of more than 300 of his men if he hadn't gone ahead to greet them all. That's what his whole life was about, it wasn't about Father Mike, it was about helping everyone else, and that's why he was so loved. He had an AIDS ministry before he became a fire chaplain.

Why do you think Father Mike was taken at that time?
Because God needed him more than we did, and he's making good use of him. I'm sure there are many people who believe that this is all there is, the world we live in. I don't believe that this is it. And Father Mike is there in that next life comforting those people that have passed on from this terrible tragedy. His work has just begun. God is using him in ways we can't even begin to imagine. I once heard someone say that the pain we carry with us to the next life is the love we leave behind in this life. So if that's true, then Father Mike is helping them understand that everything will be OK.

Have you seen *Newsweek*? Look in the back; Father Mike is there. In the summer of 1996, TWA Flight 800 went down. Father Mike and I usually talked around midnight, and that night I called him and he didn't yet know what was going on. I said, "Father Mike, did you hear what happened? A plane just crashed in the ocean off Long Island." Right away, he had to get off the phone. He flew in his car to Kennedy Airport. He was there for 2 weeks or more with those families, and for the last 5 years he's been very important to them. In *Newsweek* there's a

Cherish the sound of your partner's breath as they sleep peacefully by your side tonight. And let everyone you care about know how much they mean to you today.
9/11/01 6:46 P.M. Rtnrlfy: Apart from any political or   »

great picture of Father Mike looking out on the Atlantic Ocean, and underneath the picture it has a quote from him: "When they look down, they see your love." He was consoling people here, and now he's up there consoling those who are carrying that pain with them. What they're experiencing is far better than what we can ever imagine, but still they know the loved ones they left behind are in pain. Jesus is using Father Mike to comfort them.

I know that forgiveness is something you care deeply about. You forgave your attacker. In the present situation, what can you say about forgiving those who have caused so many people such harm?

That's something that Father Mike helped me with so much. I was angry and frustrated, unable to talk because of the gunshot wounds. I was really locked into my body, the paralysis and all. And from that came my hostility, which I'm sure the young man was the focus of. Father Mike would come over and say mass, and his homily was about Christ's love. Forgiveness is not easy, even for us Christians, though we have the greatest example of forgiveness.

Holding on to feelings of hatred and revenge destroys you inside. And talking about it helps the healing process as well. I don't think it's possible to ever forget what happened to you. But if you forgive the person, organization, or whatever it is you forgive, you're releasing yourself from those very difficult emotions. We're made out of love, God's love, and we're made to love. I think by doing this and sharing with others, we return to that love.

What about the idea of justice—are you saying that those who hurt us should go unpunished?

No—I believe in justice as well. The family of my assailant wanted me to help him get out of prison. I said if I do that, who

ideological opinions I might have, Jesus still asks me to pray for my enemies. I have spent much of the day trying to understand the mindset of 'those whose lives felt so desperate...' and I simply cannot. So I pray, because I cannot comprehend.

is going to help him steer clear of trouble? A judge had returned him to his family and to a social agency once before when he was arrested for attempted robbery. The judge hoped it would turn him around, but that didn't happen. A year or two after I forgave him, he called from prison and he apologized to my wife and to me. Father Mike was a big part of this. I would call him up and I would tell him what I was going through, what I was struggling with, and he came over for dinner just to talk. He would bring that Franciscan faith, that simple faith in Christ. He was a living example of Jesus Christ for me. Christ's parting gift to us was an act of forgiveness on the cross. Father Mike was the living face of Jesus Christ in our lives. It's true he had a great sense of humor, was clever, smart, and loving, but what's more important than being God for each other?

Your son Conor has known Father Mike since birth. What has he said about him and about the World Trade Center attack?
Conor's very upset; he's devastated. They were very close. Early on in my hospitalization, I was unable to travel, so Father Mike, my wife, Patti Ann, and Conor went to Disneyland. Conor was 3 years old, and Father Mike was like the father figure. We have some great pictures of Father Mike and Conor going on some kind of saucer ride. When I told him Father Mike was dead, Conor ran out of the house screaming, and he ran all the way to his grandmother's. Why would a loving God allow this to happen? The answer we're given as Catholics is because of free will. God gave us free will, and those men determined that they were going to destroy human life. But the reward—if I can say it that way for those people on the plane, those in the Twin Towers—is that now they're experiencing eternal life with the Father, and it's better than any trip to Disneyland could ever have been.

Deus nobiscum.
9/11/01 7:04 P.M. redcherokee: And it's happening already, people are lumping Muslims all into the same category and collectively blaming them for this tragedy. Yes it's true that »

If you could give a message to the families whose loved ones died, what would you say?

I have my problems, but nothing like what they're going through. I have made it these 15 years by turning my life over as best I can, in an imperfect way, to God. My wife said hours after I was shot, "I'm going to trust in God." I also say, "Allow people to help you." Many of us have difficulty in doing that. You'll find a stronger, deeper self when you turn yourself over to God and the help of others.

STEVEN MCDONALD is a former New York City police detective.

A GOSPEL CANTICLE OF GOOD TUESDAY
By Father Edward Hays

O God, come to our assistance; O Lord, make haste to help us.
The day awoke with blue skies bright in a September sun, plus
morning coffee and, of course, business as usual.

Then, suddenly, billowing dark clouds of fire and smoke
swallowed up the sun, plunging the world into blinding darkness,
as towering tidal waves of terror came crashing over us.

Thousands were crucified by crushing concrete and steel
on that fiery Good Tuesday, each innocent of crime—
as were you, O Christ, on your terror-filled Good Friday.
The wounded, those deeply lacerated in heart and spirit,
tally in the thousands of millions around the globe,
now united in sickening shock and moral outrage,
their eyes forever stigmatized with scenes of horror.

As heroic helpers hurriedly climbed into that smoking hell
to rescue the countless trapped and wounded,

there are Muslims dancing in the streets in the Middle East celebrating what happened today. But there are also countless innocent Muslims who will be persecuted for their religious affiliation. Heavenly Father we pray for guidance. Give us the

your voice swirled up out of the fire and smoke:
"There is no greater love than to lay down one's life
for one's friends—especially one's unknown friends,
one's anonymous brothers and sisters." Grant, O Jesus,
to the grieving families and friends of loved ones lost,
the fullness of the blessing of compassion you promised:
"Blessed are those who mourn, for they shall be comforted."

Amidst flashing red lights and wailing sirens,
we struggle to seal our ears to the echo
of your agonizing cry from high on your cross,
"Father, forgive them, for they know not what they do."
Now, as battle bugles trumpet us to a Crusade, a Holy
    War,
raise God's shofar to your lips, O Christ, and call us again:
"No war, not even a Holy War! No Crusade of hate!
Love your enemies. Bless those who injure you.
Forgive those who terrorize you."
O God, come to our assistance, forgive us our personal sins,
as well as our communal sins, as we forgive those who sin
    against us.
O Lord, make haste to help us, and gift us with the grace
of a divine courage to love our enemies.

The brutal murder of the innocents screams out for justice,
and so with a burning primitive lust our hands itch
to become angry instruments of reprisal and retribution.
O God, make haste to help us, come quickly
and wash not our feet but our itching hands
from their prehistoric craving for revenge.
Touch with your healing fingers our long-deaf ears

temperament and wisdom to not cast stones upon innocents.
9/11/01 7:53 P.M. lineboo: THERE ARE MANY YOUTHS IN MY
NEIGHBORHOOD THAT ARE GOING AROUND SO UNCON-
CERNED. THEY'RE DANCING, PLAYING LOUD CAR RADIOS, »

so we can once again hear your commands:
"Do not judge and you will not be judged.
Do not condemn and you will not be condemned!

"My disciples, I understand your thirst for justice,
your hunger that those who died did not die in vain,
your craving that all who are guilty be held responsible.
Yet, you who are my disciples have given me a holy name;
you call me, 'The Judge of the Living and the Dead.'
So place your urgent need for justice in my pierced hands,
and God will fairly balance the scales of Divine Justice."

O Lord, make haste and relieve our helplessness,
and show us how to respond to these vicious attacks.
"My friends, be clever as serpents, and innocent as doves.
Ask the ever-creative Spirit of God to inspire you
to abandon the ancient weapons of war, proven to be impotent,
and to find astonishingly new ways to defend yourselves
from those who terrorize you and seek your destruction.
Trust that God aches for your creative nonviolent solutions."

O Holy and Good Tuesday, deep as the Grand Canyon is your
     pain
and profound is our powerlessness and vulnerability.
A mighty Mississippi of our agonizing tears of loss
flows broadly across the land from shore to shore.
Like an early morning fog, now forever vaporized,
is our once carefree, innocent sense of security.
O Lord, come to our assistance, make haste to help us.

O Lord, our Risen Christ, come and visit our disasters,
placing a fresh Easter lily of hope and victory
high upon the peak of that Calvary mountain of twisted steel

DAMAGING PROPERTY. NOW IS THE TIME THAT WE MUST AP-
PEAL TO OUR YOUTH AND LET THEM KNOW THAT THIS IS
THEIR WORLD AND THEY MUST SHOW CONCERN AND RESPECT
FOR IT

and smothering crumbled ruins that entombs thousands,
and so encourage all of your disciples of peace and pardon,
whose Christian creed is forever the same one as yours:
Life is stronger than death,
and love is stronger than hate.

FATHER EDWARD HAYS is a Catholic priest and the former director of a
contemplative retreat center. He is currently prison chaplain at Kansas State
Penitentiary. A prolific author, he has published collections of contemporary
parables and prayers including two masterworks, *Prayers for a Planetary Pil-*
grim and *Prayers for the Domestic Church.* To read more about his books and
posters and cards based on his inspirational artwork, visit his publisher's
Web site at www.forestofpeace.com.

WHAT CAN WE DO BUT PRAY?
By Mata Amritanandamayi (Amma)

Words cannot possibly do full justice to what Amma wishes to
convey. In her heart, Amma experiences the profound feelings
of loss and pain that this unspeakable tragedy has inflicted on
the innocent people of America.

Indeed, people throughout the world have been deeply hurt
by this. And now that this utterly inhuman, blood-curdling act
has taken place, what can we do but pray, and try to resolve the
tense situation through peaceful means?

Amma knows that it is very difficult to keep one's composure
and not react to an atrocity of such magnitude. The human
mind can be the most destructive weapon if negative thoughts
are not properly handled. There is a lot of anger boiling within
people at present, and this is understandable. However, we
shouldn't let that anger manifest outwardly in the form of vio-

9/11/01 8:38 P.M. seetha: Today in school a girl came up to me
during lunch. "Are you one of the terrorist people?" she asked.
"No. I'm Hindu," I said. She looked at me with suspicion as
she walked away.   >>

lence. It is best to let it cool down with the help of prayers and reflection on the consequences of a war.

Of course Amma is concerned about the future of the world. But Amma feels particularly sad right now thinking about those innocent people who were killed when the planes crashed into those buildings; and Amma feels immensely sad when she thinks about the countless people who lost their loved ones, and all those children who lost their parents. Amma feels such tremendous sadness, and her heart reaches out to all those affected by that terrible, destructive act, which was an act against all of humanity.

May the Supreme Being bless everyone with enough strength to overcome their grief, and may the dark forces of negativity and ignorance give way to the light, love, and peace of God.

MATA AMRITANANDAMAYI is the beloved religious leader now known as Mother of Immortal Bliss, or Ammachi, or Amma, and travels the world holding "hugging audiences" and raising money for her numerous charities.

Do It Again, Lord
By Max Lucado

Dear Lord,

We're still hoping we'll wake up. We're still hoping we'll open a sleepy eye and think, "What a horrible dream."

But we won't, will we, Father? What we saw was not a dream. Planes did gouge towers. Flames did consume our fortress. People did perish. It was no dream, and, dear Father, we are sad.

There is a ballet dancer who will no longer dance and a doctor who will no longer heal. A church has lost her priest, a classroom is minus a teacher. Cora ran a food pantry. Paige was

---

9/11/01 8:48 P.M. PERSIANCHICKA: as a muslim, i am sickened by what has happened today. i pray that whoever is responsible for this ugly and cowardly act will be punished severely. what made me more angry is those palestinians who were celea counselor, and Dana, dearest Father, Dana was only 3 years old. (Who held her in those final moments?)

We are sad, Father. For as the innocent are buried, our innocence is buried as well. We thought we were safe. Perhaps we should have known better. But we didn't.

And so we come to you. We don't ask you for help; we beg you for it. We don't request it; we implore it. We know what you can do. We've read the accounts. We've pondered the stories and now we plead, "Do it again, Lord. Do it again."

Remember Joseph? You rescued him from the pit. You can do the same for us. Do it again, Lord.

Remember the Hebrews in Egypt? You protected their children from the angel of death. We have children, too, Lord. Do it again.

And Sarah? Remember her prayers? You heard them. Joshua? Remember his fears? You inspired him. The women at the tomb? You resurrected their hope. The doubts of Thomas? You took them away. Do it again, Lord. Do it again.

You changed Daniel from a captive into a king's counselor. You took Peter the fisherman and made him Peter an apostle. Because of you, David went from leading sheep to leading armies. Do it again, Lord, for we need counselors today, Lord. We need apostles. We need leaders. Do it again, dear Lord.

Most of all, do again what you did at Calvary. What we saw here that Tuesday, you saw there that Friday. Innocence slaughtered. Goodness murdered. Mothers weeping. Evil dancing. Just as the ash fell on our children, the darkness fell on your Son. Just as our towers were shattered, the very Tower of Eternity was pierced.

And by dusk, heaven's sweetest song was silent, buried behind a rock.

But you did not waver, O Lord. You did not waver. After 3 days in a dark hole, you rolled the rock and rumbled the earth

brating. may they be ashamed of themselves. what happened today is the acts of some sick animals. they do not represent the over a billion muslims around the world, nor the 10 million muslims here in the united states. what many may forget is >>

and turned the darkest Friday into the brightest Sunday. Do it again, Lord. Grant us a September Easter.

We thank you, dear Father, for these hours of unity. Christians are praying with Jews. Republicans are standing with Democrats. Skin colors have been covered by the ash of burning buildings. We thank you for these hours of unity.

And we thank you for these hours of prayer. The Enemy sought to bring us to our knees and succeeded. He had no idea, however, that we would kneel before you. And he has no idea what you can do.

Let your mercy be upon our president, vice president, and their families. Grant to those who lead us wisdom beyond their years and experience. Have mercy upon the souls who have departed and the wounded who remain. Give us grace that we might forgive and faith that we might believe.

And look kindly upon your church. For 2,000 years you've used her to heal a hurting world.

Do it again, Lord. Do it again.

Through Christ, Amen.

MAX LUCADO is the pastor of Oak Hills Church of Christ in San Antonio, Texas, and a Christian author of more than 25 books.

SEEING GOD IN MY NEIGHBORS
By Sharon Linnéa

Last month, I thought I knew my neighbors. We'd wave at each other as we drove by, chat in the supermarket, and have cookie swaps at Christmas. Nice folks. I also thought I knew New Yorkers. I lived in the city for 20 years before I moved to the suburbs, and I still go in to work on 23rd Street when I'm not

that Americans—christians, jews, muslims, hindus, etc. were all victims today.
9/11/01 9:38 P.M. Leftomaniac: Y'know, I've always kinda disliked the whole "Patriotism" deal, but this really makes me

telecommuting from home. New Yorkers are gruff, straight-talking people who are nicer than reputation leads you to believe, but always in a hurry.

Then came Tuesday, September 11, and I found out I didn't know New Yorkers—or my neighbors—at all. Maybe you discovered the same thing.

That morning, I drove my 6-year-old son, Jonathan, to school. When I returned to my home office at 9:19 to start my day, there were two phone messages from my husband. His office is one block from the World Trade Center. The first said, "There's been a big explosion. Someone says a small plane hit the Trade Center." The second said, "Hey, there's been another explosion." I called him back, then turned on the television. As I watched, the first tower imploded. And then my husband was gone. He could not be reached by landline or cell phone. As it had for countless thousands of others, my long day of waiting had begun.

Thankfully, my husband's journey would take him through "nuclear winter" into the open arms of help and kindness. Joyce Baldassarri lives in Staten Island just across the harbor from the southern tip of Manhattan, in full view of the World Trade Center. As soon as the magnitude of the tragedy became clear, Joyce rushed to the local police department to see what she could do to help, but they were on high alert themselves and had no time to coordinate civilian efforts. So Joyce took matters into her own hands.

She realized that thousands of people who work in lower Manhattan could not be moved north; there was no way to get past the disaster site. There was only one other way out: onboard the ferry to Staten Island. And so they began arriving, hundreds of men and women who were escaping with their lives but not much else. Jackets, purses, briefcases, and shoes had been left in offices quickly abandoned.

want to wave a flag and sing "God Bless America." Funny how precious something is when the danger of losing it is made real.
9/11/01 9:44 P.M. karenmhc: Please keep my cousin in your »

Joyce swung into action. She had three phone lines in her house; she lined them up against one wall and called her friends and the local pizzeria and asked them to bring food. Then she sent these same friends out to scour the waterfront, looking for people who didn't know where to go.

Before long, they began arriving. Shell-shocked and weary, they found themselves in a warm, pleasant home. Joyce herself signed them in when they arrived, took their contact numbers so that they could be found, and handed them her phone number so they could give loved ones a contact number. Once they were finished, they were directed to her upstairs terrace for food and breathing space. Several people needed to take showers and were given a change of clothes, including one woman who had fled the New York Marriott-WTC in pajamas and no shoes. Scores of people found sanctuary in Joyce's home that day. My husband, Bob, was one of them. I saw God in Joyce's selfless giving.

I also didn't know the determination lurking in Kay Wild, the wife of my husband's colleague Peter. When we finally located our husbands and their coworkers on Staten Island, radio and television reported that traffic was a tangled mess all around Manhattan. All the bridges and tunnels were closed. No one could get close to New York City by car; no one would be leaving Staten Island at all that day.

None of this mattered to Kay. She got in her car in Connecticut and drove south, determined to rescue Peter and Bob and their colleague Linda. She parked on the opposite side of a closed bridge to Staten Island and waited—and waited—until our husbands convinced a taxi to drive them to the bridge, and emergency workers to drive them across. Bob was home by 9:00 that night. I saw God in Kay's love and determination.

My neighbor Cliff Thomson retired as a New York City firefighter 2 weeks before the tragedy. Thank heavens! I thought.

prayers. He is a NYC firefighter who was inside the WTC complex when the towers collapsed. I hope for the best outcome for him, but it's looking pretty grim.
9/11/01 10:08 P.M. BudlongBrown: ...In the meantime, let me

He's out of harm's way. But not Cliff. He immediately headed in to Ground Zero in Manhattan, and has been pulling shifts ever since. The on-duty firefighters working there are getting paid time-and-a-half as overtime for the horrible, dangerous, life-shattering work they're doing. Cliff is being paid nothing. I see God in his selflessness.

Yesterday, Dorothy Randall called me from her Army post at the World Trade Center. I met Dorothy when she was a gangly, grinning 9-year-old who was assigned to me as a "little sister" by the Big Brothers/Big Sisters of New York. I have watched her blossom into a lovely young woman, a single mother (bereaved by a drunk driver), who has done a masterful job of raising her son in the projects of Brooklyn. She called on break because she is an Army Reservist called up to protect those clearing debris at the disaster site. "I can see the bodies," she said, "but thank God I don't have to deal with them." She called to make sure we were all right and to say she loved us. I see God daily in Dottie's perseverance and love.

This disaster has shown me depths of ordinary people I never knew were there before—in many, many different ways. Not everyone can go to help at the World Trade Center. But I'll bet there's a reaching out, a wanting to help others, in your neighborhood that perhaps wasn't as evident a week ago.

My son, Jonathan, discovered this week that local farmworkers were going to bed without blankets as the nights here dipped down below 40 degrees. He began a drive to collect blankets. My 4-year-old daughter has insisted on accompanying him as he makes the rounds, handing out flyers. I see God in their innocent compassion. I also see him in the Muslim store manager who said, "If these blankets are for the poor, I want to help, too," and did. I see him in the girls in our neighborhood who were gathering bouquets of wildflowers to sell today, and when I said we were walking

share a true story...happened late this afternoon. My son's best friend, a 12-year-old Assyrian boy (Orthodox) ...is the sweetest and gentlest boy. But he was jumped by a group of high school boys and beaten into unconsciousness. The entire time >>

distributing flyers but not carrying money, they conferred and shyly returned to present us each with bouquets and to ask if they could help us distribute flyers to gather blankets. Would they have done so a week ago? Perhaps. But they certainly did it today.

My colleagues at Beliefnet certainly do not expect me to say this, but they came into our Manhattan offices that Tuesday when no one knew if it was safe, and every day thereafter, and stayed into the wee hours because they were determined to provide our users with a place of solace and community at a time of urgent need. This was not an easy task, as our server was located down by the Twin Towers and is out for the foreseeable future.

Let me finally tell you about my across-the-street neighbor, James Shanahan. James is an obstetrician. Early Wednesday morning, September 12, he delivered a baby to a mother who has a 6-year-old son, whom James also delivered. The little boy has an inoperable brain tumor. The father is a New York City police officer who came to witness the birth on his break from disaster duty at the Trade Center. The baby was a planned Cesarean, and as the team worked, James and the parents discussed the tragic events, and how different the world was that they were bringing this child into than it had been even the day before. Their hearts were heavy, their discussion subdued.

And then the baby was born. It is a little girl. And the parents, who were facing the worst that this world has to offer, held her tight and welcomed her and surrounded her with love. God was there. And the world went on.

SHARON LINNÉA is Beliefnet's Inspiration Producer. Her most recent books include biographies of Raoul Wallenberg and Hawaii's Princess Kaiulani. She is also an editor of the *Chicken Soup for the Soul* series.

they were screaming that he was a killer and that his people had killed all those people in New York. He's awake now...with multiple skull fractures and broken ribs...a fractured jaw and broken arm.

Prayer of Protection
By Colleen Zuck

Silent Unity has been praying with people for over 100 years. We have prayed in times of peace and times of war. We have prayed in times of depression and prosperity. In every season of change or challenge, we have placed our faith in God.

In light of the recent tragedy in the United States, we as a human family are experiencing a vast range of emotions. We feel numb and ask ourselves, "How could this happen?" We feel a void, a great sense of emptiness. Whether or not we know or loved someone who died or someone who lost a loved one, we all to some degree feel a sense of loss, because a huge life force has left our planet. As a nation, we are outraged that innocent lives have been so violently taken from us. We are appalled that such an act could take place on American soil.

What can we do as a nation as emotions surface in this uncertain time? What can you do as an individual? The answer is pray.

When you feel alone, pray and know that you are not alone; God is with you.

When you hurt, pray and let God's love comfort you.

When you don't know what to do, pray and let God's wisdom guide you.

When you feel that life is in chaos, pray and let God's assurance of divine order fill your heart.

This situation has made many people feel fearful of economic downturn. If you fear lack, pray and know that God is in charge. God is your provider and source of supply.

Some people in our country are now responding to their fears by resorting to vengeful and violent actions toward innocent people who happen to look or believe differently than they do. What can we do about this? Once again we can pray. We can

9/11/01 10:32 P.M. sammah: I am a flight attendant for United in new york. I would like to ask for everyone's prayers for the victims, their families and the survivors, thank you.
9/11/01 10:38 P.M. latinomuslim: ...I am a Muslim man, I am   >>

pray and look to God for the strength we need to see others, no matter how different they appear, as children of God. We can pray and let God's love and peace fill us and radiate through us as expressions of tolerance and acceptance in a diverse world.

There are those who may be so fearful that they feel as though they are frozen in their tracks. They don't want to leave the security of their homes. They fear that their children will be exposed to more violence or put in danger. They want to hold their friends, family, and loved ones close and never let them go.

What can we do for these people or for ourselves if we feel this way? We can pray! To live in fear truly is to not live at all. So we pray and release our fears to God. We can live in faith, taking one step at a time, one day at a time.

Rebuilding on faith. We want to rebuild our lives, beginning with physical, mental, and emotional healing. Faith in God will help us do this. Faith replaces fear. The heart that lives in faith does not live in fear. The heart that lives in faith trusts God for strength, for peace, for wholeness in every aspect of living.

Faith helps us turn our attention away from doubt, hurt, or confusion to refocus on healing, to reach out to others who are also hurting or confused. We may want to help but not know how, or perhaps we feel that we are not physically or financially able to help. In Silent Unity, our answer to the question, "What can I do to help?" is always: Pray.

Prayer is our connection to God. Prayer builds faith in God, for it is through prayer that we build a greater awareness of God within us and around us. We in Unity believe that each person is always in the presence of God, so you can think of prayer as a way to become aware of God in your life. We pray affirmatively and positively, which means that we pray in the knowledge that the good we desire is ours through God. We pray, knowing that God loves us unconditionally.

from NY, and I have dozens of friends and family who worked in the building and in downtown manhattan. They witnessed unspeakable horrors today. All I ask from the general public and beliefnet members is for everyone to use common sense. Islam

We have heard people say, I want to pray, but I don't know how. And our hearts reach out to everyone who feels this way. Let us assure you that there is no right or wrong way to pray. There are as many ways to pray as there are people.

Prayer is the act of turning your thoughts to God, for to pray is to experience the presence of God. Simply uttering the word "God" can be a prayer.

One way to pray is to tell God what is on your mind and in your heart. Release all of these things to God and trust God for results that will be the best for everyone concerned.

Once you have surrendered your heartfelt thoughts to God, take time to listen to God. Take time to listen for reassurance of divine help. Try this: Close your eyes, take a deep breath, and exhale slowly. Do this a few times as you let your body and mind relax. Begin to let go of the things that are on your mind and focus your thought only on one word: "God." As you become focused on God, you might begin to bring other words to mind—the positive qualities of God: peace, love, wisdom—things that you would like to experience. Listen for God to speak to you, not in audible words, but as inspirational thoughts, as feelings of peace.

You may wonder in a circumstance like the one that we are facing today, what to pray for. You can always pray for the good of another: to be healed, to find comfort and understanding, to be guided or protected. As you pray, either for yourself or others, pray in the knowledge that answers are being revealed, that right results are taking place.

Moving forward. Some people have expressed that in their deep sadness, they feel no joy and cannot bear to hear another person laugh. Is our laughter in the midst of tragedy sacrilegious? Are we dishonoring those who lost their lives and the families and friends who are grieving? These are excellent questions and they reveal great feelings and sensitivity toward our

does not condone ANY KILLINGS. You will not find a single true Muslim that is not horrified and disgusted by today's events. I pray for the families of the victims, as well as the victims' souls. I pray they are at rest.   >>

fellow human beings. But joy is as much a part of our inner makeup as any of the other emotions mentioned before.

Joy is God-given. It is part of our spiritual nature. It is not wrong to laugh or feel joyful. We can let joy and laughter be part of the healing experience. If you can find something to be joyful about right now, allow yourself the experience. If you can't find any joy, even the smallest thing to touch your heart, you can pray. Prayer is also a great healer. Prayer will help you begin to once again live from a perspective of faith.

The senseless acts that occurred on September 11, 2001, have changed our lives forever. They have once again reminded us of our mortality. But they have also reinforced our knowledge of the precious gift of life that we all have been given. As we pray and strengthen our faith, we can move forward. We can begin to live again. We can rebuild our lives on a firm foundation of faith.

The following "Prayer for Protection" was written by Unity's beloved poet laureate, James Dillet Freeman, for men and women serving our country in the military during World War II. We invite you to join us in praying this prayer for our nation and for our world.

The light of God surrounds us;
The love of God enfolds us;
The power of God protects us;
The presence of God watches over us.
Wherever we are, God is!

Silent Unity is keeping the faith. We are available to pray with you 24 hours a day, and we hold every prayer request sacred and confidential. God bless you!

COLLEEN ZUCK has been an editor of *Daily Word* magazine since 1985. Silent Unity is the prayer ministry of Unity School of Christianity in Unity Village, Missouri, publisher of *Daily Word*.

9/11/01 11:16 P.M. bcbarrett: ...While my first impulse was to demand revenge and turn Afghanistan into a sheet of glass, I know deep within my heart that is not the answer and will only compound the problem.

A PRIEST ON THE FRONT LINE
By the Reverend Lloyd Prator

That Tuesday morning began with deceptive banality: a visit to the gym, morning prayer, and a breakfast meeting. Walking south on Seventh Avenue, I noticed an uncharacteristically stationary group of New Yorkers. Someone said, "Look up!" I looked to see the World Trade towers wreathed in smoke. I went back to the rectory to change into clerical attire and arranged for the parish staff to open our church, located just a block from St. Vincent's Hospital, a principal destination for the injured and dying. The rest of the day, I stayed on the street, meeting ambulances, blessing the sick, commending the dying, and talking to people who waited.

There was an air of unreality about everything that was happening, the unreality manifested in the way that we accepted and seemed resigned to the most improbable and awful things. I met many of the ambulances as they delivered their patients to the hospital, and usually gave a blessing and touched each patient as I blessed them. As I stepped into the street to meet one ambulance, I casually glanced south and saw the towers aflame. After I had given the blessing and the patient had been taken away, I looked up again and the towers were gone. And I went on to the next patient.

It is certainly important that triage procedures relay clinically accurate information along the patient care chain so that proper care can be given immediately. But the crisp, clinical assessment seems, somehow, to mask the reality of what has happened. An ambulance door swings open, and a woman barks "Gurney!" The next EMS technician snaps, "Patient struck in upper abdomen with heavy object!" I look at the patient gasping for breath, straining against probable broken ribs and covered with a dense layer of fine, gray dust. Struck by a heavy object, indeed. He was struck by a building. He was struck by an airplane. He was struck by international ter-

> **9/11/01 11:33 P.M. lleyke:** Dear God, please console the inconsolable. Please comfort the bereaved. Please help us to know what to say to help those terribly broken by this tragedy. Please help. amen.   »

88   FROM THE ASHES

rorists. He was struck by hate. Those are some very heavy objects.

Touching is important. New Yorkers often don't like to be touched, and certainly there are important boundary issues to be observed in pastoral care. But, a couple of times, when I got close to a patient and gave a blessing, the patient would, after I had made the sign of the cross over him, reach for my hand, as if he were clinging—clinging perhaps to the cross, perhaps to me, perhaps to the God whom I try to serve. This was an occasion for touching lives.

Last night, we celebrated the Eucharist for the repose of the souls of all who were killed. These days, funeral liturgies and memorial services are usually celebrated using white vestments because such services are understood to be part of the Easter mystery—that as Christ rose from death, so shall our dead rise, and so will we one day. That assurance makes the commemoration of the dead a joyful, Easter liturgy.

But this was not a time for victory, it was a time for sorrow, and so we used the black vestments. And we began with the ritual called the Supplication, for particular use in times of war, national emergency, or disaster. Its haunting words, "With pity behold the sorrows of our heart . . . graciously behold our afflictions . . . O Lord, arise and help us," seem more to touch the heart of the day than acclamations of triumph and victory. After the liturgy, I went back to the hospital and visited with four firefighters who had just been admitted to the hospital. Each one of them—sturdy young men all—was eager for prayer. One of them was being treated for a respiratory problem by lying on his back, head over the edge of the gurney, and having his nasal passages attended. I asked if he wanted a prayer, and before I could even finish the sentence, even with his airways crowded with paraphernalia, he eagerly assented. This is a day when people are reaching for meaning, reaching for each other, reaching for God.

And waiting. As the afternoon wore on, fewer and fewer am-

9/12/01 12:00 A.M. amyalon: Each prayer sent out into the world throws weight on the side of good. We add our prayers and metta to the collective force for peace and healing. May all beings be happy. May all beings be safe and protected.

bulances arrived. It's not hard to determine what it means to have very few people brought to the hospital. The silence and the waiting completed the profile of this disaster, and the picture that emerges is increasingly grim.

I write this the morning after the attack. I have just returned from the family triage center two blocks away, where people come looking for records of family and friends. I spoke there with a Puerto Rican family whose son worked on the 102nd floor of the first tower. As his mother looked at me, she gave me a glance that seemed to say, "Don't give me any nonsense about this being all right." I couldn't; there seems but a small chance that her son survived.

She showed me a picture, creased in the corner where it had fit into the edge of a mirror, positioned perhaps so that the mother could see her son first thing every morning. The young man sat on the sofa next to his niece. She withdrew the picture and she and her husband held it tightly, together. It seemed to be all they had.

A young lady approached me and asked, "Are you an honest-to-goodness priest?" I was unsure what sort of a cleric that might be, but I admitted my vocation and she took me to a beautiful young woman, married only a year-and-a-half, who spent an hour with me talking of her young husband. Thankful she was—thankful that they had kissed before they left each other at Grand Central Terminal Tuesday morning. "Everyone keeps telling me," she said, "that things are going to be all right. They aren't going to be all right ever again."

In the normal course of things, I would take a few moments now to conclude with some theological analysis, an orderly reflection before closing an article. Writers are supposed to do that. But I don't have time. I have to get back to the hospital.

THE REVEREND LLOYD PRATOR is an Episcopal priest and the rector at St. John's in the Village in New York City. He ministered to the injured and dying at St. Vincent's Hospital in New York after the attack.

May all beings be supported in their suffering. May all beings feel the healing energy of Divine Love.
9/12/01 12:06 A.M. luzaroon: Even if I'm not American, and am in London, and am not directly involved, how can I sleep? >>

Bright, Brighter, Brightest
By Sri Chinmoy

At this juncture, our only bounden duty is to identify our prayerful hearts with the innocent, harmless, and helpless victims and their beloved ones. Our tearful eyes and the bleeding hearts of the relatives and friends have already touched the compassion-feet of our Absolute Lord Beloved Supreme. He is with his infinity's compassion-affection-love-sweetness-fondness taking care of his supremely chosen children who have recently arrived at his heaven-home. May America the Beautiful forever shine bright-brighter-brightest in the heart of God the Creator and God the creation.

SRI CHINMOY, for the past 37 years, since coming to America from his native India, has dedicated his life to the pursuit of world peace. The Sri Chinmoy Oneness-Home Peace Run relays a peace torch through all 50 states and more than 120 countries. He is a New York City resident.

The Root of Love
Notes for a National Day of Mourning: September 14, 2001
By Paul Ferrini

I am proud of my country
because at a time when thousands of people
have been brutally executed
by a few heartless men,
the tears in our president's eyes
speak louder than his vows of retribution,

because, at a time when you could expect
the voices of hatred and vengeance

Prayers are said with every breath. And yet, amidst all this, I received news that my godson was born. Life.
9/12/01 12:08 A.M. withwonderingawe: "But I say unto you, Love your enemies, bless them that curse you, do good to them

to be loudest in the land,
it is the voices of caring and compassion
that resonate like hundreds of chimes
moving in the wind:

men digging for brothers in the rubble,
families of victims comforting other families,
volunteers from all walks of life—
doctors, nurses, firemen, policemen,
people of all races and religions
coming together as one family.

I am proud of my country
because it stood undefended and trusting at the edge of land
where the lady of sorrows holds her flame,
welcoming strangers to a place
where differences in ideas and backgrounds
are not only tolerated,
but integrated into the fabric of our lives,
making us all stronger.

I am proud of my country
because its borders have always been open
to those from other lands
who are mistreated or oppressed,
because we hold the hope of freedom and justice
not just for ourselves
but for all the peoples of the world.

I am proud of my country
not because we are perfect (we aren't)
nor because we always practice what we preach (we don't),
but because we aspire to be fair, generous, and kind,
and because, no matter how difficult or embarrassing it is,

that hate you, and pray for them which despitefully use you, and persecute you," Matthew 5:44. So I offer a prayer tonight for those who did this awful thing. I pray that their hearts may be softened. I pray that they will leave their hate and »

we try to acknowledge our mistakes
and learn from them.

Like most countries, we have a dark side too.
That's why we are learning to apologize
to our Black brothers and sisters
for years of slavery and abuse,
and to our Japanese citizens for sending their families
into internment camps during World War II.

There are very few Americans who do not feel in their hearts
the pain of Hiroshima or My Lai.
Most of us are not proud of our mistakes.
Most of us do not dance in the streets
when we see the pain and suffering of other people.

Today is a day to mourn the deaths of our citizens
and to send our prayers to their families and friends.
It is a day to be righteous in our anger
and stalwart in our resolve to see justice done.
But it is also a day to remember who we are
and who we are not.

We are not the people these terrorists take us for.
Even those who celebrated this act of brutality
in the streets of Jerusalem
can see if they look:
We are a nation of people who love each other.

We don't have one religion or one color of skin.
We don't have one economic or political idea.
Our differences are monumental,
but so is our capacity to bridge those differences
and come together when our freedom is threatened.

turn to God. I pray for their children that they will not follow in their father's footsteps. I pray for the leaders of the world that they will turn their hearts to God the Father of us all. May we beat our swords into plowshares amen

Those who don't know this about us
will learn of it now.
They will learn that we value not just our own freedom,
but theirs as well; not just our own lives,
but their lives too.

That is why we will act with equal measures
of courage and restraint.
We will not target innocent people
in other countries or in our own.
We will defend ourselves and, in so doing,
We will defend them too.

We are a nation of people who care about each other.
It is not just our military might and our material wealth
that define America.
It is our love, our trust, and our compassion.
It is our fairness and commitment to equality.
That is who we are.

And that is why those who attack us cannot prevail,
for to prevail against us would be to destroy
the very values that enable human beings
to live spiritual lives,
to live in a world where fear is stronger than love,
where freedom and trust are absent.

We do not want to live in such a world.
I don't think they do either.

I don't know a lot about Islam,
but I know this.
Muhammad was a man who loved God
and he loved all of us equally.

9/12/01 12:20 A.M. Wiccana: Dear God and Goddess, Please guide the way to all the innocent lives that were lost today, help them in their crossing. Let them truly rest in peace.
9/12/01 12:40 A.M. boudica: Divine Beloved, ...Please wrap　》》

He would not condone killing for any reason.
Like Jesus, Moses, Buddha,
and the other great spiritual teachers of the planet,
he wanted us to respect our differences
and learn to live in peace together.

He knew that no war is holy and only madmen
call for death and destruction in God's name.
Hurting other people is not spiritual.
Not in Islam, in Christianity, or in Judaism.
That I know.
And I think all of us know it.

What is spiritual is to find the Source of love
in the midst of our fear and our pain,
to learn to reach out to each other
when history and culture
threaten to divide us into two warring camps.

That isn't easy to do, but there is no other choice.
And in that respect, America will lead the way.

You can see it in the faces of our leaders,
our media people, and our citizens.

America is awake
and digging down deep
not just to bury its victims
but to draw strength
from the deepest place in our souls
where love is rooted.

PAUL FERRINI is the founder and editor of *Miracles* magazine and a nationally known teacher and workshop leader. He is the author of 21 books and has helped thousands of people deepen their practice of forgiveness and open their hearts to the divine presence in themselves and others.

your loving arms around those who are grieving. Please help us
to remember who we are and that we do indeed believe that
Love will prevail. Blessed Be.

Chapter 4
EVIL
AND THE
ENEMY

And if a whisper from
Satan reach you, then seek refuge in
Allah. Lo! He is the Hearer, the Knower.
—The Koran, Book of Sura 41 v.34–36

WHAT I WOULD SAY TO OSAMA BIN LADEN
By Thich Nhat Hanh (Interviewed by Anne Simpkinson)

If you could speak to Osama bin Laden, what would you say to him? Likewise, if you were to speak to the American people, what would you suggest we do at this point, individually and as a nation?

If I were given the opportunity to be face-to-face with Osama bin Laden, the first thing I would do is listen. I would try to understand why he had acted in that cruel way. I would try to understand all of the suffering that had led him to violence. It might not be easy to listen in that way, so I would have to remain calm and lucid. I would need several friends with me who are strong in the practice of deep listening, listening without reacting, without judging and blaming. In this way, an atmosphere of support would be created for this person and those connected so that they could share completely and trust that they are really being heard.

After listening for some time, we might need to take a break to allow what has been said to enter into our consciousness. Only when we felt calm and lucid would we respond. We would respond point by point to what had been said. We would respond gently but firmly in such a way to help them to discover their own misunderstandings so that they will stop violent acts from their own will.

For the American people, I would suggest that we do everything we can to restore our calm and our lucidity before responding to the situation. To respond too quickly before we have much understanding of the situation may be very dangerous. The first thing we can do is to cool the flames of anger and hatred that are so strong in us. As mentioned before, it is crucial to look at the way we feed the hatred and violence within us and to

9/12/01 1:12 A.M. Carmela818: Oh Lord, Let those in sorrow, feel your comfort. Let those in fear, feel your courage. Let those in need, feel your strength and protection. Let those who feel alone, feel your love. Let those in charge, feel your guidance. In

take immediate steps to cut off the nourishment for our hatred and violence.

When we react out of fear and hatred, we do not yet have a deep understanding of the situation. Our action will only be a very quick and superficial way of responding to the situation, and not much true benefit and healing will occur. Yet if we wait and follow the process of calming our anger, looking deeply into the situation, and listening with great will to understand the roots of suffering that are the cause of the violent actions, only then will we have sufficient insight to respond in such a way that healing and reconciliation can be realized for everyone involved.

In South Africa, the Truth and Reconciliation Commission has made attempts to realize this. All the parties involved in violence and injustice agreed to listen to each other in a calm and supportive environment, to look together deeply at the roots of violent acts and to find agreeable arrangements to respond to the situations. The presence of strong spiritual leaders is very helpful to support and maintain such an environment. We can look at this model for resolving conflicts that are arising right in the present moment; we do not have to wait many years to realize this.

You personally experienced the devastation caused by the war fought in Vietnam and worked to end the hostilities there. What do you say to people who are grief-stricken and enraged because they have lost loved ones in the terrorist attack?

I did lose my spiritual sons and daughters during the war when they were entering the fighting zone trying to save those under the bombs. Some were killed by war and some by murder due to the misunderstanding that they were supporting the other side. When I looked at the four slain corpses of my spiritual sons murdered in such a violent way, I suffered deeply.

I understand the suffering of those who have lost beloved

your name we pray.
9/12/01 1:40 A.M. CatRescuer: Dear God — I really don't know what to say at this time except to please help us. Please hear our prayers and make all of this insanity stop. Please try and   »

ones in this tragedy. In situations of great loss and grief, I had to find my calm in order to restore my lucidity and my heart of understanding and compassion. With the practice of deep looking, I realized that if we respond to cruelty with cruelty, injustice and suffering will only increase.

When we learned of the bombing of the Bentra village in Vietnam, where 300,000 homes were destroyed, and the pilots told journalists that they had destroyed the village in order to save it, I was shocked, and [racked] with anger and grief. We practiced walking calmly and gently on the Earth to bring back our calm mind and peaceful heart.

Although it is very challenging to maintain our openness in that moment, it is crucial that we not respond in any way until we have calmness and clarity with which to see the reality of the situation. We knew that to respond with violence and hatred would only damage ourselves and those around us. We practiced [so that we might] look deeply into the suffering of the people inflicting violence on us, to understand them more deeply and to understand ourselves more deeply. With this understanding, we were able to produce compassion and to relieve our own suffering and that of the other side.

What is the "right action" to take with regard to responding to terrorist attacks? Should we seek justice through military action? Through judicial processes? Is military action and/or retaliation justified if it can prevent future innocents from being killed?

All violence is injustice. The fire of hatred and violence cannot be extinguished by adding more hatred and violence to the fire. The only antidote to violence is compassion. And what is compassion made of? It is made of understanding. When there is no understanding, how can we feel compassion? How can we

comfort the victims' families and friends. Please help the ones still trapped and please help find the person that did this. Please just help us all.
9/12/01 1:50 A.M. JChurch: I don't usually post on message

begin to relieve the great suffering that is there? So understanding is the very real foundation upon which we build our compassion.

How do we gain the understanding and insight to guide us through such incredibly challenging moments that we now face in America? To understand, we must find paths of communication so that we can listen to those who desperately are calling out for our understanding—because such an act of violence is a desperate call for attention and for help.

How can we listen in a calm and clear way so that we don't immediately kill the chance for understanding to develop? As a nation, we need to look into this: how to create the situations for deep listening to occur so that our response to the situation may arise out of our calm and clear mind. Clarity is a great offering that we can make at this time.

There are people who want one thing only: revenge. In the Buddhist scriptures, the Buddha said that by using hatred to answer hatred, there will only be an escalation of hatred. But if we use compassion to embrace those who have harmed us, it will greatly diffuse the bomb in our hearts and in theirs.

So how can we bring about a drop of compassion that can put out the fire of hatred? You know, they do not sell compassion in the supermarket. If they sold compassion, we would only need to bring it home and we could solve the problem of hatred and violence in the world very easily. But compassion can only be produced in our own heart by our own practice.

America is burning with hatred. That is why we have to tell our Christian friends, "You are children of Christ." You have to return to yourselves and look deeply and find out why this violence happened. Why is there so much hatred? What lies under all this violence? Why do they hate so much that they would sacrifice their own lives and bring about so much suffering to other

boards, but as a "pacifist retard" who does have a friend buried under the rubble of the World Trade Center, I felt it necessary. I had a friend who worked there, and now my friend is gone. The US military might kill all the people of Afghanistan but none of >>

people? Why would these young people, full of vitality and strength, have chosen to lose their lives, to commit such violence? That is what we have to understand.

We have to find a way to stop violence, of course. If need be, we have to put the men responsible in prison. But the important thing is to look deeply and ask, "Why did that happen? What responsibility do we have in that happening?" Maybe they misunderstood us, but what has made them misunderstand us so much to make them hate so much?

The method of the Buddha is to look deeply to see the source of suffering; the source of the violence. If we have violence within ourselves, any action can make that violence explode. This energy of hatred and violence can be very great, and when we see that in the other person then we feel sorry for them. When we feel sorry for them, the drop of compassion is born in our hearts and we feel so much happier and so much more at peace in ourselves. That [empathy] produces the nectar of compassion within ourselves.

If you come to the monastery, it is in order to learn to do that, so that whenever you suffer and feel angry, you know how to look deeply, so that the drop of compassion in your heart can come out of your heart and can put out the fever of anger. Only the drop of compassion can put out the flames of hatred.

We must look deeply and honestly at our present situation. If we are able to see the sources for the suffering within ourselves and within the other person, we can begin to unravel the cycle of hatred and violence. When our house is on fire, we must first put out the fire before investigating its cause. Likewise, if we first extinguish the anger and hatred in our own heart, we will have a chance to deeply investigate the situation with clarity and insight in order to determine all the causes and conditions that

it will bring my friend, or anyone else killed today, back to life.
9/12/01 1:51 A.M. chaplain100: Dear Lord, ...Your children are so terribly pained, Lord, Your pain must be even greater than ours. amen

have contributed to the hatred and violence we are experiencing within ourselves and within our world.

The "right action" is the action that results in the fires of hatred and violence being extinguished.

Do you believe that evil exists? And, if so, would you consider terrorists as evil persons?

Evil exists. God exists also. Evil and God are two sides of ourselves. God is that great understanding, that great love within us. That is what we call Buddha also, the enlightened mind that is able to see through all ignorance.

What is evil? It is when the face of God, the face of the Buddha within us, has become hidden. It is up to us to choose whether the evil side becomes more important, or whether the side of God and the Buddha shines out. Although the side of great ignorance, of evil, may be manifesting so strongly at one time, that does not mean that God is not there.

It is said clearly in the Bible, "Forgive them for they know not what they do." This means that an act of evil is an act of great ignorance and misunderstanding. Perhaps many wrong perceptions are behind an act of evil; we have to see that ignorance and misunderstanding is the root of the evil. Every human being contains within himself or herself all the elements of great understanding, great compassion, and also ignorance, hatred, and violence.

In your new book Anger, *you give an example of "compassionate listening" as a tool to heal families. Can that tool be used at a national level, and if so, how would that work?*

This past summer, a group of Palestinians and Israelis came to Plum Village, the practice center where I live in southern

9/12/01 1:57 A.M. ashai: Tomorrow is time for justice. Let all who think they can do this, know the price of their cowardice.
9/12/01 2:09 A.M. mujahid: ...I can tell you about my reaction as a human being who considers himself Muslim as well as   »

France, to learn and practice the arts of deep listening and loving speech. [About 1,600 people come to Plum Village each summer from over a dozen countries to listen and to learn how to bring peace and understanding to their daily lives.] The group of Palestinians and Israelis participated in the daily schedule of walking meditation, sitting meditation, and silent meals, and they also received training on how to listen and speak to each other in such a way that more understanding and peace could be possible between them as individuals and as nations.

With the guidance and support of the monks and nuns, they sat down and listened to each other. When one person spoke, no one interrupted him or her. Everyone practiced mindfulness of their breathing and listening in such a way that the other person felt heard and understood.

When a person spoke, he or she refrained from using words of blame, hatred, and condemnation. They spoke in an atmosphere of trust and respect. Out of these dialogues, the participating Palestinians and Israelis were very moved to realize that both sides suffer from fear. They appreciated the practice of deep listening and made arrangements to share what they had learned with others upon returning to their home countries.

We recommended that the Palestinians and Israelis talk about their suffering, fears, and despair in a public forum that all the world could hear. We could all listen without judging, without condemning in order to understand the experience of both sides. This would prepare the ground of understanding for peace talks to occur.

The same situation now exists between the American people and people of Islamic and Arabic nations. There is much misunderstanding and lack of the kind of communication that hinders our ability to resolve our difficulties peacefully.

American. I'm shocked, horrified, grieved, and distressed. ... I pray to God that the guilty are put to justice and that this never happens again. I pray that the hate of the terrorists who did this does not become contagious and spread to the bystanders. I

Compassion is a very large part of Buddhism and Buddhist practice. But at this point in time, compassion toward terrorists seems impossible to muster. Is it realistic to think people can feel true compassion now?

Without understanding, compassion is impossible. When you understand the suffering of others, you do not have to force yourself to feel compassion; the door of your heart will just naturally open. All of the hijackers were so young and yet they sacrificed their lives for what? Why did they do that? What kind of deep suffering is there? It will require deep listening and deep looking to understand that.

To have compassion in this situation is to perform a great act of forgiveness. We can first embrace the suffering, both outside of America and within America. We need to look after the victims here within our country and also to have compassion for the hijackers and their families because they are also victims of ignorance and hatred. In this way, we can truly practice nondiscrimination. We do not need to wait many years or decades to realize reconciliation and forgiveness. We need a wake up call now in order not to allow hatred to overwhelm our hearts.

Do you believe things happen for a reason? If so, what was the reason for the attacks on the U.S.A.?

The deep reason for our current situation is our patterns of consumption. U.S. citizens consume 60 percent of the world's energy resources, yet they account for only 6 percent of the total world's population. Children in America have witnessed 100,000 acts of violence on television by the time they finish elementary school. Another reason for our current situation is our foreign policy and the lack of deep listening within our relationships. We do not use deep listening to understand the suffering and the real needs of people in other nations.

pray that prejudices and fears are quelled. I pray that the world may unite as one to put an end to terrorism and make sure that nothing of this kind ever happens again.
9/12/01 2:13 A.M. amerIrish26: It is my prayer that we   »

What do you think would be the most effective spiritual response to this tragedy?

We can begin right now to practice calming our anger, looking deeply at the roots of the hatred and violence in our society and in our world, and listening with compassion in order to hear and understand what we have not yet had the capacity to hear and to understand. When the drop of compassion begins to form in our hearts and minds, we begin to develop concrete responses to our situation. When we have listened and looked deeply, we may begin to develop the energy of brotherhood and sisterhood between all nations, which is the deepest spiritual heritage of all religious and cultural traditions. In this way, the peace and understanding within the whole world is increased day by day.

To develop the drop of compassion in our own heart is the only effective spiritual response to hatred and violence. That drop of compassion will be the result of calming our anger, looking deeply at the roots of our violence, deep listening, and understanding the suffering of everyone involved in the acts of hatred and violence.

THICH NHAT HANH is a Vietnamese monk in the Zen tradition, who worked tirelessly for peace during the Vietnam War, rebuilding villages destroyed by the hostilities. Following a lecture tour in the United States for the Fellowship of Reconciliation, an American-based peace organization, he was not allowed back in his country and settled in France. He was nominated by the Reverend Martin Luther King Jr. for the Nobel Peace Prize in 1967. Thay, as he is affectionately called by his followers, has since become internationally known for his teaching and writing on mindfulness, and for his work related to "socially engaged Buddhism," a call to social action based on Buddhist principles.

Americans realize that on September 11, 2001, we all died together: died together: NOW it is our time to LIVE TOGETHER in the beauty of the multiplicity of our Faiths and Cultures
9/12/01 2:15 A.M. Starfire2: Father Mother God, Please bless all

THE EVIL OVER WHICH WE MUST TRIUMPH
By Daisaku Ikeda

In the aftermath of the terrible shock of the tragic events of September 11, 2001, I extend my deepest sympathies to all those affected. From the bottom of my heart, I pray for the victims, and I pray that their families may find inner strength, healing, and, eventually, renewed happiness.

It is impossible not to be outraged at the senseless loss of so many lives. And yet it is not the numbers that make this tragedy so horrific. Every single person lost was irreplaceable and immensely precious—a much-loved sister, father, son, mother, or friend. Each individual's life contained infinite possibilities waiting to be realized. In the most terrible manner imaginable, we have been reminded of the immense value of human life.

In all its teachings, Buddhism stresses how sacred and precious life—especially human life—is. One scripture reads: "A single day of life is worth more than all the treasures of the universe." Terrorism, which so cruelly robs people of life, can never be excused or justified by any reason or cause. It is an absolute evil. And when such acts are committed in the name of religion, it demonstrates the utter spiritual bankruptcy of the perpetrators.

As human beings sharing a common home, we have all been impacted by this terrible deed. In the words of Dr. Martin Luther King Jr., "Injustice anywhere is a threat to justice everywhere." We must unite across differences of nationality and faith in order to create a world free of injustice, violence, and terror.

While it is vitally important that all efforts be made to identify responsibility for this heinous act and bring those involved to justice, international cooperation against terrorism cannot be limited to the short term. At a deeper level, it requires a pro-

who suffer tonight. Bless all the world with the gift of compassion. We know there will be a rush for vengeance. Help us take time and consider Wisdom. Let not the innocent suffer from misplaced blame. Free us from prejudice. Grant us peace. Grant us mercy... >>

found reexamination of the nature of human civilization. For much of our history, humanity has been trapped in vicious cycles of hatred and reprisal. We must redouble our efforts to break this cycle and transform distrust into trust. I believe that this is the most effective and fundamental antidote to terrorism and its repugnant worship of violence.

It is the function of evil to divide; to alienate people from each other and divide one country from another. The universe, this world, and our own lives are the stage for a ceaseless struggle between hatred and compassion, the destructive and constructive aspects of life. We must never let up, confronting evil at every turn.

This attack was an ultimate manifestation of evil and shows us the vilest depths to which human nature can sink.

In the end, the evil over which we must triumph is the impulse toward hatred and destruction that resides in us all.

Unless we can achieve a fundamental transformation within our own lives, so that we are able to perceive our intimate connection with all our fellow human beings and feel their sufferings as our own, we will never be free of conflict and war. In this sense, I feel that a "hard power" approach, one that relies on military might, will not lead to a long-term, fundamental resolution.

I believe that dialogue holds the key to any lasting solution. Now, more than ever, we must reach out in a further effort to understand each other and engage in genuine dialogue. Words spoken from the heart have the power to change a person's life. They can even melt the icy walls of mistrust that separate peoples and nations. We must expand our efforts to promote dialogue between and among civilizations.

I am utterly convinced that we were not born into this world to hate and destroy each other. We must restore and renew our faith in humanity and in each other. We must never lose sight of

9/12/01 2:34 A.M. Ezyduzit: It's hard for me to understand how the terrorists had any love for God, their fellow man, or any religion.
9/12/01 2:42 A.M. daggor: Dear Lord please help heal the pain

the fact that we can still make the 21st century an era free from the flames of war and violence—an era in which all people may live in peace. To this end, we must strive to make a profound reverence for life the prevailing spirit of our times and our planet. I believe that this is the greatest and most enduring way to honor the memory of the victims of this enormous tragedy.

DAISAKU IKEDA is president of Soka Gakkai International, a Buddhist association with 12 million members in over 175 countries and territories. Its activities to promote peace, culture, and education are based on the long-standing traditions of Buddhist humanism.

THE MYSTERY OF EVIL
A Sermon by the Reverend Billy Graham

National Day of Prayer and Remembrance

President and Mrs. Bush, I want to say a personal word on behalf of many people. Thank you, Mr. President, for calling this Day of Prayer and Remembrance. We needed it at this time.

We come together today to affirm our conviction that God cares for us, whatever our ethnic, religious, or political backgrounds may be.

The Bible says that he's "the God of all comfort, who comforts us in all our troubles."

No matter how hard we try, words simply cannot express the horror, the shock, and the revulsion we all feel over what took place in this nation on Tuesday morning. September 11 will go down in our history as a day to remember.

Today we say to those who masterminded this cruel plot, and to those who carried it out, that the spirit of this nation will not

9/12/01 2:48 A.M. tjdentonj: Lord I pray that you will fill us with love and a sense of unity, so that we (the USA) defeat the forces of evil that have been thrown at us. In Jesus' glorious name I pray, amen.   >>

be defeated by their twisted and diabolical schemes. Some day, those responsible will be brought to justice, as President Bush and our Congress have so forcefully stated.

But today, we especially come together in this service to confess our need of God. We've always needed God from the very beginning of this nation, but today we need him especially. We're facing a new kind of enemy. We're involved in a new kind of warfare, and we need the help of the Spirit of God. The Bible's words are our hope: "God is our refuge and strength, an ever present help in trouble. Therefore we will not fear, though the earth give way and the mountains fall into the heart of the sea" (Psalm 46:1–2).

But how do we understand something like this? Why does God allow evil like this to take place? Perhaps that is what you are asking now. You may even be angry at God. I want to assure you that God understands these feelings that you may have.

We've seen so much on our televisions, and heard on our radios, stories that bring tears to our eyes and make us all feel a sense of anger. But God can be trusted, even when life seems at its darkest.

But what are some of the lessons we can learn?

First, we are reminded of the mystery and reality of evil.

I have been asked hundreds of times in my life why God allows tragedy and suffering. I have to confess that I really do not know the answer totally, even to my own satisfaction. I have to accept, by faith, that God is sovereign, and he's a God of love and mercy and compassion in the midst of suffering. The Bible says that God is not the author of evil. It speaks of evil as a "mystery." In 2 Thessalonians 2:7, it talks about the mystery of iniquity. The Old Testament prophet Jeremiah said, "The heart is deceitful above all things and beyond cure. Who can understand it?" He asked that question, "Who can understand it?" And that's one reason we each need God in our lives.

9/12/01 3:19 A.M. naomimaile: So sorry to hear of your tragedy it has been a constant broadcast throughout australia for 18 hours. We too are devastated at this tragedy. May all of the people of the united states be united. Keep safe, be strong may

The lesson of this event is not only about the mystery of iniquity and evil, but secondly, it's a lesson about our need for each other.

What an example New York and Washington have been to the world these past few days! None of us will ever forget the pictures of our courageous firefighters and police, many of whom have lost friends and colleagues, or the hundreds of people attending or standing patiently in line to donate blood. A tragedy like this could have torn our country apart, but instead it has united us, and we've become a family. So those perpetrators who took this on to tear us apart, it has worked the other way. It's backlashed; it's backfired. We are more united than ever before. I think this was exemplified in a very moving way when the members of our Congress stood shoulder to shoulder the other day and sang "God Bless America."

Finally, difficult as it may be for us to see right now, this event can give a message of hope—hope for the present, and hope for the future.

Yes, there is hope. There's hope for the present because I believe the stage has already been set for a new spirit in our nation.

One of the things we desperately need is a spiritual renewal in this country. We need a spiritual revival in America. And God has told us in his word, time after time, that we are to repent of our sins and we're to turn to him and he will bless us in a new way.

But, there is also hope for the future because of God's promises. As a Christian, I have hope, not just for this life but also for heaven and the life to come. And many of those people who died this past week are in heaven right now, and they wouldn't want to come back. It's so glorious and so wonderful. And that's the hope for all of us who put our faith in God. I pray that you will have this hope in your heart.

This event reminds us of the brevity and the uncertainty of

you all be blessed with the courage to carry on and not let evil prevail
9/12/01 3:39 A.M. ImANewMom: Hail Mary, full of grace, the Lord is with thee. Blessed art Thou among women and ≫

life. We never know when we too will be called into eternity. I
doubt if even one of those people who got on those planes or
walked into the World Trade Center or the Pentagon Tuesday
morning thought it would be the last day of their lives. It didn't
occur to them. And that's why each of us needs to face our own
spiritual need and commit ourselves to God and his will now.

Here in this majestic National Cathedral, we see all around
us symbols of the cross. For the Christian—I'm speaking for the
Christian now—the cross tells us that God understands our sin
and our suffering, for he took upon himself in the person of
Jesus Christ our sins and our suffering. And from the cross, God
declares, "I love you. I know the heartaches and the sorrows and
the pains that you feel. But I love you."

The story does not end with the cross, for Easter points us beyond the tragedy of the cross to the empty tomb. It tells us that
there is hope for eternal life, for Christ has conquered evil and
death, and hell. Yes, there is hope.

I've become an old man now—and I've preached all over the
world—and the older I get, the more I cling to that hope I
started with many years ago and proclaimed in many languages
to many parts of the world.

Several years ago at the National Prayer Breakfast here in
Washington, Ambassador Andrew Young (who had just gone
through the tragic death of his wife), closed his talk with a quote
from the old hymn, "How Firm a Foundation."

We all watched in horror as planes crashed into the steel and
glass of the World Trade Center. Those majestic towers, built on
solid foundations, were examples of the prosperity and creativity
of America. When damaged, those buildings eventually plum-
meted to the ground, imploding in upon themselves. Yet, underneath the debris is a foundation that was not destroyed.
Therein lies the truth of that old hymn that Andrew Young

blessed is the fruit of Thy womb, Jesus. Holy Mary, Mother of
God, pray for us sinners now, and at the hour of our death.
Dear God, please grant us the strength to overcome this
heinous act. Please give all the rescue workers the strength and

quoted, "How Firm a Foundation." Yes, our nation has been attacked, buildings destroyed, lives lost.

But now we have a choice: whether to implode and disintegrate emotionally and spiritually as a people and a nation—or, whether we choose to become stronger through all of this struggle—to rebuild on a solid foundation. And I believe that we are in the process of starting to rebuild on that foundation. That foundation is our trust in God. That's what this service is all about, and in that faith we have the strength to endure something as difficult and horrendous as what we have experienced this week.

This has been a terrible week with many tears but also has been a week of great faith. Churches all across the country have called prayer meetings, and today is a day that they are celebrating not only in this country but also in many parts of the world.

And in the words of that familiar hymn that Andrew Young quoted, it says:

Fear not, I am with thee; O be not dismayed,
For I am thy God, and will still give thee aid;
I'll strengthen thee, help thee, and cause thee to stand,
Upheld by my righteous, omnipotent hand.

My prayer today is that we will feel the loving arms of God wrapped around us, and will know in our hearts that he will never forsake us as we trust in him.

We also know that God is going to give wisdom and courage and strength to the president and those around him. And this is going to be a day that we will remember as a day of victory.

May God bless you all.

THE REVEREND BILLY GRAHAM is a renowned Christian leader, televangelist, and one of the premier religious voices in the United States.

courage to continue their valiant effort. Please take care of the victims and their families. In Your Name we pray.
9/12/01 3:52 A.M. MissSara: Dear Lord, my heart is heavy today as I feel a piece of me has died with all the victims. I ≫

112   From the Ashes

The Goddess of Democracy:
A Sacred Archetype to Heal the World
By Thom Hartmann

We live in a time of extraordinary opportunity, poised on the edge of events that may literally reshape the world and the world mind.

People argue that the terrorist attacks against the United States reflect a war between one religion and another, or between the poor and the rich of the world. While there may be an element of truth to each, I'd suggest that the real war here is between the 11th century and the 21st century. And until our leaders figure that out, we may miss some great opportunities.

Back in the Dark and Middle Ages, the Catholic Church ruled Europe. Women were often forbidden to go out in public unless properly covered and were explicitly the property of men. Justice was swift and severe, ranging from disfigurement to torture to death in horrific ways, and most often meted out with the approval or supervision of clerics. The power behind the power of all the royal families of Europe was the Pope.

On November 27, 1095, Pope Urban gave one of history's most famous speeches to the Council of Clermont in France, calling for a holy war against Islam to unite factious Europe. Dr. E. L. Skip Knox of Boise State University in Idaho summarized the Pope's speech:

> The noble race of Franks must come to the aid of their fellow Christians in the East. The infidel Turks are advancing into the heart of Eastern Christendom; Christians are being oppressed and attacked; churches and holy places are being defiled. Jerusalem is groaning under the Saracen yoke. The Holy Sepulchre is in Moslem hands and has been

pray that the only good I can imagine will come out of this—
that we can pull together in this time, regardless of religion or
ethnicity— and take the time to be kind.
9/12/01 4:08 A.M. amelda: Dear God, We can not begin to de-

turned into a mosque. . . . The Franks must stop their internal wars and squabbles. Let them go instead against the infidel and fight a righteous war. God himself will lead them, for they will be doing His work. There will be absolution and remission of sins for all who die in the service of Christ. Here they are poor and miserable sinners; there they will be rich and happy. Let none hesitate; they must march next summer. God wills it!

Thus began a war between two different medieval cultures: the 11th-century Catholic and the 11th-century Muslim. Over the next few centuries, the Catholics, with their battle cry of "Deus vult!" (God wills it) were often victorious against the Muslims, whose only crime defined by the Pope was that they were living on a land holy to the Catholic Church.

Medieval historian Raymond of Agiles wrote the following eyewitness account of the attack and seizure of Jerusalem in 1099 by the triumphant Crusaders:

Some of our men cut off the heads of their enemies; others shot them with arrows, so that they fell from the towers; others tortured them longer by casting them into the flames. Piles of heads, hands, and feet were to be seen in the streets of the city. It was necessary to pick one's way over the bodies of men and horses. But these were small matters compared to what happened at the temple of Solomon, a place where religious services were ordinarily chanted. What happened there? If I tell the truth, it will exceed your powers of belief. So let it suffice to say this much at least, that in the temple and portico of Solomon, men rode in blood up to their knees and bridle reins.

scribe the feeling of being overwhelmed by what has happened in the USA. This prayer goes out from all of us in South Africa and Lord we pray for your enfolding love to enfold those who need it in this time of intense sadness and anger.   >>

In the 900 or so years since the early Crusades, both Christianity and Islam have undergone profound changes. The Protestant Reformation shook Christianity to its core, and the Renaissance in Europe wrought huge transformations in both Christianity and Judaism. Perhaps the most critical change came about in the18th century when Jefferson, Madison, Franklin, and others synthesized the highest ideals of Greek, Roman, and Iroquois thought and culture to create the United States of America. In doing that, they ignited the flame of liberty, bringing into the world an archetype that to this day inspires hope worldwide.

As America grew and our ideas of republican democracy spread around the world, further transformations of the world took place. Another turning point was when modern science challenged the medieval worldview of the Church in the Scopes Monkey Trial of 1925. Although Clarence Darrow lost that case, its widespread publicity began a dramatic and lasting process of change across the world.

The American Dream is a powerful and pervasive force in the world, even if the sometimes-imperialistic behavior of our transnational corporations is often at odds with our own ideals. The Dream has wafted over the entire world and is still so powerful that people are willing to die for it: In China, the Tiananmen Square protesters marched to their doom in 1989 carrying a 37-foot-tall papier-mâché replica of the Statue of Liberty, which they had renamed The Goddess of Democracy.

Of course, there are still pockets of medieval perspective in the Christian world. The postdisaster comments of Jerry Falwell and Pat Robertson that we had just witnessed the "wrath of [their] God" who "lifted the veil" and "allowed" the terrorists to act because of their God's anger over "homosexuals, liberals, and the ACLU [American Civil Liberties Union]," reveals

9/12/01 4:16 A.M. swaller: Dear God, A message from the UK in Soho, London. Please take care of everybody in NY and Washington and all their loved ones. We are thinking of you...
9/12/01 5:03 A.M. ichim: My thoughts are with the people of

that such a worldview is still alive and well in a small fringe of Christianity. Some Christians are still today willing to commit terrorist acts of murder or mass murder: Timothy McVeigh and those who have murdered numerous abortion providers all claimed their acts are grounded in Christianity and biblical teachings.

Just as 21st-century Christianity still has its own pockets of medieval worldview, so does 21st-century Islam. Pulitzer Prize-winning writer David Moats, once a Peace Corps volunteer in Afghanistan, tells the story in the September 23, 2001, issue of the *Montpelier Times Argus* of a discussion he had with an Islamic Afghani in 1971. "I remember the evening when I explained to my Laghmani friend that in America we believed the world was round," Moats recounts. "I used a teapot and a lantern to show how the earth revolved around the sun. He was skeptical. He was an educated man, but he also knew that the Koran referred to the four corners of the Earth, which suggests the Earth is flat."

The difference these days, however, is that as a percentage much more of Islam than of any other religion is still living out 11th-century values. In many of Islam's most wealthy and modern countries (Saudi Arabia, for example, among others), women are still veiled and forbidden to work or drive. In many Islamic nations, such as Pakistan, it's forbidden for girls to go to public school. And in a communiqué to America, Osama bin Laden cited the 11th-century Christian Crusades against Islam—a war he clearly sees himself as still fighting—as part of his justification for terrorism and a holy war or jihad against the West.

As much as Robertson, McVeigh, and Falwell would like to portray themselves as warriors for the heart and soul of Christianity, the vast majority of Christians see them for what they

America, especially the victims of this terrifying attack. May they know that people all over the world are thinking of them in this time of sorrow and have had them in their thoughts all day. We hope for justice but not revenge &   >>

are: anachronisms with medievalist perspectives. Thank goodness in America they've been marginalized and, along with the
abortion-clinic bombers, can only stand, even with the mega-
phones of their millions of dollars and television networks, on
the extreme fringes of a mainstream American culture.

Similarly, even the most orthodox and conservative of the
sects of Judaism, the Hasidic movement, interacts fully in the
modern world. None among them, to the best of my knowledge
(and I've lived and worked among them), would invoke the
name of God in a war against any other group unless in self-defense. Buddhist and Hindu traditions, as well, are largely
modern around the world (although they, too, struggle with minorities still stuck in the 11th century).

But, uniquely in the world, the Falwells among Islam actually
control entire nations. A small but significant portion of Islam
still lives the values of the Middle Ages, and the evangelists for
that medieval worldview in Islamic context are gaining ground,
particularly among the world's poorest nations. Thus, a September 22, 2001, editorial in *The News*, a large daily paper in Is-
lamabad, Pakistan, said that the time has arrived "to decide
whether they want this country to remain under the ever
looming threat of Islamic fundamentalism, with a tiny but militant minority refusing to let Pakistan pull itself out of the medieval ages . . . or join hands to purge the polity of terrorism,
blackmail, and retardation."

If this is, in fact, a battle between the 11th century and the
21st century, then it's not a battle that will be won with bombs,
threats, or intimidation. No matter how high-tech they may be,
these are the tools of the 11th century.

Instead, America and the free world must hold high our ar-
chetypal vision of freedom, individual liberty, and religious

---

for world peace. From New Zealand.
9/12/01 6:49 A.M. maythorp: I am in the UK and I want to say
how shocked and horrified we are here. We don't regard the
USA as a foreign country, and our Prime Minister has pledged

tolerance—and change the world with *ideas* instead of bombs. The Reformation and Enlightenment were times when *ideas* swept across the world and transformed every one of the world's nations and major religions, to greater or lesser extents. In past centuries in much of the world polygamy has been outlawed, women and minorities freed, and the lines between religion and government are drawn sharply in ways that no theocracy could ever again rise to power. None of these *idea*-based changes have yet happened among the most fundamentalist of the Islamic nations (nor, to be fair, among small but marginalized pockets of the world's other medieval and premedieval-based religions).

We have the means, through printing presses and radio-transmitting towers, to carry 21st-century ideas to people still living in the mind of the 11th century. If we were to set aside the internal politics of the Voice of America, we could quickly join BBC and Deutsche Welle (German radio) in reaching out to contemporary 11th-century-worldview Muslims in their own languages, and begin to give them the ideas that could bring them into the 21st century. We may also even be able to modernize a few of our homegrown Christian terrorists, if we do it right. And we have the obligation to do this: Not only were we one of the victims of fundamentalism but we are also the holders of the most sacred archetypes of the modern era: the Statue of Liberty and the Bill of Rights.

While Islam itself has not gone through a huge, systemic transition into relative modernity as did Christianity with the Protestant Reformation or Judaism with the end of the Second Temple period, nonetheless there are many modern Moslems and Moslem clerics. Islam also has a long and beautiful tradition of nonviolent mystics, those who passionately seek God

our support. My condolences to all who lost loved ones, and my sorrow for those misguided people who celebrate. It is really hard not to wish them ill. However, they undoubtedly reap what they sow....   »

rather than political power: The most well-known in the West are Rumi and Kahlil Gibran, but there are many others. Persecuted, imprisoned, and murdered in countries like Iran, the Baha'i sect of Islam is among the most outspoken in its advocacy for a 21st-century worldview within the context of Islam and its holy scriptures.

Now is the perfect time and opportunity for us to give the mystics and moderns among Islam a voice, to help them lift their brothers and sisters around the world out of the 11th century and into the 21st century, so we can live together in a world of shared visions and ideals, even while maintaining our respected differences.

If this is the outcome of this tragedy, it will prove to be a fitting tribute to those who died, and has the potential to positively transform the entire world. If, instead, our reactions are grounded entirely in force and fear—the tools and ghosts of the 11th century—then we risk plunging the world back toward the Crusades, and possibly even creating what Joseph Chilton Pearce calls *Evolution's End*.

Let us pray that our leaders will make the right choices in the days and years to come, and the Goddess of Democracy will always be a beacon of light and hope for the world.

THOM HARTMANN is an author of several books on spirituality, social issues, and the environment, including *The Last Hours of Ancient Sunlight*.

9/12/01 7:06 A.M. sassygirl1957: I pray for the living, that we may be able to go on, I pray for the dead, that their souls may reach their appointed destinations, I pray for the perpetrators of this horrific event, both living and dead, that they will be for-

The Candle and the Closet
By Rushworth M. Kidder

On September 11, the terrorist attacks at the World Trade Center permanently altered the New York City skyline. Less noticeably, but perhaps more powerfully, they changed something else: the moral thoughtscape of America.

The intense public cruelty of that day has driven us to the windows of the soul—to new depths of introspection, moral searching, and spiritual questioning. All across this otherwise pragmatic and down-to-earth nation, the air is suddenly filled with oddly metaphysical questions: Who are we? Why are we here? How do we understand our purpose? What can I do?

That last question concerns the individual's role in the face of evil. That's a profoundly moral question. And for most people the answer is, "I ought to get involved, lend a hand, help out in some way." But there's a nagging doubt. Can my involvement really change the world? Even if I, and all my friends and all their friends, banded together to help, could we make an impact? Compared to the six billion people in the world today, we're but a rounding error. Can we really make a difference?

Yes. Let me explain with a kind of parable.

Some years ago, I interviewed a number of people here and overseas for a newspaper series on global education. Among the interviewees were several American men in their thirties. Each had grown up in a terrible ghetto environment. And each, in some way, had "made it" and was successful.

Why, I asked them, had they succeeded? Why had they not been gunned down at age 18 in a neighborhood alley as, statistically, they might well have been? Each, using different specifics and a different name, told me the same story: It was

given, I pray for safety, sanity and peace for those of us who remain. I most fervently pray that we will achieve peace; that this heinous event will be the turning point and the building blocks on which peace will finally come. My sadness is endless, »

old Mrs. Smith in the fourth grade who really turned them around.

"But wait," I asked them. "You've just told me about your schooling, where you had dozens of awful teachers. You've just told me about your large and dysfunctional family, where hardly anyone seemed to care. You've just told me about your scores of friends—many now in jail, others now dead—who set all the wrong examples. And now you're telling me that, in face of that relentless downdrag of depravity, Mrs. Smith alone lifted you up?"

"Yes," each said, "that's what I'm telling you."

In itself, that fact doesn't surprise us. We all know, intuitively, the enormous power of a single right example. The question is, Why should it be so? Why is it not equally true that a child raised in caring, attentive surroundings can meet one bad teacher and be plunged into a life of crime and vice? Somehow that's far less observable.

To understand why, perform the following experiment. Find a closet that's been closed up for years. It's been shut so tight that no light can get in. If there's any place darkness could grow thick and rich and ugly, this is it.

Now light a candle. Turn off the lights in the room outside the closet. Open the closet door, and watch closely. Does this appalling darkness gush forth with such virulence that it extinguishes the candle and plunges you into utter blackness? No. In the entire history of the world, that has never once happened. Always, unfailingly, the candlelight illumines the closet and dispels the darkness.

That, too, is observable. But why should it be so?

Because light is not the opposite of darkness. It's the absence of darkness.

If light were the opposite, we'd be playing a zero-sum game

my grief overwhelming. Father in heaven, protect your children. This is my prayer.

9/12/01 7:48 A.M. enots: Where does it end? What do we do from here? We must punish the criminals who did this!!! I

with the forces of anti-light—where, about half the time, darkness would win. Maybe, if we pulled together a thousand candles, we could just barely defeat such a grisly accumulation of blackness—but only for a while, until the closet-forces regrouped and came back to defeat the candle.

Put that way, it sounds silly. Yet notice how our metaphors work to persuade us that darkness and light are equal but opposite powers. We're so used to thinking in terms of opposites—positive and negative charges in electricity, north and south poles in magnetism, up and down, left and right, yin and yang—that we let our metaphors overwhelm us. "Oh, yes," we assert, without examining our premises, "The world is made up of opposites. Light and dark—they're opposites, too. After all, night and day appear to be evenly balanced—in the course of a year, there's about as much of one as of the other. So darkness must be the opposite of light."

That mistake might be relatively harmless, were it not for one final logical misstep, where we seize on light and dark as our principal metaphor for good and evil. Result? We think of ourselves as locked in battle with powers of evil that are balanced on a knife edge against the forces of good. What will it take, we ask, to defeat such a terrible force? Surely all the goodness in the world, if we could scrape it together, would barely be enough to overcome this equal and opposite power.

But what if—just what if—we've missed the real message of the metaphor? What if evil is less the opposite than the absence of good? Doesn't that explain how old Mrs. Smith could single-handedly overcome the inertia and emptiness of our young friends' ghetto upbringings? Wouldn't it seem odd, in fact, if evil ever seemed to prevail in final combat with good?

Don't get me wrong. I don't mean to minimize the complexity and perversity of the world's evil. I don't for a moment

watched the building burn, I ran in the city streets and cried while I was running. The city was like a movie set and we were just waiting for the director to yell "cut"...and go back to NORMAL... Are we ever going back to NORMAL?   »

imagine that the forces of depravity will evaporate just because
we shift metaphorical gears—or that, in our current situation,
terrorism will instantly disappear because we analyze it in a different way. But I'm equally sure that, until we think clearly about
evil, we will never master it successfully. Such clarity begins with
the understanding that, however massive the assertions of evil,
they bear witness only to an absence, not to an opposite.

And that helps explain something else: That just as a single
candle can destroy a whole closetful of darkness, so a single life,
lived in the light of goodness, can make an enormous difference
in overcoming the reverberating void that calls itself terror and
blackness. If that's the case, is it any wonder that any one of us,
accurately assessing the moral nature of reality and banding together with a few others in unity of action, really can change the
world?

RUSHWORTH M. KIDDER is founder and president of the Institute for
Global Ethics in Camden, Maine (www.globalethics.org), and author of *How
Good People Make Tough Choices: Resolving the Dilemmas of Ethical Living.*

THE NEW FACE OF THE ENEMY
By Sam Keen

We have to start off with the fact that there *are* enemies. We were
attacked and, at the moment, the dominant thing that people
have to deal with is the grief, the sorrow, and the sense of loss,
not only of the lives lost but also of our lost innocence.

We have been perched up on this high catbird seat of our
own special privilege, wealth, and safety since the Second
World War—even during that war. But, as the Buddha reminds

9/12/01 07:58 A.M. SayNoMore: Please pray for my brother who
was in the WTC and has not been heard from.
9/12/01 8:17 A.M. icci22: Last night was the first night that I
went to bed afraid...I was afraid that this "safe country" isn't as

us, life is suffering. Most human beings live in daily danger, with wars and rumor of wars, with refugee problems. We thought that we were just about to enter into the alabaster city undimmed by human tears. We've suddenly been jolted into reality, and from now on we're going to be living with a sense of danger.

So what do we do? Our first response is to use a very old idea of the enemy to try to get us back to the old world. With the old faces of the enemy—the ones in the book—we're dealing primarily with the emotions of fear and hate. Here's an enemy: We fear him. We know who he is: He's a Hun or he's a "Jap" or he's an American pig, but he has a face. Then over that face we put another face, of an atheist or a barbarian or some kind of an animal, and this allows us to kill him. We retaliate; we strike out. And that makes us feel better, relieves our anxiety.

Now what's happened is very, very different. I'm just talking psychology, not actual fact, but, according to the mass mind, we have been hit by somebody. We don't know who they are. We don't know where they came from. We don't know why and we don't know when they will strike again. All we know is that everything is different.

What that has created is not fear but anxiety, and there is a vast difference between the two. Fear has a concrete object; anxiety doesn't. You can't marshal much against anxiety. When we use the old image of the monster, of Satan, and of pure evil, we're trying to get into that old enemy psychology. We would feel so much better if we could bomb somebody, especially if it's Osama bin Laden.

Whether he is or is not in back of this tragedy hardly matters in terms of our "enemy" psychology. A faceless enemy makes us anxious. What makes us outraged and grief-stricken, of course,

safe as we once thought it was....I cried most of yesterday and being out here in the mid-west there was nothing I could do except for cry and pray.
9/12/01 8:21 A.M. callalily: Has anyone heard from WayneLu? >>

is that we've been hit. What makes us uncertain is we don't know what kind of a world this act is calling us into. So we are apt to react very quickly. I think this is all wrong, of course. As I tried to point out in *Faces of the Enemy*, the only way to lessen the eternal circle of violence is by stopping knee-jerk retaliation. We have to sit and think for a long time about what we want to do and how to punish those who are guilty.

There was a picture in the paper that shows followers of Osama bin Laden holding up a great big sign that says, "Americans, think. Why are you hated all over the world?"

That's a hard question for us at a time like this. But it's the only question that is going to get us out of the mind-set of war and get us into dealing with what the real issues are. The real issues have to do with American success and the envy and the resentment of it, and the way that we have ignored the Middle East except for Israel. But before we know how to respond in a creative way, we have to know how they see us.

Naturally right now, we're looking at the incredible sorrow and outrage of this monstrous destruction and loss of lives, and it is good and inevitable that we should do that. But we have to ask ourselves what are we not seeing when we use this image of the enemy. The most embarrassing thing that we don't want to talk about is that, in the Iraqi war, we killed somewhere between half a million and a million, maybe a million-and-a-half people—nobody knows how many—and we rained who knows how many times this amount of destruction on Baghdad.

This is not to say that Saddam Hussein was not an evil man. He was doing evil things. But our response to it was so massive that it was an overreaction. Then we walked away and forgot about it. They haven't forgotten. When they look at us, that's what's on their minds. And when they attacked the World Trade

Did he get home to his wife?
9/12/01 08:28 A.M. flxcat: Please God, support those who have lost loved ones and those who still don't know where their loved ones may be. Please be with any survivors who might still

Center, what they see is that we have ruthlessly attacked people in the Middle East.

I think also—and this is very hard to say because there are certain things we can't say; I'm going to tell you what we can't say—that we are unfairly pro-Israel. Our media is unfairly pro-Israel, and our religious leaders are unfairly pro-Israel. Now, I don't know why we can't say that when all of the Arab world knows it and feels it and hates us for it. We have to say that out loud; we have to say to Israel, "No more support from us until you give the Palestinians a homeland." How many Americans realize that we give Israel $3 billion a year?

I think we're way too timid in these things. The *Wall Street Journal* outlined the reasons why we're hated: for what we did to Iraq; for the way in which, although we talk about civil rights, we support kings and tyrants as long as they keep our oil supply going; and because of our uncritical support of Israel.

If we want to change, we've got to change those things. We've never talked about Iraq in terms of what our aims were, what the threats were versus what our response was. Do you remember those horrible pictures of the Highway of Death? We killed everything living and then bombed everything else. That is not a way to wage war. You know, even if you go to war, there are rules of warfare, and we broke those rules.

Understanding the enemy is very crucial because only then can we prepare creative, reasonable, and just responses. But I think that as long as you have an image of the enemy, you can't make a distinction between reaction and responding. We *do* have to respond, and we *do* have to seek justice, but a reaction is not a response—it's unthinking.

Nationally, our process has to be, first of all, our grief; we need to feel the loss and mourn the people who were killed,

be trapped underneath the rubble and keep them strong while they wait for rescue. And also please be with the many people who are attempting these rescues. Keep them strong for all the horrible things they will be witness to and keep them safe »

mourn the destruction of those symbols, and grieve our lost innocence.

The second thing to do is do nothing. Sit. Pause. Wait. There's no reason that we have to respond militarily right away; that is, no good reason.

The third thing is to study the enemy. Pay attention. Who is it? The *Wall Street Journal* had it right. They had a headline on one article, "Why Do They Hate Us So Much?" We need to know the answer to that before we are prepared to give a good response.

Then after that, I would say deal with the guilty, but not with the innocent. The final thing that is we really have to rethink our entire foreign policy and the way that we're going to be in the world. It will never be the same, and that means that the old Marlboro Man of America, the independent nation standing tall and alone, is gone.

SAM KEEN is the best-selling author of several books, including *Fire in the Belly: On Being a Man.*

CALL EVIL BY ITS NAME
By Tom Bethell

In the past weeks, many writers have observed that those who flew planes into the World Trade Center had reasons for what they did: They disapproved of U.S. foreign policy, and they disapprove of our support of Israel in particular. For the purposes of debate, let us accept that these observers are right, at least in their attribution of motives. But discerning motives on the part of terrorists by no means exonerates them from the charge of evildoing. Are we to believe that only those who act in a pur-

while they do thier jobs.
9/12/01 9:06 A.M. genatemory: ...Is this what it takes for us to forget our differences and come together as one entity? To reevaluate our priorities, to truly appreciate the freedom and

poseless manner can legitimately be accused of evil? I think we can see how inappropriate, indeed silly, that would be. People like the author Sam Keen seem to be under the impression that only those who do bad things for no reason other than the fact that they are bad can be accused of evildoing.

If so, Mr. Keen fails to understand the underlying concept of evil. As it has been understood by a wide range of theologians (such as St. Thomas Aquinas) and popular writers (such as C. S. Lewis), evil is not to be thought of as the opposite of good but as the perversion of good. Theologians are in agreement that there is no such thing as pure evil, and in denying that the terrorists manifested just this attribute, Keen is shielding them from a charge that he has himself invented. Not just sometimes, but always, evil is done by those who aspire to some ultimate goal that is good. So we should not be surprised if the same applies to those who destroyed the World Trade Center.

Here is the relevant observation from C. S. Lewis's best-known book, *Mere Christianity*:

> In real life people are cruel for one of two reasons—either because they are sadists, that is, because they have a sensual perversion which makes cruelty a cause of sensual pleasure to them; or else for the sake of something else that they are going to get out of it—money or power or safety. But pleasure, money, power, and safety are all, as far as they go, good things. The badness consists in pursuing them by the wrong method, or in the wrong way, or too much. I do not mean, of course, that the people who do this [commit cruel acts] are not desperately wicked. I do mean that wickedness, when you examine it, turns out to be the pursuit of some good in the wrong way.

security of our everyday life? Did we need this to teach us that hate kills but love heals? My prayer is that we all come to see that rainbow at the end of the storm.
9/12/01 9:45 A.M. bmooring: I would like to pray for all the   >>

You can be good for the mere sake of goodness. You cannot be bad for the mere sake of badness. You can do a kind action when you are not feeling kind and when it gives you no pleasure, simply because kindness is right; but no one ever did a cruel action simply because cruelty is wrong. Badness cannot succeed in being bad in the same way in which goodness is good. Goodness is, so to speak, itself. Badness is only spoiled goodness."

So, too, the terrorists were no doubt pursuing some ultimate "good," as they saw it (autonomy for the Muslim world, for example), but they were also most decidedly pursuing it "in the wrong way" (by murdering innocent people). Our natural inclination to call the terrorist attacks evil is therefore sound from any reasoned moral or theological perspective. In pursuing a goal that may well have been good in itself, the recent acts of terrorism were no different from other evil acts, except that they were far more heinous than most such acts.

Some people have difficulty with this analysis of evil, I believe, because we have so much fallen out of the habit of thinking in terms of evil at all. Routinely, we fear that anything we say might give offense. Are we being too judgmental? Our relativized understanding of truth has taken its toll. We say to one another: "What is bad for us may be good for others, so who are we to say what is good or bad?" That is the way many of us think, even when confronted with the enormity of the events of September 11.

We have become so sensitive to the absolute overtones of the word "evil" that to a great extent we avoid using it, and it has acquired a special aura. When the *Washington Post* used it in a big headline on the day after the attack—"Under a Cloud of Evil"—

victims and their families and friends. I pray for their strength and protection during this difficult time. I also ask for your prayers for my brother Eugene as we are waiting for word as to whether he was a passenger on one of the flights leaving Boston

it carried a high voltage for that reason. We treat the notion of evil as though it were our 16-inch gun—to be wheeled out and fired only on very special occasions; in reference to the Holocaust in World War II, or perhaps to some hate crime in America.

Of course, the terrorist attack and the consequent murder of thousands of innocent people was itself no ordinary event. On that ground alone, therefore, it should qualify for the dreaded label evil. But my point is not that the attack deserves to be called evil because of its enormity, but because a very large number of routine events in our lives partake of evil to some degree. And it goes without saying that the terrorist attack did so to a large degree.

We are all immersed in evil, great and small, every day of the week. We do bad things routinely, when we lie or cheat or steal or succumb to any number of temptations. We are urged in the Lord's Prayer: "And lead us not into temptation, but deliver us from evil." Catholics in the pews are urged to go to confession regularly not because evil is a thing of rare enormity, but because it is so everyday.

When Jesus enjoins us to pray that God might "deliver us from evil," it is not because we might otherwise be tempted to blow up buildings filled with thousands of innocent people, but because we might do something so inconspicuous as thinking ill of our neighbor. And if small animosities fall under the rubric of evil, as they do, then the large hatreds manifested by the terrorists certainly do likewise.

TOM BETHELL is the Washington correspondent for *The American Spectator* and one of Beliefnet's Catholicism columnists.

9/12/01 10:13 A.M. covenantsecurity: It is now 24 hours after the attack. I can't get myself going so I can get some work done today. I am still at home, glued to the TV.... How could this happen? Who could have planned this so precisely? I have »

WHY DOES GOD ALLOW EVIL?
A Sermon by Pastor Rick Warren

The Bible explains the root of evil: "This is the crisis we're in: God's light streamed into the world, but men and women everywhere ran for the darkness . . . because they were not really interested in pleasing God" (John 3:19). We're far more interested in pleasing ourselves.

The horrific mass murder of innocent Americans leaves all rational people shocked, angry, grief-stricken, and numb. Our tears flow freely and our hearts carry a deep ache. How could this happen in our nation?

As mothers, fathers, brothers, sisters, friends, neighbors, and coworkers begin to share their stories of the horror, this tragedy will become even more personal. As this tragedy becomes more personal it will become more painful, and as our pain deepens, so will the questions. Why does God allow evil to happen? If God is so great and so good, why does he allow human beings to hurt each other?

The answer lies in both our greatest blessing and our worst curse: our capacity to make choices. God has given us a free will. Made in God's image, we have been given the freedom to decide how we will act and the ability to make moral choices. This is one asset that sets us apart from animals, but it also is the source of so much pain in our world. People, and that includes all of us, often make selfish, self-centered, and evil choices. Whenever that happens, people get hurt. Sin is ultimately selfishness. I want to do what I want, not what God tells me to do. Unfortunately, sin always hurts others, not just ourselves.

God could have eliminated all evil from our world by simply removing our ability to choose it. He could have made us pup-

heard from friends in Thailand, Bhutan, and Nepal, who indicate that the whole world is dumbfounded. May the Lord Bless us all, and lift up His Souls.
9/12/01 10:14 A.M. becben: Help us know what to tell our chil-

pets or marionettes on strings that he pulls. By taking away our ability to choose it, evil would vanish. But God doesn't want us to be puppets. He wants to be loved and obeyed by creatures who voluntarily choose to do so. Love is not genuine if there is no other option.

Yes, God could have kept the terrorists from completing their suicidal missions by removing their ability to choose their own will instead of his. But to be fair, God would also have to do that to all of us. You and I are not terrorists, but we do harm and hurt others with our own selfish decisions and actions. You may hear misguided minds say, "This must have been God's will." Nonsense! In a world of free choices, God's will is rarely done! Doing our own will is much more common. Don't blame God for this tragedy. Blame people who ignored what God has told us to do: "Love your neighbor as yourself."

In heaven, God's will is done perfectly. That's why there is no sorrow, pain, or evil there. But this is Earth, a fallen, imperfect place. We must choose to do God's will every day. It isn't automatic. This is why Jesus told us to pray "Thy will be done on earth, as it is in heaven."

There are many other questions that race through our minds during dark days. But the answers will not come from pollsters, pundits, or politicians. We must look to God and his Word. We must humble ourselves and admit that each of us often chooses to ignore what God wants us to do.

No doubt this weekend houses of worship across America will be packed. In a crisis we cry out for a connection with our Creator. This is a deep-seated, universal urge. The first words uttered by millions on Tuesday were, "Oh, God!" We were made for a relationship with God, but he waits for us to choose him. He is ready to comfort, guide, and direct us

dren to calm their fears. Help us so that we can again feel safe. **9/12/01 10:42 A.M. erica_c:** It's 24 hours later. Now what? I ask myself. I just got out of my Biostats class. I made some lame remark at the beginning of class about how we need to move >>

through our grief. My prayer is that you will attend a house of worship this weekend and reconnect with God. But it's your choice.

RICK WARREN, D.M., is a founding pastor of America's second largest congregation, Saddleback Church, in Lake Forest, California.

on and try to continue with our lives. (I'm not an eloquent person). Then I stood there and proceeded to lecture on probability. And it all seemed so hollow. Why am I doing this? What does it matter?

Chapter 5

THE QUESTION
OF ISLAM

O you who believe! When you conspire together,
conspire not for crime and
wrongdoing and disobedience to the messenger,
but conspire together for
righteousness and piety and keep your duty
toward Allah, unto Whom you will
be gathered.
—The Koran, Book of Sura 58 v. 9

IS ISLAM VIOLENT?
By Karen Armstrong

What kind of Muslim is Osama bin Laden, and what is the background of his movement? Osama bin Laden is from Saudi Arabia, where a particular form of Islam, Wahhabism, is practiced. Wahhabism was an 18th-century Muslim reform movement, not unlike Puritanism in Christianity. It was an effort to get back to the sources of the faith, get rid of accretions and additions, and all foreign influence. Thus, Wahhabis wanted to eliminate the practice of Sufism, the mysticism of Islam, which developed after Muhammad's time; it was deeply opposed to Shiite Islam, another later development. And Wahhabis wanted to rid Islam of all foreign influence. Instead, they wanted to go back the bedrock message of the Koran and renew the faith by going back to the sources.

Bin Laden believes that the Saudi rulers are corrupt and that the Kingdom of Saudi Arabia is not living up to the purity of the Islamic ideal. Like most Sunni fundamentalists, he has been influenced by the Egyptian ideologue Sayyid Qutb, who was executed by President Jamal Abdul Nasser in 1966.

Qutb's story shows why so many fundamentalists believe that secularism is aggressive and inimical to faith. Nasser paid lip service to Islam and used the rhetoric of religion when it suited him. But he was a secularist, committed to a form of socialism and nationalism. The vast majority of Egyptians, who had not had a modern education, found his secularism alien and baffling; they responded far more warmly to the Muslim Brotherhood, which thus constituted a rival. After an attempt on his life, Nasser imprisoned hundreds of the brothers without trial. Many of them had done nothing more incriminating than attend meetings or hand out leaflets.

9/12/01 11:21 A.M. wardc: ...I pray that the innate Buddha nature in all beings manifest at this time of suffering and grief... may the families and loved ones of the victims find peace and may the people of the world react with compassion and un-

Qutb went into the concentration camp as a liberal, but after 15 years of physical and mental torture, he came to the conclusion that Muslims had a duty to conduct a jihad against their secular rulers. He developed a form of liberation theology: Because God alone was sovereign, no Muslim had any obligation to obey any authority—religious or secular. Egyptian society was evil: It was like the *jahiliyyah*, a term Muslims use to describe the Age of Ignorance in Arabia before the coming of Islam. Muhammad had fought the *jahiliyyah* of his own day, and now Muslims must continue this struggle, even against their own people, who were only Muslims in name.

Qutb devised a program of action, which included a withdrawal from the world, a period of preparation, and finally an offensive against the enemies of Islam. This program completely distorts the meaning of the life of the Prophet Muhammad, who was forced to engage in war but who achieved victory by an ingenious and inspiring policy of nonviolence. Bin Laden roughly subscribes to this kind of Sunni fundamentalism. His quarrel with the United States is not, however, over theological differences. He resents what he regards as its partisan and one-sided support for Israel; its support of such unpopular leaders as the Saudi kings and President Mubarak; and the continued bombing and sanctions against Iraq, which have deprived the Iraqi people (though not Saddam and his cronies) of food and drugs, as a result of which thousands of Iraqi children have died of cancer. All this bin Laden regards as an act of war against the Arab peoples. All this seems to him, and to many people in the Middle East, an American war against Islam.

He is not simply concerned with fighting the United States. He also wants to get rid of regimes that he regards as apostate in the Muslim world: His targets include Saudi Arabia, Egypt, and Shiite Iran. He is not fighting democracy or freedom per se. He

derstanding, particularly with regard to religious and ethnic minorities within the U.S. I pray to relieve the suffering of all beings.
9/12/01 11:42 A.M. gk11673: Dear God, please help us to re- >>

simply wants the United States out of the region and is fighting a war against what he regards as American imperialism.

Only a small minority of Muslims would support bin Laden's full program, but most of the middle classes would share his dislike of "American imperialism." There are many business people and professionals who believe the United States now controls the region, economically and politically, and they deeply resent this. Because much of this opposition is mainstream, this creates conditions sympathetic to the radicals. People in the mainstream do not like American foreign policy, and even though they utterly deplore the events of September 11, they continue to believe that America and the West have no concern for their welfare or their views. They believe, rightly or wrongly, that the United States regards their needs and concerns as unimportant.

Fundamentalism is nihilistic because it denies crucial and sacred values of the faith. The ideology of Qutb and bin Laden is un-Islamic, because Islam condemns violence, aggression, and killing, and like Judaism, holds that to kill even one person is in a sense to kill the whole world. The Koran will permit only a war of self-defense. It holds that killing is always a great evil, but that sometimes it is necessary to fight in order to preserve decent values. This is similar to the mainstream Western ideal of the just war: In World War II, the Allies deemed it necessary to fight Hitler.

What does the Koran say about violence? The word "Islam," which means surrender, is related to the Arabic *salam*, "peace." When the Prophet Muhammad brought the revealed scripture called the Koran ("recitation") to the Arabs in the early 7th century B.C.E., one of his main purposes was precisely to stop the kind of indiscriminate killing we saw on September 11.

At the time, the Arabian Peninsula was in crisis. The tribal system was breaking down, and the various tribes were locked

member we are a people of strength and faith, not a people of vengeance. Please help us to heal our anger and pain so that we don't continue this endless circle of violence.
9/12/01 11:57 A.M. IanPF: Many of you have expressed a need

into a murderous cycle of vendetta and counter-vendetta. For a weak tribe, or a man who lacked powerful protection, survival was nearly impossible. The Prophet himself suffered several assassination attempts, and when his religious and social message ran him afoul of the establishment of Mecca, the small Muslim community was persecuted. Things got so bad that the Muslims had to migrate to Medina, some 250 miles to the north, and there they were subject to attack by the Meccan army, the greatest power in Arabia.

For about 5 years, there was war, and the Muslims narrowly escaped extermination. Terrible things were done on both sides. But when Muhammad sensed that the tide had just begun to turn in his favor, he completely changed tack. He concentrated on building a peaceful coalition of tribes and initiated an inspired, brave, and ingenious policy of nonviolence. This proved so successful that eventually Mecca opened its gates to the Muslims voluntarily, without a single drop of blood being shed.

Because the Koran was revealed in the context of an all-out war, several passages deal with the conduct of armed conflict. Warfare was a desperate business in Arabia. An Arab chieftain was not expected to take prisoners; it was a given that he would simply kill everybody he could get his hands on. Muhammad knew that if the Muslims were defeated, they would all be slaughtered to the last man or woman.

Sometimes the Koran seems to have imbibed this spirit. Muslims are ordered by God to "slay [the enemy] wherever you find them (4:89). Muslim extremists like bin Laden like to quote these verses, but they do so selectively, never quoting the exhortations to peace and forbearance that in almost every case mitigate these ferocious injunctions in the verses immediately following. Thus, "If they leave you alone and offer to make peace with you, God does not allow you to harm them" (4:90).

for prayer. If this makes you feel better, then do it. But please, donate blood, as I did. I am an atheist, and these were my fellow human beings, too.
9/12/01 12:39 P.M. ViddyD: Dear God, Please show me the   >>

Therefore, the only war condoned by the Koran is a war of self-defense. "Warfare is an awesome evil" (2:217), but sometimes it is necessary to fight in order to bring the kind of persecution suffered by the Muslims to an end [2:217] or to preserve decent values [22:40]. But Muslims may never initiate hostilities, and aggression is forbidden by God [2:190]. While the fighting continues, Muslims must dedicate themselves wholly to the war in order to bring things back to normal as quickly as possible, but the second the enemy sues for peace, hostilities must cease [2:192].

The word "jihad" is much misunderstood. It is rarely used as a noun in the Koran, but in a verbal form, meaning striving, struggle, or effort. This jihad denotes the determined effort that Muslims must make to put God's commands into practice in a terrible and evil world. Sometimes this will mean armed struggle, but the jihad also refers to a spiritual, moral, intellectual, social, domestic, or purely personal effort. There is a very famous and much quoted hadith, or tradition, about the Prophet Muhammad, which describes him returning home after a battle and saying to his companions, "We are returning from the Lesser Jihad [the battle] to the Greater Jihad," which is the far more important and urgent struggle to reform one's own heart and one's own society.

Consequently, the Koran is quite clear that warfare is not the best way of dealing with difficulties. It is much better to sit down and reason with people who disagree with us, and to "argue [with unbelievers] in the most kindly manner, with wisdom and goodly exhortation." If Muslims are forced to respond to an attack, their retaliation must be appropriate and proportionate to the wrong suffered, but forbearance is preferable: "To bear yourselves with patience is far better for you, since God is with those who are patient in adversity" (16:125–27).

way. amen.
9/12/01 12:42 P.M. dfuhs: Love, fear, and anger cannot coexist in the same place at the same time. This is a defining moment for each of us. I believe that we can choose to be the peace we

The Koran also quotes the Jewish Torah, which permits the *lex talionis*—an eye for an eye and a tooth for a tooth—but adds that it is a meritorious act to be charitable and to refrain from retaliation (5:45).

Muslims must be realistic. If God had wanted all peoples to be the same and have identical opinions and policies, then he would have made them into one nation and made them all Muslims. But God has not chosen to do this, so Muslims must accept his will (10:99; 11:118). If there is an irreconcilable difference, Muslims must simply go their own way, as the Prophet himself did when he found that he could not agree with the Meccan establishment, saying, "Unto you your moral law, and unto me, mine" (109:6). You go your way, and I'll go mine.

Above all, "There must be no coercion in matters of faith" (2:256). The grammar here is very strong, very absolute ("La ikra fi'l-din"). It is similar in form to the Shehadah, the Muslim profession of Faith: "There is no God but Allah!" ("La illaha 'l Allah!") The Unity of God is the basis of all Muslim morality and spirituality. The principle of *tawhid* ("making one") is the Muslim task par excellence. Nothing must rival God—no ideology, material goods, or personal ambitions. A Muslim must try to integrate his entire personality and his whole life to ensure that God is his top priority, and in the unity that he will discover within himself when this is achieved, he will have intimations of that Unity which is God. It is, therefore, significant that in the Koran, the prohibition of force and compulsion in religious matters is made as emphatically as the assertion of the Unity of God. The principle is as sacred as that.

Muhammad did not intend to found a new world religion to which everybody had to subscribe. The Koran makes it clear that he considered that he was simply bringing the religion of the One God to the Arabs, who had not had a prophet before and

want to see around us....
9/12/01 1:25 P.M. drdeb2: Lord, walk with us, fill our hearts with love so that hate will not consume us. Help us come together and find each other in our despair, let us see your light.   >>

had no scriptures in their own language. The Koran insists that its revelation does not cancel out the revelations made to previous prophets: to Abraham, Moses, David, Solomon, Enoch, or Jesus. Every nation on the face of the Earth has been sent some kind of revelation, which it expresses in its own cultural idiom. So every rightly guided religion comes from God.

In the Koran, Muslims are commanded to speak with great courtesy to Jews and Christians, "the People of the Book," who believe in the same God as they do (29:46). These were the world faiths that Muslims were familiar with; today, Muslim scholars argue that had the Prophet known about Buddhists, Hindus, the Native Americans, or Australian Aborigines, the Koran would have endorsed their religious leaders too. Muhammad simply thought that he was bringing the Arabs, who seemed to have been left out of the divine plan, into the religious family founded by the other great prophets.

This is reflected in the symbolic story of the Prophet's spiritual flight from Mecca to Jerusalem, where he is welcomed by all the great prophets of the past on the Temple Mount, preaches to them there, and then ascends to the Divine Throne, greeting and sometimes taking advice from Moses, Aaron, Jesus, John the Baptist, and Abraham on the way. It is a story of religious pluralism: The prophets all affirm one another's visions and teachings; they gain help from one another. And it also shows the Prophet's yearning to bring the Arabs in far-off Arabia into the heart of the monotheistic faith.

So when Osama bin Laden declared a jihad against Christians and Jews, he was acting against basic tenets of the Koran. It goes without saying that any form of indiscriminate killing (*qital*), which is strongly condemned in the Koran, is also un-Islamic.

So too is suicide, which is forbidden in Islamic law. True, the

9/12/01 1:35 P.M. Mich17: Yesterday was possibly the worst day of my life... I have never felt so fearful, vulnerable and unsure of the future. Today so far has been better but still this event holds a grip on my life... I was even haunted in my dreams by

Koran promises that those who fall in battle while fighting for their lives against Mecca will surely go to paradise. It was certainly not encouraging Muslims to rush out and expose themselves to the danger of certain death.

KAREN ARMSTRONG is the author of a celebrated account of Christianity, Judaism, and Islam, *A History of God*, and *The Battle for God*, on fundamentalism in the major religions. A former Catholic nun, she teaches at Leo Baeck College, a seminary for Reform Judaism, in London.

WHAT WOULD MUHAMMAD SAY ABOUT TERRORISM?
By Alex Kronemer

Terrorism as witnessed on September 11 is not directly addressed in the Koran, the Muslim holy book, which was the basis for all Muhammad's actions. However, a certain category of crimes outlined in the Koran in verses 5:33–34 comes close to a definition that would apply to terrorist actions. These are crimes committed by a few that spread fear, destruction, and havoc in society at large. Among the most hated offenses addressed in the Koran, examples traditionally include gangsterism, banditry, and serial murder. Terrorism would almost certainly fall into this category, since the hallmark of these crimes is their almost radioactive power to inflict harm long after they are committed. For this reason, such crimes as terrorism carry the harshest penalties in Islamic justice: execution in the worst case, banishment from the land, or the cutting off of a hand and a foot to prevent the perpetrator from threatening society again.

A story from the life of the Prophet not only illustrates why

images of people stuck in a destroyed building in downtown LA (visible from my apt) waving out of windows at rescuers.
9/12/01 1:53 P.M. jhhastings: My world is lost in fire and heat, But the terrible wind does not dry my tears. My heart is   >>

such crimes are so harmful, but is eerily reminiscent of the current situation. Quoted in Bukhari, Muslim, Abu Dawud, and several other authenticated stories of the Prophet's life, it tells about a small group of nomadic men who wandered from the desert into Medina when Muhammad lived there, and finding him, claimed to be Muslims and asked for shelter. Winter had come to the region, and the men were sick and badly malnourished. Feeling pity for them, Muhammad gave them shelter, food, and allowed them access to several female camels for milk. They lived among the Muslims in Medina for a long period, gaining the trust of many and seeming to have joined the society. But one night, after the weather had improved and their health was restored, they killed the attendant who cared for the camels and disappeared into the night with the animals.

Arabia at that time was full of such nomadic people, and they often attacked and pillaged desert caravans. But this crime was different and unexpected to the Muslims. These men had come to the city, claiming to be one of them—claiming to be Muslims—and had been accepted. But they had lied and murdered. Who among the other nomads living now among them in Medina and claiming to be Muslims were also murderers, waiting for the right moment to strike?

Then as today, such suspicions quickly can undermine a society, making people deeply distrustful of one other, creating fear and anarchy.

For this reason, not only does the Koran spell out the judicial punishment, but also warns that an "awesome" suffering awaits in the afterlife.

But as is the case with the execution of any Islamic punishment, justice is tempered with mercy and must be guided by certitude. A tradition of the Prophet says that it is better to err in

cracked and bruised but it will not be broken. Evil cannot take me into itself and deliver me to hatred. I long for vengeance but I pray for justice. I will bear the weight of unspeakable sorrow, But I will not bend. I will not break. This is my pledge.

acquitting a guilty person than in punishing an innocent one. It would therefore be important that the crime be proven by a decisive event without any doubt, and that all the requirements of Islamic justice, which include a fair trial and the humane treatment of people in custody, be fulfilled.

Once proven, the guilty would probably find at least one mercy still available to them, even as they faced their punishment. While the judicial requirement must be met, truly repentant people would be told that they could hope for God's forgiveness and mercy in the afterlife. As the Koran frequently reminds the people who go to it for guidance, God is all-forgiving, merciful beyond boundaries, and compassionate to those who seek it.

ALEX KRONEMER is an Islamic expert and formerly a State Department officer for human rights and religious freedom. He is currently coproducing a documentary on the life of the Prophet Muhammad.

FINDING THE VOICE OF ISLAM
By Ingrid Mattson

The terrorist attack on September 11 exacerbated a double bind American Muslims have been feeling for some time now. So often, it seems, we have to apologize for reprehensible actions committed by Muslims in the name of Islam. We tell other Americans: "People who do these things (oppression of women, persecution of religious minorities, terrorism) have distorted the 'true' Islam."

And so often we have to tell other Muslims throughout the world that America is not as bad as it appears. We tell them: "These policies (support for oppressive governments, enforce-

This is my prayer.
9/12/01 2:19 P.M. BeJeTe: Many are missing; pray for Peter Klein. May God hold you in the palm of His hand
9/12/01 2:39 P.M. kblackthorne: Words fail. Grant us all   >>

ment of sanctions responsible for the deaths of almost a million
children in Iraq, vetoing any criticism of Israel at the UN) contradict the 'true' values of America."

What is clear is that now, today, Muslims in America must finally commit to speaking out against injustice—wherever it occurs.

The freedom, stability, and strong moral foundation of the
United States are great blessings for all Americans, particularly
for Muslims. Here in America, we have been able to free Islam
from many of the negative cultural practices that have developed
in other countries.

But God has not blessed us with these things because we are
better than the billions of humans who do not live in America.
We do not deserve good health, stable families, safety and
freedom more than the millions of Muslims and non-Muslims
throughout the world who are suffering from disease, poverty,
and oppression. Muslims who live in America are being tested
by God to see if we will be satisfied with a self-contained,
self-serving Muslim community that resembles an Islamic
town in the Epcot global village, or if we will use the many opportunities available to us to change the world for the better.

The dilemma is that we must be lovingly self-critical of our
nation and our faith community, without appearing to betray
either. At first glance, it may seem easier to speak out against injustice committed by our nation. We have free speech in this
country. But it's not that simple. If our speech in this country
has no effect on policies that harm Muslims throughout the
world—at the same time we're criticizing injustice committed
by Muslims—our loyalty to the global Muslim community will
be questioned. American Muslim leaders will have no credibility
as authentic interpreters of Islam. Our opinions will have no authority. Only the voices of the radicals will be heard.

In his speech to the nation, the president of the United States

healing
9/12/01 2:40 P.M. Anwan Girl: My thoughts, hopes, and prayers
go to the people who died (may they be kings/queens in their
next life) and the people who were left behind. I got sick with

argued that American Muslim leaders and other "moderates" represent the true voice of Islam. This is only true if we are recognized as authentic interpreters of Islam among the global Muslim community. According to Islamic doctrine, after the death of the Prophet Muhammad, no Muslim has the right to claim infallibility in interpreting the faith. This does not mean that all opinions are equal, nor that everyone has the ability to interpret religious and legal doctrine. Solid scholarship and a deep understanding of the tradition are essential. But not all scholars are considered authoritative. Most Muslims will accept a scholar's opinions as authoritative only if they are convinced he or she is truly concerned about the welfare of ordinary people.

There have been times when forces hostile to Islam attacked or occupied Muslim lands—for example, the Mongol invasions, (Christian) Crusades, European colonialism, and the Soviet invasion of Afghanistan. At those times, people needed revolutionary leaders; those who were unable to unite the people against aggression were considered irrelevant.

Throughout most of Muslim history, however, religious leaders who advocated aggression against the state were marginalized. After all, most Muslims did not want to be led into revolution—they simply wanted their lives to be better. The most successful religious leaders were those who, in addition to serving the spiritual needs of the community, acted as intermediaries between the people and the state.

The question we need to ask is, at this point in history, what do Muslims need to hear from their leaders? What voices will they listen to? So many Muslim lands have undergone unending turmoil since the beginning of European colonialism. Continued occupation by foreign powers allowed revolutionary zeal to take root in the Muslim world. Oppression has made many

disgust, I was down with fear, I cried with sadness, I smile for hope.

9/12/01 3:02 P.M. IronButterfly3: The people of Canada (I'm in Montreal) are also feeling the same way that has been ex-   >>

Muslims blind to the possibility of peaceful change and deaf to the arguments of Muslim scholars who teach that revolt and lawlessness cause more harm than government corruption.

This is the reason why it is so difficult to find authentic, authoritative Muslim voices. Religious leaders who speak out in a peaceful way against injustice will remain marginalized if their speech has no effect. The majority of Muslims will not recognize such people as leaders. On the other hand, in many parts of the world, those who speak out against corruption are jailed, tortured, and killed. In such circumstances, very few people— only those who are willing to risk losing their property, their families, their security, and their lives—will continue to speak out. Only the radicals will remain.

So how do American Muslims convince the rest of the Muslim world that peaceful social and political change is possible and, indeed, preferred by Islamic theology and law? How do we prove that America is neither a crusading nor a colonizing power? How do we demonstrate that the American Constitution forms the basis for a state that does not fit the old models of statehood articulated in Islamic law? How can we convince other Muslims that the true essence of America is a love for freedom and human rights?

We can do all of this only if America abandons policies that contradict our arguments. We cannot silence the radicals. Our only hope is to render their arguments unbelievable, their voices unauthoritative.

INGRID MATTSON, Ph.D., is a practicing Muslim and professor of Islamic Studies at the Duncan Black MacDonald Center for the Study of Islam & Christian-Muslim Relations at Hartford Seminary in Connecticut. In 1988, she traveled to Pakistan where she worked with Afghan refugee women. She is the vice-president of the Islamic Organization of North America.

pressed here already. It's a little difficult to keep this dialogue simplified dealing with only one facet of what has happened. It's emotion, religion, politics, etc. I'm not thrilled about the idea of war - but there must be a retaliation to this. An eye for

I'M AN AMERICAN MUSLIM—
AND I'M AFRAID
By Rhonda Roumani

On September 11, like many others around the country, I felt my heart sink, my throat tighten, and my eyes fill with tears. How could this happen here? This act of terrorism and the loss of life are something that as a nation we can't understand—and it leaves us vulnerable and scared. We have lost loved ones and friends. Our security and safety have been violated. We cannot even begin to understand how someone could orchestrate such horror.

I feel afraid, not only for America at large, but for a specific group: American Muslims. Because I am one. I'm not really worried about myself. I blend in with most others on the street. I don't look particularly "ethnic," since I'm fairly light-skinned and I don't wear a head scarf. But one of my close friends here in New York wears hijab (the Islamic head dress), and she's afraid to walk outside today. Another of my friends who wears hijab is not allowed to leave the house because her parents fear for her safety, even though she lives in Los Angeles. Another is considering taking the hijab off. And I understand why.

My parents immigrated to this country in search of the freedoms not available to them in their home country. Although they did not face religious persecution at home, they knew that religious freedom was guaranteed in this country, and they cherished the opportunity to live in a society where freedom of expression is protected under law. So it worries me now to think that Muslim Americans are no longer feeling they can enjoy rights and freedoms guaranteed to them under our Constitution. As a society, it is our duty to make sure that their freedoms are protected.

As I was walking the streets of New York the day of the at-

an eye.
9/12/01 3:52 P.M. snellchatfield: God, please be with those who have lost loved ones and with those who may still be trapped in the rubble. »

tacks, I could hear the words "Muslims" and "Islam" being whispered. One person even said that this was a time for "extermination." There are reports that Muslims and mosques are being targeted. I don't know how many of the reports are true, but I do know that Muslims are keenly aware of the image that is out there—and they are worried for their religion, for their community, and for their country. We need to remember that the majority of Muslims in this country are American citizens. Islam in America has many colors—black, white, East Asian, Middle Eastern—but our common thread is that we are all American. American Muslims are grieving too.

Still, in our own country, the words "Muslim" and "Islam" are wrongly associated with terrorism. The problem is that Americans know very little about Islam as a religion and so are susceptible to rumors, suspicion, and misinformation. We are quick to associate Islam with the Middle East and with the conflict around the world. Yes, there are conflicts, and yes, there are many zealots. But Islam is a religion that does not condone terrorism. It is a religion rooted in the Abrahamic tradition. Muslims pray to the same God as Christians and Jews, and they believe in many of the same teachings and prophets. Islam is a religion that in its history has provided for years of peace and prosperity among different religious groups.

When I was young, like many people in search of their faith, I went through a time of doubting and questioning Islam because of the very images that are still out there today. As a Muslim growing up in America, it was not always easy to distinguish between Islam and the images that the media has used to define Islam. Was it possible that Islam could be so different than the religion being shown on television? How could my friends, members of my family, and members and leaders in my

9/12/01 3:53 P.M. mom2bonnie: Dear Jesus, let the terrorists see your face and repent for what they have done. Let their sympathizers see your face and turn away from their evil deeds. Let all who mourn see your face and be comforted. Let

community find solace in a religion that was depicted as so extreme, intolerant, and radical? How could such disparate images of the same religion exist?

Needless to say, it took many years of research, reading, and soul searching to realize that the Islam described in the Koran and that has been a guiding light for so many people around the world is in fact a practical and beautiful religion. When I was able to isolate Islam from the images and rhetoric that have become commonplace in our society and on TV, I found a religion that was simple, that stood for justice, that placed the utmost importance on revering God and tolerating other faiths. It placed the responsibility for justice on the people. And, for me, most important, it made God and your relationship to God a personal one for which you were responsible.

Far too often, the word "jihad" has been misused and taken out of context. Jihad is not another word for terrorism. Jihad is a term that refers to a person's struggle to uphold justice. It can take many forms—from an inner struggle to do right to an armed struggle against aggression. But what is clear is that an armed struggle cannot target innocent people—that is just plainly against Islam. Terrorism is in no way justified or condoned in Islam. It's as simple as that.

There is the possibility that this event could drastically change the way our society works. Suspicion may run rampant, and our freedoms may be threatened. In the past few years, Muslims have had to fight the "Secret Evidence Act." More than 20 Arabs and Muslims have been held for up to 3 years without being told of the charges and evidence against them. A repeal of the act passed the House of Representatives this year, but there is still a long way to go. What we thought could never happen in America already has—we have lost some of our freedoms. We must be careful not to let this wave of fear foreshadow some-

all of us see your face and give thanks that we are alive and have your love. "May the souls of the faithful departed rest in peace." amen
9/12/01 4:21 P.M. Wilted Rose: Why do we kill people who kill >>

thing even greater and more dangerous to our individual liberties as Americans.

How we handle the situation now is crucial. As people search for an outlet for their anger and frustration, we need to make sure that emotion and anger do not cloud the need for due process. We cannot return to a McCarthy-like era where everybody becomes suspect; this would threaten the very foundations upon which our country was built.

We have a long process of healing before us. May God guide us all.

RHONDA ROUMANI is the Islam producer for Beliefnet.

MUSLIM AMERICANS: A PRAYER
By Imam Izak-El Mu'eed Pasha

Delivered September 23, 2001

With God's name, The Merciful Benefactor, The Merciful Redeemer, it is God we beg for assistance, we beg for strength and guidance, and his mercy. We witness that he is one and we witness to all of his messengers and Prophets.

Dear God, Creator of all things in heaven and Earth, guide us this day to bring comfort to those who have lost loved ones and give hope to those who are still waiting to hear.

We, Muslims, Americans, stand today with a heavy weight on our shoulders that those who would dare do such dastardly acts claim our faith. They are no believers in God at all. Nor do they believe in his messenger Muhammad, the prayers and peace be upon him. We condemn them and their acts, their cowardly acts, and we stand with our country against all that would come against us.

people to show people that killing people is wrong?
9/12/01 4:28 P.M. Dur: Blessed be those that are suffering. Blessed be those that are dying. Blessed be those that are mourning. Blessed be those that are helping. Blessed be those

We are members of one human family, one human dignity, one human worth. That worth that God has given to us, the goodness that he has created us in, no single group or nation will be able to destroy. We are one with the Creator of the heavens and the Earth. We are one with members of faith, both Jewish, Christian, and others here today and those who are absent. We are believers.

We will not be deterred. So let those of you who are here today take this word out that we are one America made up of all the beautiful faces and beautiful persons and beautiful colors, and that's what makes us unique in the world, and we will not change.

God is bigger. God is greater.

These families here today, we are here for you and we will forever be here for you. We are among those who are saddened and troubled by the world we have today. We call on all of our religious leaders, all of our political leaders, all good people: This must stop. We cannot tolerate oppression of any type.

I close by saying a short Surah from our holy book, the Koran. In its English translation, in that Surah, which is called "Time Through Ages," it says, "By time, verily mankind is in loss, except such as have faith and do righteous deeds and join together in the mutual enjoining of truth and of patience and constancy."

May God guide us. May God bless our mayor, our governor, our president, and all of you. Do not allow the ignorance of people to have you attack your good neighbor.

We are Muslims, but we are Americans.

IMAM IZAK-EL MU'EED PASHA is imam of Malcolm Shabazz Mosque in Harlem and the first Muslim chaplain of the New York City Police Department.

that can do nothing but wait. Lord and Lady give us strength.
9/12/01 4:31 P.M. t00ldissectional: I don't know what I believe but I can and I will pray for those lost in the terrorist attacks....

Chapter 6
THE DESIRE
FOR JUSTICE

Injustice anywhere is a threat to justice everywhere.
We are caught in an inescapable network of mutuality,
tied in a single garment of destiny. Whatever affects
one directly, affects all indirectly.
—Martin Luther King Jr.
"Letter from Birmingham City Jail," April 16, 1963

HEAL THE WORLD: A MULTIFAITH RESPONSE
TO AN ASSAULT ON OUR HUMANITY
By Arthur Magida

Tuesday's carnage was an assault on not just the core of our nation, but on something deeper and more fragile: It was an assault on our sense of who we are and what we are and how we are to live our lives.

Every faith issues exhortations toward goodness:

Engage in *tikkun olam*, says Judaism: Repair the world. Make it a good world, a decent world, a world worthy of its Creator, who had such high hopes for it.

Practice *dhimmi*, say Muslims: Protect the minorities who live within your borders so they can practice their religions and their customs.

Be compassionate, say Christians: Let your love envelop the world. Let it even envelop your foes.

Engage in *ahimsa*, say Jains and Buddhists and Hindus. Don't inflict injury on any creature. Recognize the specialness of all of us, our worth, our decency.

And now something very indecent has happened, and it makes us wonder why we even try to repair the world when it can collapse so easily down on us. And we wonder if it is possible to be compassionate toward all when we find that, after the sort of horrors that engulfed New York and Washington, a visceral, primal urge for revenge—bloody revenge—drowns out all the sweet kindnesses and soothing homilies.

What can we do at such moments? Be kind to ourselves and remember that we are not saintly, but very human—and very pervious to calls for rage and revenge. Be kinder than usual to the innocents around us for they, too, are victims of this slaughter that fell from the skies. Try to be loyal to the best part

> **9/12/01 4:57 P.M. akallel:** May Lord Vishnu welcome those who died into his solar heaven. May their bad Karma be purged by the horrible suffering they had to endure and my Lord Hanuman be with our nation as we find the strength to comfort

of ourselves, for without the remembrance that we harbor goodness and decency (although regarding this particular instance of
terror, possibly *not* forgiveness), more is taken from us than two
landmarks and yet-to-be-counted lives: Spurning such remembrance scours us of our humanity and our decency, both of
which are too precious to be defiled by that Tuesday's frightful
carnage—and too splendid to be sacrificed on the rotten altar of
blind and bitter revenge.

ARTHUR MAGIDA is a contributing correspondent to PBS's "Religion &
Ethics Newsweekly" and a consultant to the United States Holocaust Memorial Museum in Washington, D.C. He is also the author of several books, including *Prophet of Rage: A Life of Louis Farrakhan and His Nation* and the
two-volume set, *How To Be a Perfect Stranger: A Guide to Etiquette in Other
People's Religious Ceremonies*. He has received numerous awards from Jewish
press organizations.

THE MORALS OF MIGHT:
HOW DO WE RESPOND WITHOUT
STOOPING TO THE TERRORISTS' LEVEL?
By Gregg Easterbrook

Some sort of U.S. military response to the terrorist attacks on
the United States has begun. Only a true pacifist—someone who
would not kill in self-defense—would urge inaction; true paci-
fists are rare. Since something has to happen, the question becomes: What can America do without stooping to the tactics of
the other side? Probably the nation will quickly find itself on the
classic slippery slope from justified to questionable to wrong.

Surely, air strikes can be justified, so long as they are accurate and are specifically targeted at someone or something re-

the survivors and rebuild. May the Great Mother comfort us all.
May she cradle us all as infants and dry out our tears.
9/12/01 6:23 P.M. ms_wings77: I pray for forgiveness, for my
own angry thoughts and the desire to punish those whom >>

lated to Tuesday's events. There seems little that doubt Osama bin Laden and Saddam Hussein have sponsored terrorist attacks against the helpless (both have links to the first, the 1993 World Trade Center bombing), and there's growing indication that at least one of them had a hand in Tuesday's horrors. This despite bin Laden's weird statement of quasi-innocence, saying he hadn't sponsored any terrorism lately because the Taliban asked him to stop. This is little different from Henry Kissinger complaining that since he hadn't ordered the bombing of civilians in years, why do people keep pestering him about that?

If it became possible to target a cruise missile on bin Laden, Hussein, or any of their immediate lieutenants, the argument for pressing the launch button would be strong, even knowing that there might be bystanders and that there is a small chance the missile would go haywire and strike in the wrong place. Similarly, if U.S. planners had solid evidence of the location of terrorist training facilities, meeting places, or similar targets, the argument for blowing these places up would be strong.

Morally—oddly—this causes us to root for the cruise missile and similar high-tech "precision guided munitions," condemned as high-tech nightmares. But in the last decade of use, such weapons have rarely missed, and their accuracy allows warheads to be fairly small, limiting the risk of killing bystanders. (The fuel load of each jetliner that hit the World Trade Center towers had the explosive equivalent of about 1,000 tons of TNT; standard U.S. cruise missiles carry a half-ton warhead.)

By the same logic, if planners knew where to find bin Laden, Hussein, or similar figures, the argument for dropping in commandos to capture or kill them would be strong, even though a bystander might be shot. Commandos may act secretively and stealthily, but so long as they are going after specific armed bad

God should punish. Forgive my troubled spirit and my shattered illusions that cry out to be avenged. Forgive my angry flailings at the injustices and for the senseless violence that has darkened the skies and minds and hearts of the country I love and

guys, there's no relationship between what they do and terrorists who strike the unarmed at random.

Using missiles or commandos to get specific terrorists would
represent the deliberate attempt to kill a named person—something U.S. forces have been prevented from doing since Jimmy
Carter signed an antiassassination directive a quarter-century
ago. Carter's directive was rooted half in his moral beliefs and
half in the anti-CIA fervor of the mid 1970s, when congressional
denunciations of spying were all the rage. (Sadly, it may be that
the growth of the world terror network that struck that second
week in September was made possible by the de-toothing of the
CIA, begun under Carter and not reversed by any subsequent
president, including Ronald Reagan.)

The notion that government leaders can act as judge, jury,
and executioner for foreign individuals is obviously unsettling.
But there are instances where killing specific people may save
much larger numbers. It would have been far more humane to
specifically target Hussein during the Gulf War than to generally
bomb Baghdad. Bush administration officials are about to re-
scind Carter's directive—which is an executive order, not a law,
and thus may be altered at any time. If they can kill bin Laden or
whoever is responsible, this would be far preferable morally to
any general military action.

The moral picture gets hazier when we don't know where the
bad guys are—obviously, a problem when chasing terrorism.
Bombing Kabul to coerce the Taliban into doing something
about bin Laden would cause great suffering to the Afghan
people, already reduced to near–Stone Age existence by two
decades of constant war and by depredations imposed upon
them by the Taliban.

Planners would try to pick Afghan military and infrastructure sites since U.S. forces have not deliberately bombed civilian

our friends in other nations. Forgive my humanity and imperfec-
tion. Let me see Your way and let go of the hate in my heart.
9/12/01 6:49 P.M. join4me: ...May you be free from anger may
you be free from sadness may you be free from pain may you »

areas since Kissinger's immoral Cambodian campaign, and then the tactic was widely opposed within the Pentagon. But at this point, there are few left and none would have any direct link to the terrorism. We'd just be inflicting pain to see if it helps our position.

This haziness thickens considerably when the subject is Iraq. If the United States attempted to bomb Hussein into abandoning terrorism, it would cause still more suffering for an Iraqi population that has lived for a decade in a country impoverished by the Gulf War bombs and Western sanctions, and rendered miserable by Hussein's tyranny.

A decade ago, the Gulf War bombing, which targeted Iraq's military and infrastructure, was sufficiently accurate that most estimates now hold that "only" a few thousand civilians were killed. That was fewer than expected—estimates of 100,000 Iraqi civilians dead from bombing were common when the air war began—but still horrible. Many Iraqi civilians, surely, were indirect casualties, victims of lack of food and health care. To be potent enough to make Hussein yield, any new bombing campaign inflicting harsh harm to his military apparatus and oil revenues would also mistakenly kill more civilians, and a new wave of poverty and repression would sweep Iraq.

Similar calculations apply to possible efforts to coerce the governments of Iran, Syria, Lebanon and—depending on how things go—Pakistan. Even effective, accurate strikes on morally defensible targets might backfire by inspiring a new generation of fanatics to try to kill unarmed American civilians.

Some of the moral issues could actually be lessened if the United States invaded. Invading Iraq would enable us to depose Hussein and liberate the Iraqi people, leaving the country better off than we found it. Imagine, too, how much Islam would benefit if Iraq were free and prosperous, rather than a

be free from difficulty may you be free from all suffering may you be healthy may you be happy may you be whole may you be at peace may all beings be happy, healthy and whole. May there be Peace Om Mani Padme Hum Nameaste

tyranny run by a madman. But with thousands of U.S. casualties, huge expenditures, years of quagmire, and so on, invasion feels like a last resort.

The ethics of a war to counteract terrorism will need to be worked out in the months and years to come; let's hope this subject is not brushed aside in a rush to say we blew things up. Much as Americans long for retribution against a horror, it may turn out there's relatively little we can do without stooping to the other side's level.

Or it might turn out that shocking application of force is justified. Suppose, for example, it was discovered that Hussein is building a facility in the desert to make atomic weapons. Based on what we know from that week in September, it might be acceptable to stage an immediate tactical nuclear strike to reduce such a facility to hot slag. Please don't ask me what the ethics would be if it were discovered that Hussein is building an atomic weapons plant in a civilian area.

Of course, a true pacifist might object to everything proposed in this essay. And as the counterstrike gears up, American Christians must bear in mind: Jesus was a true pacifist. There may simply be no solution to the dilemma that Jesus opposed fighting, but fighting is justified here as the lesser evil. If we act, some will die. If we don't act, more might die.

GREGG EASTERBROOK is the author of *Beside Still Waters* as well as being a prizewinning reporter and contributing editor for *Newsweek* and *U.S. News & World Report*.

9/12/01 7:02 P.M. EveM: Dear God, Please protect those working at this tragedy's site, for they are still in danger.
9/12/01 7:21 P.M. michellemillerschmidt: I pray for our country, for those who are lost, for their friends and families, and for >>

A WAR AGAINST TERRORISM IS MORAL
By Rabbi Joseph Telushkin

It is sobering to realize that if our government had learned what was being planned a week before this tragedy and had gone in and killed the people coordinating the attack, we would have been denounced by Arab leaders and much of the world for being assassins. I think it would behoove us all to realize that in the war against terrorism, trying to kill terrorists before they strike again—as Israel has been trying to do in the face of international condemnation—is actually the most moral of acts, an attempt to stop the most guilty from doing the most evil.

As we will find over the coming days, there undoubtedly are many lessons to be learned from this wicked attack, but the above is perhaps the most important, a lesson that puts us in mind of a 2,000-year-old teaching from the Talmud: "If someone comes to kill you, wake up early and kill him first."

Unfortunately, there are groups in the world now that see it as a holy act to kill Americans and Jews. If we and the rest of the world do not learn from this that we must coordinate an international war against terrorism and suicide bombers (and against the mentality of those people on the West Bank and in Egypt who greeted the news of American deaths with celebrations and shouts of "God is great"), then the likelihood is that more and more good and innocent people will die, and the most evil of people will achieve more and more power.

JOSEPH TELUSHKIN, a rabbi, is the author of several books that have made Jewish philosophy, theology, and history accessible to the broad public. He lectures throughout the United States and serves as an associate of the National Jewish Center for Learning and Leadership and as spiritual leader of the Synagogue for the Performing Arts in Los Angeles.

our President and Congress. God be with us all, of all faiths. **9/12/01 8:04 P.M. Soulfire1:** To all Americans everywhere. Canada sends our support, love, and hope for peace. My children and myself have been forever changed by the suffering we

THE ANGER TRAP: WE CANNOT BECOME THE IMAGE OF WHAT WE PURSUE

By Rodger Kamenetz

The sight of the buildings burning. The smoke pouring out the rows of windows. A body sailing in the air. Another plane flying into the second building, exploding. The building seeming to give like cloth. The piles of dust and debris, faces coated with it. People walking among the rubble, body parts under the dust. Human beings connecting with one another via cell phones—a husband saying goodbye to a wife, a wife to a husband, knowing the other is going to die.

The hundreds and hundreds of individual deaths: burned by fire, crushed, bones broken. A moment before, drinking coffee, answering the phone. Now, trapped on a rooftop, the heat from below, the fear. A couple holds hands and drops together through the air, better than burning, desperate choices.

Numbness and shock sets in. We dig in the rubble of our own hearts, looking for the feeling. When we understand the pain of individuals, we are touched. When we view the whole panorama abstractly, as televised images repeated, we lose touch. The spectacle erases the particular: the giant building, the huge plane, the enormous rubble. These images take over, and only when we are reminded of particular human suffering can we begin to feel again. Our fear begins, then in time our fear is layered over in dust. We too are buried under the rubble of our everyday lives. We don't want to feel, don't want to know.

But we are afraid and also, at the sight of death, we are angry. We cannot help being angry. We do not yet know the enemy, but we already have an enemy because anger needs an object. It is impossible to sustain our anger without an object.

Yes, anger is normal, healthy in the sense that it is not numb-

have witnessed. Hang on to those you love for they could be gone in a second. PEACE to you all.
9/12/01 8:04 P.M. ejess: Heavenly Father, may thy will be done.
9/12/01 8:23 P.M. decisions: God cannot fix the mess we   >>

ness. Anger, rage at our helplessness, fear—these are normal responses. The desire to help, to give blood, to give money, to come up with answers, to rally behind political leaders—all this is normal. But is the anger a good long-term condition?

Those who live in anger, whose consciousness is daily stewed in it, over time are damaged. We know this physiologically; we know this psychologically. We need to understand it spiritually. At the physiological level, a constant state of anger is bad for the heart. Anger produces toxins and poisons, irritants in the blood.

At the psychological level, anger is a feedback loop. Anger produces anger. There is no evidence that releasing or expressing anger relieves it. Those who use angry words, conjure up angry images, get angrier and angrier. Their consciousness becomes steeped in anger.

The angry person is convinced there is only one way of seeing a situation. An angry person is out of touch with reality in the sense of being out of touch with the wholeness of life, with the interconnectedness of life. An angry person stands outside that interconnectedness, that web of life, and sees all that belongs with him on one side, and all that threatens him on the other. It is the world of dualism, us and them—magnified and intensified. Anger prevents wisdom.

Anger is preoccupying. Anger takes over consciousness. Anger sees more causes for anger everywhere it looks. Anger is self-satisfied and self-justifying. Anger is righteous and right. And so anger becomes a god. That is, anger controls a person's every action and every perception. Anger's knowledge pretends it is omniscient; anger's power pretends it is omnipotent over the individual possessed by anger, as a person in a trance is possessed by a deity. This is why the Talmudic sages equated anger with idolatry. "Regard," they said, an angry person "as an idolater, because such are the wiles of the Tempter: Today he says to

create. What God can do, and will do, and does all the time is give us the courage and presence of mind to do whatever needs to be done to rectify our errors. What we must do is ask for guidance, and trust it will be okay.

him, 'do this,' tomorrow he tells him, 'do that' until he bids him, 'Go and serve idols,' and he goes and serves them (Shabbat 105b). Anger replaces judgment. It is so overwhelming that it comes between the person and the divine.

According to the Jewish philosopher, Maimonides, the sages have "hyperbolized in denouncing anger and fury, and the severest among their teachings is their saying, 'Everyone who is given to anger it is as if he has worshiped an idol.' They juxtaposed this with the statement, 'Neither let there be a strange god in you [i.e., anger] nor shall you bow down to a foreign god [i.e., idolatry]' (Psalms 81:10), meaning to say that the two matters are equal."

Elsewhere Maimonides writes, "An angry person—his life is not worth living." We are in a trap today. We feel anger and we cannot help feeling it, but we should know that constant anger is a danger to us physically, psychologically, and spiritually.

How do we end anger and violence? We find our way out of the cycle. This is not the easy thing to do. It is the hardest struggle, both individually and collectively. Do we love our enemies? Do we love those who murder us and murder our children and our family and friends? Can we even think in those terms?

I don't know. I feel conflicted in my own soul. I would say though that in this state of anger, I am also numb to my connection to others. As I have been numb in the past. This pain and anger we are feeling, others in the world have felt. We have walled ourselves off from it, with indifference, with ignorance, with our own sense of self-satisfaction. We have built huge walls against it psychologically, as tall as the Twin Towers—and now those walls have fallen down and we are in agony, and anger tells us we must do to someone else what was done to us.

Does anyone's anger justify the violence of September 11? No.

9/12/01 8:45 P.M. joyousoz: A deep sadness overcomes me and many others in Australia. I pray for peace for all everywhere in the world. May such an event NEVER happen again and may the world find some way to heal   »

Absolutely not. Does our anger at that violence justify violence of our own in return? If we are able, we have the right to pursue, discover, and punish those who committed, planned, or aided these attacks. If the sponsor is a foreign power, we have the right to declare war. If we love our loved ones, we have that right and duty. But at the same time, if we go along with the anger, contempt, and revenge in our hearts that normally accompany such duty, then we will become the image of what we pursue: bloodthirsty, heartless, and cruel. For those are the attributes of the idol, anger.

People in America today don't use the word "revenge"; they speak of closure, settling accounts. But if anger and violence are cycles, there is no closure and there is no settling of accounts. Our anger costs us every time we use it. There's no simple end to it. There is no simple answer, and those who, in their rage, think there is are turning themselves into what they hate.

RODGER KAMENETZ is a poet, essayist, and author of eight books, including *The Jew in the Lotus*. He is known for his work in Jewish-Buddhist dialogue.

THE CHRISTIAN CRITERIA FOR RETRIBUTION
By Richard Land

As the U.S. government contemplates its response against those who unleashed a reign of terror upon us, we must consider the ethics of war. From its earliest days, the church has debated when it is morally legitimate to wage war.

For many centuries, Christians have employed the "just-war theory" as a framework for the discussion of issues of war and peace. This theory was adopted by early church leaders, partic-

> **9/12/01 9:10 P.M. bondsman:** Why is it that no one has expected something like this to happen? Evil never sleeps. We have been interfering in the internal affairs of other countries for decades while at the same time building this false sense of security here at home.

ularly Augustine, to deal with the reality of war in a fallen, sinful world of empires and nations.

There are two dimensions to just-war theory—one that weighs whether to engage in armed conflict (*jus ad bellum*) and the other that examines how to conduct the military exercises (*jus in bello*). The aim of any armed conflict should be to keep the peace and maintain justice.

The proper response to the destruction unleashed against America by an illusory, stealthy enemy is a declaration of war. We have a duty to answer acts of terrorism. As Christians, we must pray for our enemies, and we cannot seek personal vengeance. However, we should expect our government to exact justice. Any military action should be designed to thwart the ability of this enemy to continue its ghastly campaign of terror.

Sadly, the resort to armed conflict is the price human beings must periodically pay for the right to live in a moral universe. We must always remember that eternal vigilance is the price of liberty, and we must bring these perpetrators of evil to justice.

There is a similar episode in America's early history. In the early 19th century, pirates from North Africa were destroying American and European shipping and taking crew, passengers, and cargo hostage for ransom. The Barbary States (Morocco, Algiers, Tunis, and Tripoli) were allowing them safe harbor. Presidents Washington and Adams acquiesced to the tyrannical practice by paying tribute to these rulers for safe passage for their ships.

But President Jefferson was repulsed by this practice and declared war when the ruler of Tripoli tried to increase the tribute. He sent a fleet of ships into the Mediterranean in what became known as the Tripolitan War (1801–1805), which concluded with a peace favorable to the United States. We need to learn from Jefferson's wisdom and follow his example.

9/12/01 10:25 P.M. LemurGirl: Blame the media for showing the images of celebrating Palestinians. Only one channel here in Australia has shown images of Palestinians lighting candles and mourning, which are far more representative of how   >>

Can resorting to military force be justified? If so, under what circumstances? While there have been persistent elements of pacifism within the Christian tradition, for most Christians, in most places, at most times, the answer has been: Yes, military action by legitimately constituted civil authority is justifiable.

Just-war theory was never intended to justify war. Instead, it tries to bring war under the sway of justice as understood by Christians and to ensure that war, when it does occur, has limits to reduce its barbarity. In fact, if all parties accepted just-war criteria, there would be no wars or acts of terrorism, because the theory's first rule clearly states that only defense against aggression can be just. Hence, if everyone adhered to just-war theory, aggression would be eliminated.

In other words, only defensive war is defensible. The intent must be to secure justice for all involved. It is to be a last resort, authorized only by legitimate civil authority. There must be limited goals, and the question of proportionality must accompany all actions. Underlying all of these criteria is the question of noncombatant immunity. No war that does not disqualify noncombatants as legitimate military targets and that does not seek to minimize collateral civilian casualties can be just.

Can such goals be achieved without disproportionate casualties? Are there no effective alternatives to avoid conflict? Will measures be taken to ensure the minimizing of noncombatant casualties? If so, then resorting to armed force is justified.

Perhaps most important, a legitimate authority must authorize the use of armed force. For Americans, the duly constituted authority is the government of the United States.

The key Scripture passage supporting just-war theory is Romans 13:4. The Apostle Paul writes that it is God who ordains the secular state to reward good and to punish evil. God established the state to "bear the sword"; that is, to use lethal force to

they feel. Don't tar everyone with the same brush.
9/12/01 11:06 P.M. oblio: As a truly omnibenevolent and omnipotent being, it would have been easier than breathing to save ten thousand people who are all now in Hell. Why isn't

keep the peace and maintain justice. This limits the use of force. Peace, not vengeance, is always the object of war.

We should never surrender to, nor compromise with, cowardly villains who sneak about and in their madness spill the blood of innocent men and women. We need to pray for all those who have lost loved ones and who are in the midst of anguish and suffering. We also need to understand that one of the prices we pay for being a free and open society is vulnerability to this kind of attack.

We must be eternally vigilant to minimize these horrors and to bring their perpetrators to justice. I salute President Bush for his determination to conduct an all-out campaign "to root out and whip terrorism." In the face of the unrefined evil of terrorism, this is the only "just" thing to do.

RICHARD LAND is president and CEO of Ethics & Religious Liberty Commission of the Southern Baptist Convention.

RESTORE OUR SOULS
By Denise Breton and Stephen Lehman

Human beings suffer,
They torture one another,
They get hurt and get hard.

These lines from Irish poet Seamus Heaney's *The Cure at Troy* sum up the events of September 11. Human beings suffer and inflict suffering, sometimes of staggering proportions. When this happens, we cry for justice. But what is justice? What does seeking justice mean following such horrendous events? Justice lies at the center of this crisis; justice must be done, we all agree. But what does it mean to do it?

your God held as culpable for the deaths as the terrorists? **9/12/01 11:26 P.M. Katyr:** Goddess, where were you? Why did this have to happen? Why couldn't you stop it? Did you weep along with us? Did you scream in outrage and horror? Did   >>

When the terrorists said "justice must be done," it meant flying airplanes into buildings. When we've heard of justice since, it's meant waging war. Calls for revenge are understandable: We're all human, and such emotions come with such suffering. When we saw innocent people die senseless, cruel deaths, we cried out in shock and outrage. But the terrorists' cultures have experienced similar destruction over decades. Happy people do not agree to suicidal missions of mass destruction. As trauma research suggests, violence takes over a mind and heart when trauma upon trauma beats upon them, until all normal feeling is lost. That violence follows holds true not only for individuals and families but for nations and cultures as well.

If, in our suffering, we too lash out, will it be justice? When evidence indicated an organization of fundamentalist Muslims behind the attacks, Muslim Americans were insulted, threatened, spit at, shot at. Certainly this is trauma acted out, but is it justice?

Indeed, since September 11, "justice" has mostly meant "vengeance." Do unto them as they have done unto us. As philosophers, we suggest this is not true justice. True justice must act as remedy. It must take what is broken and make it whole. Because vengeance cannot do this, it is shadow justice. It not only fails to restore harmony to the discordant world but also adds to the discord. Vengeance sates our wrath momentarily, but it cannot make things whole. And because it adds to the suffering, it becomes the seed of future violence.

Nonetheless, vengeance is the prevailing model of justice, adopted by terrorists and governments alike. Vengeance, or just deserts, is based on reward and punishment, a form of behavior management embraced by schools and religions and taught to us in childhood. This technique of social control becomes so in-

you fall to your knees in despair? Where were you? You were there with us every step of the way. You were leading the survivors to safety. You were comforting the dying. You were sitting next to the airline passengers. You were giving a Nation

grained that we do not object when it stands in as a model of justice.

But is it justice? Can it heal our hurt? Philosophically, the problems with the model are legion, problems raised 2,500 years ago by Socrates and Plato but also by many psychologists and educators today. For one thing, rewards and punishments blast out our intrinsic, soul-connected motivation and replace it with externals. We lose our inner compass, as externals dictate our responses. Worse, this model collapses into "might makes right," for whoever controls the externals controls our options: Those who wield the "might" rig the game. Revenge, requiring a show of might, cannot bring justice because it cannot be fair, since inequities are its currency. Nor can it heal.

We need justice to right things, but we need a radically different model of justice, one that "restores our souls" from trauma and heals our broken relations. Before we sketch an alternative, however, let us agree that those who commit crimes must be stopped and held accountable. Trauma may explain the roots of violence, but understanding causes does not belie responsibility. Harming others, especially innocent others, is never acceptable. Yes, complexities arise that make our choices of how to protect ourselves without doing harm difficult, but we need to be clear about our principles. Justice as inflicting harm will not create a just world. Because it expands suffering, it creates its opposite: further violence.

Fortunately, a healing, constructive model of justice exists. Socrates and Plato hinted at it, while many indigenous communities practice it as their cultural heritage. This model of justice makes different assumptions about who we are, what we're doing here, and most relevant, how we can best respond to hurts and conflicts. The Hollow Water First Nation on Lake Winnipeg, Canada, states:

strength. For all of this, we thank you.
9/12/01 11:26 P.M. stefnbabystefan: I do not regret giving birth to my beautiful boy. But what the hell was I thinking bringing a child into this world. I am in a daze, probably will be for a   >>

Our tradition, our culture, speaks clearly about the concepts of judgment and punishment. They belong to the Creator. They are not ours. They are, therefore, not to be used in the way that we relate to each other. People who offend against another (victimizers) are to be viewed and related to as people who are out of balance—with themselves, their family, their community, and their Creator. A return to balance can best be accomplished through a process of accountability that includes support from the community through teaching and healing. The use of judgments and punishment actually works against the healing process. An already unbalanced person is moved further out of balance.

Today the restorative justice movement, which has grown worldwide over the last 30 years, offers a model of justice devoted to healing, "restoring our souls," mending broken relationships, and above all, using conflicts to strengthen communities by correcting imbalances and building understanding. But how does this relate to our terrible crisis? What can restorative justice say to something of this magnitude?

Let's begin with actual responses that practice the principles of restorative justice. First, the bravery, tireless dedication, and profound sacrifices of the police and firefighters. Second, the national outpouring of assistance, including record blood donations. Third, the expressions of grief offered from cultures around the world. Because these behaviors respond to tragedy in selfless, heartfelt ways, striving to make whole what is broken, they express true justice.

Like these responses, restorative justice presupposes a deep, unseen community. Absorbed in life's details, we tend to shrink our community, from world to nation to city to family to self.

long time. All that I can think about is my son's future. I haven't even thought about mine.... The violence has been unspeakable. The pain has been unbearable. Please comfort all
9/12/01 11:28 P.M. JodOfArc: Dear God: those who grieve,

Unseen ties remain unseen. But in times of crisis, our hearts open. We sacrifice for the larger good, feel empathy for strangers, consider the needs of others, and work to heal hurts. These are acts of justice, because they make our invisible community visible. Our community emerges as we try to make it whole.

But justice as healer needn't require the catalyst of crisis. Justice lives in any act that creates respect, understanding, and wholeness. What might justice suggest about how we drive our cars, regard coworkers, or treat children? How might it change our relationship with nature, how we grow food and handle waste? Care and consideration in daily life are acts of justice because they nurture our relationships, thereby strengthening our local and national communities. They are by definition acts of patriotism, just as meanness, selfishness, and exploitation are by definition unpatriotic.

Today we're challenged as never before to practice this justice on a global scale. How? First, America could mindfully enter the global community, embracing the peoples of other nations (not necessarily the governments) as our relations. Without community—inclusive rather than exclusive—there is no justice. In community, hurt to one affects all.

Second, we could pledge that, while we protect ourselves (and others as well) from terrorist attacks, we will not murder civilians anywhere. We could reject the concept of acceptable "collateral damage"—not just innocents killed in bombings, but those dying from disease and starvation years after war's end from embargoes and the destruction of water supplies and hospitals. (The murder of innocents is, after all, why September 11 is so horrible. But these terrorists didn't invent this. Think of Nanking, Dresden, the Battle of Britain, the Holocaust, Hiroshima, Nagasaki, the killing fields of Laos and Cambodia.) We could also rethink our role in selling arms, developing

soothe all those in pain, help all the rest of us who are confused and angry and sad....
9/12/01 11:39 P.M. akallel: I pray that Lord Krishna, Lord Hanuman, and Mother Durga manifest themselves. I implore **>>**

biological and chemical weapons, and intervening militarily worldwide.

Third, we could promise not to ignore the daily suffering of others in our world community and to work for healing solutions—to keep this larger family of ours in our minds and hearts when we act politically and economically. After September 11, exploiting foreign labor and environments for profit may seem less profitable.

Such commitments could bring true healing justice to our world far more than could deploying all our missiles. Will they stop terrorists? Short term, no. But long term, as we seek a truer justice, we will build a global harmony that could eventually leave terrorists no place on Earth to lay their heads.

We need to see the big picture if we're going to solve the big problems, and this big picture turns around how we understand and practice justice. Shifting our paradigm from retributive to restorative justice entails huge transformation, personally and culturally, but that's what the search for justice asks. Once more, Seamus Heaney, a longtime Dubliner who knows terrorism close up, guides the search by calling us to

> . . . hope for a great sea-change
> On the far side of revenge.
> Believe that a further shore
> Is reachable from here.

To find true justice, we cannot look in the ruins of the World Trade Center or toward missiles falling on Afghanistan. Justice lies on a further shore, a shore we must first believe is reachable from here.

After that, we must start rowing hard—together.

DENISE BRETON AND STEPHEN LEHMAN are coauthors of *The Mystic Heart of Justice: Restoring Wholeness in a Broken World*.

them to aid our country. i beg them to comfort us and every one who was directly struck by this tragedy. Also I ask Indra to strenghten our collective army as we prepare the blow of righteous retribution. and may Lord Krishna teach us to act without

YIELDING TO HATE GIVES
VICTORY TO TERRORISTS
By His Eminence Bernard Cardinal Law

September 21, 2001

We are living in a different world. The terrorist attacks of September 11 have changed our lives in more ways than we yet recognize.

We know that God does not make death. What this nation and the world experienced on that fateful Tuesday was the work of evil.

God's presence in the midst of this tragedy is encountered in the outpouring of love and generosity by literally millions of people in this country and around the world.

That love has found its most poignant expression in the self-sacrifice of police, firefighters, medical technicians, steelworkers, and others involved in rescue efforts.

God's grace has also awakened faith in the hearts of so many. Churches have been filled as seldom before. One man said to me after the special Mass at the cathedral on September 12, "Thank you for reminding me how important faith is to my life." I heard of another person saying, "This tragedy has brought me back to the Church." I do not think that this expression of faith is simply an emotional response. What it is, it seems to me, is that people for whom faith has been at the periphery of their personal lives have suddenly realized that faith must be central to all we do and are. Faith has been awakened. It is a time when we should sustain in prayer and surround with love and support the families and friends of the victims. Our priests, pastoral staffs, and people of the parishes most affected are doing an extraordinary job in ministering to those in sorrow.

While the signs of faith and love have been sources of light in

attachment. may he teach us to act and not hate.
9/12/01 11:44 P.M. chicagoan: Lord, please be with your children in this time of devastation. Please hold the hands of those that are dying alone and comfort them in their last moments. ...   >>

an otherwise dark time, the expressions of hate and discrimination directed against Arabs and Muslims in our midst are reprehensible and intolerable.

To ascribe to all Muslims the acts of the terrorists is, in effect, to hand victory to the terrorists. Muslims throughout the nation and the world have denounced the attacks of September 11 as a perversion of Islamic faith. Where such hateful acts of prejudice occur, they should be denounced for what they are, and each of us should seek ways to express our solidarity with our Muslim neighbors. With all our hearts we should apologize for the acts of those whose anger and frustration have simply continued the cycle of violence. What are we to think about the way ahead for ourselves and the nation? What principles should inform our response? To help me in my own analysis of our situation, I have developed 11 points that, it seems to me, must be a part of our moral reasoning:

1. We are in solidarity with our president in prayer and in love for our country.

2. The warlike acts of September 11, 2001, were perpetrated against our nation, but they threaten the international community as a whole.

3. We have a moral right and a grave obligation to defend the common good, which remains threatened by such terrorist acts.

4. Our nation and the global community must seek out and hold accountable those nations that are responsible.

5. It is incumbent upon all citizens to recognize this common threat and to support our nation's efforts to respond in a moral way. This support will entail sacrifice on the part of each citizen.

6. Any military response must be in accord with the just-war theory and should be applied taking into account the unique nature of this new terrorist threat.

9/13/01 12:15 A.M. Muslim911: Why are the lives of Americans and that of its allies considered innocent only? Why are the Americans the only species on planet earth allowed to take revenge and retaliate?...

7. The grave obligation to protect innocent human life must govern our political and military decisions.

8. In our foreign policy, new emphasis should be given to strengthening ties with Arab and Muslim nations, and indeed all nations.

9. Every effort should be made to press for a just and peaceful resolution to the Israeli-Palestinian conflict and other armed conflicts throughout the world.

10. Even as we undertake the heavy burden to defend ourselves and others, we must not forget that the goal is a peaceful and stable world.

11. We condemn acts of violence and discrimination directed against Arab and Muslim persons in our midst. To yield to hate is to give victory to the terrorists.

HIS EMINENCE BERNARD CARDINAL LAW is archbishop of Boston.

IS FORGIVENESS POSSIBLE?
By Johann Christoph Arnold

In the days following the terrible attacks on New York and Washington, all of us are torn by powerful emotions. In many hearts, the overwhelming horror and grief have already given way to powerful currents of anger and hatred.

Each of us faces one of the most difficult choices of his or her life. There is no escaping it. Will we respond with hatred or with compassion? Will we seek vengeance or healing? How we choose will determine our future, individually and collectively, one way or another. It will affect the course of history, the lives of our children and of children to come.

We are at a turning point rarely seen in history. These days

9/13/01 1:15 A.M. kab123: "God is our refuge and strength, a very present help in trouble. Therefore we will not fear, though the earth should change." Psalm 46:1- Hold steadfast in compassion and mercy, for war breeds war   »

present our nation with an opportunity for a flood of compassion or for a bloodthirsty drive for revenge. Which will it be? Will we hate those who hate us, and become like them? Or will we respond by loving each other more? If we do, evil will be broken, suffering eased, and we can start the long process of healing.

Already there has been a tremendous outpouring of goodwill. Thousands have volunteered to help in the relief effort, donating time, services, money, food, and even their own blood. Millions have lit candles and sent up prayers. Many gave their lives trying to save others.

One of those killed in Manhattan was a fellow pastor and close friend of mine. A true man of God, Father Mychal Judge was killed while administering last rites to a fireman injured during the rescue effort. Through Father Mychal and the hundreds of police, firefighters, and other rescue workers who lost their lives while helping others, the words of Jesus have become newly alive: "No greater service can a man do than to lay down his life for his friend."

Father Mychal's service was not limited to New York. Over the last years he traveled to Northern Ireland three times with me and our mutual friend, New York Police Department Detective Steven McDonald, to spread a message of reconciliation there. We were planning a similar trip to Israel this October.

In these places torn by years of violence, Steven, shot in the line of duty by a teenager and paralyzed from the neck down, would tell people, "The only thing worse than a bullet in my spine would have been to nurture revenge in my heart. Such an attitude would only have extended my tragic injury into my soul, further hurting my wife, son, and others. It is bad enough that the physical effects are permanent, but at least I can choose to prevent spiritual injury."

9/13/01 1:43 A.M. Katherina1: My heart goes out to all of you!!!My uncle John and my cousin Jimmy are still missing, both with the NYPD, in my own time of grief...my heart and prayers are with you all!!!!!!

At Steven's side, Father Mychal said, "When peace comes to this country, and it will come some day, there will be memories, there will be families that were torn apart. Forgiveness is a tremendously long, ongoing process and it needs great grace and strength from above. I have my own problems, my own hates, my own harsh feelings; I am as human as anybody else. So I have to have this ongoing forgiveness in my heart, too."

Unfortunately, many Americans' anger has been misdirected at Muslim Americans and innocent civilians in the Arab world. Some religious figures have even suggested that America's homosexuals and liberals are to blame for the carnage. In this hour of national grief and mourning, we need to hold hands, not point fingers. Every human being, no matter their race or creed, has been created in the image of God. As I watched images of desperate people jumping from the Twin Towers, I became more convinced than ever that God is loving and merciful, and that everyone who died fell straight into his arms. The television images didn't show it, but I believe the skyline of lower Manhattan was filled with angels receiving the souls of the departed and bringing them to God.

Unrestrained, our thirst for vengeance may lead to thousands more dying overseas—including many American sons and daughters, if our leaders' pronouncements are any indication. But such anger can also destroy us personally. As a counselor, I have watched many beautiful people become emotionally paralyzed by a bitterness that eats at their souls like a cancer.

I have also met ordinary people who, like Steven McDonald, have suffered greatly, yet refused to let anger control their lives. Another example that comes to mind is my friend Bud Welch, whose daughter was one of 168 people killed in the Oklahoma City bombing. In my book *Why Forgive?*, I quote Bud's words: "I still have moments of rage. Forgiving is not something you

9/13/01 2:29 A.M. linus-furious: This I pray... May we come to recognize the unity of all sentient beings. To injure one is to injure us all.
9/13/01 2:52 A.M. nisutAUS: For the first time in my spiritual   >>

just wake up one morning and decide to do. You have to work through your anger and your hatred as long as it's there." My counseling experience confirms these words, as well as those of Alan Paton, the South African author who wrote, "There is a hard law. . . . When a deep injury is done to us, we never recover until we forgive."

Granted, in the present situation, in which the horror of Oklahoma City is multiplied a hundredfold, the pain may still be too near, the loss too real, and the idea of letting go of hatred too hard to fathom. But we should bear in mind the ancient Chinese proverb that states: "Whoever opts for revenge should dig two graves." Like Bud, we are all in this for the rest of our lives.

Each of us can contribute to the good in the world or add fuel to the fires of fear and hatred. What future will we choose: one filled with fear or one filled with hope? If we choose revenge, the victims will become mere statistics in an endless tit-for-tat that will eventually destroy our civilization. We know from history that violence only begets more violence in a vicious cycle. If, on the other hand, we choose forgiveness, we give the victims dignity, so that they will not have died in vain. America can become a stronger, more united, and more caring nation through this ordeal.

In a show of true leadership, President Bush refrained from instant retaliation, and instead called on all Americans to observe a national day of prayer and remembrance. Even if his tone has changed since, we as citizens should respect and support the God-ordained authority placed on our leaders to punish evildoers, as Paul writes in Romans 13. The forgiveness I describe in no way absolves the killers or negates the need to bring them to justice. It is rather a process involving those who have been hurt, not the perpetrators. It is something we can do for ourselves, for

life and I hope the last, I entered my shrine after learning of these unspeakable acts and heard nothing but sobbing. The very gods Themselves were weeping within my shrine. There were no words even from Them at this time when it feels as if the Uncreated it-our own healing. Otherwise we become paralyzed with hatred that in the end will destroy the moral fiber of our nation.

As we pray for the souls of the departed, for their families, and for our country, let us pray that hearts are not hardened by what has happened. Let us pray that we as citizens can find it within us to rise above the urges of hatred and vengeance that gave birth to this horrible atrocity, and which will surely spawn even more dastardly deeds if we respond in kind. And let us pray for our leaders, who are facing the same life-or-death choices we are.

Beyond that, as we continue to search for meaning amid all the suffering visited on our country on September 11, may we be guided by this remarkable prayer, found on an old wrapping paper in the Ravensbrück concentration camp at the end of World War II:

Lord, remember not only the men and women of good will, but also those of ill will. But do not remember all the suffering they have inflicted upon us. Remember rather the fruits we brought, thanks to this suffering: our comradeship, our loyalty, our humility, the courage, the generosity, the greatness of heart that has grown out of this. And when they come to judgment, let all the fruits we have borne be their forgiveness.

JOHANN CHRISTOPH ARNOLD is senior pastor of the Bruderhof Communities and author of 10 books, including *Why Forgive?*, *Seeking Peace*, *Be Not Afraid*, *Cries from the Heart*, *Endangered*, and *Escape Routes*.

self thrust through the barrier of Creation and sank in its fangs...
9/13/01 3:27 A.M. Emily25: I would like to thank all people of America for their posts here. I am european and through your words you allowed me to understand better. Please do not   >>

VENGEANCE IS THE LORD'S
(BUT SOMETHING IN ME WANTS TO
"BOMB THE HELL OUT OF THEM")

A Sermon by the Reverend Mary Lynn Tobin

The days since the terrorist attacks have been horrible for all of us. At first I felt as if I had been kicked in the stomach. A few days later, I felt like I was walking around in a cloud of lethargy and depression. One day I even fell asleep twice. And I was not even directly affected by personal loss in this tragedy. Imagine the state of those who have lost parents, sisters, brothers, children, friends, and coworkers.

The only times the load of grief and sorrow lifted for me has been while listening to words of Scripture. The words, "My God, my God, why have you forsaken me?" were certainly written by someone who knew the experience of having his known world collapse.

Today, we hear Jeremiah say, "Death has come up into our windows, it has entered our palaces, to cut off the children from the streets and the young men from the squares. . . . Human corpses shall fall like dung upon the open field . . . and no one shall gather them."

We know that experience. New York City and Washington are our Zions, our "holy cities." For better or for worse, they represent the heart and soul of America. They are our alabaster cities gleaming; they contain our temples of honor and history. And they have been struck with a deadly vengeance that has resulted in horrific images that will stay with us for the rest of our lives.

And Jeremiah says, "Call for the mourning women to come. . . . Let them quickly raise a dirge over us so that our eyes may run

hurt innocents. Be better than those who did that. Show the world how great a nation you REALLY are.
9/13/01 3:50 A.M. Mary44: As I sat in my comfortable chair all the way over here in Australia without a care in the world

down with tears . . . for a sound of wailing is heard from Zion: 'How we are ruined!' "

We need to wail and mourn. Bring in the professionals to help us do it. We need to cry and yell and scream because all of those feelings are normal and appropriate. It is horrifying. It is tragic. It is terribly unfair.

Some very angry people have attacked us. We have to be careful when we call them "terrorists" because by doing so, we run the risk of forgetting that they are also human beings. The people responsible for the actions on that Tuesday are angry at the United States. They are angry to the point of hatred and revenge, and even suicide. They have acted in extreme and indefensible ways.

But here's the thing I've been thinking about. I've learned in my personal life that when someone is angry with me, I need to look at myself and find out what piece of truth that person sees in me that I don't want to see. Their anger may be completely out of proportion to what I did or said, or their picture may be terribly incomplete and unfair, but usually there is a gnawing sense that I may have given them, perhaps unconsciously, a hook for their anger. They are responsible for how they express their anger, but I am responsible to look inside and pay attention to the truth of what I find there.

In the case of the attacks on our country that Tuesday, the actions of these people are absolutely deplorable. There is no excuse for wreaking the kind of unmitigated devastation on innocent people that they unleashed that day. None at all. I want to be clear about that.

But let's look at the end of our passage from Jeremiah: "Thus says the Lord: 'Do not let the wise boast in their wisdom, do not let the mighty boast in their might, do not let the wealthy boast

laughing and chatting away, I tuned into CNN just as the second plane hit the WTC, all of a sudden the laughter died and a sick feeling of helplessness and anger came over me as I watched the devastation. Church services were held here in australia,   >>

in their wealth; but let those who boast boast in this, that they understand and know me, that I am the Lord; I act with steadfast love, justice, and righteousness in the earth, for in these things I delight,' says the Lord." Isn't that a sobering passage for this very proud American culture? Is it at all possible that we have been guilty of boasting in the wrong things? That we have put our trust in wealth and might instead of in the steadfast love, justice, and righteousness of God? That in our arrogance we have stepped on other people in the world and they are justifiably angry? Can we look at that? And if found guilty, can we repent?

While I am furious that people would treat human life so casually in organizing such a catastrophic attack, I am also concerned that our leaders are planning to turn around and do exactly the same thing. Perhaps you remember our collective revulsion when Timothy McVeigh referred to the deaths of 19 children in the 1995 Oklahoma City blast as "collateral damage"? Well, Senator Zell Miller (D-Georgia) said in the week following the events, and I quote, "I say, bomb the hell out of them. If there's collateral damage, so be it." That kind of language, while understandable in the heat of the moment, scares me when it persists.

The black and white rhetoric of good and evil that we have heard the week after the tragedy is inviting us into our own version of a "holy war," not unlike that we have witnessed and criticized in places like Northern Ireland, Israel, the former Yugoslavia, and Nigeria.

And as if in answer to that invitation, we hear these words from Paul to Christians who were suffering unfair persecution in another time and place: "Do not repay anyone evil for evil, but take thought for what is noble in the sight of all. If it is possible, so far as it depends on you, live peaceably with all. Beloved,

to pray for those people who died, for their friends and relatives, for the injured and also for those who witnessed the devastation in person. We prayed for the people of America.
9/13/01 7:15 A.M. maryeo: Tayata om bekhandze bekhandze

never avenge yourselves, but leave room for the wrath of God; for it is written, 'Vengeance is mine, I will repay, says the Lord.' No, 'if your enemies are hungry, feed them; if they are thirsty, give them something to drink; for by doing this you will heap burning coals on their heads.' Do not be overcome by evil, but overcome evil with good."

Believe me, friends, I read these words to you with utter humility. When I was bemoaning to my husband the direction my writing was taking, he asked, "Are people going to be mad?" I said, "Yes, they're going to be mad. It's the gospel. And the gospel makes us all mad." It makes me mad. There is something inside me that wants to "bomb the hell out of them" as well. I want revenge. There is part of me that wants to personally be able to spit in the eyes of those responsible. I am furious and I want payback. I want firebombs and loud noises. And if you can find a place in the New Testament that tells us to respond in that way, let me know and I'll preach it!

It is in the character of evil to beget evil. The greater the evil, the more evil it begets. That's what Satan intends. That's what keeps the cycle going. God calls me to a different way. God calls us, as a Christian community, to a different way. I don't presume to dictate what our national strategy should be, but if our actions are based on an attitude of retribution and revenge, we are sure to bring nothing but calamity upon our heads. Words like "retribution" and "revenge" are not part of God's vocabulary. If they were, we'd all be in bad shape.

I can't prescribe how we follow that way of God, that way of justice that acts in mercy. But I trust that somehow, by the grace of God working through the love and support of fellow Christians on this journey, we may just find strength to convert our anger into actions that embrace the ultimate cost of the cross.

mahabekhandze randzasamungate soha. May all hearts and minds be healed before further madness occurs.
9/13/01 7:30 A.M. jschultheis: Our Father, Who art in Heaven, Hallowed be thy name. Thy Kingdom come, Thy will be done,   >>

As Lenore Yarger wrote in *From the Other Side Online* in October 1999:

> For it is there, at the cross, that the living God is finally revealed. Not in a firestorm raining down from heaven or in the anxiety of a tired heart. God comes as the suffering in the Kosovar, the sick Iraqi child, the wounded Serb [the burned and crushed men and women and children in New York and Washington and Pennsylvania]. God comes in our own arms, outstretched in reconciliation and hope, and in a vision that reshapes our violent hearts in the way of love.
>
> The mountains of our nation have shaken. As we weep and mourn the devastation that has been wrought upon our country and upon our people, can we put our hope and trust in God rather than in our own violent instincts? Can we rest in the arms of the God who comes in the still small voice? Can we act out of our confidence and hope in God rather than fear of our enemies? Can we walk the narrow tightrope between justice and revenge? May God help us as we struggle with what it means to be faithful in the face of terror.
>
> Amen.

THE REVEREND MARY LYNN TOBIN is minister of Davis Community Church in Davis, California.

on Earth as it is in Heaven. Give us this day, our daily bread and forgive us our trespasses, as we forgive those who trespass against us. And lead us not into temptation, but deliver us from evil. For thine is the Kingdom, the Power, and the Glory, forever and ever.

Chapter 7

TEACHINGS
AND TRADITIONS

It is the principle of the pure in heart
never to injure others,
Even when they themselves have been hatefully injured.
Hating others, even enemies who
harmed you unprovoked,
Assures incessant sorrow.
—Tirukkural 32:312–13, sacred Tamil text

THE POPE'S MESSAGE
By Pope John Paul II

Wednesday, September 12, 2001: General Audience

I cannot begin this audience without expressing my profound sorrow at the terrorist attacks that yesterday brought death and destruction to America, causing thousands of victims and injuring countless people. To the President of the United States and to all American citizens, I express my heartfelt sorrow. In the face of such unspeakable horror, we cannot but be deeply disturbed. I add my voice to all the voices raised in these hours to express indignant condemnation, and I strongly reiterate that the ways of violence will never lead to genuine solutions to humanity's problems.

Yesterday was a dark day in the history of humanity, a terrible affront to human dignity. After receiving the news, I followed the developing situation with intense concern and with heartfelt prayers to the Lord. How is it possible to commit acts of such savage cruelty? The human heart has depths from which schemes of unheard-of ferocity sometimes emerge, capable of destroying in a moment the normal daily life of a people. But faith comes to our aid at these times when words seem to fail. Christ's word is the only one that can give a response to the questions that trouble our spirit. Even if the forces of darkness appear to prevail, those who believe in God know that evil and death do not have the final say. Christian hope is based on this truth; at this time our prayerful trust draws strength from it.

With deeply felt sympathy I address myself to the beloved people of the United States in this moment of distress and consternation, when the courage of so many men and women of good will is being sorely tested. In a special way I reach out to the families of the dead and the injured, and assure them of my

9/13/01 7:38 A.M. Elderberry: my speechless, heartfelt prayers go out to all who are affected. The whole earth is encircled by prayer now - let us unite our hearts so that peace may prevail.
9/13/01 9:44 A.M. Atheleas: May all the victims of this tragedy

spiritual closeness. I entrust to the mercy of the Most High the helpless victims of this tragedy, for whom I offered Mass this morning, invoking upon them eternal rest. May God give courage to the survivors; may he sustain the rescue workers and the many volunteers who are presently making an enormous effort to cope with such an immense emergency. I ask you, dear brothers and sisters, to join me in prayer for them. Let us beg the Lord that the spiral of hatred and violence will not prevail. May the Blessed Virgin, Mother of Mercy, fill the hearts of all with wise thoughts and peaceful intentions.

Today, my heartfelt sympathy is with the American people, subjected yesterday to inhuman terrorist attacks that have taken the lives of thousands of innocent human beings and caused unspeakable sorrow in the hearts of all men and women of good will. Yesterday was indeed a dark day in our history, an appalling offense against peace, a terrible assault against human dignity.

I invite you all to join me in commending the victims of this shocking tragedy to Almighty God's eternal love. Let us implore his comfort upon the injured, the families involved, and all who are doing their utmost to rescue survivors and help those affected.

I ask God to grant the American people the strength and courage they need at this time of sorrow and trial.

A Letter to the President
From His Holiness the Dalai Lama

I am deeply shocked by the terrorist attacks that took place involving four apparently hijacked aircrafts and the immense devastation these caused. It is a terrible tragedy that so many innocent lives have been lost, and it seems unbelievable that

find their way home, whether to the life beyond or to their loved ones in this world. May their families find peace. May the rescuers move swiftly and find those who can still be saved. The love of us all shines around them, helping them find their >>

anyone would choose to target the World Trade Center in New York City and the Pentagon in Washington, D.C. We are deeply saddened. On behalf of the Tibetan people, I would like to convey our deepest condolence and solidarity with the American people during this painful time. Our prayers go out to the many who have lost their lives, those who have been injured, and the many more who have been traumatized by this senseless act of violence. I am attending a special prayer for the United States and its people at our main temple today.

I am confident that the United States as a great and powerful nation will be able to overcome this present tragedy. The American people have shown their resilience, courage, and determination when faced with such difficult and sad situations.

It may seem presumptuous on my part, but I personally believe we need to think seriously whether a violent reaction is the right thing to do and in the greater interest of the nation and the people in the long run. I believe violence will only increase the cycle of violence. But how do we deal with hatred and anger, which are often the root causes of such senseless violence? This is a very difficult question, especially when it concerns a nation and we have certain fixed conceptions of how to deal with such attacks. I am sure you will make the right decision.

A VIEW FROM THE HINDU HEART
By Satguru Sivaya Subramuniyaswamil

Issued September 13, 2001

Every high-minded and good soul on Earth has been hurt and shocked by the appalling images of the buildings being destroyed in New York and Washington and the resulting deaths

way and keeping them safe. May they find their way in the Tao. **9/13/01 9:50 A.M. farhiya:** In the name of Allah, the most merciful, please Allah we pray to you, this is the moment we most need you, Ya Allah, please give hope to the people who are still

of untold thousands of innocent human beings. Hindus everywhere in the world, of every tradition, are praying for those who have suffered and are rightfully calling for the terrorists to be brought to justice and for terrorism itself to be stopped in every nation of the world so people everywhere may live in security. Leaders must be vigilant, and governments have the duty to protect all citizens and to punish the guilty. We must all rely on the integrity of the U.S. leadership to do the right thing to assure a future free from such terrorism.

Hindus everywhere are reminding themselves and those they meet of the great principle of *ahimsa*, noninjury, which Mahatma Gandhi lived so faithfully and which lies at the heart of all Hindu thought and culture. Not to injure others is the highest path.

The ancient South Indian scripture, Tirukural, says, "It is the principle of the pure in heart never to injure others, even when they themselves have been hatefully injured. Harming others, even enemies who harmed you unprovoked, surely brings incessant sorrow." The wise never let hateful people fill them with hate, never give permission to the angry to arouse their own instinctive nature of anger. They cling to the Divine, trust in the Divine in all circumstances, and thus are channels for the divine process of human transformation and evolution.

As unimaginable as this tragedy is, we must all not respond to violence with more violence in our homes and streets. Trust our government and the governments of the world to perform their military duty to assure our safety in the future. We must be the peacemakers, the arbiters of differences, and the protectors of goodness. The world has always been populated by people of the lower nature and those of a higher nature. Immature souls, young souls in spiritual evolution, live in the chakras below the *muladhara*, where fear, anger, hatred, jealousy, confusion, self-

alive trapped in the building! please Allah, they need you most, please give them strength! Allah please give us strength too, we need to overcome this, this is the moment we need you most! walk with us, help us, help the victims, and please give »

ishness, and maliciousness without conscience reside. Old souls live in the higher chakras, where reason, will, understanding, and love prevail. Life on Earth has always been happiest, safest, and most rewarding when the higher-consciousness people are in control, both of themselves and of those who follow a lower path. Each one can make a choice in the days ahead to remain in the light and illumine the world or be drawn into the darkness of hate, fear, and revenge. Our Siva is a God of love, and our traditions and scriptures assure us that this love will overcome every lesser force.

SATGURU SIVAYA SUBRAMUNIYASWAMIL is publisher of *Hinduism Today* and *Hindu Press International*.

WHAT WOULD JESUS DO?
By David P. Gushee

It was totally predictable that the horrific terrorist attacks on our nation last week would elicit angry calls for punishment, retaliation, even a crusade against evil. It was also totally predictable that, while many Christians unequivocally joined in such calls, others hesitated because of their understanding of the life and teachings of Jesus Christ. The same pattern of response has existed for centuries. The difficulty is rooted in two primary sources: the complex nature of the biblical witness, and the question of where the loyalty of the Christian truly lies.

To the biblical issue first. It would have been easier if the Bible's stance on violence were clear-cut. But the Scriptures offer us instead a mix of materials. The Old Testament, or Hebrew Bible, ranges from the idyllic peace of the Garden of Eden to the

us hope, please especially me, tell me more survived, Allah please, we need you now! Inshaallah, amin!!!!
9/13/01 11:29 A.M. lisabryan: Dear Lord, please help the leaders of our nation and give them the wisdom to do the right thing.

holy-war motif in the Book of Joshua, to the wars of self-defense in the later historical books, to the bitter lamentations over the destruction of Jerusalem in the Prophets, and then to the eschatological hope for and promise of peace in the last days.

The New Testament tells us that those last days have come in the person of Jesus Christ. Jesus himself teaches that the kingdom is dawning, that peacemakers are blessed, that his disciples are to turn the other cheek and love their enemies. He rejected revolutionary Jewish nationalism and related humanely even to the Roman occupiers, whose leader ended up crucifying him without Jesus offering any physical resistance. The rest of the New Testament tells the story of a persecuted yet courageous band of evangelists who were always prepared to suffer but never to inflict suffering for the cause of Jesus Christ. The blood of those martyrs changed the world.

No thoughtful Christian finds it easy to work out a synthesis of this diverse material.

The loyalty issue is just as difficult to disentangle. When Jesus was asked whether it was right to pay taxes to Caesar (that is, Rome), his response was cryptic: "Give to Caesar what is Caesar's, and to God what is God's" (Matthew 22:21). Christians have sensed a tension between loyalty to nation and loyalty to God ever since.

So what does belong to the Caesars of our own time, and what belongs to God alone? A range of answers is possible, including a stark subordination of national loyalty, a stark subordination of religious loyalty, or some effort to accommodate or even marry the two.

In the time since that Tuesday's horrible attacks, we have seen all of these responses, though clearly the latter has predominated. Yet isn't it true that for Christians, Jesus Christ alone is

9/13/01 11:33 A.M. xenotzu: I live in a country where 2/3 of the population are muslims, whilst the remaining 1/3 are non-muslims. It is sad to say this, but the majority of the muslims that I have spoken to here, either do not condemn or do condone »

Lord? If so, what would we do if his will for our lives didn't seem to match up with the will of our own leaders, or the sentiments of the nation as a whole? Would we even be willing to acknowledge that this conflict of loyalties could possibly occur?

By framing the discussion in this way, I have hoped to clarify the difficulty of these issues and move us away from any focus merely on retaliation itself. Any Christian who feels no tensions here, either in terms of biblical interpretation or loyalties, is missing something pretty important. But still, a response is needed.

Choices must be made. What counsel would I offer to those attempting to navigate these treacherous waters?

I would begin by saying that while the whole biblical witness is authoritative, the witness of Jesus must be the final word. Similarly, while loyalty to nation has an appropriate place, our loyalty to Jesus Christ as Lord must also be, on that matter, the final word.

But this does not lead to a counsel of passivity or nonresistance in the face of evil. I believe that Jesus neither taught nor practiced nonresistance to evil. This is a historic misunderstanding. Yet neither did he seek to defeat the world's evils through the world's own strategies.

Instead, he came preaching the kingdom of God and inaugurated it in his very person. He did this not only through his saving death and his resurrection, but also through his moral teachings and practices. Christians are those who not only receive the eternal benefits of his atoning death but also joyfully participate in advancing God's reign—the deliverance of the world from every kind of evil, including violence and murder, a deliverance initiated by Jesus at his first coming and to be consummated by the same Jesus when he comes again.

When Jesus taught enemy-love and cheek-turning and going the second mile, he did not teach his followers to allow evil to reign. He himself resisted evil and the evil one every day. But he

the WTC terrorist attacks, on the basis that it could have been done by muslims. Without any exception, all the non-muslims that I have spoken to are utterly shocked by the attacks, and condemn it.

did so, as people like Mahatma Gandhi and Martin Luther King Jr. noticed, by practicing and teaching the overcoming of evil through courageous, creative, and transformative resistance—through a kind of resistance that refuses to settle for evil as the means to resist evil.

Matthew 5:39 should be translated: "Do not resist by evil means"—but do resist. It makes a good summary of Jesus' approach. It's how evil is defeated and the reign of God advanced.

Practically, in this situation, the Christian has various responsibilities before God, such as the work of praying for the enemy and acting on behalf of the victimized. We also have a particular witness to government. I think it should include the following exhortations:

• Take appropriate steps to ensure the basic security of innocent civilians in their daily lives.
• Discover who exactly was responsible for this terrorist attack and see to it that they are held fully accountable for their deeds and their network is destroyed so that it can never harm innocent people again.
• Exercise sober restraint in whatever use of violence may be necessary to accomplish these goals, with special attention to avoiding civilian casualties.
• Open improved lines of communication to the Middle East in order eventually to understand the grievances that some hold against us and address legitimate concerns in appropriate ways, including acknowledging any wrongs done on our side.
• Work to strengthen ties to Middle Eastern states in order eventually to increase mutual understanding and cultural contacts.
• Discourage any form of racial/ethnic stereotyping or hatred of Arabs or Arab-Americans.

9/13/01 11:40 A.M. astro5: I am mostly Buddhist, and my thought is that this was a tragedy of the worst kind of human suffering. But we must separate ourselves from anger and revenge, so that we can think clearly as to what is the wisest ac- >>

• Reaffirm the cardinal values of democracy, human rights, and religious liberty both in our own response and in the interactions we undertake with other nations.

• Double-check our own judgment as to how to proceed through conversation with friends, allies, and representatives of the international community.

• Maintain a dignified tone that reflects the best of our national moral heritage.

Perhaps the very gravity of the evil inflicted on so many innocent people that Tuesday can shock us out of the too-comfortable categories we usually apply to issues of war and violence.

Suffering so deeply ourselves, perhaps we can contemplate the effects of imposing harm and suffering ourselves, and ask what a resistance beyond retaliation would look like.

If mere retaliation were a sufficient response to perceived or actual wrongs, then the daily headlines coming out of, say, the Middle East, would look a lot different than they have for the last 50 years or so. The cycle of an eye for an eye and a tooth for a tooth leaves a lot of people without eyes and teeth, and the initial problem no closer to solution.

Retaliation is a deeply instinctive reaction to being wronged. But mere retaliation, even when justifiable as it would be here, is not a strategy for an enduring, secure, and just peace. Jesus— God in the flesh, after all, the one who knows better than anyone God's design for us—shows us a better way.

DAVID P. GUSHEE is the Graves associate professor of Moral Philosophy and senior fellow at the Center for Christian Leadership at Union University in Jackson, Tennessee.

tion to follow. Meditation is very important right now.
9/13/01 11:44 A.M. laughing_owl: Kuan Yin, Mother of Compassion, please cradle all in need in your arms. Wipe their tears away in loss, and help them grieve, and stand behind them as

WHAT WOULD BUDDHA DO?
By Lama Surya Das

What would the Buddha do? No one can really say for sure, any more than anyone can say in truth why God sent death to 6,000 innocent people that week at the hands of a terrorist attack. (I personally consider it the handiwork of man, not God, and that we might do well to look among and within ourselves for the causes.)

However, I am sure that the Compassionate Buddha would stop for a prolonged moment of mindfulness and total attention—silent, centered, and present—to pray for all those who have suffered and are suffering, feeling their pain and grief as his own. Buddha would stop and pray for the victims and their families, and all worldwide who suffer and have suffered; he would join Jesus in blessing the peacemakers, while also praying for those who have perpetrated such horrendous crimes.

What would Buddha do? Buddha would move among the wounded, grief-stricken, and despairing, with gentle healing hands. Buddha might remind us of the fleeting, ephemeral nature of life in all its forms, and remind us that we might profit by turning toward lasting values and the deeper meaning of life, to help instill in us a sense of the long-range view and the bigger picture.

We condemn wanton acts of violence and destruction. The criminal perpetrators and their aides and abettors must be brought to justice, and terrorism erased from our world as an acceptable form of political or social action in any country of the world.

However, I feel quite sure that we should not rush into vengeful retaliatory acts, which will make us into the mirror image of those who have attacked us and could bring more

they move forward in their lives. Mother Kuan Yin, hold us all in your embrace.
9/13/01 11:46 A.M. scottgriz: Seeing people of all faiths gathered in common prayer gives me a wonderful feeling. God is >>

problems rather than provide lasting solutions. The Enlightened One would no doubt advocate restraint, reason, compassion, and understanding in the face of violence and aggression.

What would Buddha do? Buddhism would teach that the enemy and those who harm us can be our best teachers. We can actually benefit now and in the long run by learning to generate sincere feelings of compassion for the perpetrators' negative actions and bad karma. Buddhist wisdom consistently reminds us to recognize how interconnected we all are in this small world, while emphasizing the universal spiritual verity that hatred does not cease through hatred but through love alone, for loving-kindness and compassion are greater than hatred, greater than death. Twenty-five hundred years ago the Buddha himself said: "Hatred is never appeased by hatred in this world; by love alone is hatred appeased. This is an Eternal Law." (The Dhammapada, Verse 5)

Buddha might well advise us to be very cautious about allowing anger and righteous indignation to drive us toward further violence, extreme nationalism, jingoism, and the further loss of innocent life. As a person of Asian origins, the Buddha might remind us that the Afghani people are starved, exhausted, incapacitated, suffering, even as one billion people on our planet are starving and one-third of the world's population is suffering from hunger today. (A few years ago, the United Nations estimated that there are 500,000 disabled orphans in Afghanistan—a country with no economy, no food, and millions of widows.) New bombings would mainly stir only the rubble of earlier Soviet bombs. Would they get all the bin Ladens and remove the Taliban from power? Not likely.

I think Buddha would ask us to consider the karmic causes, origins, and conditions that have given rise to the kind of hatred

with us all. My prayers are with those who need the love and support of God. We are voices for God. Let love speak through every one of us as we progress through our lives.
9/13/01 12:22 P.M. KathyA: Dear God Please help our children

and animosity that drove the perpetrators of this criminal act. Buddha's vision encompassed the fact that everything in this universe has a cause, and that nothing happens by accident. This is known as the law of karma, or causation, pointing out that each and every effect has its web of myriad causes and conditions. Individuals or nations who shortsightedly deny causality by ascribing blame to others short-circuit the profound introspection necessary to see our own karmic responsibility for whatever befalls us and for our own lives, character, and destiny—our karma, in short.

The Buddha, as an embodiment of the wisdom of spiritual experience, would exhort us to reflect and explore deeply and conscientiously about what, if anything, can be done to address the causes of those ongoing conditions, and to strive to redress the great imbalances and iniquities we find in our world as well as long for a higher, better spiritual world to come. I suppose Buddha would note the economic, social, political, and religious differences between we Americans and those who seem to have attacked us, and observe how our own foreign policies, postmodern consumer culture, and material lifestyle might contribute to arousing the spite of others with radically different worldviews and extreme fundamentalist religious beliefs. I think Buddha would point out that unless we get to the roots of these seemingly intractable problems, no solution is in sight.

The events of September 11, their prelude and aftermath, are a rare and terrible gift in our hands, a broken heart. When our hearts are broken open we may find a moment of vital opportunity. Only out of suffering comes understanding. Great suffering can turn to great compassion and beneficial action. We pray for the healing and turning of the perpetrators of these crimes whose damaged hearts and clouded minds have created

erase the images of the last two days from their minds, so that they can become innocent again.
9/13/01 1:34 P.M. oswcmom: Lord, this is a huge door that has closed upon us,...help us to find the open door you wish us to ≫

vast suffering in the present and into the future. We count on the wisdom, patience, and loving-kindness of the world's leaders, that they may be just and exercise restraint and care in all their actions. Every decision they make should be motivated by compassion.

LAMA SURYA DAS is a leading spokesman for Buddhism and contemporary spirituality and a lama of the Tibetan Buddhist order. He is the best-selling author of several books, including *Awakening the Buddha Within*.

MITAKUYE OYASIN
By Michael Hull

Mitakuye oyasin is a phrase my Lakota friends taught me to use to both begin and end Lakota ceremonies. *Mitakuye oyasin* is often translated to mean, "Amen to all my relations." An exact translation is not possible, yet "all people are my family" or "all people are my people" might be more accurate.

Since the attacks, my inbox has been flooded with e-mails from my spiritually minded friends with quotes from Gandhi, Martin Luther King Jr., and others calling for peace, nonviolence, for a loving response. One example from my friend who runs the Boulder office of the Tibetan Global Peace Foundation reads, "Nonviolence is the greatest force at the disposal of man. It is mightier than the mightiest weapon of destruction devised by the ingenuity of man." With each message I wonder, How are they so sure in the face of such loss, grief, pain, and suffering?

I have staked my life to the belief that God exists, love matters, and prayers are answered. I have signed on to the proposition that love, whatever that means, will win in the end; that a loving response is the only rational, sane way for me to live in

find. Keep our faith strong because above everything you are our Rock and our Redeemer. On Christ the Solid Rock we stand. **9/13/01 1:55 P.M. surfer:** My thoughts and prayers are with all the people who have perished in this tragedy. I'd like to add a

the world. I stand for the belief that if I live grounded in that proposition, and ask every day for a loving God to tell me in prayer what the loving response is in any situation, that I will receive that guidance, and I have agreed to follow it.

In the midst of my piety about love and God and a loving response, some very devout people who presumably thought they believed in God, acting from what I assume they thought was divine guidance, hijacked four planes. Now thousands of folks have died, and our lives are forever altered.

In prayer I ask for guidance but drown in a galaxy of grief. The enormity of the loss crushes me. The sheer incomprehensible size of the pain, sorrow, and sadness overwhelms me, makes me lose my way, and makes me doubt and question. The tragedy raises questions about all I believe. How, I wonder, can a loving, just, divine God permit such a seemingly senseless slaughter? All the parts of me that demand justice, that yearn for fairness, stare in shock at the TV, hour after hour, numbed by the outright wrongness of it all.

When I take a step back, I must concede that we in America have been victimized on other occasions. Intellectually I know my government has victimized others: My Lakota friends are living proof of this. Others in the world have been victimized in brutal fashion before and will be again. But in some curious way, this has become a collective brutalization; it is ours in some way that times before were not.

I struggle with my internal voice that cries out for retribution, for a violent response. It is a voice that wants to inflict pain and suffering on those who are responsible for the pain I feel, for the loss we have all experienced. I am shocked at the insistence of this violent voice after so many years spent in devout pursuit of a spiritual life. Thankfully, I am not asked today to decide what military response the United States should make to these attacks.

special prayer for Mike Seaman, a father, friend and neighbor who was at the World Trade Center and is missing. To see the human spirit of the firefighters, policemen and medical workers who are helping is incredible...   >>

I am called upon to pray for those who are in a position to decide, to pray that they too will seek divine guidance, will act out of the Golden Rule, and not out of resentment or fear, that the steps that are taken reflect the best guidance in the situation.

In response to my numerous questions about why things happen the way they do, my grandpa would shrug and say that if God ever held a question-and-answer session, he would be sitting on the front row. That response is probably the best I can do here. I must settle into knowing I likely never will understand this tragedy. There are things, however, I do know because of these events.

The events of September 11 mean I must redefine what God looks like to me. Whatever understanding I have is too shallow to encompass this tragedy. Michelle, my 4-year-old, asked me what God looked like. Struggling, I replied that God did not exactly resemble a person. Michelle said, "Well, does God look like a refrigerator?" I wonder what God looked like to the hijackers, or to us when we financed those who now allegedly terrorize us, or to me when I walk past an outstretched hand?

I must redefine my relations with you. I have been too remote, too distant. I have looked the other way one too many times, have failed to extend the hand of friendship when doing so might have made a difference. I must reexamine my commitment to life, to the fundamental proposition that what I do and what I think affects all of us. Everyone is my family. I am responsible for what I do, and for what I think about doing.

When I agreed to the practice of a loving response, I also agreed to be guided by several principles. My Lakota friends taught me one of them, the idea that we are all related. All means all. I am related to those I like and to those folks who perpetrated this massacre. Being related to those I like or admire is easy. Those who hurt me and mine throw me for a loop.

9/13/01 4:06 P.M. Shebachick2002: Where was God? God was there waiting to embrace his children as they entered Heaven with perfection. And he was there looking sadly at the terrorists as he sent them to their chosen fates...the dark, fiery pits of hell.

My 12-step friends taught me to pray for those who harmed me. They said to ask for help, knowing the victimizers were sick, and to ask that the victimizers get the help they need as I was relieved of the burden of anger and resentment. "Pray that they get what they need," I was told. When I complained that I could not do this, they said, "Then ask that they get what they deserve."

I struggle with my Baptist upbringing and how to reconcile the Jesus who taught the Golden Rule, the Jesus who taught us to turn the other cheek, the Jesus who died rather than retaliate, with the Jesus who cursed the fig tree and the Jesus who overturned the tables in the temple.

I know resentments, even justified ones, cut me off from the sunlight of the spirit. Resentments clog my ears, so that when I seek divine guidance, I often hear the voice of my resentment instead. To hear divine guidance, I must be free of resentment, an outcome that requires me to examine my part in any situation, including this one.

In America and across the world, people are suffering from a lack of the most basic items of food and clothing. We have the means and ability to provide for those basic needs, yet people still suffer. When those who are slighted retaliate, when they strike out from a place of desperation and need, I scratch my head and wonder why.

Fear can also clog my hearing. I confess I fear the incredible hatred and resentment that fueled these acts of violence. Some contend fear is the absence of faith. Faith, for me, is going forward with my fear, not denying it, but also not being controlled by it. Here, no matter what fears I may have, I refuse to live my life being controlled by them.

I have also been taught to be grateful where I can. Who would have thought a tragedy of this magnitude would bring religious tolerance to the forefront of American thought? Forty years ago

9/13/01 4:18 P.M. NoGods: Dark, Fiery Pits? HA! These men thought God was on their side! I'll tell you where your various gods were on Tuesday. The same place they are today. In your own twisted imagination. These delusions motivate   »

a substantial question existed about the wisdom of electing a Catholic for president. Now, our president utters the name "Allah" in a joint session of Congress and declares that Muslims practice a religion of peace. On CNN a Mississippi farmer declares his support for Muslims, stating, "They pray in 'Musqs' to the same God we do."

The tragedy has brought us together as a nation. Support for the victims, their families, the relief and rescue workers, and others runs across party, gender, age, and ethnic boundaries. For this brief time at least, there is less of "them and us" and more, much more, of "they and we." Language of tolerance, open displays of grief and sadness, substantial acts of kindness and generosity are the orders of the day.

The attacks have helped solidify an awareness that we are all related, that what I do here affects you there, that the line between you and me, we and they, is thinner and more blurred than we might have previously believed. I am related to the victims, the victimizers, to those who decide what our response will be, to those affected by those responses, and to those who respond in the absolute divine circle of our existence.

We are all related. *Mitakuye oyasin.*

MICHAEL HULL is the first white man to be awarded a Sun Dance bundle and recognized as a Sun Dance chief by traditional Lakota elders. A practicing attorney in Austin, Texas, he is also the author of *Sun Dancing: A Spiritual Journey on the Red Road.*

some to do good and some to do evil. Hold your breath and wait for divine justice. I'll take human justice everytime. **9/13/01 5:01 P.M. RevSusanne:** Send Thy peace, O Lord, which is perfect and everlasting that our souls, may radiate peace. Send

WHAT WOULD THE GODDESS DO?
By Starhawk

The world has changed since Tuesday, September 11, 2001. All of us have come face-to-face with death on a massive scale, with the immense power of the forces of destruction, with our fragility, and with fear. The loudest voices around us in the U.S. are calling out for retaliation and revenge, led by the president and most of our public officials. In such a situation, what would the Goddess do?

In the Pagan tradition that I practice, the Goddess is not a role model. She's the great forces of birth, growth, death, and regeneration that move through the universe. In thealogian (a feminist theologian) Carol Christ's words, the Goddess is "intelligent, embodied love." Her many aspects are the faces we put on these forces so we can interact with them. She is immanent within us as well as in nature. So for me, the question shifts and becomes, "What can we do in the name of the powers of creativity and regeneration? How can we intelligently embody love in this crisis?"

First, we can mourn the dead. Death kills the body but not the spirit. Thus, the prayers and energies people of all religions have been offering truly help the spirits of the dead pass to a place of peace.

We can support the families and friends who have lost someone by offering comfort and practical help, by being willing to listen, by sending prayers and love.

We can feel our grief. Our grief is not just for the dead, but for the world that existed before that Tuesday. Grief can be an opening; it can make us rethink our values and our priorities and make us more compassionate.

We can speak for justice, not revenge. Retaliation is the quick fix that might restore our sense of being mighty and powerful,

Thy Peace, O Lord, that we may think, act, and speak harmoniously. Send Thy peace, O Lord, that we may be contented and thankful for Thy bountiful gifts. Send Thy peace, O Lord, that amidst our worldly strife we may enjoy Thy bliss Send Thy peace, >>

but it can't actually make us safer. Revenge will simply exacer-
bate the tensions that led to the attack. If we bomb civilian populations, if we kill innocent women, men, and children who had
no part in these activities or voice in their governments' decisions, we become terrorists ourselves. The intelligent, embodied
love of the universe does not value some groups of people over
others, does not weigh the lives of Americans more heavily than
the lives of Afghanis.

Witches know that words have power. If we continue to call
this attack an act of war, we turn the perpetrators into martyrs
and heroes. A criminal act of murder is seen as despicable, but
an attack on the heartland of the enemy in wartime is seen as ad-
mirable. If we go to war over this, we dignify the perpetrators.
Instead, we should call for them to be brought to justice and
tried in a court of law.

Justice restores balance. But to wage justice, we must also
look at ourselves. If we begin a campaign against terrorism, we
must look honestly at the many ways in which the U.S. has supported and uses terror as a political tool. When the Israelis as-
sassinate Palestinian political leaders with U.S.-made rockets
fired from U.S.-funded helicopters, when we support death
squads in Colombia, are we not supporting terror? Our
bombing of Iraq's water system and our sanctions cost the lives
of 500,000 children a year from contaminated water and lack of
medicine. The CIA trained bin Laden and funded his group
from 1979 to 1989. We supported the Taliban and helped put
them into power as part of our Cold War with the Soviets.

These are painful issues to look at because they undercut our
belief that the U.S. is a free and just society. But only by facing
hard truths can we grow. And I do believe that out of this terrible time can come growth and transformation. The Goddess,
who is the cycle of rebirth, teaches us that death is followed by

O Lord, that we may endure all, tolerate all in the thought of Thy
grace and mercy. Send Thy peace, O Lord, that our lives may become a divine vision, and in Thy light all darkness may vanish. Send
Thy peace, O Lord, our Father and Mother, That we Thy children

regeneration. We need to hold that possibility in our minds through the moments of fear and despair.

As witches, we know that energy follows imagination and leads to manifestation. We need to imagine a world in which love can flourish and the cycles of regeneration are cherished. We need to envision a world at peace.

We can speak and act for that vision. We can embody it in the ways we speak and treat each other, in every action we take. And we need to take action. We need our voices to be heard.

When we speak out, we may receive unexpected support. Just a day after the attack, my friend Nancy went out with her children in her small town and held a peace banner on an overpass. They expected to receive hostility or even threats, but instead people cheered, honked in support, or came over and said, "I'm so glad you're doing this. I was afraid to speak out. Can I join you?"

What would the Goddess do? Ultimately, any answer I give to that question is more honestly what I would do, what I urge you to do: Hold the vision. Speak for it. Act for it. Don't make decisions out of fear. Take risks because there is no longer any safety in inaction. Fill the streets and connect with one another. In times like these, we need support. Create places of healing, rituals, circles where people can come together and speak of how they feel. We can be the intelligent, embodied love of the Goddess for each other. Right now, we need each other as never before.

STARHAWK is the author or coauthor of eight books that link an Earth-based spirituality to action, including *The Spiral Dance* and *Dreaming the Dark*. A feminist and peace activist, she is one of the foremost voices of the Goddess movement and ecofeminism. She travels widely in North America and Europe giving lectures and workshops.

on earth may all unite in one family —Hazrat Inayat Khan
9/13/01 5:26 P.M. shannonc: Lord, we know that we are living in the last days and all that is happening is what you have already warned us about through your holy word, I pray that ≫

WHAT WOULD MOSES DO?
By Joshua Wolf Shenk

Moses was the great prophet of the Hebrew Bible, but he was not a Hebrew, not fully, not without struggle. Born a slave to un-named parents and raised as an Egyptian, he spent his adult-hood among the Midianites, and married the daughter of a Midianite priest. When they had a child, Moses named him Ger-shom (from the root "to drive out"), explaining, "I have been a stranger in a strange land."

The absence in Moses' life of a true geographical or cultural home and his ambiguous relationship with the Israelites is but one aspect of his complex character. As I reread portions of the Torah and interviewed rabbis and scholars about what Moses would do in response to an awful attack, apparently by Islamic fundamentalists, on the World Trade Center and the Pentagon, it is this complexity that most struck me. Moses is both powerful and powerfully flawed; courageous and fearful; an exalted prophet and a most humble one. You may have in mind an image of Moses akin to the role Charlton Heston played in *The Ten Commandments*, a broad-chested, bronze-skinned man, a sublime figure, a perfect servant of God. But though Exodus does show a very special relationship—"The Lord would speak to Moses face-to-face, as one man speaks to another" (33:11)—this is as much a burden as a blessing for Moses. He has to trans-late the will, execute the wishes, and placate the temper of the fiery, unpredictable God and at the same time manage a nation of downtrodden, unruly, perpetually dissatisfied people.

Two early scenes from his story help illustrate Moses' char-acter. In the first, Moses is still in Egypt, apparently living as a prince of the Pharaoh. He sees an Egyptian beating a Hebrew slave. "He turned this way and that, and seeing no one about he

we will all be prepared to meet you and stand before you. **9/13/01 5:31 P.M. lisawhite:** And this is the beginning of sor-rows. It's ironic to me that before this happened people all thought we evolved from apes. Now we're singing "Amazing

struck the Egyptian and hid him in the sand." Then Moses sees
two Hebrews fighting among themselves. He asks one why he
strikes the other. "Who made you chief and ruler over us?" the
man snarls. "Do you mean to kill me as you killed the Egyptian?"

In my reading, Moses has a visceral reaction to the mistreat-
ment of slaves. He hesitates because he knows there would be
great danger if he acted on that instinct. Seeing no one about, he
does act. Then, from that place of strength and moral authority—for the removal of the Israelites from slavery is the
great purpose of the drama about to ensue—he comes upon two
Hebrews quarreling. Again, his instinct seems to draw him near,
to lead. But even his question provokes a backlash. This un-
named Hebrew seems to see Moses as outsider, not a helper or
savior.

It is no wonder that, when God calls to Moses from the
burning bush and instructs him to lead "my people, the Israelites" from slavery, Moses demurs. "Who am I that I should
go to Pharaoh, and free the Israelites from Egypt?" he asks. Notice that God uses the possessive pronoun, but Moses does not
repeat it. God answers, "I will be with you, and it shall be your
sign that it was I who sent you." This is a lovely moment, for
Moses' question can be read as either a kind of self-effacement
("Who am *I*?" he asks with shoulders scrunched near his ears)
or as an earnest pleading ("Who *am I*?" he demands, wanting to
know his ancestry, his identity). God's answer is not an answer
at all, actually, but merely a repeat of the call.

This dance between God and Moses goes on, for Moses
queries God not once or twice, but five times before accepting
the job asked of him.

Moses: "Suppose I go to the Israelites and say to them, 'The
God of your fathers has sent me to you,' and they ask me, 'What
is his name?' Then what shall I tell them?"

God: "*Ehyeh-Asher-Ehyeh* (variously translated as 'I am what I am,' 'I will be what I will be,' or even 'I am what I do.') Thus you shall say to the Israelites, *Ehyeh* sent me to you. . . . They will listen to you."

Moses: "What if they do not believe me and do not listen to me, but say: 'The Lord did not appear to you?'"

Here God performs two miracles—turning Moses' rod into a snake and back again; then turning his hand leprous and then healthy again. This frightens Moses.

Moses: "Please, O Lord, I have never been a man of words, either in times past or now that You have spoken to Your servant; I am slow of speech and slow of tongue."

God: "Who gives man speech? Who makes him dumb or deaf, seeing or blind? Is it not I, the Lord? Now go, and I will be with you as you speak and will instruct you what to say."

Moses: "Please, O Lord, make someone else your agent."

At this point, God grows angry with Moses and promises his brother Aaron as his spokesman. Thus God finally gives an (indirect) answer to Moses' original question, "Who am I?" Moses now knows that he is a brother of Aaron, the son of Aaron's mother.

It is rare in the Bible to see God questioned by humans, let alone negotiating with them. That he suffers such impudence may be taken as a sign that Moses is not an incidental choice. God *wants* Moses, and it may be that his strange qualities recommend him for the job ahead: He is an ancestral Hebrew but a lifelong outsider. (Moses is 80 years old by this time.) He is quick to anger at injustice, but he also has what a psychiatrist might call appropriate fear.

It may be that God appreciates these qualities because the times ahead will require a series of complex responses. Moses will need, at times, to be ruthless (even with his own people) and

are thinking. "Kill them and let God sort them out." God knows we can't. Whether they will go to heaven, hell or purgatory is not our business. That is between them and God- all we can do is pray for them as we pray for anyone. So yes: pulling together,

at other times forgiving. He will need to be philosopher, judge, and warrior. He will need both supreme confidence and abject humility. He will need to displace some other nations, and to "blot out" (or exterminate) at least one. And yet he will also preside over a new legal order that applies to all people. (It is "Thou shalt not murder," not, "Thou shalt not murder other Israelites.")

The Israelites were to be a holy people, a model to other nations. To the extent that they succeeded, it is because of the ethical and democratic traditions they nurtured: an adherence to divine laws, not temporal wishes; an injunction that all study Torah, not just the priests. We in the United States also have a tradition that we have a right to be proud of. But it is our burden to articulate just what we stand for; where we, too, have faltered; and what struggle lies ahead for us and others.

President Bush, in his address 10 days after the bombing, said, "The course of this conflict is not known, yet its outcome is certain. Freedom and fear, justice and cruelty, have always been at war, and we know that God is not neutral between them." Immersed in the story of Moses, I found his assurance of divine favor to be curious: An important theme of the Torah is that no people, no leader can ever be so assured. In fact, at the end of Deuteronomy, God foretells the Israelites' demise. And Moses, his faithful servant for 40 years in the desert, is rebuked for his insufficient faith. We now remember Moses as a great leader. If modern leaders wish to emulate him, they might remember that he was humbled, even in death.

JOSHUA WOLF SHENK is an essayist and historian based in New York City. His first book, *The Melancholy of Abraham Lincoln*, is forthcoming from Viking Press.

donating blood, money and helping their neighbors. People are praying on the streets. Maybe this is the wake up call we needed, and if it is (and I believe it is) our freedom, especially of religion is as worth fighting for today as it was in 1776.

Chapter 8

FEAR AND VULNERABILITY

Oh, only for so short a while you
have loaned us to each other,
because we take form in your act of drawing us,
and we take life in your painting us,
and we breathe in your singing us.
But only for so short a while
have you loaned us to each other.
Because even a drawing cut in obsidian fades,
and the green feathers, the crown feathers,
of the Quetzal bird lose their color,
and even the sounds of the waterfall
die out in the dry season.
So, we too, because only for a short while
have you loaned us to each other.
—Aztec Indian prayer

IN PRAISE OF SMALL AMBITIONS
By Hugh O'Neill

Our country has been wounded. We're grieving the losses from the attacks on the World Trade Center and the Pentagon, and the deaths of the passengers who took on the terrorists in midair and perished in a field outside Shanksville, Pennsylvania, saving other folks the bad guys sought to slaughter.

Right after the attack, like most Americans, we've found ourselves trying to salvage some lesson that might be salve for the ache. But lessons often come in language, and in the brutal terrain of thousands immolated for no reason, words seemed paltry things. Silence seemed most like home.

But in the days since, a TV-screen image has emerged as a truth worth clinging to, whatever happens in the future. Whether the dogs of war are loosed, or wisdom and love can find a way around necessity, the memory of the rescuers, hundreds of police officers and firefighters and ironworkers and emergency medical technicians and civilians, good and true, moving methodically over great, gruesome heaps of rubble will remain an inspiration for dealing with a crisis and, what do you know, with plain-old daily life as well.

With a stubborn mix of strength and care, those people just worked. One chunk of concrete, one bucket of concrete dust at a time, they set about moving the mountain of I-beams and glass that entombed their countrymen.

We were struck by the simple doggedness of their work, the relentless simplicity of lift and carry and continue. Facing an undoable task, they set about doing it. They did what strong folks do best—they began. Nothing fancy. Just muscles and wills at work. They just looked about them, bent and bore away

9/13/01 7:52 P.M. Micka: I am so touched and saddened by the way the folks in NYC and DC are coming together. I mean, we might have our problems here in the U.S. with each other, we might hurt each other and hate each other, but By God, if

the nearest burden. Their ambition extended only to the end of their arms.

The lesson we're determined to learn is that we're most useful when, like those rescuers, we focus on the small circle around us. Too often, we get lost in big plans, vague angers, and old regrets, and forget that the job is right here and right now. The opportunities aren't *out there*. They're asleep upstairs—wearing Spiderman pajamas. They're at the supermarket, buying stuff for dinner, and now, after the attack, a little more fearful for the people they love. The assignment, Lieutenant, is to focus on the task at hand, to seize opportunities that are right in front of you—within your arms' reach—instead of lamenting chances missed or dreaming of others yet to come.

The word "ambition" has come to mean the drive to achieve wealth or standing. But in truth, our 'ambit' is nothing more nor less than the circle in which we move, the compass of our connections. We hereby decree that ambition is the more modest, but more demanding urge to enrich all the rooms you walk into—whether you're a Wall Street player or a firefighter from Bay Ridge who runs *up* the stairs of infernos.

It's a good bet that we'll feel better. It's also a good bet that Thomas Moore is right: Melancholy carves out a space in the soul where wisdom can grow.

We're determined to shrink our circle, commend our attention to the chances on our doorstep. We're going to deploy our love and energy in classrooms, on ball fields, in churches, in bars, in bedrooms, in backyards, in very tall buildings where deals get done, throughout the ambit of our lives.

Make no mistake. We remain four-square behind great achievements—including rebuilding whatever time reveals to be right on the site of the Twin Towers. But a few weeks out from

someone else tries it, the way these terrorists did, we won't stand for it! We are truly the UNITED States... Please remember that these terrorists wanted to instill terror in our hearts. Let us show them that instead, we are a strong united nation ral- >>

this tragedy, we find ourselves committed to stewardship. In all the great people we've known, their strength came from a sense of duty. Left foot, right foot. We're at war, all right. And terrorism is just one of the enemies. The other is carelessness. To honor the memory of those who died, and the service of those who dug, we're going to try our best to make ourselves useful.

HUGH O'NEILL is an editor of *Men's Health* magazine and the author of several books, including *A Man Called Daddy*.

WE ALL LIVE IN A SUKKAH
By Rabbi Arthur Waskow

Just a few weeks after the attacks of September 11, the Jewish community celebrates the harvest festival of Sukkot. Many Jewish families and organizations will celebrate by building a *sukkah*. What is a sukkah? Just a fragile hut with a leafy roof, the most vulnerable of houses. Vulnerable in time, where it lasts for only a week each year. Vulnerable in space, where its roof must be not only leafy but leaky—letting in the starlight, gusts of wind, and rain.

In the evening prayers, we plead with God—"Ufros alenu sukkat shlomekha"—"Spread over all of us your sukkah of shalom."

Why a sukkah? Why does the prayer plead to God for a "sukkah of shalom" rather than God's "tent" or "house" or "palace" of peace?

Precisely because the sukkah is so vulnerable.

For much of our lives we try to achieve peace and safety by building with steel and concrete and toughness. Pyramids, air-raid shelters, Pentagons, World Trade Centers. Hardening what

lying together for a common cause and you can kick us but you can't keep us down! peace....
9/13/01 8:37 P.M. NREMTP: Dear God, please wrap your loving arms around all that hurt. may you give them comfort in this

might be targets and, like Pharaoh, hardening our hearts against what is foreign to us.

But the sukkah comes to remind us: We are in truth all vulnerable. If "a hard rain gonna fall," it will fall on all of us.

Americans have felt invulnerable. The oceans, our wealth, our military power have made up what seemed an invulnerable shield. We may have begun feeling uncomfortable in the nuclear age, but no harm came to us. Yet, September 11, the ancient truth came home: We all live in a sukkah.

Not only the targets of attack but also the instruments of attack—the sleek, transcontinental airliners—were among our proudest possessions. They availed us nothing. Worse than nothing. Even the greatest oceans do not shield us; even the mightiest buildings do not shield us; even the wealthiest balance sheets and the most powerful weapons do not shield us.

There are only wispy walls and leaky roofs between us. The planet is in fact one interwoven web of life. The command to love my neighbor as I do myself is not an admonition to be nice: It is a statement of truth like the law of gravity. For my neighbor and myself are interwoven. If I pour contempt upon my neighbor, hatred will recoil upon me.

What is the lesson, when we learn that we—all of us—live in a sukkah? How do we make such a vulnerable house into a place of shalom, of peace and security, and harmony and wholeness?

The lesson is that only a world where we all recognize our vulnerability can become a world where all communities feel responsible to all other communities. And only such a world can prevent such acts of rage and murder.

If I treat my neighbor's pain and grief as foreign, I will end up suffering when my neighbor's pain and grief curdle into rage. But if I realize that in simple fact the walls between us are full of holes, I can reach through them in compassion and connection.

time of need. i understand in a part their feelings, i was a rescue worker in the Oklahoma bombing my prayers will be with you all each and every day

9/13/01 9:06 P.M. LibbyS: God, Thank you for being with us   »

216

FROM THE ASHES

Suspicion about the perpetrators of this act of infamy has fallen upon some groups that espouse a tortured version of Islam. Whether this turns out to be so, America must open its heart and mind to the pain and grief of those in the Arab and Muslim worlds who feel excluded, denied, unheard, disempowered, defeated.

This does not mean ignoring or forgiving whoever wrought such bloodiness. They must be found and brought to trial, without killing still more innocents and wrecking still more the fragile "sukkot" of lawfulness. Their violence must be halted. And we must reach beyond them—to calm the rage that gave them birth by addressing the pain from which they sprouted.

From festering pools of pain and rage sprout the plague of terrorism. For some reason, some people think we must choose between addressing the plague and addressing the pools that give it birth. But we can do both—if we focus our attention on these two distinct tasks.

To go to war against whole nations does neither. It will not apprehend the guilty for trial, and will probably not even seriously damage their networks. It will not drain the pools of pain and rage; it is far more likely to add to them.

What would be a policy of precision? Let me offer one possible example:

The U.S. government could draw together what serious evidence it has against the bin Laden network it has accused. It could go to the United Nations Security Council and treat the UNSC as a grand jury, providing it with the evidence and requesting its authority to arrest those charged.

Under the present circumstances, it seems extremely likely the UNSC would give that authority. That is exactly the way the UN Charter was designed: When there is ethical agreement among those who around the world hold great political power,

during this trying time. You are here and my faith has been renewed in you and in mankind. Victims waged their own war against the hijackers to save our lives, victims called family members for what was for some a final "I love you". Strangers

then force can be used. Given the imperfections of human society, it is not a bad way to go.

Then not the U.S. alone, not the world's one superpower acting from a place of wounded arrogance, but the united opinion of humanity would be demanding from the nations where the accused live their extradition for trial, maybe including the possibility of trial by an international court of crimes against humanity (the court the U.S. has opposed creating) or trial by U.S. law in another country (like in the Lockerbie, Scotland, case).

If that Security Council warrant for extradition and arrest were refused, then the Security Council's writ could be enforced by carefully focused use of armed force, if necessary.

This approach would enhance the rule of law instead of further shattering it, and focus on the perpetrators, not on raining death on whole communities. It might ultimately mean using armed force. But it would come as close as possible to using it as the police do.

And meanwhile, we would be addressing pools of pain and rage.

How do we establish the goal and encourage the emergence of a peaceful relationship between Israel within, approximately, the Green Line of 1967 (with a few tiny mutually respectful emendations) and a viable, peaceful Palestine?

Of course not every demand put forward by the poor and desperate and disempowered becomes legitimate, just because it is an expression of pain. But we must open the ears of our hearts to ask: Have we ourselves had a hand in creating the pain? Can we act to lighten it without increasing the overall amount of pain in the world?

Instead of entering upon a "war of civilizations," we must pursue a planetary peace.

RABBI ARTHUR WASKOW is the director of The Shalom Center in Philadelphia and the author of *Godwrestling—Round Two*.

helped strangers out of the buildings, even though their own lives were in danger. Thousands of people have come together to help. There is beauty beyond the devastation. There is hope. There is life. Praise God   >>

HARBINGERS OF HOPE
By Suzy Yehl Marta

Grief is painful enough to experience, but witnessing it in children is heartrending. As adults, we are charged to be protectors and elders of all children—not just our own. In that role, we have wanted childhood to remain a time of security, wonder, and innocence. We know too well that soon enough, the struggles intrinsic to adulthood will be our children's.

September 11, 2001, irrevocably changed everything. Security is now tenuous. Wonder has been replaced by fear. Innocence has been snatched from all our hearts.

As the young and old alike learn the tools for grieving together, we need to be the harbingers of hope to the youth in our midst. Tears and sadness are inevitable during great loss. Both affirm the magnitude of what has happened. Both allow us to heal and hope again.

Hope is at the center of all loss. This feeling is what carries us from darkness into light. Hope suggests that suffering does have a purpose. Hope says we do have the strength to survive what has happened. Hope is much more definitive than a wish. To hope is to have a determined, clear vision for the future and how it can be.

We, as harbingers of hope, must teach our youth how to turn this incomprehensible crisis into a meaningful lesson of life.

- We must assure children and teens with our *presence* so they can reclaim their security.
- We must affirm the genuine goodness of people by *acknowledging* the kindness, generosity, and integrity of individuals.
- We must model *delight* in the wonder of ordinary days.
- We must *encourage* children to continue to live with their arms open rather than with their fists clenched.

9/13/01 9:09 P.M. ImpulsiveAnnie: I pray to Almighty GOD to give strength to all the families, including mine, who are waiting to hear word from a loved one. Forgive us the hatred we may feel in our hearts for our enemies. I pray that YOU Dear

Hope embraces tomorrow. Every day well-lived is the door that welcomes it.

Dear God,
As I reaffirm my commitment
To reach out to the children and adolescents around me,
Please give me the words to help them
Sort through their feelings,
Let them know how really special they are,
How good life really is,
And to be that Harbinger of Hope for their tomorrows.
I ask you to help me
Be the role model children require.
May my voice speak the words they need to hear.
And be able to offer the support that provides them
*   consolation.*
For these are the gifts that instill hope.
God, I shall try to be your arms for hugging,
Your ears for listening,
And your heart for loving.
Through these times of terror and unprecedented fear,
Strengthen my resolve
so that I will be strong for all that the children need.
Amen.

SUZY YEHL MARTA is founder and president of RAINBOWS, a not-for-profit organization that offers training for more than 8,000 peer support groups for children and adults of all ages and religious denominations who are grieving a death, divorce, or any other painful transition in their families. To find a RAINBOWS group in your area, call (800) 266-3206 or visit www.rainbows.org.

GOD help mankind realize that we must live in harmony and not take out our hatred on each other. PLEASE PRAY FOR MY NEPHEW RONALD BUCCA, A NYC FIRE MARSHALL WHO WAS IN THE FIRST TOWER AND IS MISSING SINCE TUESDAY. GOD >>

RESILIENCY IN THE FACE OF FEAR
By Dan Baker

The horrific images of September 11 have been indelibly imprinted upon our collective psyche. And the emotions that accompany these images—grief, shock, and a deep, soul-shaking
anger—have washed over us like a tsunami, threatening to
overwhelm our sense of our life's order and stability, perhaps
even causing some of us to question our very existence.

It is apparent that great pain leaves its mark upon us; we're never
again the same. Some of us are weakened, never to recover. But
others, somehow, gather the strength to survive and even thrive.

The difference between those who thrive and those who
don't is not luck-of-the-draw genetics. Those who ultimately
come through a momentous tragedy have somehow learned the
skills they need to cope. And to some degree, every one of us
can learn them.

While the September 11 attacks are almost without precedent
in our nation's history, it's important to remember that people in
other nations and in other times—for example, Londoners during
the Blitz and the survivors of the concentration camps in Nazi
Germany—have lived through and ultimately thrived after the
similarly devastating and even horrific events that befell them.

When your feelings of sadness or anger threaten to overwhelm you, please try one or all of these coping skills. They can
help you cope with your cataclysmic emotions—or, perhaps,
help someone you know.

Stop asking "Why?" It's a natural question—and, at times, it
feels like the only one that matters. But generally speaking,
"Why?" is not a question that will help us understand or process
a negative life event. Implicit within this poignant, one-word
question is another question: "Why would God, or the Power of

---

BLESS ALL MANKIND AND GOD BLESS AMERICA
9/13/01 10:20 P.M. MatthewS: In times like this we turn to our
families and our beliefs for comfort. I spoke to my Dad last
night. It was one of our best conversations in years. He helped

the Universe, allow such a thing to happen?" Humans are creatures of free will, and the fact is, there is no satisfactory answer.

So when you catch yourself asking "Why?" redirect. You might ask instead, How can I grow from this pain? What are the lessons that this event can teach me? How can it help me gain wisdom, forge a stronger sense of connectedness with my fellow human beings, help me to discover what I truly value in this life?

These are questions that are within your power to answer.

Practice survivor's responsibility. Many psychologists have spoken about survivor's guilt, which is an offshoot of the question "Why?" Feeling guilty for having survived this tragedy helps no one—not the dead or wounded, and certainly not those you love.

A far more constructive reaction to this tragedy is to assume the mantle of survivor's responsibility. There is no satisfactory answer to why we are alive while others died. But the fact is, you are alive. You have survived. What will you do now? What must you do now?

Think about and commit yourself to your responsibilities to your family. To your friends. To your neighborhood and community, and to your country. Acting in others' best interests can help you feel like you're making a meaningful difference.

Take action. One of the best antidotes for a sense of helplessness is to participate in an activity that has a beginning, a middle, and an end. For example, you might donate blood, participate in a memorial service, or help raise money in your community for the families of those who died in the tragedy.

But don't confine your actions to those that memorialize the tragedy. Life goes on. Try to continue to take action, to serve others in need. You will honor the memory of those who have suffered and died, and their lives will have indeed made a difference.

Focus on someone else. Never underestimate the power of altruism to heal a wounded heart. So in the midst of your pain, try

me understand the gravity of these barbaric actions. Find comfort in your loved ones and your beliefs. Call them, tell them you love them. I pray for all.
9/13/01 11:09 P.M. Lindadee: On my drive home from work »

to empathize with others. Shop for an elderly neighbor. Knock on your single next-door neighbor's door and ask if they'd like a cup of coffee. Smile at the harried mother of two screaming toddlers behind you at the supermarket checkout counter—then help her unload her filled-to-the-brim shopping cart.

Continue to express your emotions. In his book *Opening Up*, James Pennebaker, Ph.D., of the University of Texas reports that there's research suggesting that people who have experienced trauma and talk about it cope far better and heal far more effectively than those who keep a stiff upper lip.

Chances are, you've shared your shock, grief, and anger with your family, friends, or colleagues. You may feel all talked out. But when these emotions wash over you, it's important to honor them by expressing them as often as you need to. (Keeping a journal of your feelings may help, too.) Expressing how you feel, whether by word or pen, can trigger a catharsis, which helps us cope.

Believe in something beyond yourself. For some people, this something beyond is God. But it doesn't have to be. Believe in anything that takes you out of the center of the universe but includes you as part of it. Nature, for example. There is beauty and wonder to be found on a quiet path, a body of water, the peace and silence of the woods.

Forge deeper social ties. In the face of the tragedy that befell us as a nation, it is essential that we make a conscious effort to connect with each other more deeply. If we are to move from merely surviving to thriving, it is essential that we turn to one another for social support. We are social creatures, and there is, indeed, strength in numbers. So do whatever you can to engender stronger, deeper, more meaningful social relationships. Dare to risk a hello and a smile to a complete stranger. Invite someone you've wanted to get to know better out to lunch or for a quiet stroll.

this afternoon I thought suddenly how sorry I feel for the ones who did this terrible deed. That may sound like lunacy at the very least, but let me explain. They feel they have done something great. They have no idea what they have really

Search your memory for survival successes. Remember back to a difficult time in your life. Ask yourself: What did I do? What support did I seek out? How did I think, and what did I believe? What values did I hold on to? Then ask yourself if any action you took then can help you cope today.

Also, study those around you whom you perceive to be coping well. Ask them how they're managing to survive and thrive. Perhaps something they're doing can also help you help yourself. Mayor Rudy Giuliani of New York reportedly has been reading books about the survivors of the London Blitz. The point is to look for models of people who cope well in times of adversity. Study them. Learn from them. Then incorporate some of the traits or practices in your own coping styles.

Adopt an attitude of gratitude. When your sadness threatens to overwhelm you, remember the good people and the good times in your life. Reflect on the unity and fellowship that have arisen in the aftermath of our great loss—of the heroism, of the kindness, of the sensitivity that has become commonplace, all over our country.

Love, service, and gratitude are the enemies of those who would bring us to our knees.

Focusing on gratitude does not mean that you won't be sad, depressed, or angry. But you will manage these emotions far better if you interrupt them by honoring, for a moment, all that you do have—for all that we, the survivors, still have. Many of us will never directly know those who lost and sacrificed their lives, but we can live out a legacy of tribute to all who simply wished to live, work, and maybe make the world a better place.

DAN BAKER, Ph.D., is the founding director of the Canyon Ranch Life Enhancement Center and the author of the forthcoming book *What Happy People Know*.

done. Our souls make this earthly journey to learn and to progress closer to the Maker. The good we do here, the ways we help others, the love we show to others, these are the things that make progress for our souls. I believe that »

WHAT DO YOU TELL CHILDREN?
By Jean G. Fitzpatrick

In times of national crisis, many of us keep vigil in front of the television. News shows often repeat the same scenes, such as the one with the second plane flying into the south tower of the World Trade Center and the subsequent explosion. As adults we may watch scenes like this repeatedly, almost to help the reality sink in. But if you have a child in the room, this can be overwhelming. It's especially a good idea not to play graphic television scenes at your child's bedtime.

Even if it were possible, there is no need to put on a stoic front and try to hide all your feelings. Tears about tragedy show our children that we feel connected to others, that we care.

Nonetheless, it's important not to elaborate upon your fears, imagining out loud, in the presence of your child, all the other terrible things that could happen. You may worry that your town hall or the school will be blown up, but keep this anxiety to yourself.

Share your grief and fear with other adults. You may wish to talk to a friend or a clergyperson. Our church organized a prayer vigil. It's good to be gathered together with other people. The comforting presence of others bears witness to our belief in and desire for a better world. The chance to hug or just stand together with others can do a great deal more than wordy explanations.

Try to keep a balance. I guess what I want to convey to my kids is that sometimes terrible things happen, but there is always grace, most people are basically good, God is always present. Watch CNN for 2 hours but then take your child for a walk, go buy some chrysanthemums, have a cuddle, get together for your family dinner.

Teenagers may respond with cynicism or anger at God. This is not the time to try to persuade them that they are wrong. Your

hell after death is knowing... really knowing and feeling the impact our lives have had on others. Oh dear, I can't help but feel sorry for them. I am angry also, but mostly I am sad, so very, very sad for the American people and for the fools who

simple presence, your willingness to accept their feelings and thoughts, whatever these may be, will do more to convey the love of God than any parental sermonizing could do.

Keep in mind that your child's response to this event will depend on his or her temperament as well as on experiences of loss or violence he or she has had, and how these were dealt with. Some kids will want to discuss the logistics and politics of the situation; for others that will be overwhelming or will interfere with their processing their fear. There is no single formula to helping a frightened child. The most important things are to be present and to listen.

Remember that children will not be able to process the whole series of events right now. They will be reflecting on it for the rest of their lives. When John F. Kennedy was shot, all I remember is Sister Marie Loretta, the principal of my elementary school, telling us over the loudspeaker, "Children, the president is dead." But I have thought of that day often in the 30-plus years since.

JEAN G. FITZPATRICK is a pastoral psychotherapist and the author of *Small Wonder: How to Answer Your Child's Impossible Questions about Life.*

PROTECTING OUR RELATIONSHIPS
By Hugh and Gayle Prather

If there was any doubt that we are all connected, the terrorist attacks of September 11 brought home the reality of our unity in both shocking horror and transcending nobility. Even the aftermath of this tragedy continues to teach us about our oneness. Yet in our relationships, especially with our partners, many of us now see heightened evidence of what divides us. For instance, many couples are noticing a tendency to indulge their irrita-

have done this terrible thing....
9/13/01 11:26 P.M. jef35faith: I pray for Mark Bingham, who most probably selflessly helped divert Flight 93 from its target in Washington, DC. I pray for those brave passengers who,   »

tions, to feel misunderstood, and to forget the purpose of relationship, which is to come together to give comfort, to share burdens, and to make life easier on one another.

On the surface, this sickening event was unmasked hatred directed at innocent strangers. They were just ordinary people going about their daily lives, when suddenly and inexplicably they were caught in the crosshairs of madmen. But the anguish and grief were not confined. It was instantly felt around the world. And millions of hearts also opened in prayer, good will, self-sacrifice, and altruism, and they have stayed open.

Today much of the world's population shares in a conflicted mind-set that operates on several levels—it is affecting our marriages, health, motivation, job performance, and parenting attitudes. It is a complex of thoughts and feelings that includes unity, patriotism, tolerance, and generosity, all of which are much talked about in the media. But it also includes somberness, anxiety in the present, increased fears about the future, and, interestingly, an overall decrease in motivation. These combine into a single mood or mind-set that often results in distraction and preoccupation. As one of our talk-show listeners said, "My idle thoughts are much louder than usual."

So it is clear that we now must begin to heal, to bring together the shattered pieces of ourselves and become whole. But we need each other to accomplish this. Without oneness in our primary relationships, we have little chance of experiencing inner oneness.

In addition to our contacts with our friends and the people we counsel, our radio program has put us in touch with people in disparate locations and walks of life. Almost to a person they are having difficult and contradictory experiences. On one hand, they feel more closeness with their families and friends, and on the other, they experience more discord with many of these same

along with him, no doubt saved our nation from an even greater tragedy. I pray for the crew and passengers on that flight who gave their lives so that many more in this country could be saved. I pray for Mark's father, my family's dear friend,

people. Their ordinary day is also affected. They feel a spiritual unity at unexpected moments, as if suddenly they catch a glimpse of great wings of love sheltering them and all others. Yet at other times nothing makes sense, nothing seems important, and there is a nagging feeling that everything in their lives are going to pieces: circumstances, relationships, emotions, health.

"We are all in this together" is no longer a cliché. That means we can no longer escape the fact that we are in each other's hands. If we undeniably can help, if we can understand and bring comfort, then it is our duty to do so. We now must heal ourselves by offering healing to our loved ones. The means of healing are many, but the following are three principles that we personally have found helpful during these times.

The first element of healing is acceptance. What has happened has happened. The attitudes of our partners, families, and friends are as they are. This means that to heal, we must allow the people in our lives to react to our national tragedy in their own ways—to be sad, angry, optimistic, depressed, dysfunctional, or withdrawn all in their own ways. In our attitudes toward them, we take the pressure off. We don't judge. We don't point out mistakes. We resist drawing our own private conclusions about how they should be. We don't even demand consistency.

By giving this gentle tolerance to others, it is easier to extend it to ourselves. If from one moment to the next we are confused about what to do, let us admit that. Is it right to celebrate a birthday or have a joyous gathering of friends? Is it okay to let our housework slip—or our diets? Should our partners slack off in their chores? Should we volunteer or give more to charity than we have? Perhaps we should cut back on our demands of our kids.

If we don't know how we should be handling this crisis, then obviously we don't know how someone else should either. So ac-

and for all who know and love him and his son. I pray for all those who have died in this terrible thing, and for their families and acquaintances. I pray for the recovery of those who are injured or lost. And, I pray for those who must deal with the >>

ceptance applies to ourselves as well as to our partners, children, and coworkers. However, it is an American tradition to "demand the best" of others and to be even harder on ourselves. Thus it is easy to fall into the trap of thinking that to lecture or shame ourselves is a virtue. But this is a time of healing, and healing requires patience and inner rest. Acceptance of our own and others' moods and reactions brings rest to our entire experience.

The second element of healing is faith. We acknowledge the place of wholeness and stillness within us, even if at the moment it seems remote or irrelevant. This is something that in normal times we would do automatically, but now there are several lines of thought that are blocking the spiritual efforts of many people.

One hindering thought is the doubt that God is Love. This comes in many forms: that God caused this and it is part of his plan. That God decided not to protect our nation. That God works in mysterious ways and we are left to figure this out for ourselves. That Divine Law or Divine Consciousness is removed from human suffering. That the world is a dream or illusion and absolute Truth is without concern or anguish over unreal events. Regardless of the form this doubt takes, it blocks us from thinking of God as a consoler, as a present help, as One who understands, as One we can turn to as we experience the increase of personal problems that inevitably follows an event this shocking and unsettling.

Another obstacle to healing is the assumption that if we only find the right concept, the right thing to believe, we will understand this tragedy. This tempts us to think philosophically about horror and devastation, substituting intellectual concepts for direct experience and blocking our sensitivity. But the people around us need us to act on the insights we have about what makes them happy and what doesn't, what brings them comfort and what needlessly stirs them up. Even a little child or

horror of not knowing...
9/14/01 6:14 A.M. justmehere: Dear Savior, do not weep for our ignorance. Protect all children of the world, so they do not grow up neglected or hateful. Please save us from ourselves

animal can give love and comfort. We don't need a philosophy to be kind.

A third obstacle is the belief that the subject most deserving of our attention is not our partners or other loved ones but the actions of world leaders, that our primary duty is not to seek the peace of our family and friends but to influence our government to do the right thing. For example, we may think that we should have strong opinions on all the issues that swirl around this tragedy and express them often. We should spend long hours daily watching news reports on speculations about governmental decisions. We should send lots of e-mails stating our moral stands to our friends. But how we use our time is important. A gentle use of time is always more healing than being right.

The third element of healing is expression. For acceptance and faith to have transforming power, they must take form. In short, we must act on them. Here are eight guidelines that we recently have tried to incorporate into our daily routine.

1. Do not tell yourself when your disturbing or upsetting emotions must end.

2. Do not tell your partner, child, or anyone else how they should be feeling.

3. If you have been having a particularly disquieting thought, and if there is no action to be taken, put in place a plan for how you will release it the instant it begins.

4. Instead of seeking a breakthrough, try for a little gain each day; whether it is exercise, job performance, housework, or meditation, do what you can do in the present.

5. Even if you don't feel like being kind, be kind; even if you don't feel overwhelming love, be a friend.

6. Seek to think peacefully about your partner, and seek your partner's peace.

9/14/01 8:48 A.M. wjfisher: This morning I pray for all those against whom I reacted in anger. I pray for guidance for all people, not just for myself. May all people know peace. I pray for my dear nephew Noah, who is three, who I hoped would ≫

7. Turn to God and let go of the day at the end of the day so that tomorrow you can begin anew.

8. During the day, talk to God often. Do not be afraid to say anything in your heart. And know that God knows how to reach your heart with the answer.

HUGH AND GAYLE PRATHER are ministers of the United Methodist Church and inspirational writers on relationships and marriage. Hugh Prather's most recent book is *The Little Book of Letting Go.*

PROCESSING A NATIONAL TRAGEDY
A Sermon by the Reverend Bill Hybels

September 15, 2001

. . . A few days ago, I was talking to one of the wisest people I know, and at one point in the conversation the guy said, "Bill, this weekend people are going to stream into your church having been inundated with information and assaulted by horrific images. But they probably haven't done much learning from all this yet . . . really hasn't been much time for learning." He said, "If there's no learning that comes from last week's events, then this tragedy is just compounded." So I prayed about his counsel and felt prompted by the Spirit of God to try to articulate some of the early learnings that are already rising from the rubble heaps on our eastern seaboard.

The first learning has to do with the fragility of life. Deep inside all of us there's a subconscious awareness that our lives are quite precarious. Deep down we know disease can strike and accidents can happen, unforeseen events can interrupt our carefully planned lives. Bad things might happen to other people. We're pretty sure we're insulated . . . they won't happen to us.

never know something like this in his lifetime. ...
9/14/01 9:40 A.M. RevBayes: The fact that humans must endure suffering is sufficient evidence for me that a loving and omnipotent god simply does not exist. It should be

And when we live calamity-free for long periods of time, not only do we feel a kind of invincibility, but we slowly begin to take life itself for granted. We stop thanking God for the gift of it—for the daily blessedness of it. We stop thanking God for sunrises and sunsets and for spring rains and fall colors. In a way we get too accustomed to the privilege of living, until a day like Tuesday comes.

Joe Ditmar, a Chicago business guy, was on the 105th story of the World Trade Center when the terrorist strike began. He was fortunate enough to find his way out just before the building collapsed. In an interview with the press he kept saying, "I will never, ever take life for granted again." See, he came very close to the alternative. Each day since Tuesday he's been looking at nature differently, people differently, his faith differently, and especially he's been looking at his family differently. He was quoted as saying that when he was running for his life, he just had that image of his family in front of his face and he was running to them with all of his might. This guy's pretty thankful just for life this weekend.

Did you notice in all these cell phone calls that were made from hijacked airplanes and burning buildings in the final moments of someone's life . . . I mean, when the alternate to life was near, you know what most folks did with those last gasps of breath they had? They just said, "I love you. I love you. Tell Dad. Tell Mom. Tell the kids." There's a learning in this, friends. Life is fragile. Life is relatively brief against the backdrop of eternity. It's a scandalously gracious gift from the hand of a good God. A gift that should be sincerely celebrated each day by those of us whose hourglass still contains some grains of sand. And what better way to celebrate this gift than by carrying out the instruction of the giver of the gift who said, "If you love God with all your heart, soul, mind, and strength. . . ." If you love others,

sufficient evidence for any sentient being. No amount of human suffering can be justified by any mysterious plan of such a god...
9/14/01 10:39 A.M. pegsbaby: The Lord is my shepherd; I shall >>

family and friends, you will experience the gift of life in all its
fullness. There's a lesson in this for us. A lesson about this glorious gift of life.

. . . There's a second learning from last Tuesday: Evil is alive
and well. Need we spend much time on this one, really? When
times are peaceful and crime rates are falling and circumstances
have been kind to us, we sometimes get lulled into forgetting
that there's a ferocious battle being fought in this cosmos; a
battle between the forces of good and evil. The Bible teaches
from cover to cover that this spiritual war that's going on between the forces of good and evil is real. It's not folklore. It's not
some religious fantasy idea. It's real. The Bible tells us that this
battle goes on, that it's fought on the battlefields of individuals'
minds and hearts. And the Bible teaches that the outcome of
these individual battles between good and evil will have enormous impact on a society.

In recent days, we've all had front row seats to what happens
when the tide of the battle goes in the favor of evil forces.
Unimaginable deeds are done. Tuesday morning in my office, as
I and my son and a few friends were watching thousands of innocent people being burned and crushed, the thought happened
into my mind that quite possibly in another office somewhere
on the other side of the world, the instigators of this carnage are
high-fiving one another, breaking out the champagne and
saying, "We did it. We did it." And when that thought came into
my mind, I almost got physically ill. I remember thinking, if that
happened, it's as evil as evil can be. But the man of the station of
evil is not limited to the relatively small group of people who
planned this. What about all the accomplices who have been
taking money for these past few years helping these few pull this
off? That's pretty evil. What about people in various parts of the
world who broke out in dancing and partying in the streets

not want. and I will dwell in the house of the Lord forever. thou
anointest my head with oil; my cup runneth over. for thou art
with me; thy rod and thy staff they comfort me. he leadeth me
in the paths of righteousness for his name's sake. he leadeth me

when they saw the television coverage of this catastrophe, rejoicing in the bloodshed of innocent people? I'd call that evil. And what about the gas station owners right here in the U.S., right here in the state of Illinois, who doubled and tripled their gasoline prices to profiteer from the slaughter of fellow Americans? That qualifies as evil in my book. And then what about the frustrated and angry Americans whose tempers boiled over and started accosting and assaulting innocent Arab-Americans, dragging them out of cabs, beating them, throwing Molotov cocktails into their homes and places of worship? There's an Arab-American who serves me coffee some mornings here in the area, and the last few mornings when he gives me my coffee I say, "You okay? Are you being treated well? Are you okay?"

And then let's bring it close to home. What about the evil in me? Because, boy, I felt it this week. Did you feel any darkness in you the last couple of days? What about some of us who get so outraged by the scope and the savagery of this last week's events that . . . we're no longer content to want them to come to justice. We want more than justice. We want revenge. Now the Bible's very clear that when there's wrongdoing in the world, people should yearn for justice. That's the work of the Holy Spirit in the life of those of us who know and love God. The Holy Spirit pulls out of us this call, this yearning, this cry for justice. And justice in this case would be that the wrongdoers be found and arrested and brought to a fair trial in an international court where they would have a fair trial and then be sentenced and the sentence carried out. Don't ever feel bad about longing for justice. But what about the darkness that happened in me several times the last couple days where I wanted a lot more than that? What about the darkness in some of you we're hearing on the radio and television that want massive amounts of retribution to fall on large groups of people's heads, even innocent

beside the still waters. He maketh me to lie down in green pastures: He restoreth my soul: Yea, though I walk through the valley of the shadow of death, I will fear no evil: Thou preparest a table before me in the presence of mine enemies: >>

people? We'll call it collateral damage so it doesn't seem so personal. What about that? . . . I felt it in me. Did you feel it in you?

. . . Jesus said, 2,000 years ago, if you keep returning evil for evil, eventually you'll escalate hostility levels to all new heights; you'll give birth to yet another generation of hate-filled, vengeance-seeking extremists and pretty soon millions of people will be eating and drinking and sleeping hatred and violence, and this will not be a fit planet upon which to live. You see sooner or later, we're going to have to figure out here on Earth how to flesh out the counsel of Jesus, who said evil is going to happen and when it does, you have choices to make. . . . You can choose the strategy of ever-escalating amounts of revenge and retribution and retaliation. Here's where it's going to go. Take it to the bank, that's what's going to happen.

Or somebody can take the huge risk of trying to figure out how to move toward returning good for evil. Pursuing reconciliation and humility as opposed to retaliation and revenge. Again, some of you right now are saying, "I don't want to hear this right now." Let me remind you, Jesus didn't just espouse empty words. He lived them. When he, history tells us and Scripture tells us, was illegally, falsely accused, illegally arrested, illegally beaten, and then illegally pounded to a cross . . . when the executioners were putting nails through his hands and feet, he had the recourse to call 10,000 legions of angels to come down and destroy those who were doing this illegal stuff to him. He had recourse to the powers of heaven. He didn't take that strategy when evil was done to him. He said, "Father, forgive them. They know not what they do." And then he voluntarily went to the cross and procured the redemption of his executioners—the potential redemption for them—and he procured our redemption as well. The world has never seen anyone like Jesus Christ. The world rarely sees anyone who will follow his

Surely goodness and mercy shall follow me all the days of my life: Psalm 23

9/14/01 11:34 A.M. nyangel1: Lord, Jesus we ask you to comfort all Americans and others who have lost loved ones in this ter-

wisdom in situations like these, and the world is the worse for it.

This past week, I read some from Gandhi and I read some from Martin Luther King Jr., who wrestled with these very words and tried in nonviolent ways to stand up to evil brought against them. I've been very challenged by this. I'm not pretending for a moment that it would be real easy to figure out how to implement the wisdom of Jesus in this current situation. Frankly, it's much easier to drop bombs. And yet only a few hours after bombs are dropped and a whole bunch of other innocent people are killed, you know what happens to the American consciousness? We slowly begin to realize that we have sunk to the level of those who attacked us and we've got blood on our hands now too. These are days when we have to pray for our leaders. These are days when God needs to speak to those who are in positions of responsibility to figure out our response. And friends, I understand that sometimes evil gets so entrenched in a situation that sometimes military reaction, sometimes military attack is the only way to root out entrenched evil. Sometimes it comes to that. But that should never be the first choice.

. . . Well, my third and final learning from Tuesday's nightmare is going to require additional mental rigor . . . this third learning pertains to a spiritual principle that's particularly difficult for American Christians to embrace. Some scholars refer to it as the "kingdom inversion principle." I sometimes call it the "winning through losing principle." It pertains to how God manages to produce something out of good even when the most difficult circumstances are what cause you to know this activity in the first place. I want to be very clear about this—no thinking person could attribute Tuesday's actions to the hand of a good God. God did not author what happened on Tuesday. God was repulsed by it. God stood and watched people whom he created, in whom he invested a free will; he watched them make deci-

rible tragedy. Thank you for sparing my family and friends who were there and somehow survived. This is one time it paid to be late for work.

9/14/01 1:08 P.M. spiritjordan: I am praying for all of you out >>

sions that broke his heart. But then, in the middle of this horrendous catastrophe, God moved into action in curious, behind-
the-scenes ways, and he's been working and he's been creating
something that we need to notice and wonder about. . . .

Let me just come right out and say it. Last Tuesday we suffered a terrible, national defeat. We lost two times the number
of lives that we did on Pearl Harbor day. We lost a collective
sense of security that may never be regained in our land. We lost
face before a watching world. As one newspaper put it, "America
the invincible became America the vulnerable." But what did
our loss evoke in our citizens and our people since last Tuesday?
Let me ask that another way. What has God been raising up out
of the rubble on the eastern seaboard? What kind of work has
God been up to against the backdrop of that horrendous loss?
Well, first, we've seen unforgettable acts of heroism. Friends, I
will never look at a firefighter the same way the rest of my life.
Hundreds of them running toward the burning inferno instead
of away from it; running up the steps of the Trade Center while
people are racing for their lives coming down. And they're in
there trying to save people they don't even know and they're not
going to get bonus pay for it. They were stirred to do something
that defies human logic; to overcome the fear that would be in
play in each of our lives were we in their shoes. Their bravery becomes part of our collective national legacy. It lifts us up as a
people. Their bravery dignifies all of us. It's God at work, friends.
The same could be said of police officers and other rescue
workers. And what about the airplane passengers who used their
cell phones to figure out that the hijackers were probably headed
for Camp David or the Capitol or the White House? As best
the story can be pieced together, these passengers stormed the
cockpit where the hijackers were, they drove the plane into the
ground to their own deaths in order to avert a greater tragedy.

there who are looking for the people you love. I can't imagine
how excruciating it must be to not know, so I send you the best
energy I can muster to comfort you.
9/14/01 2:38 P.M. patsbanjo: ...Don't despair. God was, and is, in

Who does that kind of thing these days in our pacifistic, fear-driven society? Who's prompting these acts of heroism? These acts ennoble a nation.

And what about the outpouring of volunteerism that Tuesday's loss evoked? The stories take your breath away. Doctors driving hundreds of miles away from their own high-paying jobs to go to New York City to serve, without pay, wherever they can be used. People opening their homes, offering food and refreshments to hundreds of rescue workers. Construction workers leaving their job sites, driving great distances with their own equipment in tow to help the rescue efforts. So many willing volunteers showing up in downtown New York that rescue officials had to fence them out. . . .

And have you ever seen greater displays of unity in our land? Republicans and Democrats arm in arm singing together on the Capitol steps. I hope you videotaped that. It will probably never be seen again in our lifetime. Unbelievable. Governmental agencies cooperating with each other, flags waving all over from homes and cars and so. And some cynics say it's just emotion-driven patriotism and that will be short-lived. I tend to differ. I think this is the result of our relentlessly redemptive God working behind the scenes raising something good out of the rubble heap.

And then what about the return we're seeing to our spiritual core, to our spiritual foundations? On a normal weekend, in our country, more than half our population makes the decision not to worship at a church, not to declare their faith in God, not to confess their sins and pray and grow and build their souls. It doesn't mean they're bad people, it just means they drifted, they put other things first, they've lost their way a bit. What's happened since last Tuesday? Against the backdrop of this horrendous loss—I mean no one's given a big "everybody go to

New York. Look at the people working together on your TV. There is, and always will be signs of God's love all around you in the deep green of the grass and the clear blue of the sky. We were never alone, and we are all loved and we are always free. >>

church" charge—secretly God has been using this catastrophe to remind people everywhere we need his help. We need his wisdom. The world needs his wisdom. We need his love, we need his assurance, we need his guidance, we need his strength. Churches have been jammed since Tuesday. Nine thousand people showed up here Wednesday and Thursday night to pray. The whole nation watched a church service this past Friday. When's that happened last? My prediction is, we will set a record this weekend for church attendance in our country. Again, I remind you, a victory didn't product this. A defeat did, and here's God producing a wonderful new thing out of rubble heaps and broken lives.

I don't know about you, but what I've seen happen since Tuesday has given me greater hope for our country, not less. I think we're learning the kinds of lessons from this national nightmare that will serve us for a long, long time. . . . So here's my challenge to you now, to every one of you. Why don't you do what so many of us are doing these days? Why don't you just open up your chest cavity? Just say, "God, work in my life in these dark days. Speak to me, God, I'm listening. Teach me, God, I'm willing to learn. Prompt me, God. I will obey. Tell me what to do and I'll do it." And friends, if all of us in this church and all of us around the nation and the world will open ourselves up to the leadership and the love of God in a new way, something unbelievably redemptive will come out of this, which is what I'm hoping and praying for.

THE REVEREND BILL HYBELS is the senior pastor of the 12,000-plus member Willow Creek Community Church located in South Barrington, Illinois, a Chicago suburb.

9/14/01 3:09 P.M. longhornmo: Lord, Comfort those who mourn...Heal those in pain...Encourage those who wait...Inspire those who minister...Lead those who govern...and gather each one in our grieving nation near to your heart.

Chapter 9

REPENTANCE

We have to alter the structure of our society, its injustice, its appalling morality, the divisions it has created between man and man, the wars, the utter lack of affection and love that is destroying the world. If your meditation is only a personal matter, a thing which you personally enjoy, then it is not meditation. Meditation implies a complete radical change of the mind and the heart. This is only possible when there is this extraordinary sense of inward silence, and that alone brings about the religious mind. That mind knows what is sacred.

—Jiddhu Krishnamurti

Is This an Apocalyptic Event?
By Jerry B. Jenkins (Interviewed by Deborah Caldwell)

What are you hearing from readers about how they believe the terrorist attacks and the impending war fit into God's plan for the end times?

Many want to know if this is a sign of the end and if Antichrist will soon emerge. Some even ask if Osama bin Laden could be Antichrist, but of course he cannot. The prophecies are clear that Antichrist will be charismatic, attractive, charming, winsome, and that almost everyone will believe he is not only a wonderful person but perhaps even Jesus reincarnate. I don't think anyone thinks that of bin Laden.

What do you believe about how this event fits into the end times?

It makes everything we've been writing about that much more immediate and real. Even I sometimes viewed the devastation scenes in the novels as futuristic and fantastic. Having been in Manhattan when this happened, I will never again be separated from such carnage by decades and oceans. Jesus told his disciples that one sign, not of the end but of the beginning of the end, would be wars and rumors of wars and nations rising up against nations.

Although you don't subscribe to the idea that the Bible provides an exact prophecy of when Jesus will return, can you tell us where you think we are on the time line heading toward the end?

We believe that nothing more needs to be fulfilled before the coming of Christ. The last prophecy that was even debatable was whether the gospel had been preached to all the nations. After the memorial service, in which Billy Graham made plain the

9/14/01 4:22 P.M. tlgregory: How wonderful, what an amazing, supernatural blessing to watch our nation's leaders gathered together in prayer, worship, and hope, rather than petty partisan political posturing. In the wake of this terrible tragedy, I pray

gospel, was broadcast to every country in the world, few can doubt that that has been fulfilled.

That is not to say that God is now obligated to send Christ back tomorrow. He may, in His mercy, wait one more day—which, in his economy of time, is as a thousand years. On the other hand, it could be today. We are instructed to live as if it could be any moment. Then, whether it happens that soon or not, our lives and those we come into contact with should be impacted.

Would this kind of attack have ever fit into one of your plot summaries?

While it's unlikely I would have come up with that exact scenario, it's the very type of heartless attack that appears in many places in the *Left Behind* series. In fact, in my new book *Desecration,* Antichrist launches attacks on unarmed, defenseless civilians (a million of them) in the Holy Land, using all the technological weapons of mass destruction at his disposal. The manuscript was finished in mid-April.

Does it worry you that end-times thoughts are reemerging in the popular imagination?

On the contrary. While, like any other rational person, I am amused and sometimes annoyed at the extremists who run to the hills waiting to be whisked away, I believe a true study of end-times prophecies will change how people live. We are not to have our eyes so fixed on heaven that we're no earthly good. If we truly believe Christ will return someday, it should make us more aggressive and urgent in living out our faith, in being tolerant and loving and persuasive, but not holier-than-thou or condemning. We know not everyone will agree with us or accept our message or embrace Christ. But since we truly believe what

this will signify the beginning of something wonderful for all Americans, and the entire world. Praise God!
9/14/01 6:42 P.M. sheryn: I must say that I was very disheartened today. My Daughter came home from school upset, in   »

we're writing, we would be remiss not to at least clarify for people what the issues and choices are. If my neighbor honestly believed that wearing a purple necklace would save my soul, I would not likely believe him or take him seriously. But if he really believed that, I would be offended if he didn't at least tell me so I could decide whether there was any merit to his belief.

What role do you and Reverend LaHaye believe that you should play in helping people through these fears?
We hope that if nothing else, people will be led back to studying the Bible to see what it says about the end of time, and especially about the relationship between God and his creation. We believe there is a personal God who cares about every individual. We don't understand any more than anyone else does why he allows such tragedies, but we believe he is sovereign. He wants us to seek Him. He never promised to deliver us from trouble, but he does promise to be with us in trouble.

What is the ultimate message of the series?
That Jesus is coming back someday and that everyone has the opportunity to be ready. We're not saying we know better or that we have an inside track or that if a reader disagrees with us, he or she is less worthy a person. We're just saying, we've studied this, we believe it, at least investigate what the Bible says and make up your own mind.

JERRY B. JENKINS is the coauthor, with Tim LaHaye, of the best-selling *Left Behind* fiction series. He is author of more than 100 books and the former editor of *Moody* magazine; his writing has appeared in *Reader's Digest* and *Parade* magazine. Jenkins also writes the nationally syndicated sports story comic strip *Gil Thorp*.

---

tears and concerned. Apparently, a close friend of hers is of Middle Eastern descent. Can you imagine the look on my face when I heard that this little girl was spit on, tripped and harassed by her peers? This little child is a citizen of the U.S. She was

Our Estrangement from God
By Rabbi Michael Lerner

There is never any justification for acts of terror against innocent civilians—it is the quintessential act of dehumanization, one that does not recognize the sanctity of others. The violence being directed against Americans today, like the violence being directed against Israeli civilians by Palestinian terrorists, or the violence being directed against Palestinian civilians by the Israeli army occupying the West Bank and Gaza, seems to point to a world increasingly irrational and out of control.

It's understandable why many of us will feel anger. Demagogues will try to direct that anger at various "target groups" (Muslims are in particular danger, though Yassir Arafat and other Islamic leaders have unequivocally denounced these terrorist acts). The militarists will use this as a moment to call for increased defense spending at the expense of the needy. The right wing may even seek to limit civil liberties.

To counter that potential of mass panic, or the manipulation of our fear and anger for narrow political ends, a well-meaning media will instead try to narrow our focus solely on the task of finding and punishing the perpetrators. These people, of course, should be caught and punished.

But in some ways, this exclusive focus allows us to avoid dealing with the underlying issues. When violence becomes so prevalent throughout the planet, it's too easy to simply talk of "deranged minds." We need to ask ourselves, "What is it in the way that we are living, organizing our societies, and treating each other that makes violence seem plausible to so many people?"

It's true, but not enough, to say that the current violence is a reflection of our estrangement from God. More precisely, it is

wearing our flag on her. I was horrified and frankly disgusted.
9/14/01 9:23 P.M. Dobee: Our entire nation is still in a deep shock. We don't know how to stop the tears.
9/15/01 12:26 A.M. mujahid: In the name of Allah, the Benefi- >>

the way we fail to respond to each other as embodiments of the sacred. We may tell ourselves that the current violence has "nothing to do" with the way that we've learned to close our ears when told that one out of every three people on this planet does not have enough food, and that one billion are literally starving.

We may reassure ourselves that the hoarding of the world's resources by the richest society in world history and our frantic attempts to accelerate globalization with its attendant inequalities of wealth have nothing to do with the resentment that others feel toward us. We may tell ourselves that the suffering of refugees and the oppressed have nothing to do with us—that's a different story that is going on somewhere else. But we live in one world, increasingly interconnected with everyone, and the forces that lead people to feel outrage, anger, and desperation eventually impact our own daily lives.

When people have learned to desanctify each other, to treat each other as means to our own ends, to not feel the pain of those who are suffering, we end up creating a world in which these kinds of terrible acts of violence become more common. No one should use this as an excuse for these terrible acts of violence—the absolute quintessence of desanctification. I categorically reject any notion that violence is ever justified. It is always an act of desanctification, of not being able to see the divine in the other.

We should pray for the victims and the families of those who have been hurt or murdered in these crazy acts. Yet we should also pray that America does not return to "business as usual," but rather turns to a period of repentance and atonement, a turn in direction of our society at every level, a return to the most basic biblical ideal: that every human life is sacred, that "the

cient, the Merciful, I pray for all the men, women, and children who have lost their lives, as well as for those who were injured, in the horrific blasts today. May peace be upon the deceased and may the injured be healed. May the hatred of the terrorists

bottom line" should be the creation of a world of love and caring, and that the best way to prevent these kinds of acts is not to turn ourselves into a police state, but to turn ourselves into a society in which social justice, love, and compassion are so prevalent that violence becomes only a distant memory.

RABBI MICHAEL LERNER is the editor of *Tikkun* magazine and the author of numerous books, including *Jewish Renewal: A Path to Healing and Transformation.*

REPENT

By Frederica Mathewes-Green

Here's a checklist for post-9/11: Rescue survivors. Comfort the bereaved. Execute strategic response. Revise security protocols. Repent.

That last one clangs like a cymbal in a flute solo. We're Americans; when slapped by suffering, we get practical. We move ahead soberly and briskly, with confidence and resolve. Introspection isn't our style. A call to repentance may even seem cruel, as if it implied that this disaster was our own making. When we can see hard-faced mug shots of killers on TV, we're not confused about who the bad guys are.

Yet there's good spiritual precedent for taking a moment for reflection and assessment in any time of sorrow. The Hebrew scriptures show a consistent pattern: A devastating loss was a signal to repent, turn, and change. That didn't mean that the enemy was right or that God liked them better, just that it was time to learn a hard lesson.

A lesson, that is. The Bible wasn't talking about mere pun-

not spread to us and may innocent people not be wrongfully accused or harassed.
9/15/01 1:28 A.M. WillowWolf: ...The pledge means something different now to me and those I've talked to. Our flag »

ishment. The goal was renewal. As Ezekiel wrote, Jerusalem would fall to forces of sacrilege and terror, but the plan went further. The beloved people of God would be changed. "Thus says the Lord God: 'I will give them one heart, and put a new spirit within them; I will take the stony heart out of their flesh and give them a heart of flesh.'"

For us, some of this assessment began instantly and without too much pondering. It was obvious that now was not the most tasteful time to release a Schwarzenegger flick about a man avenging the death of his family at the hands of terrorists. Likewise pulled: a hip-hop CD cover that showed the artist about to detonate the World Trade Center. For the past week, entertainment violence has not been included in the category of general fun. We've had decades of peace and plenty, and the persistent human need for thrills was met by lots of spatter. When the real thing comes, it makes playacting look stupid.

Since entertainment drives our culture, it's not surprising that this would be the first noticeable arena of change. Let's push it further. Can we ditch the reality TV shows now? As a friend of mine said, "I don't want to turn on the TV and see real people being unhappy."

In fact, let's dump entertainment based on insult, loss, and ridicule. Smart-mouthed sitcom kids and their potty-mouthed parents just aren't funny any more, not when families have been ripped to shreds. There used to be other kinds of humor—sheer silliness and absurdity, the Marx Brothers and screwball comedies. Does anybody remember how to do that any more?

The same thing goes for the visual arts. How about this: no more rotting carcasses encased in glass. No more stuff designed merely to shock. We've seen the truly shocking now and it's not a game. Get over the idea that art must be ugly in order to be

means something different now too, to those, like me, who didn't completely notice before. I am thankful for the fact that I understand this now. We are more of one nation now then ever before, one people too. Let us hope it stays that way, and our

true. Most generations before us have had the idea that truth was connected to beauty. We're hungry for some beauty now.

And can we stop being ironic? Can we just say what we mean, instead of saying it backward for the sake of sarcasm? Wouldn't it be refreshing if people were just genuine?

This attitude adjustment is broad but not deep. Let's go further. Can we do a better job of protecting the innocence of children? It's tragic that even 7-year-old girls are trained to think of themselves as tempting. They deserve better than this. Can we see their purity as something beautiful and precious, and protect it?

At this point we reach touchy topics, things on which Americans have disagreed for a long time. Perhaps we can agree, though, that something has been out of order, something has been sick, with the way things stand. We'd gotten complacent about it; we'd even taken sneaky pleasure in things ugly and sick because our safe lives were so boring. Maybe this sudden battering will wake us, to lay aside old feuds and work together for the kind of society our nation deserves—something healthy, loving, and fine. If so, we can glean good in the midst of tragedy and crush our enemies' hopes. We can say to them the words of Joseph: "As for you, you meant evil against me, but God meant it for good."

FREDERICA MATHEWES-GREEN is a writer, renowned thinker, and member of the Eastern Orthodox Church.

understanding stands solid.
9/15/01 4:11 A.M. henryvii: There is a difference between anger and hatred. Make sure that you, as a Christian, don't step over that line between anger and hatred. Just remember that we »

BREAKING THE CYCLE
By Paul Rogat Loeb

It's hard to look deep into our souls. It's harder still when we feel profoundly violated, when the boundaries of our world have instantly crumbled. But we need to look deep if we want more than revenge for the crimes that killed more than 6,000 innocent people. As citizens, we must help prevent these kinds of horrors from continuing, generation after generation, in the United States or any other place on this Earth.

Our president has called this "a war between good and evil." He vows to "rid the world of evildoers." Overwhelmed with outrage and loss and wanting to feel united, most Americans cheer him on. The attacks were evil—unequivocally so. Nothing could ever justify them. Yet U.S. policies may have sowed some of the seeds for this terrible day. And we can't afford to fuel the cycles of indiscriminate violence. To help prevent still more innocent deaths, we need to use the lessons of what happened to chart a different path. The future depends not only on our government's actions but also on our own, as individual citizens.

For all our anger and sorrow, and for all the monstrous and inexcusable deeds of the hijackers, we still need to ask what made them so bitterly despairing that they were willing to murder thousands in the name of their cause. Even as we work to bring them to justice, it's not naïve to ask what made them act as they did. It's essential for breaking the endless cycles of vengeance.

A few months back, I read a newspaper article about a Palestinian terrorist. He crossed the Israeli border and blew himself up along with a group of Israelis. Originally an apolitical man, he worked as a jailor, assigned to guard a top official from one of the militant West Bank groups. The two became friends, but

are just as bad as the terrorists that perpetrated these terrible acts. While we were still sinners, Christ Died for us. God was so merciful that even when we killed his only begotten son, he forgave us and reaches out to us, to give us an oppurtunity to be

the jailor remained uninterested in politics. Then an Israeli bomb blew up his friend. The jailor lost hope, abandoning everything but retribution. He took his own life—and as many innocent Israeli lives as he could. They could have been my cousins in Tel Aviv.

Just as something turned this man, something turned the hijackers. Maybe it was watching corrupt dictatorships like Saudi Arabia inviting U.S. bases onto their soil. Maybe it was seeing Palestinians shot and bombed by Israeli soldiers with American backing. Maybe it was the Gulf War and the one million Iraqis who have died because the war and our continuing embargo have destroyed their most basic health and sanitation systems. Or our bombing of Sudan's only pharmaceutical factory, on what turned out to be false charges that it was producing biological weapons and was tied to Osama bin Laden.

The ordinary Americans whose inexcusable deaths rend our hearts may have died in part because of our own government's past actions. As always, the sins of the fathers are visited upon the innocents. Unless we create a more just world, desperate men from voiceless communities will continue to destroy more innocent lives, here and abroad.

How then, as citizens, do we respond? In a crisis of this magnitude, people understandably want to unite. I see flags and red, white, and blue ribbons on houses and cars, purses, and persons. The flags are a way for people to say their spirits won't be cowed and to do something tangible, along with donating blood, supplies, and money. But they can also promote a self-righteous crusade of good versus evil.

I saw this on a beach near my Seattle neighborhood, where people had surrounded our local 10-foot-tall version of the Statue of Liberty with an impromptu shrine commemorating the dead. They'd left candles and flowers, crosses and American

with him forever in heaven. I ask you to pray for the terrorists and their families, that they'll realize God's love for them.
9/15/01 4:54 A.M. Spider2k99: Everywhere I turn, I see the stars and stripes a-flying. I can't describe the pride that swells >>

flags, peace signs, a New York City firefighter's shirt, and messages of mourning. But then a fundamentalist megachurch descended to hold a rally, overwhelming the original circle of diverse messages with new ones proclaiming, "An eye for an eye" and "Kill a terrorist for Jesus!"

If we feel like wearing or flying the flag, we should. But maybe we need to display it next to banners or buttons asking for true justice, not vengeance. And ribbons of mourning that recognize our common humanity—even with the men who lost theirs by being so tangled with rage that they didn't care who they killed.

It's tempting to say that in a time like this, we need to trust our national leaders. They're probably right that some force will be needed to apprehend the perpetrators of these inconceivable crimes. But our responses need to focus on individuals, not populations. And proceed in a way that gives them the broadest possible legitimacy, including in the communities from which the bombers were recruited. Think of Iran, and the delicate path toward democratization pursued by reformer Mohammad Khatami. Bomb enough Islamic civilians, and his already-beleaguered regime will surely fall, replaced by the Ayatollahs. Think of Pakistan, with its nuclear capabilities. If we don't proceed with caution, acknowledging past misdeeds, we'll only incite more terrorists. No one could argue with the trial of the bombers who destroyed the Pan Am jet over Lockerbie, Scotland. They blew up innocent people. They were tried with full due process. Their jailing created no more martyrs or cycles of hatred.

I don't intend to encourage self-righteousness among those of us who question our government's response (God knows we all need humility now), but to describe the real context in which we act. For it's going to be up to ordinary citizens to raise the hard issues, including which crises we consider urgent.

Congress authorized $40 billion to rebuild New York and beef

in me when I see all the flags flapping in the breeze. Every house down every block ... multiple cars ... all showing their patriotism, not because some holiday requires it, but because they realize what it means to be American.

up antiterrorist security. Much of this investment is appropriate. But why have we chosen not to make other investments addressing crises equally real? According to Bread for the World, six million children die every year of hunger-related causes in developing countries—the equivalent of three World Trade Center attacks every day. For an annual appropriation of $13 billion—that's a third of what our Congress just authorized, or 5 percent of our existing $260 billion defense budget—we could meet the basic health and nutrition needs of the world's poorest people every year. I cite these examples not to diminish the horror of these unjustifiable attacks, but to stress that all shattered lives are just as real, and to ask why some cataclysms disturb us so little.

I fear that this tragedy will pave the way for needless and provocative military buildups and interventions that will spawn further spirals of vengeance.

But it doesn't have to be this way. Imagine if these terrible events inspired us all to take on the difficult work of creating a more just world, and making the necessary common investments so indiscriminate violence and needless suffering do not prevail.

The crisis has already produced a wealth of individual acts of courage and compassion. We saw tremendous heroism in the firefighters, police officers, and ordinary citizens who gave their lives trying to help others live. We've seen an outpouring of personal generosity: people giving blood, comforting their neighbors, collecting supplies. American Christians and Jews have held vigils to help protect threatened mosques, and a Jewish family volunteered to walk with a Muslim woman who felt threatened just stepping outside. For the moment, we're common mourners: People seem careful, vulnerable, and extraordinarily kind to each other. These events just might be able to break us away from our gated communities of the heart.

9/15/01 7:19 A.M. acamp4boys: Yahweh, Allah, Lord Jesus Christ, be with us! Bring us comfort, peace, and justice. Deliver us from evil and lead us not into temptation. Your will be done. amen.
9/15/01 10:12 A.M. theinterpreter: Our blessed Lord and   >>

But by itself, individual compassion won't create a just world. To do that requires asking what common choices would respect the humanity of all human beings—and then working to make those choices a reality.

This means acting in common, raising our voices, continuing to speak out no matter how hard it becomes. We need to be kind to ourselves and nurture our souls while we act: whether through walking in nature, playing with children, dancing to music, or communing with our God and the people we love. We also need to take public action—including reaching out to those who disagree with us on how to respond to this brutal cataclysm. Because from what I've observed, there's ample common ground once we make clear we share the goal of preventing these horrors from continuing to be visited on innocent humans again. We need to act with enough faith and strength to keep on raising the difficult questions, demanding paths that are both just and wise.

If we really raise the hard questions, we'll probably take some heat and be called some names. It might help to carry flags at our vigils and protests, since true patriotism requires taking responsibility for the choices of our nation.

We can never know every facet of this situation. We will not know every detail of how our government responds. We may not know whether our actions will prevail. But we need to speak out, whatever the obstacles or costs, for our own human dignity. And also because this is the only way that the cycles of vengeance have a chance of finally ending.

PAUL ROGAT LOEB is the author of *Soul of a Citizen* (www.soulofacitizen.org) and three other books on citizen involvement with war, peace, and social justice issues.

> Savior, who promised to not bring peace but a sword (Matthew 10:34), I pray not for peace but for war as also all the martyrs in heaven pray, that their deaths may be avenged (Revelation 6:9,10), and that this remaining face of evil be wiped out.

Chapter 10
FROM
THE ASHES

Mother of waters,
Father of rain,
You have taken back your own.
As a stream flows into a river,
as a river flows into the sea, may spirit flow
to the waters of healing,
to the waters of rebirth.
—Pagan Book of Living and Dying

GOD STILL ANSWERS PRAYERS
By Bruce Wilkinson

The horror of the terrorist attacks on September 11 is indelibly etched in the hearts and souls of all Americans. Who of us will ever be able to forget the image of hijacked passenger airliners diving into the Twin Towers, the Pentagon, or the hills of Pennsylvania? Or the thousands of innocent lives lost, and the painful shredding of our national sense of well-being? It's a calamity that none of us could have imagined only a short time ago.

Are goodness and hope and God to be found in the ashes? I believe so. Certainly, for those most directly affected, it may be too soon to believe any answers or to receive any comfort. But I believe that answers and comfort will come. As a nation, we've only begun to emerge from the shock, and the grief and loss will be with us for years. Yet for every life lost, we're already seeing thousands upon thousands of acts of heroism and generosity.

These are times that strip away the places, feelings, routines, and assumptions that had seemed most real to us and had been most often the measure of our wealth. We're left feeling impoverished, vulnerable, and perhaps abandoned by God. Feeling, in other words, utterly mortal.

These are times when we turn to prayer. And in that turning I find great hope. My friend Max Lucado wrote recently, "This is a different country than it was a week ago. We're not as self-centered as we were. We're not as self-reliant as we were. Hands are out. Knees are bent. This is not normal. And I have to ask the question, 'Do we want to go back to normal?' Perhaps the best response to this tragedy is to refuse to go back to normal."

I agree with Max. In fact, these are times when "normal" living and real prayer flourish best. Each time we sing "God Bless America," the nation is crying out for God's blessings and favor

---

9/15/01 10:56 A.M. solmcdonald: In the name of God, who is the God of Abraham, Isaac, and Jacob, Who gave his revelation upon Mt. Sinai through your prophet Moses. You are the one who affirms life, and you create the wonders of the universe.

and help. Though we might wish them to be, God's blessings are not an insurance policy against the sufferings and tragedies that exist in our fallen world. The Apostle Peter advised, "Do not think it strange concerning the fiery trial which is to try you, as though some strange thing happened to you" (I Peter 4:12).

But the experience of such pain doesn't mean we aren't also able to experience God's blessings. When we're in the midst of these sufferings, our Heavenly Father longs to pour out his supernatural favor on all who are willing to ask. If ever people from all walks of life sense a need for divine aid and blessing, it is now.

For Christians who are sensing a new readiness to live out their faith, this is a most promising moment. By God's grace and power, now is the time to step up to a larger life of ministry and impact for eternity. Jesus' passion was that his disciples would bless the whole world—people of every race and creed and circumstance. Our passion can be for nothing less.

That's why it's so heartening to see churches, communities, and individuals rising to incredible feats of service. And as we stretch beyond our comfort zones in God's service, we discover that his hand is available to empower us. I recall an example from the Old Testament of how God works through us in desperate times. Many years after Jerusalem had been left in ruins by enemy forces, it fell to a man named Zerubbabel to lead in the effort to rebuild the city. When he balked at the task, God reminded him that he would succeed "not by might nor by power, but by My Spirit." Therefore, I encourage Christians everywhere to pray boldly, not only for significant ministry in Jesus' name but also for the power of the Spirit to accomplish it.

Last, since we do not know where or when evil forces may strike again, I urge you to continue to pray that God will keep us from evil. Ultimately, only God has the power to keep violence

Shower us with your compassion in this dark hour, grant us your mercy as we move forward from this unholy tragedy.
Barukh Atah Adonai, Elohenu Melek Ha-ol am.
9/15/01 1:23 P.M. andyjo: Lord God help me and others know >>

and hatred on this scale from succeeding. We must plead, then, for protection from the evil that is now so nakedly apparent—in the world, in others, and in our own hearts.

One comfort for Christians at times like this is that our faith is matter-of-fact about evil. The Bible calls it sin. We know that it is real and ubiquitous on this planet, and that our Savior came to rescue us from its grip now and from its consequences for eternity. In fact, the night before Jesus gave himself up as a sacrifice for our rescue, he comforted his friends with spiritual advice that was large enough to account for both the joy and horror in life. He said, "I have told you these things, so that in me you may have peace. In this world you will have trouble. But take heart! I have overcome the world."

Despite our sorrows, I urge you to remember that what counts most hasn't changed at all since September 11. Truth is still truth. Love still endures (and ultimately wins over hatred). And God still answers prayer. Join with me and millions of others in beseeching him for peace, justice, and healing for our nation and our world.

BRUCE WILKINSON is the author of *The Prayer of Jabez* and *Secrets of the Vine*, which are *New York Times* bestsellers.

AN EARLY ATTEMPT AT GRATITUDE
By Brother David Steindl-Rast

Imagine a country whose citizens—maybe even its leaders—are brave, calm, and open toward each other; a country whose people realize that all human beings belong together as one family and must act accordingly; a country guided by common

that just because i cannot smile more than just a few seconds—i will again smile. because i can not sing with joy, my heart will again soar.. Lord show us that these tears although bitter are the waters of growth...

sense. To the extent to which we show ourselves not hateful but grateful, this becomes reality.

But gratefulness? The very word seems utterly out of place, even offensive, under the given circumstances. And yet, that we speak of "given" circumstances is significant. Whatever is given is a gift; and the appropriate response to any gift is gratitude. But what could be the gift in this case?

The gift we were given by the wake-up call of September 11 is an unprecedented opportunity: to wake up, wake up to the madness of violence and counterviolence. What happened to New York and Washington was as much and as little a first as what happened to Hiroshima and Nagasaki. After all, we witnessed merely the most recent link in a chain of revenge for revenge. This recent retaliation is certainly not the first, but it gives us a unique opportunity to wake up and to make it the last.

Strange though it is, many of us were able to ignore the vicious circle of violence against violence—our own and that of others—as long as it was happening far away. We were asleep. This was a rough awakening. What now? We can show ourselves grateful for the wake-up call by staying awake, by acting wakefully. A danger recognized and faced is cut in half. The danger is violence, regardless who commits it—terrorists or legitimate governments. No rhetoric, no posturing can any longer obscure the fact that violence breeds violence. We must break that cycle of madness.

Violence has its roots in every heart. It is in my own heart that I must recognize fear, agitation, coldness, alienation, and the impulse to blind anger. Here in my heart I can turn fear into courageous trust, agitation and confusion into stillness, isolation into a sense of belonging, alienation into love, and irrational reaction into common sense. The creative imagination of

9/15/01 5:54 P.M. Johanna4: Our country was founded on the principles of faith, survival and Love of God. For surely what has happened is that the wisdom of Love has been woken up by the dagger of evil going into the heart of all Americans. We are >>

gratefulness will suggest to each one of us how to go about this task. I will list here five small gestures that have helped me personally show my gratitude for the wake-up call and stay awake.

All gratitude expresses trust. Suspicion will not even recognize a gift as gift: Who can prove that it isn't a lure, a bribe, a trap? Gratefulness has the courage to trust and so overcomes fear. The air has been electrified by fearfulness these days, a fearfulness fostered and manipulated by politicians and the media. There lies our greatest danger: Fear perpetuates violence. Mobilize the courage of your heart, as the truly awake ones are doing. Say one word today that gives a fearful person courage.

Because gratitude expresses courage, it spreads calm. Calm of this kind is quite compatible with deep emotions. In fact, the mass hysteria rampant all around betrays confusion rather than deep feeling—superficial agitation rather than a deep current of compassion. Join the truly compassionate ones who are calm and strong. From the stillness of your heart's core reach out. Calmly hold someone's hand today and spread calm.

When you are grateful, your heart is open—open toward others, open for surprise. In the days since the wake-up call, we have seen remarkable examples of this openness: strangers helping strangers often in heroic ways. Others turn away, isolate themselves, dare even less than at other times to look at each other. Violence begins with isolation. Break this pattern. Make contact—eye contact, at least—with people whom you normally ignore: the agent at the toll booth, the parking lot attendant, someone on the elevator. Look a stranger in the eyes today and realize that there are no strangers.

You can feel either grateful or alienated, but never both at the same time. Gratefulness drives out alienation; there is not room for both in the same heart. When you are grateful, you know that you belong to a network of give-and-take, and you say "yes"

more united, more giving, more kind and more inclined to pray than ever before. And that is a wonderful gift that has come from an evil act. We have been woken up to Love on a universal, global community level. The deed, in that regard, gave us a blessing.

to that belonging. This "yes" is the essence of love. You need no words to express it; a smile will do to put your "yes" into action. Don't let it matter to you whether the other one smiles back. Give someone an unexpected smile today and so contribute your share to peace on Earth.

What your gratefulness does for you is as important as what it does for others. Gratefulness boosts your sense of belonging; your sense of belonging in turn boosts your common sense. Your "yes" to belonging attunes you to the common concerns shared by all human beings. We have only one enemy, our common enemy: violence. Common sense tells us: We can stop violence only by stopping to act violently; war is no way to peace. Listen to the news today and put at least one item to the test of common sense.

The five steps I am suggesting here are small, but they work. It helps that they are small: Anyone can take them. Imagine a country whose citizens—maybe even its leaders—are brave, calm, and open toward each other; a country whose people realize that all human beings belong together as one family and must act accordingly; a country guided by common sense. To the extent to which we show ourselves not hateful but grateful, this becomes reality. Who would have foreseen that gratitude could shine forth with such new brightness in these dark days? May it light our way.

BROTHER DAVID STEINDL-RAST, O.S.B., is a Benedictine monk and the author of many books, including *Gratefulness, The Heart of Prayer*. His Web site is www.gratefulness.org.

9/15/01 10:44 P.M. CatRescuer: God please be with us and watch over us. Please console the people who are looking for loved ones. I pray for a miracle. Please let the people who did this come to the realization that they have done wrong.   >>

LOVING-KINDNESS
By Sharon Salzberg·

Loving-kindness, or *metta* meditation, is a traditional Buddhist practice that helps us to move from a sense of dislocation and isolation into a more true sense of connection with ourselves and, ultimately, with all beings everywhere.

It's traditionally taught with three other practices; namely, compassion; sympathetic joy, feeling delighted in another's happiness rather than feeling jealous; and equanimity or balance of mind. All four of these qualities can be experienced within any one of them. Loving-kindness, for example, has strands of compassion, sympathetic joy, and equanimity within it.

One of the confusions about loving-kindness is that the word is not very common, which is a shame. Often the word *metta* is translated as "love," which is also confusing. Sometimes when we say "love," we mean attachment or an exchange of some sort, such as: "I will love you as long as you love me in return or as long as the following 15 conditions are met." Sometimes we mean a kind of sentimentality, which isn't willing to open up to pain, dislocation, and torment.

Metta doesn't refer to either one of those conditions. The literal translation of the word is "friendship." So *metta* means knowing how to be a friend to ourselves and a friend to all of life. Its foundation is connection.

So because loving-kindness meditation deals with a sense of dislocation, it is a highly appropriate practice for the situation we find ourselves in today. I had an acupuncture treatment three days after the September 11 event. When the acupuncturist put a needle in me, it hurt so much I practically leaped off the table. I asked her, "What point was that?" And she said, "That's the getting-back-into-your-body point." I was in shock, as were

9/15/01 11:58 P.M. irism1: Lady catch my tears and place them in our ocean of sorrow that I may not sorrow alone. Give me strength to maintain a forgiving heart and open mind in the face of such hatred. Let our love touch the hearts of those who

many people. Now it's a process of coming home to ourselves, coming home to a deeper sense of community.

It's also coming back to being in the moment, because all of those states of mind that we experienced—fear, anxiety, dread, grief—take us out of the moment: We either ruminate about the past or project into the future.

There's a great quote from Mark Twain, who said, "Some of the worst things in my life never happened." Truly terrible things *have* happened, but our minds spin out into the future and we create some kind of certainty about the terrible truth of tomorrow. We need to come back into the moment to enter a way full of wisdom that accepts the uncertainty of things.

The *metta* meditation. Loving-kindness begins with ourselves. It's a tremendous sense of tenderness and care for ourselves, which is not our usual way of being. The classical progression of this meditation is that we begin the practice first toward ourselves, opening to and befriending all aspects of ourselves, not just those parts we like or that we present to the world, but even those things we'd rather keep hidden or those things that we have a vague knowledge of.

So we practice by repeating certain phrases: "May I be happy" or "May I be peaceful," but the content of the phrases isn't so important; it's the aiming of the mind toward embracing one's self.

Then we go from there to repeating the phrases for someone called a benefactor, someone who has been generous toward or inspired us. Someone we respect, someone we feel grateful for.

Then we move to a friend; then to a neutral person, someone we don't strongly like or dislike. In our society, it would be somebody who serves a kind of function in our lives, like the checkout person at the supermarket, someone whom we see from time to time but don't have a particular feeling about.

The next step is offering loving-kindness to someone with

grieve. Blessed be.
9/16/01 12:28 A.M. brian_allen: When I saw the terrible events Tuesday morning, I knew allies would support us. When I realized war was on the way, I knew there would be allies to fight >>

whom we have difficulty. This is a very tricky and complicated thing because we're not aiming for a state of acquiescence or collusion or unwholesome action. The suggestion in the teaching is that you start with somebody that you have mild difficulty with. You don't begin with somebody who has hurt you, or has hurt the world really terribly. You begin with someone who annoys or irritates you. Part of the nature of the practice is developing confidence in the nature of love and our ability to love. If you find any one person or group of people too hard, it doesn't matter; just go back to someone who's easier.

There are ways of offering *metta* to different groups as long as you include pairs of opposites, like all females and all males. If you are partial toward one group, it doesn't matter. You just make a point of including both.

Then the next step is offering *metta* to all beings everywhere without distinction, without exception. There's a great line from poet Wendell Berry, in which he says, "The smallest unit of health is a community." And health, of course, means healing too. People are doing loving-kindness meditation everywhere for themselves and for what they consider their community.

The way to do this meditation is to sit quietly with your back erect. Sit comfortably with your eyes closed. Then choose three or four phrases that express what you wish most deeply for yourself. Repeat them over and over, allowing your mind to rest in the phrases. Classical phrases are: "May I be happy." "May I be peaceful." "May I live with ease of heart." You can choose these or any others that work for you. Develop a rhythm and a cadence, a very gentle pacing.

Beginning with yourself, gently repeat the phrases without trying to force any particular kind of feeling. Rather, gather all of your energy behind each phrase, just one at a time. After a time, if you have someone who has been really good, kind, or

along with us. But I saw something else that I never expected. I saw and heard the U.S. national anthem played at Buckingham Palace in London. I saw children at a school in Asia standing at their desks with their heads bowed in silence. I saw a crowd of

inspiring, you can visualize them or say their name to yourself, get a feeling for their presence. Offer the phrases of loving-kindness to them, wishing for them just what it is you've wished for yourself.

Then move on to a friend, and after some time, a neutral person, then a mildly difficult person if you have somebody like that in your life. And then various groupings, all females, all males, all wise beings, all those in ignorance, whatever categories you would choose as long as you make the point of using pairs of opposites or complementary sets: those known to me, those unknown to me; those near, those far; those being born, those dying. Then, finally, all beings everywhere in all directions. All creatures in existence. "May they be happy. May they be peaceful. May they live with ease of heart." Just repeat the phrases of loving-kindness that you've chosen and extend them to all things everywhere without division, without exclusion.

At the end, there should there be a period of silence. Sit silently for a few moments.

Sharing merit. There's also another practice called sharing merit. Merit is a concept in Buddhism that every time we turn our mind toward the good, there's an energy created. Every act of generosity and kindness, even sitting down to meditate, generates positive energy. It's believed that the force of that energy is a conduit to those who have died. In traditional cultures like Burma, when somebody dies, the family will come to the monastery and feed the monks, then dedicate the merit of this gift to the person who has died. They share the merit of that action.

Once a friend of mine died before I went to sit a retreat. I told the teacher this on the first day, and he said, "Well, now you'll have to do the retreat for both of you." So every night, I did a sharing of the merit. You don't have to have spectacular medita-

thousands gathered at Brandenburg Gate in Germany paying respects to the U.S. and those who died in the attacks. I saw people in Australia in tears. I saw people in Israel in prayer. I saw a huge crowd of people gathered before Saint Peter's   >>

tions, just the fact that you did it generates merit. It's like aligning yourself with an energy of goodness. Throughout the retreat, I would dedicate my meditations to him and to all things everywhere.

Just like with the *metta* meditation, you start with people who have helped you in some way. You say, "May so-and-so be happy. May they be peaceful." Then you move to those who have died, those who are suffering, and then you include all things everywhere. You can create your own progression, whatever seems right.

Our heavenly messenger. The Buddha, before his enlightenment, was living a luxurious life in his father's palace. His father pampered him because he didn't want him to leave home and look for a deeper truth, a deeper sense of happiness. He tried to have him avoid the sight of suffering at all costs. According to the legend, when the Buddha left the palace at the age of 29, he saw a sick person, an old person, a corpse, and a mendicant monk. One corpse was his wake-up call. That was his heavenly messenger, as they say in the classical tradition. That was enough for him to deeply question where the foundations of happiness could be found, and if there was something in life that wouldn't crumble, that wouldn't be destroyed no matter what else happened. September 11, 2001, was a giant heavenly messenger.

SHARON SALZBERG is cofounder of the Insight Meditation Society in Barre, Massachusetts. She is the author of several books, including *Lovingkindness: the Revolutionary Art of Happiness* and *A Heart as Wide as the World.*

Basilica in Rome. I saw the world observe three minutes of silence to remember the dead. I was stunned. I expected support from allies, but not like this. Not when there has been so much criticism directed at the United States in recent years. Not with

What Good Can Come from this Evil?
By the Reverend William Webber

It has been amazing. "Today our nation saw evil," President Bush told the country on September 11. He reported that thousands of lives were "suddenly ended by evil, despicable acts of terror." There has been blanket coverage by the media, with newscasters relaying every detail of the horrific events as soon as they were known.

Perhaps even more amazing has been the constant counterpoint that has often become the dominant theme: that from this evil, good will come. President Bush affirmed this truth, stating that the intended goal of the terrorists will fail; that the United States will emerge united, stronger, and better after this carnage. Again and again the belief that good will come from this evil has been repeated by public officials, commentators, rescue workers, and ordinary citizens.

What good can come from this evil? The fact that we are asking this question is in itself a tremendous benefit. Every one of us faces problems and difficulties in our lives, some minor and some life-threatening. Because we have heard this axiom so often in the light of the tragedies of that week, people today more than ever are confronting their own life situations, asking, "What good can come from this?" What a tremendous shift of paradigms!

I asked a group of fifth- and sixth-grade children, "What good has come from this evil?" "People are more generous," they replied. On television they had seen the professional rescue workers joined by volunteers, even though it meant they were risking their lives. The children were aware of the many ways people were working together to aid the victims and their families and the countless others whose lives were impacted in

the increasing hatred of our country. I never would have expected this. I was moved to tears. I believe it is time to be a little more humble in our attitudes toward the rest of the world. They are indeed our friends. »

New York and Washington. But they had also told me that people around them had become more helpful and generous. Was their observation correct? Yes! Several studies by psychologists have uniformly documented that people observing someone being a good Samaritan were more likely to help another person they saw in need. A carefully crafted, groundbreaking study by psychologist Jon Haidt found that spectators who simply observed someone who helped another received feelings of "elevation." What we have seen in the wake of recent terrorism bears this out.

People have had strong feelings of anger, hurt, sorrow, and grief because of the carnage. At the same time, in response to seeing the selfless acts and heroism of many, people have experienced feelings of elevation. The observation of the children was accurate. People across the nation are being both more generous and more helpful and feeling better. The cruel acts of terrorists have had the unexpected result of creating a kinder, more caring American populace.

Suddenly things have been put in a different perspective. As we have listened to reports of the last conversations from the hijacked planes or the Twin Towers, we have been reminded of the importance of families. Not just the families of the victims. We have been jolted to a new awareness of the importance of our own families. Even when we knew our family members were not in any of the cities where the destruction had reigned, we felt it was important to call. A teen told me he was aware that those in his home had become more sensitive, more caring. Parents were trying to find the words to explain the events to their children. For many, this was the first serious conversation families have had for a long time. Sometimes words failed, and the family members were silent—but there was a togetherness in their si-

9/16/01 3:00 P.M. subhalakshmi: Om Shanti, Shanti, Shanti
May Lord Siva grant us peace in this time of destruction.
9/16/01 9:52 P.M. katkar2: Dear Lord, I pray for all the victims of
the past weeks terrorist acts. I know heaven has some pretty

lence. One mother told me, "We sat on the floor, just holding hands and praying. It's the first time we have done that."

A nurse in the cardiac intensive care unit observed a great difference. Usually many of the heart patients are in denial about the seriousness of their condition, but as they watched the continuing coverage on television they were impressed with the suddenness of life and death. Patients with tears in their eyes began to deal honestly with their own mortality in a healthy way, speaking openly with the medical staff about their concerns, rearranging their priorities, and accepting the necessary changes in regimen.

Outside the hospital, ordinary folks in every walk of life report that they have new feelings of thanksgiving for life itself. No longer taken for granted, each day is viewed as a gift, and individuals are discovering the joy of grateful living.

In villages and cities across America there are new feelings of community. Many people told me that neighbors are talking to neighbors with whom they never passed the time of day. In the office, people who were barely acquaintances are showing concern for each other. Neighborhoods are pulling together. There is a new sense of camaraderie. Flags are being flown from houses and on autos. Candlelight vigils are being held. Donors spend hours in line to give blood.

There has been a new national unity. Democrats and Republicans are working together in a common cause. People at every level are pulling together. Despite frequent warnings that the war against terrorists may be long and require sacrifice, the response of people in general is that Americans do better in hard times. In the face of the prospect of fewer material advantages, they see a return to the more basic moral and spiritual values.

Americans are a religious people, with the overwhelming

terrific angels right about now.
9/17/01 1:02 A.M. CatRescuer: God please help us in this moment of fear. Please be with us and help us get through this. Please comfort us and ease our minds. Be with the victims.   >>

majority professing faith in God. During this time of national emergency the houses of worship have been filled. Those in grief have found solace and comfort in faith. Others have found strength and courage to face an uncertain future. And it has not only been individuals and communities of faith that have turned to religion. In a real sense it has been a national response. The nation watched as the leaders of the country gathered in the National Cathedral for an ecumenical service. Billy Graham and other religious leaders sounded a call to righteousness as well as the benefits of trust in Almighty God. A national Day of Prayer was observed. Clergy of all faiths were prominent in the news coverage. Many believe this may be the beginning of the turning of a nation from materialism to a new spirituality.

There has been a tremendous international response. In this time, when the United States was seen as vulnerable, nations of the world have responded. In our time of need, envy has been replaced with sympathy. Especially since the citizens of many nations perished at the World Trade Center, this event has been seen not only as an American tragedy but also as a global problem. No program, however worthy, has brought so many nations together as the need to combat global terrorism.

THE REVEREND WILLIAM D. WEBBER has been an American Baptist pastor for 40 years and is the author of *A Rustle of Angels* and *How to Become a Sweet Old Lady instead of a Grumpy Old Grouch.*

Please help us, I'm begging you
9/17/01 10:17 A.M. kitcando: Believe it or not I have prayed for bin Laden. But in all honesty I must say this put my mind & emotions to quite a challenge and task! When I pray I try to be

DENY THEM THEIR VICTORY
Interfaith Statement

This statement was delivered on September 20, 2001, to every Congressional office and to the White House. Signers from the Christian community include Protestant, Roman Catholic, Evangelical, Orthodox, Historic Black Church, and Historic Peace Church traditions. The breadth of participation has made the document one of the most inclusive religious statements ever released.

We, American religious leaders, share the broken hearts of our fellow citizens. The worst terrorist attack in history that assaulted New York City, Washington, D.C., and Pennsylvania, has been felt in every American community. Each life lost was of unique and sacred value in the eyes of God, and the connections Americans feel to those lives run very deep. In the face of such a cruel catastrophe, it is a time to look to God and to each other for the strength we need and the response we will make. We must dig deep to the roots of our faith for sustenance, solace, and wisdom.

First, we must find a word of consolation for the untold pain and suffering of our people. Our congregations will offer their practical and pastoral resources to bind up the wounds of the nation. We can become safe places to weep and secure places to begin rebuilding our shattered lives and communities. Our houses of worship should become public arenas for common prayer, community discussion, eventual healing, and forgiveness.

Second, we offer a word of sober restraint as our nation discerns what its response will be. We share the deep anger

honest with all my emotions whatever they may be. Because I realize if not, I am only fooling myself for God already knows what lies within more than I am probably aware of myself. So, upon first doing so it was very difficult. What do you pray   >>

toward those who so callously and massively destroy innocent lives, no matter what the grievances or injustices invoked. In the name of God, we too demand that those responsible for these utterly evil acts be found and brought to justice. Those culpable must not escape accountability. But we must not, out of anger and vengeance, indiscriminately retaliate in ways that bring on even more loss of innocent life. We pray that President Bush and members of Congress will seek the wisdom of God as they decide upon the appropriate response.

Third, we face deep and profound questions of what this attack on America will do to us as a nation. The terrorists have offered us a stark view of the world they would create, where the remedy to every human grievance and injustice is a resort to the random and cowardly violence of revenge—even against the most innocent. Having taken thousands of our lives, attacked our national symbols, forced our political leaders to flee their chambers of governance, disrupted our work and families, and struck fear into the hearts of our children, the terrorists must feel victorious.

But we can deny them their victory by refusing to submit to a world created in their image. Terrorism inflicts not only death and destruction but also emotional oppression to further its aims. We must not allow this terror to drive us away from being the people God has called us to be. We assert the vision of community, tolerance, compassion, justice, and the sacredness of human life, which lies at the heart of all our religious traditions. America must be a safe place for all our citizens in all their diversity. It is especially important that our citizens who share national origins, ethnicity, or religion with whoever attacked us are, themselves, protected among us.

for? His capture? His destruction? So many different things came flooding in and what would be right. What would Jesus do? So I had to peer very deep within my heart to know what plea to make and ask for. And in the end I leave justice in God's

Our American illusion of invulnerability has been shattered. From now on, we will look at the world in a different way, and this attack on our life as a nation will become a test of our national character. Let us make the right choices in this crisis—to pray, act, and unite against the bitter fruits of division, hatred, and violence. Let us rededicate ourselves to global peace, human dignity, and the eradication of injustice that breeds rage and vengeance.

As we gather in our houses of worship, let us begin a process of seeking the healing and grace of God.

Developed by DR. ROBERT EDGAR (National Council of Churches), the REVEREND JIM WALLACE (Sojourners), the REVEREND WESLEY GRANBERG-MICHAELSON (Reformed Church of America), RABBI DAVID SAPERSTEIN (Religious Action Center of Reform Judaism), DR. RON SIDER (Evangelicals for Social Action), in conjunction with Christian, Jewish, Muslim, and Buddhist clergy. As of September 26, there were 2,800 signatories.

hands and his will be done.
9/18/01 10:36 A.M. ashai: May the souls of the victims have Ushta, radiant happiness forever! May we all have unity through serenity!

ACKNOWLEDGMENTS

First and foremost, Rodale and Beliefnet would like to thank all the contributors for their generosity, their courage, their brilliance, and their honesty. As individuals, each has inspired us to do our best and as a collection, the effect is overwhelming.

The staff at Beliefnet and Rodale poured their hearts and souls into this book, and it has started a glorious partnership that will continue to flourish. Thanks to the Rodale family for making it possible and to Steve Murphy, Marc Jaffe, Peter Spiers, and Alan Klavans and Beliefnet's Gil Henry and Tony Uphoff who mastered the countless details that make a joint effort like this possible.

To the Beliefnet community staff who worked around the clock in the days after September 11 to provide a safe place for online prayer and conversation: Martha Ainsworth, Sabreen Ameen, Susan Byrne, Neal Christiansen, Kimberly Fath, Cheryl Fuller, Edward Gates, Mary Alice Kearns, Marcia Keller, Brenda Miklish, Ted Miklish, Naomi Naughton, Kim Nava, Jerry Osborne, Erin Pearson, Kristi Winters, Evan Weeks, Joe Zazulak, and to the Beliefnet community itself, who provided many of this book's richest insights.

To Beliefnet's managing producer for the book, Wendy Schuman, and to the editorial staff: Deborah Caldwell, Sharon Linnéa, Jonathan Lowet, Paul O'Donnell, Rebecca Phillips, Rhonda Roumani, Elizabeth Sams, Lisa Schneider, Laura Sheahen, Anne Simpkinson, Steven Waldman, Mary Wilk, and designer Bill Akunevicz Jr. They worked with skill and dedication under incredible time pressure and the emotional weight of life in New York City after the World Trade Center devastation.

To the tireless Rodale employees—editors, copy editors, designers, and production and layout staff—who met an insane deadline with passion and creativity: Stephanie Tade, Troy Juliar, Lisa Andruscavage, Jennifer Kushnier, Kathy Dvorsky, Neil Wertheimer, Rich Kershner, Joanna Williams, Bob Anderson, Jennifer Giandomenico, Jackie Dornblaser, Leslie Keefe, Dale

Mack, Diane Zero Meckel, Dan Shields, Eileen Bauder, and Jodi Schaffer. Special thanks also to Sindy Berner, Jodi Quick, Erin Douglas, Kristen Scott, Dan Elwood, Dawn Traub, Linda Rutenbar, Krissa Strauss, Andrea Hall, Karen Follweiler, Cara Hungerford, Jacqueline Shaw, Jeanne Dorney, Kathy DiCataldo, and Mike Hoye for their creative efforts.

To the magazine circulation and magazine production teams of *Prevention, Organic Gardening, Organic Style, Men's Health, Runner's World, Bicycling, Mountain Bike, Backpacker,* and *Scuba Diving,* who reshuffled their plans at the last minute to support this effort.

The Maple-Vail Book Manufacturing Group is pleased to participate in the manufacturing of this book. We send our prayers and sympathies to all families touched by this tragedy and hope that in some small way this book will bring comfort and spiritual renewal to the American people.

As a supplier of printing paper needs to Rodale Inc., the Atlantic Paper Company, its management, and employees are proud to participate in Rodale's request to help support the printing of From the Ashes: A Spiritual Response to the Attack on America. *May this book not only help to provide financial support for the charities assisting those directly involved but also serve as a source of strength, courage, and perseverance for all who read it.*

To those who were lost; to those who must now stand alone; to those who have worked so courageously; to those who will fight bravely, we are with you in spirit and will remember now and forever. —The people at Glatfelter Printing

Fortran Printing, Inc., is proud to contribute in the manufacturing of this publication. Our thoughts and prayers go out to the families and friends of all the victims and to the courageous rescue workers. God Bless America!

Special thanks to Harte-Hanks Print and Dearfield Associates, Inc., whose contributions helped make this book possible.

Thanks, most of all, to the Spirit that inspired this book.

APPLEWHITES
AT WIT'S END

Also by **STEPHANIE S. TOLAN**

···

SURVIVING THE APPLEWHITES

LISTEN!

WELCOME TO THE ARK

FLIGHT OF THE RAVEN

ORDINARY MIRACLES

THE FACE IN THE MIRROR

WHO'S THERE?

SAVE HALLOWEEN!

PLAGUE YEAR

A GOOD COURAGE

APPLEWHITES
AT WIT'S END

STEPHANIE S. TOLAN

HARPER

An Imprint of HarperCollins*Publishers*

Library of Congress Cataloging-in-Publication Data
Tolan, Stephanie S.
Applewhites at Wit's End / Stephanie S. Tolan. — 1st ed.
p. cm.
Summary: Great changes are in store for the highly creative
and somewhat eccentric Applewhite family when money
problems force them to open a summer camp for gifted children,
who almost immediately begin to rebel, while a mysterious
interloper watches from the woods.
ISBN 978-0-06-057938-8 (trade bdg.) — ISBN 978-0-06-057939-5
(lib. bdg.)
[1. Camps—Fiction. 2. Family life—North Carolina—Fiction.
3. Creative ability—Fiction. 4. Eccentrics and eccentricities—
Fiction. 5. North Carolina—Fiction.] I. Title.
PZ7.T5735App 2012   2011019388
[Fic]—dc23   CIP
                                                          AC

Typography by Erin Fitzsimmons
12 13 14 15 16   CG/RRDH   10 9 8 7 6 5 4 3 2 1
❖
First Edition

← County Road

Meadow

Pond

Wit's End Playhouse

Cottages

Lodge

Camp Eureka

Hal's Map of Wit's End

Acknowledgments
Thanks to Larry Michael
of the North Carolina Department
of Environment and Natural Resources
for a delightful and very helpful
conversation concerning
camp regulations!

Thanks to Katherine Paterson
for coming up with the name Furniture of the Absurd
for Archie's work as we were writing the dramatic
adaptation of *Surviving the Applewhites*. Archie is grateful, too.

To all the Yunasa campers,
past, present, and future—
thanks for your inspiration!

P.S. Any resemblance to persons
living or dead is purely coincidental!

FAMILY
TREE

Sybil Jameson	Randolph Applewhite
WIFE	SON

Cordelia	Hal
DAUGHTER	SON

Edith (E.D.)	Destiny
DAUGHTER	SON

Zedediah
Applewhite
PATRIARCH

Archie
Applewhite
SON

Lucille
Applewhite
WIFE

Jake
Semple
BY INVITATION

The Cast of

APPLEWHITES AT WIT'S END

Permanent Residents of Wit's End

HUMAN

E.D. (Edith) Applewhite–
age thirteen, well organized and reliable
(the only noncreative member of the family),
third child of Randolph and Sybil

Randolph Applewhite–
professional theater director, husband of Sybil
and father of the four Applewhite children

Jake Semple–
age fourteen, the bad kid from the city,
the only non-Applewhite student at the family's
home school, the Creative Academy

Sybil Jameson–
author of the Petunia Grantham mystery novels, wife
of Randolph and mother of the Applewhite children

Destiny Applewhite–
age five, highly creative, extremely talkative,
youngest Applewhite child

Zedediah Applewhite–
patriarch of the Applewhite family, maker
of fine furniture, father of Randolph and Archie,
grandfather of the children

Archie Applewhite–
creator of Furniture of the Absurd, husband of
Lucille and uncle of the children

Lucille Applewhite–
poet, wife of Archie, aunt of the children,
sometime mystic and photographer

Cordelia Applewhite–
age seventeen, dancer-choreographer,
eldest Applewhite child

Hal Applewhite–
age sixteen, sculptor, painter, seriously
introverted second Applewhite child

OTHERS

Winston–
highly sensitive and slightly
overweight basset hound

Paulie–
Zedediah's adopted parrot, known for his
impressive vocabulary of curse words

Wolfbane (Wolfie)–
exceedingly bad-tempered male member
of Lucille's pair of rescue goats

Witch Hazel (Hazel)–
gentle and unassuming female goat

EUREKA! CAMPERS

Ginger Boniface–
age eleven, the green twin, poet

Cinnamon Boniface–
age eleven, the blue twin

Harley Schobert–
age twelve, son of indie rock stars, photographer

David Giacomo–
age fourteen, "angel" and Renaissance man

Quincy (Q) Brown–
age thirteen, dancer, singer, swimmer,
talent show winner

Samantha Peterman–
age twelve, passionate reader, visual artist

ASSORTED MINOR CHARACTERS

Bruno–
the Boniface chauffeur

Mrs. Montrose–
telephone voice, bane of Randolph's existence

Marlie Michaels–
Harley's considerably tattooed mother, lead singer of
Dragon's Blood

Mrs. Giacomo–
David's elegant mother

Mystery Driver of Plain Black Sedan

Daryl Gaffney–
telephone voice, assistant at the North Carolina
Department of Environment and Natural Resources

Chapter One

I t was a dark and stormy night when Randolph
Applewhite arrived home from New York to
announce the end of the world. The whole family
plus Jake Semple, the extra student at their home
school, the Creative Academy, were gathered at the
time around the fireplace in the living room of the
main house at Wit's End, while a wind howled and
snow swirled against the windows.

Like everyone else, E.D. had at first taken her father's
announcement to be hyperbole—one of her vocabulary
words for that week, which meant "deliberate and

obvious exaggeration for effect." A famous theater director, Randolph Applewhite had a habit of making exactly this announcement whenever something—almost anything—went wrong with a project of his and he felt the need for sympathy. So often had they heard it, in fact, that E.D.'s mother, the even more famous Sybil Jameson, author of the bestselling Petunia Grantham mystery novels, actually said, "That's nice, dear," as she struggled to pick up a stitch she had dropped in the scarf she was attempting to knit.

It wasn't until well into his explanation that she put down her needles and began paying attention. "What do you mean gone?"

"Just what I said! Gone! Embezzled!"

"How much of it?"

"All of it! To the last penny. The Applewhite family is destitute. We shall have to sell Wit's End and move to a hovel somewhere."

"What's a hovel?" asked E.D.'s five-year-old brother, Destiny, who was cheerfully and industriously drawing a bright spring-green pig on a large pad of newsprint.

When the whole story had at last been told—not until long after Destiny had been sent to bed and everyone else had finished a couple of mugs of hot cocoa enhanced with comforting marshmallows or alcohol, depending on their ages—it was clear that while the end of the Applewhites' world had not yet

arrived, it was looming on the horizon like smoke from a wildfire and heading their way.

E.D. had never really understood—nor felt the need to—the financial structure that formed the foundation of her family's creative compound. She only knew that the whole, extended Applewhite family had left New York when Destiny was a year old and moved to rural North Carolina, where they had bought an abandoned motor lodge called the Bide-A-Wee. They had renamed it Wit's End and had lived here since, the adults following their particular creative passions and the children, except for E.D.'s own absolutely noncreative self, *discovering* theirs. All of the adults were famous. Her grandfather and her uncle Archie both designed and created furniture—Zedediah Applewhite's handcrafted wood furniture and Archie's "Furniture of the Absurd," which wasn't really so much furniture as sculpture and which was regularly exhibited in galleries around the country. Her aunt Lucille was a poet.

What E.D. learned that stormy winter night was that they had come to Wit's End not just so the family could live together, but so that they could pool their resources in order to continue their work. The vast majority of these resources came from the worldwide sales of the Petunia Grantham mysteries; some came from Zedediah's beautiful, expensive, and entirely practical furniture; and some came from Randolph's

work directing plays. Nothing else anyone did brought in much money. All of their resources had been gathered together in a family trust. The manager who had handled that trust, and therefore the future of the entire Applewhite enterprise, had turned out to be a crook.

"He'll go to jail," Randolph said after his second cup of bourbon-laced cocoa. "There's that, at least!"

"And what good will that do *us*?" Archie asked.

"I, for one, will feel better," Randolph answered. "It will cheer the dark nights in our hovel."

Zedediah, ever practical, pointed out that the Petunia Grantham mysteries would no doubt continue to sell as they always had, to which Sybil responded that she had only that morning killed Petunia Grantham off. The current novel, which was due to be finished within the week, would be the last in the series. "I killed her because I simply can't write another one. It would destroy my very soul."

"Your soul is tougher than that!" Randolph responded. "You can simply resurrect her in the next! They do it all the time in soap operas."

"My books are not soap operas!"

Only Aunt Lucille had taken the news of their sudden poverty in stride. She breathed a series of long, calming breaths, smiled, and announced that they would get along in some unforeseen way, just as they always had. All they needed to do was trust

their creative energies, and they would surely come up with a way to solve the problem. "One step at a time," she said. "Out of the darkness, into the light."

"How long do we have?" Sybil asked then.

"If we gather up everything we have in the bank accounts, plus whatever you're owed when you turn in the current novel, plus the fees for the two directing gigs I have contracts for—assuming that Zedediah's furniture continues to sell the way it has—we can probably keep the mortgage paid through June. Maybe July. But after that . . ."

"We'll think of something," Lucille said. "Remember Shelley's 'Ode to the West Wind.' *'O Wind, / If Winter comes, can Spring be far behind?'"*

As it turned out, the winter was unusually harsh and unusually long, or at least it felt that way. By the time the Wit's End daffodils began blooming in March, the family had become obsessed with saving money in every way possible. The children's allowances had been not just cut, but actually discontinued. E.D.'s older brother, Hal, unable now to order sculpture supplies online for UPS delivery, had taken to going through the trash to find materials for his projects. "If it gets much worse," he complained, "I'll have to go back to painting! At least I have plenty of tubes of paint."

E.D.'s sister, Cordelia, had given up drinking her seaweed-and-protein health drinks. "I can't even

afford the gas to get to the store, let alone the cost of the supplements! How am I going to maintain the energy to keep up my dancing?"

Winston, their food-loving basset hound, was now living on kibble instead of canned dog food, and liver treats had become a thing of the past. Zedediah's parrot, Paulie, could no longer count on fresh peanuts, and meat had become an occasional indulgence instead of the centerpiece of most dinners for the humans in the family. Pot roast, everybody's favorite dinner, had not been seen since the end of the world was announced. E.D. thought she had seen Uncle Archie at the goat pen from time to time, staring longingly at Wolfbane and Witch Hazel, Lucille's rescue goats.

E.D. herself had begun using the back sides of papers from the recycling box to write her research papers for school. And Zedediah had sped up production of his furniture, appearing in the kitchen late for dinner, still wearing his sawdust-covered work apron, and going right back to the woodshop afterward. So busy was he that Paulie had begun picking his feathers out from loneliness and perches had to be established for him throughout Wit's End. The last person to leave a room was supposed to take Paulie along so that he wouldn't be left by himself.

It was an evening in early March when Randolph, having just been paid by the theater in Raleigh where he'd directed a production of the musical *Oliver!* with

Jake, his newly discovered star, playing the role of the Artful Dodger, called a family meeting. He waved his check in the air. "This will cover another mortgage payment," he said. The Applewhites couldn't always be counted upon to celebrate one another's successes, but this time they broke into spontaneous cheers and applause. "Even better, I have a plan to save Wit's End!"

The cheers and applause died away. No one entirely trusted Randolph's ideas. "What is it?" E.D.'s mother asked suspiciously. She had steadfastly refused—citing the arrival of her Petunia Grantham royalty check as her fair contribution to the family bank account—to resurrect Petunia or begin another book, as she felt the need to rest her brain. "Your plans have been known to require considerable effort from the rest of us."

"All for one and one for all," Randolph said. "Just listen to me, everyone. You're going to love it!" He turned to Jake, who was sitting on the floor rubbing Winston's ears. "I owe a part of this idea to Jake. I was sitting in the theater, listening to him sing 'Consider Yourself at Home,' when it came to me. The next line of the song invites Oliver Twist into the family, just as we've invited Jake into ours. So there I was, looking at this stage full of singing and dancing kids—Fagin's pickpockets—and it occurred to me that we could create just such a family."

"A family of pickpockets?" Archie said. "I hardly

think that's the best way to solve our problem!"

"A family of creative kids! We invited Jake to join the Creative Academy. Why couldn't we take in a whole lot more? Not all year round—just in the summer. We'll start a camp for creative kids. I've even got a name for it. *Eureka!*" Randolph looked expectantly around the room. "Well? What do you think? People pay big money to send their kids to summer camp. Just regular summer camp. Think what they'd pay to have their kids spend eight weeks with a family of professional artists. *Famous professional artists*!"

"Kids? Living here with us?" Hal said, his face going pale. "How many?"

"I'm thinking just twelve this first year, a pilot group."

"And what would we do with these twelve kids?" Archie asked.

"Teach them. Encourage them. Share with them our love of art, our own individual creative passions. Set them on the path to becoming creative, productive adults! *Eureka!* would not only bring in big bucks, it would be a humanitarian endeavor—helping to groom the next generation of American artists. It will be a whole family project. There will be something for everyone to do."

"Me, too?" asked Destiny.

"Of course you, too. You can be the camp mascot!"

E.D. doubted that Destiny knew what a mascot

was, but the title was enough to satisfy him.

Randolph turned to his wife. "Now that Petunia Grantham's dead, you're going to need something to do! You can't rest your brain forever!"

"Twelve children? Twelve *other people's* children?"

"Yes. Think of it. Twelve delightful children into whose meager little lives we will bring the joys of art. We do art—and children—uncommonly well. Just look at our own four, and Jake, too, of course! Who would have thought when Jake first came to us that we could turn him into a musical-theater star in a matter of weeks? We could do that sort of thing with twelve more!"

E.D. suspected that Jake wasn't willing to give the Applewhite family *all* the credit for his newly discovered talent, but she could see that he was listening carefully as Randolph laid out the details of the camp. Each of them would share with the campers what they liked to do best, Randolph told them—their own creative passion—including Jake. As the only one besides Destiny able to sing at all, he could be the singing coach.

"And what would *I* share with them?" E.D. asked.

"A play needs a stage manager, a camp needs a—a— *an executive assistant*, the person who handles the schedule and the details and makes sure everything runs smoothly. You do that wonderfully well, E.D— you know you do!"

No one but Destiny had yet accepted the idea. So Randolph went on, refusing to be daunted by their stony faces. "For heaven's sake, people. We're talking only eight weeks here! Practically no time at all. If we charge twelve families what I expect to charge them, we could save Wit's End, bring meat back to the family table, and restart allowances. Would you really rather sell out, leave here, and move to a hovel in Hoboken?"

Chapter Two

W hen Jake had first come to live at Wit's End, he had been determined to get away as soon as possible. Having been kicked out of the entire public school system of the state of Rhode Island, then out of Traybridge Middle School after he was sent to North Carolina to live with his grandfather, he had expected to get himself kicked out of the Applewhites' Creative Academy in a matter of days. The first problem with that had been that the Applewhites weren't the least bit bothered by his multiple piercings, his scarlet

spiked hair, his black clothes, or his cursing—all the things that established his identity as the bad kid from the city. The second problem was that he really had no place else to go. His parents were both serving time in minimum-security prisons for having attempted to sell their home-grown marijuana to an off-duty sheriff's deputy, and there were no foster families back home in Providence willing to take him in. E.D. had almost gleefully pointed out that his only alternative was Juvie. So he'd been forced to stay.

It had turned out to be the best thing that ever happened to him. Becoming a musical-theater star in a matter of weeks had surprised Jake as much as it had surprised the Applewhites. He'd never suspected that he had a talent for singing and acting until Randolph recruited him to play Rolf in *The Sound of Music*. The show had been a success and Jake had gotten good reviews, but that hadn't been nearly as important as his discovery of what the Applewhites called a "creative passion." Never in his life had Jake been anywhere near as happy as he was onstage, in front of an audience, becoming a person quite different from himself. He loved singing. He loved acting. And later when Randolph cast him as the Artful Dodger in *Oliver!*, he'd found out that he loved dancing, too. Everything about musical theater, in fact, turned Jake on.

Because the Creative Academy was a home school,

he had been able to take off the whole month of February to be in *Oliver!*; and not only that, he'd been able to get school credit for doing it. He was theoretically in the seventh grade with E.D., but he didn't have to be stuck all the time doing what she did and being shown up by her obsessively organized, determinedly academic, and viciously competitive version of education. This was a girl who drove herself relentlessly toward perfection and couldn't bear the thought of getting (actually, thanks to the way the Applewhites did home schooling, *giving herself*) less than an A in anything. She and Jake might be very nearly the same age, but they were wildly and impossibly different. Thanks to the Applewhite philosophy of life, which passionately celebrated individuality, that was completely okay.

Randolph's end-of-the-world announcement had scared Jake clear down to his toes, though he'd done his best to hide it. What would suddenly poverty-stricken Applewhites do with *him*? He himself had no money. His grandfather was providing him with a small allowance so he could pay for clothes and a few incidentals, but otherwise he'd really been taken in as if he were a family member. He wasn't. He was another mouth to feed. Jake couldn't stand to lose his place here—it would mean losing himself. His new self. The only one he'd ever really known or cared about!

The morning after that dark and stormy night he'd worked up the nerve to ask Archie and Lucille—it was their Wisteria Cottage that he lived in—if they thought it was going to be possible for him to finish the school year.

"Don't be silly, Jake!" Lucille had proclaimed, "You're a full-time student. Of *course* you'll finish the year."

But as time went on and the austerity measures the Applewhites had adopted began to really pinch, Jake had started worrying about what would happen in the summer. Like regular schools, the Creative Academy's year ended in June. There'd be no reason to keep him here after that, so he figured they would probably send him to the grandfather he barely knew, a grandfather who had no clue about creative passion and who had only seen one musical in all his life: *The Sound of Music* last October at Wit's End Playhouse.

So when Randolph announced his idea for *Eureka!*, Jake had mostly held his breath until he heard the words he'd been hoping for: that he was to have a job to do at the camp. He didn't care that he didn't have the first clue about how to be a singing coach. He only cared that he wasn't going to be sent off to spend the summer alone on a ramshackle farm outside of Traybridge with his grandfather. Whatever camp turned out to be, it had to be better than that! He figured he was the happiest person in the room when

the rest of the family had finally agreed to it.

Now, the very next night, the family was gathered for their first planning session. "What are we going to do with these kids all day?" Archie asked.

"Workshops, of course!" Randolph said. "Each of us, as I said in the first place, will share our own creative passion. We'll give them the whole spectrum of creative and artistic possibilities. I will do a theater workshop, of course, with an emphasis on acting."

"I can't teach twelve children how to make sculptural wood furniture in eight weeks," Archie protested.

"Well, then—how about Sculpture with Natural Materials?' Randolph said. "They can gather whatever they need from our own woods and meadows—thus saving a fortune on materials. You can certainly teach that."

Archie shook his head. "I don't want to teach! I want to do my own work."

Sybil quickly agreed.

"We're talking about saving our *lives* here!" Randolph reminded them. "There will still be plenty of time for each of you to do your own work. It isn't as if you'll have the campers the whole day!" Then he looked at Sybil. "You don't even *have* your own work, remember? A fiction workshop shouldn't be any problem at all. You *do* it so well, how hard could it be to teach?"

"I shall be in my element," Lucille said. "That poetry workshop I did at Traybridge Middle School

was a disappointment—one hour every other week. How can anyone instill a love for the sound and imagery and *soul* of poetry in five disconnected hours? Imagine having twelve young poets to mold and encourage on a daily basis for eight whole weeks, twelve young poets to introduce to the vast wealth of American contemporary poetry! I'll have them write every day, of course. We'll put out an anthology at the end of camp—or a journal of their work at the very least!"

"Children are not going to make fine wood furniture," Zedediah said.

"Of course not, Father! You can teach them the principles of design, the use of tools."

"No kids are going to get near my lathe—it would be a lawsuit waiting to happen."

"So have them make something simple. Wooden toys. Birdhouses. Focus on design. You know yourself that's the most creative part of what you do."

"I'll teach them ballet! Maybe a little modern dance," Cordelia said. "We can work up a presentation for the end of camp. Maybe a contemporary version of *Swan Lake* down by the pond."

Randolph turned to Hal. "With Archie doing sculpture, you can do a painting workshop. We've already got plenty of paint and brushes. And as short a time as you spent focused on painting, you must have a lot of canvas left over. We'll make Sweet Gum Cottage into an art studio."

"I can't do it," Hal said. "Twelve kids? No way!"

Jake tried to imagine Hal in Sweet Gum Cottage surrounded by twelve kids. He was such an introvert that Jake hadn't even laid eyes on him his first few weeks at Wit's End. When the whole family had decided to go on Facebook as an experiment in interacting with their fans, Hal had refused to friend anyone except himself.

E.D. spoke up then, counting off the workshops on her fingers. "Theater, dance, poetry, fiction, wood design, natural material sculpture, singing, and painting. If the workshops are an hour each—"

"Theater needs to be at least two hours. You can't get any momentum going in an hour!"

"So that's nine hours, not counting meals, rest periods, any kind of sports—"

"This is a creativity camp, not a sports camp!"

"Randolph," Lucille said, "these are children! They have to have physical activity of some kind."

"*Dance* is physical activity!" Cordelia said.

Lucille nodded. "True . . ." She thought for a moment and then smiled. "I can teach them yoga— perfect for balancing body, mind, and spirit. We'll start the day with it. Meditation first, then yoga— before breakfast."

"I've got the credentials to be a lifeguard," Archie said reluctantly. "I suppose we could offer swimming."

"*Gross!*" E.D. said. "Swimming in the pond? There are frogs and snakes and snapping turtles!"

"And muck," Jake added. Every time he and Winston went to the pond, the dog got covered with mud up to his stomach.

"Archie's right," Randolph said. "A camp should definitely have swimming. We can anchor a diving platform in the middle. The pond will make a wonderful picture for the brochure."

"Brochure!" Lucille said. "Yes, we have to let people know about us. We can replicate the advertising campaign we did for *The Sound of Music*. It worked splendidly!"

"Too expensive," Randolph said.

"Then we'll do most of it online," Archie said. "We'll need a *Eureka!* website."

"Somebody has to design a logo!"

E.D. was counting on her fingers again. "Swimming, yoga and meditation, meals, rest time, and all those workshops . . ."

"Campfires!" Sybil said. "Don't forget campfires. Toasting marshmallows—"

"S'mores!" Lucille added.

"Singing and storytelling," Sybil said. "We'll have to make a fire circle—over in the barn parking lot maybe."

"Don't forget free time," Zedediah said. "The creative spirit needs plenty of unscheduled time."

"There aren't enough hours in the day!" E.D. protested.

"Well then, they won't do everything every day," Randolph said. "You'll figure it out. You're a genius at calendars and scheduling."

Jake smiled to himself. His summer was secure. The Applewhites were off and running.

Chapter Three

With a jolt, E.D. realized she had fallen asleep over the computer keyboard. Again. She had been doing her online math course when the numbers had begun running together and she'd drifted off. Now she looked around at the ever-growing chaos of what had been the Creative Academy's schoolroom and sighed. Like just about everything at Wit's End, it was now partly what it had always been and partly something else. It was eleven o'clock in the morning on May seventh, almost exactly

two months after Randolph had first brought up his plan, and she was the only one here, the only one still accomplishing anything that remotely resembled school. Jake was off in the woodshop with Archie building a diving platform for the pond. She had no idea what either Cordelia or Hal was up to, but she was certain it had to do with *Eureka!*

This was going to become the camp office, so the schoolroom's furniture and materials had been shoved to one side to make room for a somewhat dented metal desk, a threadbare swivel chair, and two enormous file cabinets that Archie had found at a used furniture store. Three of the school desks had already been carted off to the storage rooms in the bottom of the barn because nobody was using them. She was the only student at the Creative Academy who was determined to finish every single thing she had planned for spring semester. Everybody else had substituted camp preparations for most of their schoolwork. Math, which all of them took online, was the only part of regular school that went relentlessly on for Hal, Cordelia, and Jake, and all three of them complained bitterly about it. With final exams approaching, they were pretty much forced to keep up.

E.D. absolutely refused to let *Eureka!* derail her. Since that first planning meeting, she had finished three research papers (for science, history, and current

events), read four books and written book reports (for language arts), kept up her vocabulary study, and maintained a steady A average in math. If camp was supposed to save their way of life, she didn't see how it could do that by destroying hers! So even though she'd been up late the night before creating the fifth—*fifth!*—version of a weekly schedule that could include all the camp activities everyone thought were absolutely necessary, she was still managing to stay on her own daily school schedule—except for occasional accidental catnaps.

She swiveled her chair around to look at the list she'd posted on the wall by the door. It was a list of all the things that needed to be done to make the camp happen, and it stretched from very near the ceiling all the way down to the floor. Everyone in the family had contributed to the list, including Destiny, who wanted them to build tree houses for the campers to live in, to bury play money all over Wit's End, and then to make pirate costumes for treasure hunting. Those, at least, didn't actually have to be done. Her father had added an enormous number of *absolutely necessary tasks* and then headed cheerfully off to Pennsylvania to direct another play. "Just like you," her mother had complained to him, "leaving the rest of us to do all the work!"

"*All* the work? Don't be ridiculous," he'd said as he stowed his suitcases in the trunk of his Miata. "I'll be

back in plenty of time to help with the most difficult job of all: winnowing the hundreds of applications we get to find the best possible candidates, the cream of the creative crop. Everything that needs to be done between now and then will be an exhilarating challenge for the whole family! Don't think of it as work; think of it as stretching boundaries, galvanizing energies. Meanwhile, I'll be all by myself in Pennsylvania, slaving away in the theatrical salt mines to keep the mortgage paid."

E.D. had thought about her father's words quite a lot in the weeks after he'd left. It had been a challenge, all right. By now a lot of entries on the to-do list had been crossed out, but there were still an unsettling number to go. Hal had designed the camp logo, and Uncle Archie had built the website. Randolph had *driven* to his directing gig in Philadelphia instead of flying, as he normally would have, so they could use the money he'd saved on airfare to finance the advertising campaign.

There hadn't yet been leaves on the trees when the brochure and website deadline had arrived, so Lucille couldn't take any new pictures. She'd gathered photographs of Wit's End from family albums and then spent days on end Photoshopping in images of happy campers she'd found on the internet so they appeared to be frolicking in what the brochure called "the summer glory of *Eureka!*'s natural setting."

23

Then there had been the problem of creating the camp application. "It needs to give us a sure way to determine who belongs to that 'cream of the crop' Randolph wants and who doesn't," Sybil pointed out. "We'll need a form for basic information, and lots of supporting materials, too—like samples of the children's creative work."

"We should require recommendations from teachers and coaches . . . ," E.D. had added.

"And an essay from the child explaining why he or she wants to attend," Lucille added. "I want to see something of their thought process."

"Not everybody likes to write," Archie had protested. "We need to let them send a video instead—let them talk if they want."

There had been several major arguments and three revisions before Zedediah was able to put the forms and instructions up on the website and cross "application" off the list.

When the advertising budget ran out, Sybil managed to get free publicity with some small stories printed in various newspapers around the country and on a great many parenting blogs. Apparently there were millions of parents across the country who believed they were raising creative geniuses, because the news of *Eureka!* quickly went viral. The *Eureka!* website's e-mail account was deluged with inquiries from parents. The trouble was that almost all of them asked

for—or demanded—scholarships for their prodigiously talented children. "I don't understand it!" Sybil moaned. "We don't mention *scholarships* anywhere!"

"Yes, but we did mention the fees," Archie said. "Astronomical fees!"

"Tell them the *Eureka!* scholarship fund has already been exhausted," Zedediah said dryly. "Like the advertising budget."

As the application deadline approached, Lucille, who'd been put in charge of collecting the applications, reported that two had arrived, then a third. "Three? Three total?" Sybil said. "From all those thousands of inquiries? This is a disaster!"

Aunt Lucille dismissed Sybil's concerns. "You know how creative people are. They put things off till the last minute. We'll get an avalanche of applications the week after the deadline."

E.D. turned back to her math now. It was the last schoolwork she was likely to get done today. Her father had arrived home last night, grumpy from the long drive. He had dragged his suitcases in from the car, kissed her mother, and gone straight up to bed, saying he couldn't possibly deal with anything *Eureka!* until he'd had a good, long sleep. The meeting to catch him up on their progress and begin winnowing applications was scheduled for this afternoon.

◯◯◯

"Seven? What do you mean *seven*?" Randolph roared when Lucille set the basket of applications on the table where the family had just finished lunch.

"Seven, seven, seven!" Paulie repeated quietly from his perch in the corner.

"She means that we have received a total of seven applications," Zedediah said. "Period."

Lucille nodded. "Think of it this way. At least we don't have to spend the whole afternoon winnowing."

There was a considerable period of silence.

E.D. thought of all the effort that had gone into creating the application. They could have just asked for names and addresses and been done with it.

"We'll just have to accept all of them then," Randolph said. "We needed twelve campers to pay the mortgage off entirely, but I think we can survive with seven. *Barely.*"

There was another silence. "What?" he said. "Why is everybody looking at me?"

"I'm not looking at you, Daddy!" Destiny said from his stool at the end of the table. "I'm drawing Pooh and Piglet in the woods!" Destiny had recently become entirely obsessed with drawing.

"You might want to look at that first application on the top of the pile," Sybil said.

Randolph picked up the sheaf of paper-clipped pages and scanned the top sheet. "Priscilla Montrose? *That* Priscilla Montrose?"

"You think there's another in Traybridge?" Archie said.

"Oh, no. No, no, no! Absolutely not! We are not having that child at our camp."

E.D. sighed. It was Randolph's utter refusal to cast Priscilla Montrose in *The Sound of Music* last fall that had led Priscilla's mother, the president of the board of the Traybridge Little Theatre, to cancel the production he had been hired to direct. That had led the Applewhites to turn their barn into a theater and create the Wit's End Playhouse so the show could go on. As successful as that show had been, Randolph had not forgiven Mrs. Montrose for canceling it in the first place.

"That child has less talent than a sea slug!" he said now. "She not only isn't the cream, she isn't even the *skim milk* of the creative crop! I will not have Priscilla Montrose at *Eureka!* under any circumstances whatsoever."

"Maybe you should consider that this is a child who really *needs* us!" Lucille offered.

"And it could certainly be argued that we need her," Zedediah added.

"Clearly," Archie said, "we can't afford to be choosy."

Randolph looked at the application again. Then he leafed through the pages. "We couldn't take her anyway," he said. "Not from this application. Look at this signature!" He pointed to the line where the

parent was supposed to sign the form. "Priscilla has quite obviously forged her mother's signature."

"Think of it as a sign of independence!" Sybil said.

"This is not a valid application. The child has gone behind her mother's back. I'll make you a bet she was *forbidden* to apply. That hateful, spiteful, vengeful woman would never allow her child to spend the summer with us!"

"I was afraid you'd take this stand," said Sybil with a sigh.

"We can survive with six campers," Randolph said. "We'll just have to cut a few corners, that's all. Be a little more frugal."

E.D. shook her head. *Frugal* had been another of her vocabulary words: "characterized by thriftiness and avoidance of waste," it meant. They'd had peanut butter and jelly sandwiches for lunch—for the third time that week. She didn't think they could be any more frugal than they already were.

Chapter Four

Once it was clear there was no application winnowing to be done, Archie left the meeting to go pick up the swimming pool ladder he had bought from Craigslist for the diving platform. He took Destiny with him and told Jake he'd need some help when they got back. Meantime, Jake was eager to hear who the campers were that he was going to have in his singing workshop.

Lucille and Sybil had spent a long time going over the applications and were now taking turns presenting

the campers to the family. It occurred to Jake halfway through Lucille's presentation of the first one—a thirteen-year-old boy named Quincy Brown—that he hadn't really thought this whole camp idea through. There had been some vague image in his mind of a bunch of little kids he could get singing with him, the way he'd done with Destiny. *Little kids.* Not somebody almost his own age who had won so many talent shows that he was paying for camp himself from his winnings!

When Sybil began talking about the next two—a pair of eleven-year-old twins named Ginger and Cinnamon Boniface—Hal began to hyperventilate. He excused himself and went up to his room. "He'll get used to the idea by the time they come," Lucille assured everyone. "It's only six kids."

After Sybil and Lucille finished talking about all of them—three girls and three boys—Jake felt a headache coming on. He'd taken a few notes so he could fill Archie in, but E.D. was going to make up a booklet of camper bios so everybody could have a copy. "It's important for all of you to *memorize* the bios," she said in her usual bossy way, "so you'll be ready to handle the campers."

Jake didn't see how memorizing all the great accomplishments these kids had put on their applications would help him get ready to handle anybody.

"One of them is the son of rock stars!" he told Archie later as he held the ladder Archie was attaching to the diving platform.

Destiny was sitting on the floor pounding nails into a board Archie had given him. "Rock stars?" he asked. "You mean those guys E.D. has pitchers of on her ceiling?"

"Not those rock stars," Jake said. "The kid's parents have an indie rock band called Dragon's Blood."

"They have a cult following among high school and college kids," Archie said.

"Yeah. His mom's the lead singer; his dad is lead guitar."

Destiny stopped pounding. "He gots a guitar for a dad?"

"His dad *plays* the guitar. The kid's name is Harley—he was named for his father's motorcycle."

Archie groaned.

"His mother wrote a note on his application that she hopes the camp will give him a new outlet for his creative abilities. Right now he's into photography, but he only takes pictures of dead things."

"Eeeww," Destiny said. "Where's he get dead things?"

"She didn't say. Then there's Quincy Brown," Jake said, "who calls himself Q. He's thirteen and the only African American. He's won something like ten talent

shows. He sings. He dances. And he's been in more musicals than I have."

"Feeling a little intimidated, are you?" Archie asked.

"A little?" Jake said. "Besides those two there's David. He's *fourteen*! My age. He's had professional coaches—singing, dancing, *and* acting coaches—since he was three! Plus, he wrote a play that was done at his private school in Virginia last semester—with him in the lead. According to his mother, David is a *genius*: God's gift to all things creative."

Archie finished screwing in the ladder. "That's his mother talking. Remember Mrs. Montrose. Don't believe what a mother says about her talented kid. Not till you meet him and see his work."

"Okay, but how am I going to be singing coach for dudes my age who've had more experience than I've had and real, professional coaching? What makes me any different from the campers?"

Archie laughed. "What makes you different? You're you and they're them! Think about what my dear wife says about you, Jake: you are a *radiant light being.* Lucille is never wrong."

Jake frowned. "Yeah, but she'd say that about the campers too. She thinks that about everyone."

"Am I a light being?" asked Destiny.

"You're practically blinding!" Archie told him. "So, Jake. There are plenty of ways to show your

individuality. Why did you get all those piercings and dye your hair red and spike it all over your head? So you'd stand out, right? So you'd scare off the people you didn't want to deal with!"

"I don't know. I guess. Is that why you got your tattoos?"

Archie looked down at the anchor on one forearm and the dragon on the other, and laughed. "Just the opposite. When I decided I wanted to work my way around the world on a tramp steamer, I was a skinny high school dropout with a ponytail who wore Birkenstocks and tie-dyed T-shirts. I wasn't sure I could even get a shipboard job, but if I did, I figured the rest of the crew would give me no end of trouble. So I worked out for a couple of months to build up some muscle, got myself a crew cut, and then went to a tattoo parlor down by the docks. I had the guy there give me his two most popular designs."

"And it worked?"

"Yep. By the time I got back to New York a couple of years later, the look had come to feel like me. So I've kept it ever since. Funny thing is that it was like *camouflage* on the ship—I blended into the background. But now it pretty much guarantees I'll stand out in an art gallery. It's not just the look that counts; it's the context. If you want to separate yourself from the campers, you could just go back to your old look."

Jake shrugged. "The hair was a pain to keep up—the dye and the gel and all."

Archie looked at Jake's dark brown hair—nicely grown out from the buzz cut he'd had in the fall for *The Sound of Music*. "You know Lucille cuts my hair—she's a whiz with the clippers. She could give you a Mohawk. You wouldn't have to do much with it—maybe a little wax—and I guarantee that, with all your piercings and a Mohawk, you'll at least *look* plenty different from the campers."

"What's a Mohawk?" Destiny asked. "Can I have one too? Does it gots colors?"

"No colors," Jake said.

"And no Mohawk for you," Archie added. "Would you please go find Hal and ask him to help us get the platform anchored in the pond?"

Destiny put down his hammer and folded his arms across his chest, his lower lip sticking out. "Not unless I gets to have a Mohawk like Jake."

"Tell you what," Archie said. "If your mother says yes, Lucille will cut your hair too."

"Yay, I'm gonna gets a Mohawk!" Destiny said, and ran out of the woodshop.

Jake and Archie went out on the porch to wait for Hal. "The thing is," Jake said, "not looking like the other campers doesn't mean I can be their singing coach!"

"You have an advantage over them. You've seen

34

their applications and know what they've done. In the camp publicity you're billed as a prodigy, and that's all they'll know. If you act like you know what you're doing, they'll just assume you do. So tell me about the girls."

"A pair of eleven-year-old identical twins—one's a poet."

"Lucille must be thrilled. What about the other one?"

Jake thought for a moment and then shrugged. "I don't remember. The third girl—Samantha—is into visual arts. The portfolio she sent looks like a set of illustrations for a fantasy novel. Lots of elves in the woods."

"It promises to be an interesting eight weeks," Archie said.

"Yeah, *interesting.*"

Chapter Five

It was June 27. The first day of camp. E.D. swiveled the desk chair and looked around what had been the schoolroom. Nothing was left of the Creative Academy except the clock on the wall, now reading 10:14, and the old computer table made of a door resting on a pair of filing cabinets. The computer and printer were still there, but instead of random piles of books and papers, the door now held a used copier and a laundry basket containing brightly colored plastic water bottles from the dollarstore in Traybridge. Her father had decreed that every camper

needed to have a water bottle at all times in case of dehydration or heat prostration. They'd bought extras on the grounds that creative kids were scattered and forgetful and would probably lose them frequently. There was a stack of canvas bags on which Cordelia had painted the *Eureka!* logo, because Lucille had decided that all of the campers needed some way of carrying a notebook, pens, and whatever else they might need as they moved from workshop to workshop during the camp day. Bags, notebooks, and pens had also been purchased from the dollarstore.

A counter made of scrap lumber and painted somewhat randomly in Destiny's favorite primary colors (by Destiny) now stretched across most of the room a few feet inside the door. On that counter were a sign saying CAMP OFFICE and a vase of silk flowers. The used office furniture was arranged in the space behind the counter, and the dented desk at which E.D. was sitting now held a new and complicated-looking telephone as well as the first-week schedules she had been stapling together for the campers. A large and rather fanciful map of Wit's End that Hal had drawn covered much of one wall, and the rest was taken up with a densely filled-in calendar with today's date circled in red, plus copies of all the materials that had been sent to the campers' families and the schedule for the day. The original to-do list had been taken down, even though several entries hadn't yet been crossed off.

Between two and five this afternoon, the campers would arrive and *Eureka!* would start, whether they were ready or not. And of course, E.D. thought, they were not! The dining tent, rented from a discount wedding supply house, was supposed to have been delivered two days ago but hadn't come till this morning. Uncle Archie was out behind the house with Jake now putting it up. He should have been in the woodshop instead, helping to finish the dock Zedediah had designed for the pond to keep campers from having to tromp through the muck to get into the water.

Jake appeared in the doorway, his dark brown Mohawk standing up down the center of his otherwise newly shaved head. His eyebrow ring and all of his earrings were in place, and he was gleaming with sweat. He held out a stack of army surplus blankets. "Your mother wants these on the beds. Do you have a few minutes to help me?"

"What're you doing here?" E.D. asked him. "You're supposed to be helping Uncle Archie put up the dining tent!"

"It's up. Archie's gone back to helping your grandfather with the dock." He wiped the sweat from his face on the sleeve of the official *Eureka!* staff T-shirt Lucille had designed. "I don't know why Sybil thinks the campers are going to need blankets. It's freaking hot out there already."

The phone rang. E.D. picked it up. "Good morning,

you've reached *Eureka!*, the unparalleled summer experience for creative kids."

She listened for a moment, put her hand over the mouthpiece, and groaned. Why hadn't she checked caller ID? The grating, heavily North Carolina-accented voice was unmistakable. "It's Mrs. Montrose," she mouthed silently to Jake as she punched the phone's speaker button.

The woman's voice filled the room. "I demand to speak to Randolph Applewhite! Who is this?"

Jake set the blankets on the counter.

"This is E.D. Applewhite, Mrs. Montrose," she said, her voice as neutral as she could make it. "I'm afraid my father is not here at the moment." Her father and Destiny had left fifteen minutes earlier for the airport in Greensboro to pick up the two campers who were coming as unaccompanied minors. She would have had to lie otherwise, of course. This was not a day for Randolph Applewhite to talk to Mrs. Montrose. "How may I help you?"

"You tell your father, young lady, that I would never have allowed my daughter to apply to his so-called creativity camp if I had known she was doing it. As far as I'm concerned, the man has not the slightest understanding of the sensitive psyche of a highly creative child—"

E.D. shook her head. Highly creative children were the *only* ones her father understood.

"There should be some sort of law to keep that man

39

from interacting with anyone under the age of thirty," the irritating voice went on. "My daughter went behind my back to fill out the forms and gather the required teacher recommendations. She submitted that application entirely on her own. But once she did so, proving to me how strong is her wish to make a career in the arts, I was naturally compelled to support her. Your father had the audacity to *reject her application*! My daughter's self-esteem has been irreparably damaged by his callous disregard for her talent and potential."

E.D. rolled her eyes at Jake.

"Refusing to cast her in *The Sound of Music* last autumn was inexcusable," the woman continued. "But rejecting her camp application was an act of pure vindictiveness. I am quite certain he only did it to get back at me. Her talent is unquestionable. I recently sent him letters from experts in three—*three*—separate fields of creative endeavor recommending that he reverse his decision and accept my daughter. If *any* child belongs at a camp for highly creative children, my Priscilla does! But he has refused."

E.D. hadn't heard about any expert recommendations. Probably her father had simply thrown them away.

"I hold your father solely responsible for the fact that Priscilla has been crying herself to sleep every night. She's devastated! She had been absolutely counting on a summer of companionship with other creatively

gifted children. *You tell him he has not heard the last of this."*

"I'm terribly sorry for Priscilla's distress, and I'm certain my father is as well." E.D. took a breath and then went on. "But really, there was nothing we could do. By the time those expert recommendations were received, the camp was completely filled up. All the places were taken within a week of the application deadline."

Jake began to laugh and hurriedly put a hand over his mouth.

"Thank you for calling, Mrs. Montrose," E.D. said. "I'll be sure to give my father your message." She hung up. "Thank goodness we didn't take her kid. Imagine that woman hovering over us all summer. Listen, I don't have time to help with the blankets. Just put them on the ends of the bunks! I bet the campers won't use them a single time all summer."

After the success of *The Sound of Music* last fall, the family had decided to air-condition Wit's End. But they had only finished the main house, Zedediah's and Archie and Lucille's cottages, the woodshop, and the dance studio before the end of the world. The campers were going to have to depend on North Carolina breezes to cool their cottages. "Roughing it" is what Randolph called it.

"At least your new haircut ought to be cool," E.D. said.

Jake ran a hand through his hair and grinned. "Cool and easy. Destiny's having fits because your mother won't let him get a Mohawk too."

E.D. sighed. Jake was an appalling role model. She had been hoping to help her little brother avoid the curse of the creative flake by instilling in him habits of organization and good sense while he was still young enough for them to stick, but the moment Jake came into their lives that hope had turned to dust. She divided her life now into BJ and AJ: Before Jake and After Jake. Until he came, E.D. had thought there were basically two kinds of people in the world: chaotic creatives like everybody else in her family, and normal, stable, sensible people like herself. Jake didn't fit into either camp. He had both an Applewhite-esque creative streak and a genuine ability for organization and follow through. Unfortunately, it wasn't the organization and follow-through side of him that appealed to Destiny.

Just then Winston began his hysterical "terrorists coming, terrorists coming" combination of howling and barking outside. Most of Winston's terrorist alarms were figments of his imagination caused by the occasional vehicle that happened to pass Wit's End on the road out beyond the driveway. But this time the alarm was followed immediately by the sound of a car on the gravel driveway.

"Who could it be?" E.D. looked at the clock: 10:27.

"It's way, *way* too early to be a camper!"

By the time E.D. and Jake got out onto the front porch, the driver of the shiny black Mercedes with heavily tinted windows that was parked in front of the main house was leaning on the horn. The sound was driving the dog into ever more frenzied howling, though by now he was backing slowly but purposefully toward the porch, the fur on his neck and back standing straight up.

"Inside, Winston," E.D. said, holding the screen door open.

The frantic dog turned, nearly tripping over his ears, and scuttled safely into the house, where he continued to bark menacingly.

The horn went still. For a moment nothing happened. The car windows were so dark it was impossible to tell who might be inside.

Aunt Lucille appeared at the door now, her cascades of blond curls coming loose from the flowered scarf she had wrapped around her head, her hands covered with flour. She pushed Winston out of the way with one foot and came out onto the porch, brushing the flour from her hands, just as the back window of the Mercedes went slowly down and two identical faces peered out. "This had better be *Eureka!*" one of the faces said. "We've been driving in circles for an hour!"

43

Chapter Six

The driver's side door of the Mercedes opened. "Of course it's *Eureka!*" a gruff voice bellowed. "Didn't you see the sign?"

A man wearing a chauffeur's cap above a New York Yankees T-shirt, tattered blue jeans, and sandals got out of the car, stretching his legs and groaning. Ignoring Lucille, Jake, and E.D., he came around and opened the back door so the identical bodies that went with the identical faces could get out.

Cinnamon and Ginger Boniface. The twins from

New Jersey. The twins were eleven years old, Jake knew, but in person they didn't look it. As thin and small as they were, they could have passed for third graders. Both had short, curly, carrot-orange hair and pale skin sprinkled with freckles. They wore matching shorts and beaded tank tops—one green, one blue— matching sequined flip-flops, and long, sparkly earrings. Their finger- and toenails were painted the color of their clothes. They stood in the gravel drive now, frowning identical frowns.

Lucille was hurrying down the steps to greet them, still brushing flour from her hands. "Welcome, welcome, welcome, girls!" she said as she went. "Welcome to *Eureka!* I'm Lucille Applewhite." She held out her hand to the nearest twin, but the girl kept hers at her side.

"The poet!" the other twin said, her frown vanishing. "I'm a poet, too."

"Of course you are," Lucille said. "You won an award!" She used her still-outstretched hand to point first to E.D. and then to Jake. "This is E.D. Applewhite and that's Jake Semple."

In spite of his fresh Mohawk, the twins barely glanced at Jake. He could feel his jaw clenching. He'd expected, at least, to be noticed.

The man nodded at the green twin, "Ginger," and then at the blue, "Cinnamon."

"Well, girls, you're a little early, I'm afraid," Lucille

said. "The other campers won't be here till—"

"Between two and five P.M., *like the schedule says,*" E.D. said with a familiar edge to her voice. She had sent the opening-day schedule electronically, Jake knew, as well as including it in the precamp packet she had sent to every family by snail mail.

"We're really, really glad to have you, though!" Lucille put in quickly. She turned to the man, who had popped the trunk and was hurriedly dragging out blue and green suitcases and duffel bags.

"Are you—are you Mr. Boniface?"

"Nope. Name's Bruno. Theodore Boniface's driver."

"I see. We were under the impression you'd be doing the whole trip today. We weren't expecting the girls to get here till around five."

"Somethin' came up, and Mr. Boniface needs me back tonight. We came as far as a hotel in Raleigh last night."

"*Motel,*" the blue twin said. "That didn't even have a pool!"

"I should'a been on the road an hour ago. Stupid GPS didn't work for—"

"I'm so sorry you got lost," Lucille interrupted. "We sent directions—didn't we, E.D.?"

"You should have received them with *the schedule,*" E.D. said to the man.

He hefted a blue-and-green plaid steamer trunk from the car and dumped it on the drive with the

other luggage. "I hope somebody can get this stuff where it belongs. I gotta be starting back right now."

The twin in blue squinted up into the sun. "Is it always this hot here? Where's the pool? There's supposed to be a pool!"

"A pond, actually," Lucille said. "It's quite lovely. Entirely natural."

"There's a tour of the grounds scheduled for *after the other campers arrive*," E.D. told her.

"Does that dog bite?" the green twin asked. Winston's barking had subsided, replaced by the occasional *whuff* to show he was still keeping an eye on things. "I'm not staying if he bites."

Jake shook his head. "He's just nervous."

Jake had intended to lock Winston in Wisteria Cottage while the campers were arriving. The dog was frightened of new people till he got to know them. There was no way Jake could have known he should do it this early.

Lucille was holding on to her welcoming smile, but Jake could tell it was taking an effort. "Jake," she said, "why don't you take those duffel bags down to Dogwood Cottage for the girls."

Jake went down the porch steps as the driver pulled a pair of tennis rackets from the trunk. "Might as well take those back with you," Jake said. "No tennis court here."

"No tennis court!" the blue twin wailed.

Bruno put the rackets back and closed the trunk. "Nice to meet you," he said to Lucille. "Good luck!" He got back into the car. "See you in August," he called to the girls. He slammed the door and started the car.

"See you," the green twin said.

"Whatever," said the other.

As Jake went to pick up a duffel bag, the Mercedes roared away, spitting gravel. He could understand the man's hurry to get away from the twins even if he didn't have to be back in New Jersey that night.

"No tennis court!" the blue twin said again. "What kind of a camp is this anyway?"

Jake had already thrown the first duffel bag over his shoulder, picked up the other one, and started down the path that led to the cottages.

Chapter Seven

E.D. heard Aunt Lucille take a *deep, calming breath*. "You go on back to the kitchen," E.D. told her. "I'll help these two settle in. Get your suitcases, girls. I'll take you to your bunk." Mercedes and a driver or not, there was no reason these two couldn't get their own bags to their bunk.

The screen closed behind Aunt Lucille. The twins had made no move toward their suitcases. The green twin was staring up into the trees next to the house, an abstracted look on her face. With disapproving eyes, the blue twin, hands on her hips, scanned the

house, then the yard, and finally what could be seen of the barn above the bushes. E.D. went down the stairs and found herself seeing Wit's End suddenly—really seeing it—as the campers would.

Some shingles were missing from the porch roof, and the main house badly needed a paint job. It was a stark contrast with the bright new sign Archie had made proclaiming it to be the Lodge. They couldn't have afforded to paint the house; but why had no one thought, when the sign was hung, to clean the heavy, gray tangles of spiderwebs from around the eaves or to scrub the green algae or mold or whatever it was creeping up the siding from the ground?

The scraggly combination of grass and various North Carolina weeds that constituted the front lawn had grown tall enough to be putting out seeds and a few raggedy flowers. And the barn, in spite of all the work that had been done last year to turn it into a theater, still looked shabby from the outside. There, too, the sign over the double doors, with its gold leaf lettering—WIT'S END PLAYHOUSE—made the dull, flaking, barn red paint look even worse by comparison.

E.D. started down the gravel path toward the cottages. "The girls' cottage is called Dogwood," she said, acutely aware of how much less picturesque it was than its name. All of the cottages at Wit's End, built in the 1940s when it had been turned from a failing farm into a motor lodge, had been white

originally but over the years had weathered to a silvery gray. Their roofs were thick with moss. The southern mixed-deciduous forest—sweet gums, beeches, hickory, and oak trees, with a few tall pines—might seem to be closing in on them. Her mother liked to say the cottages blended perfectly into their surroundings. Someone else might say their surroundings were gobbling them up.

E.D. spoke as cheerfully as she could, considering how angry she was that the girls had arrived so early. It wasn't their fault, she reminded herself. "Just grab your suitcases and come along. I'll take you there."

"What about our trunk?" the blue twin asked. Her voice, E.D. thought, was an irritating whine.

"Jake'll be back to get it any minute." She continued down the path, assuming the girls would come after her. Behind her she heard a loud, theatrical sigh. Then there was the sound of scraping gravel, followed by a series of bumps and thumps and curses. She turned back. The wheels on the two suitcases had dug trenches in the path and were now jammed against little piles of gravel. The twins were standing there, looking helpless.

"They won't go any farther," the green twin said.

"Well then," E.D. said, determinedly hanging on to cheerfulness, "I guess you'll just have to *pick them up!*" She turned back toward Dogwood Cottage.

Green twin Ginger, blue twin Cinnamon, she repeated in her head as she walked. She would take them to their

cottage, but that was absolutely all she would do with them. She wasn't their counselor; Cordelia was. She would leave them at Dogwood and go find Cordelia. It wasn't her fault they had come nearly four hours early. What kind of parents spent a fortune to send their kids to camp and then totally ignored that camp's very clear instructions about when to get them there? For that matter, what kind of parents sent two eleven-year-olds halfway across the country accompanied only by a surly chauffeur? *Green twin Ginger, blue twin Cinnamon.*

Behind her the twins were complaining to each other now about the heat and humidity and how heavy their suitcases were. "Where do you suppose Maria packed our swimming suits?" one of them asked the other. "I gotta get in the water."

E.D. wondered who Maria might be. A maid, maybe. *Maid. Chauffeur. Mercedes.* These were not kids who would take well to roughing it. When the cottage came into sight, Jake was nowhere to be seen. He had left the duffel bags on the porch and disappeared. Just like him to go off and leave everything to her.

E.D. went up onto the slightly sagging porch, stepped over the duffel bags, and held the screen door open for the twins. They bounced their suitcases up the stairs and around the duffel bags, and dragged them inside.

Cinnamon immediately left hers in the middle of the living room and began inspecting the walls, lifting

52

pictures to peer behind them and feeling behind bookcases. "Where's the thermostat? Somebody needs to turn up the air-conditioning. It's an oven in here!"

"No thermostat. No air-conditioning." E.D. pointed to the open windows. "The bunks are cooled by outside air."

"Cooled? Cooled? You have got to be kidding! People could die of heat like this."

E.D. knew this wasn't true. She had lived at Wit's End without air-conditioning for four whole summers. "It'll be better at night." This wasn't entirely true, either, of course.

"That's it! I'm out of here." A phone seemed to have materialized in Cinnamon's hand. She was biting her lip and pressing on the screen. "Dad will just have to send Bruno back for us."

Would that mean refunding the twins' deposit? E.D. wondered.

Ginger had gone off down the hall to explore the bedrooms. "Hey, the back bedroom isn't too bad," she called. "It's all shaded by trees." There was a brief pause. "And there's a breath of a breeze. Oh! Listen! Did you hear that? Shaded by trees—breath of a breeze. It's the start of a poem!"

"You two can have that room if you want," E.D. told Cinnamon.

Cinnamon swore and peered at her phone. "What's the matter? I'm not getting a ring."

"You probably don't get service here," E.D. said. "There's only one tower."

"Look at this," Cinnamon said, holding her phone out to no one in particular. "No bars! Not one single bar! I've never seen that before."

"That's because you live in New Jersey," E.D. said. "This is North Carolina. The *country*. If your phone doesn't match our one tower, you don't have service. Period. Anyway, we sent you the list of rules. Rule three: no cell phones."

"Mother said that had to mean no cell phones *during sessions*. You know, like no cell phones in class at school. You can't expect us not to have a phone! What if there's an emergency?"

"*Our* cells work here. Plus, there are land lines. This is the country, not a desert island. Count yourself lucky—since your phone doesn't work, we won't have to confiscate it!"

"Cinn, come on back here," Ginger called from the bedroom. "There's a real, live hummingbird out there by some big orange flower. Come look!"

Cinnamon swore again and put her phone in the pocket of her shorts. "First chance I get, I'm calling Dad. We're going home." She raised her voice then. "Did you hear that, Ginger? *We're going home!*" But she went down the hall.

"The bathroom's on the right," E.D. called after her. "I'll go get your counselor."

Chapter Eight

Jake had dropped the duffel bags at the girls' cottage and was on his way to the woodshop to help Archie and Zedediah with the floating dock, kicking gravel as he walked. His grandfather had told him, the day he'd dropped Jake off at Wit's End to join the Creative Academy, "Those who sow the wind will reap the whirlwind." His grandfather had been making some sort of point about the behavior that had gotten Jake in trouble, but now Jake had a niggling suspicion that starting a camp was sowing the wind, and the Boniface twins were the

first signs of the approaching whirlwind.

Before the day was out there would be four more kids besides the twins. He waved a hand in front of his eyes to shoo away a cluster of gnats. That's pretty much what he'd done with people all his life, he thought. He'd shooed them away—turned them off, scared them. He hadn't really known how to do anything else. There were some guys back at school in Rhode Island who he used to hang out with, guys who were as intimidating as he was. Kids and teachers all pretty much did their best to avoid them, which was what they wanted. The thing was, he hadn't really known those guys. They were all too busy showing how tough and cool they were to find out what any of them were like behind the image.

Now that he had the new haircut that was supposed to make him stand out from the other campers, he wondered if that was really what he wanted. Part of what he'd loved about being in the shows Randolph had cast him in was hanging out with other kids who liked what they were doing as much as he did. Like Jeannie Ng, who had played Liesl and given him his first stage kiss—his first kiss of any kind, though he hadn't admitted that to anybody. There'd been her brother, too, and most of the guys from *Oliver!* They'd all become his friends. The first friends he'd ever had.

They had understood what he felt when he was on the stage. They had the same kind of focus, the same

determination to be the very best they could be. Jake had never before in his life really worked at anything. But as much work as a show took, it didn't really *feel* like work. He'd been hoping camp would be like that. Now he wasn't so sure.

Destiny had wakened him at five thirty this morning, flinging himself onto Jake's bed and startling Winston, who left claw marks on Jake's bare arm as he scrambled out of Destiny's way. "Get up, get up, get up, Jake!" Destiny had hollered, prying open one of Jake's determinedly closed eyes. "It's *Eureka!* day! Finally! This is gonna be the bestest summer in my whole life!"

Jake wished he could be as sure of that as Destiny.

As he approached the door to the woodshop, Jake could hear raised voices from inside. Archie and Zedediah must still be arguing about how best to moor the dock they were working on to the land. Like the diving platform, it would be mounted on oil drums. It was designed to float so that it could accommodate itself to the water level, which changed according to how much rain they got. They'd had days and days of rain in the late spring, so the pond was unusually high. But as the summer went on, the pond would shrink.

Jake went in and found the two of them standing in their own halves of the woodshop's working space with the long, narrow, nearly completed dock

between them. Each side was a reflection of father's and son's very different ways of working. On Zedediah's side the hand-tools were neatly hung on Peg-Boards, the worktable was precisely organized, with screws, nails, nuts, and bolts all in labeled containers. The wood that was destined to become the rocking chairs and gliders that made up most of his catalog was stacked neatly against the wall covered with a tarp. In the corner was a cabinet that held cans of stain, varnish, polyurethane, paint, and the solvents needed to work with them, organized by both type and size.

Archie's side was a chaos of paint cans and tools, mostly strewn on the floor, some dumped without apparent order into buckets and boxes among miscellaneous piles of oddly shaped chunks of wood and tree stumps or limbs in assorted sizes that were the raw materials from which he created his Furniture of the Absurd.

They stopped arguing when Jake came through the doorway. "What do *you* think, Jake?" Zedediah said. "Tie the dock to a couple of trees like Archie says, or sink posts a little ways back from the water and fasten it to those?"

"Whichever is easier and faster," Jake said. "Two campers are here already. E.D.'s having a fit."

"Ha!" Archie said. "Trees it is then."

"All right, trees," Zedediah conceded.

"It's awfully big," Jake said. "Will it fit through the door?"

Archie sighed. "You weren't even here for the *Incident of the Buffet*!"

Jake had heard the story, of course. Several times. When the buffet, which Archie had fashioned from the massive trunk of a fallen oak tree, was completed, it had turned out to be too long and tall and wide to get out of the shop. After a major argument about whether the buffet or the front wall of Pinewood Cottage would have to be dismantled, Archie had ended up cutting the buffet in two and turning each half into a credenza.

Zedediah claimed to have won the argument, while Archie said he'd yielded only because he realized that he could sell two pieces for more than he could have gotten for one. Zedediah always insisted that the buffet would never have sold at all. "There's a limit to how 'absurd' furniture can be and still serve any useful purpose whatsoever. That buffet wouldn't have fit into any dining room smaller than a soccer field."

"Ah, but it was a thing of beauty." Very little of Archie's furniture served a useful purpose, actually. The first piece Jake had ever seen was a coffee table that looked more like a short, fat, shiny hippopotamus. "You couldn't put a cup of coffee on it," Lucille had said of it, "but then who would want to?"

"True art is seldom practical," Archie often said.

This, Jake knew, was a thinly veiled insult aimed at Zedediah's rocking chairs. The question of who among the Applewhites created "true art" was a regular and hotly debated topic around the family dinner table. Jake had come to the conclusion that art was whatever the artist claimed it to be.

"I'll get some rope from the barn," Zedediah said, "while the two of you finish the dock. Be careful of the wet paint. Destiny decided it needed decoration."

Chapter Nine

E.D. found Cordelia and Hal in Sweet Gum Cottage, which was now the visual arts studio. Surrounded by tubes of paint, they were painting elegant wooden signs for the boys' and girls' cottages with the names of the campers who would be staying in them. It was an idea they'd thought up when everybody had still been expecting a dozen campers; and though it hardly seemed necessary now that there were only three names on each sign, they had refused to give it up. Cordelia's was covered with flowers and vines. Hal

had chosen a fantasy theme of wizards and dragons and goblins. Just like them, E.D. thought, to take hours to create something only moderately useful that could have been printed out in seconds.

Paulie greeted her from his perch in the corner with a scream and a string of curses. "Hi, Paulie," she said automatically.

Hal looked up from his work. "I'm not sure I can go through with this after all. Whenever I think of staying in a cottage with three other people, I feel like I'm going to throw up."

"Quit complaining," Cordelia said. "At least you're going to have your own room, which is more than I get!"

"How long do we have till they start getting here?"

"No time at all," E.D. said. "The first two are here already. They're down in Dogwood Cottage now, complaining about the heat."

Hal's face went so white that the acne on his cheeks was more noticeable than usual. He rubbed at the sparse goatee that had taken him all spring to grow. "Now? Campers are here now? We're not ready. I'm not ready!"

"*You* don't have to be," E.D. told him. "They're Cordelia's, not yours. The Boniface twins. A really scruffy chauffeur brought them in a Mercedes! Cinnamon says they're going home, though. Between the lack of air-conditioning and the cell tower not

being the right one, she is *not* a happy camper! Do you suppose we have to refund their deposit if they go home? Dad'll have a heart attack."

"Of course they're not going home," Cordelia said. "They're my first two campers! I'm so excited! Cinnamon and Ginger, right? Age eleven. The poet and—and—I forget what the other one does. I'll get right over there." She put down her paintbrush. "Could you finish painting these last two—"

E.D. just looked at her.

Cordelia picked the brush up again. "Sorry, I wasn't thinking. Would it be okay, you think, if I just take the time to paint in these lilies? It'll only take a minute."

"It isn't as if they have anywhere to go," E.D. said. "Or even any way to call home and demand their chauffeur back since their phones don't work here."

Hal put his brush down suddenly and rushed off to the bathroom. After a moment E.D. and Cordelia could hear him retching. "You think he's going to be okay?" E.D. asked.

"Of course. He only has three boys to deal with. How bad could it be?"

"It's Hal! I couldn't believe he agreed to this counselor thing in the first place."

Cordelia finished the last lily with a flourish of her brush and shrugged. "Dad had him the moment he promised to pay us! Hal was halfway through building a computerized moving sculpture when the world

ended, remember? All the parts he needs to finish it cost a fortune. If he hadn't agreed to be a counselor, he'd have had to abandon the whole project."

"What are you going to do with the twins from now till the other campers come?"

Cordelia put her paintbrush into a jar of turpentine and stood up. "Don't know. I'm sure that when I meet them something will come to me. I got a zillion ideas off the internet. Like Uncle Archie says, 'Google is your friend!'" She picked up some papers from the end of the table. "These are the maps of Wit's End I made for the campers when you rejected Hal's version—"

"I didn't reject it; I gave it half the wall in the office."

"Maybe I'll give one to each of the twins and challenge them to a scavenger hunt."

"Ginger is green, Cinnamon blue," E.D. said.

"What?"

"You'll see."

"Okay." Cordelia took off her paint smock and tossed it on the end of the workbench, smoothed her long, wavy auburn hair, and tugged at the flowered skirt she had chosen to wear with her staff shirt. "Do I look all right?"

E.D. nodded. *All right?* Cordelia was flat-out gorgeous. She tended to dress like Aunt Lucille, in bright colors and flowing fabrics; but even in cutoffs

and a raggedy T-shirt, she would look better than E.D. on her best day.

"Here I go. Wish me luck."

As the screen door slammed behind Cordelia, Hal came out of the bathroom wiping his mouth with the back of his hand. Paulie, preening his newly grown-in feathers, swore at him gently. "It's no good," Hal said. "I can't do this. I'll be in my room. Tell Dad I'm sorry to let the family down, but I just can't do this."

"Dad's at the airport. He'll be back in a couple of hours. The Applewhite future depends on *Eureka!* You know perfectly well you can't quit."

Hal uttered a couple of parrot words and headed back to the bathroom.

Chapter Ten

When Zedediah left, Jake and Archie went back to work on the dock. After they'd nailed the last of the top boards in place, Archie dug through a pile of scrap wood in the back corner of his side of the shop and came up with an old, paint-splattered, four-rung wooden ladder. "There weren't any more swimming pool ladders on Craigslist, so I figured we could use this."

"It won't look as classy as the other ladder."

Archie sighed. "I know—but it'll do the job." When

the dock was finished, Archie stood back to look at it. "Hardly a work of art!"

"Destiny's orange and green blotches add a nice touch," Jake said.

"It's possible that absurdity can go too far. I must remind myself that this, like the diving platform, is merely practical. Let's get a dolly under the thing and move it outside."

While they were maneuvering it through the doorway, Zedediah drove up in Archie's pickup with an enormous coil of rope in the back.

"We'll take it from here," Zedediah told Jake. "You'd better go find out what's still on E.D.'s to-do list. With her schedule screwed up like this, she's probably beside herself."

Jake headed back to the Lodge. One thing that wouldn't be on E.D.'s list was getting Winston stashed in Wisteria Cottage before anybody else arrived. Nobody understood Winston's sensitivity the way Jake did—or even noticed it particularly. But in a world as intense as the Applewhites', the dog needed his own personal safe haven. As far as Winston was concerned, that haven was Jake's bedroom—in fact, Jake's bed.

The moment Jake slipped inside the front door, Winston came running, snuffling and whining with pleasure, and leaped on him, covering his knees with saliva. "Down, boy!" Jake said, shoving the dog firmly

to the floor. Winston rolled over to let Jake rub his tummy. The smell of warm chocolate wafted in from the kitchen. Lucille was making her famous triple-chocolate brownies as a treat for the first night of camp.

"Let's go," he said, "and get you stowed." But outside, instead of heading for Wisteria Cottage, Winston trotted purposefully off toward the meadow, his tail waving cheerily. Jake didn't whistle him back. If the dog wanted a walk, why not let him have one before he got cooped up in his safe haven?

Winston leaped at a butterfly—the only prey he ever went after—prey he never came anywhere near catching. It was funny to watch the big, ungainly basset hound leap up in the air after a butterfly that could float effortlessly out of his reach. For some reason, Winston never got discouraged. *Butterfly, leap. Butterfly, leap.*

Across the meadow, Winston took the woods trail in under the trees. Jake followed, watching his footing to keep from tripping over wisteria vines or the things E.D. called barbed wire vine. Lucille said they were greenbrier, but E.D. insisted that nothing as vicious as that should have such a pretty name. No matter how often the vines were cut back from the trail, they grew across it again. In spite of that, the trail was passable—cutting cross-country through the woods was nearly impossible. Between wisteria, barbed wire

vine, and poison ivy, the North Carolina woods could be treacherous, but at least they were quiet and shady. Jake began to hum "Consider Yourself at Home," his favorite song from *Oliver!*. His heart lifted immediately. *This,* Jake thought, *is what Zedediah means when he talks about joy.* In no time he had switched from humming to singing, his voice filling the green shade of the woods.

When he finished the song, he thought he heard voices from the general direction of the pond. He stopped and listened. Girls' voices. The fur rose along Winston's back, and he began making the whuffling sound he made when he was deciding whether to bark. It couldn't be E.D. or Cordelia. Winston never whuffled at anyone he knew. It had to be the twins.

"No worries," he told the dog. "We don't have to go anywhere near the pond." He had taken only a few more steps along the trail when there was a bloodcurdling shriek. It was followed by another, and another. Soon there were two voices shrieking. Whatever was going on, it sounded serious.

Jake tore through the woods toward the pond, leaping over vines and fallen limbs, shoving branches out of his way as he went, his skin getting scraped by the thorns of the barbed wire vine. Winston lumbered behind him, barking frantically. When Jake emerged from under the trees, he saw one of the twins, completely covered with black muck, standing hip

deep in the pond. Her carroty curls had vanished under the muck, as had her freckles. The only part of her that wasn't black was her mouth, stretched wide in yet another scream. The other twin, in a blue swimsuit, was dancing along the edge of the pond, staying well back from the edge, her bare feet, too, black with muck.

"Come back!" the blue twin yelled. "Right this minute! Come back here!"

"I can't! I can't! It's got me. I can't move! You gotta come pull me out!" The muck-covered twin held a dripping hand out to her sister. *"Quick, quick! It's sucking me down! I'm gonna drown!"*

"I can't come out there. It'll get me too. We'll both drown!"

Jake sighed. The girls had begun to cry now, growing more hysterical by the minute. He pulled off his sneakers and socks, ran to the pond, and splashed into the water, sinking deeper into the mud with every step he took. It was all he could do to keep his balance as he pulled one foot after another out of the mire.

Good thing she's so small, he thought. She was still gasping through her sobs that she was drowning when he reached her, pulled her free, and threw her, dripping slime, over his shoulder. Slight as she was, the extra weight forced him even farther into the mud. Still, he managed to slog his way back to shore

without falling in himself. No way this girl had been in any danger of being pulled under.

"You saved me, you saved me," she was saying as he set her down on the grass.

Jake wrinkled his nose. The feel of the muck didn't particularly bother him underfoot, but the smell was disgusting: all mold and rot and dead things. Dead fishy things. He was almost as black with it now as the girl.

The other twin had started screaming again. She was sitting among the cattails at the edge of the pond, trying to fend Winston off as he slathered her face with his tongue. Jake didn't need to have seen it to know what had happened. Winston couldn't stand to see anyone cry, stranger or not. He always did his best to offer comfort, which consisted of licking them reassuringly. And thoroughly. He must have jumped on her and knocked her backward.

Jake went over, grabbed Winston's collar, and pulled him away.

"That's it!" the girl said, struggling to her feet and trying to wipe Winston's saliva off her face with one hand and the mud off her bottom with the other. "Get me to a phone," she demanded. "Right now! My sister and I are going home."

Jake picked up a towel that was crumpled on the grass. He supposed the girls had been intending to swim out to the diving platform that floated invitingly

in the center of the pond. Kids who were used to swimming pools clearly didn't understand about ponds. He took the towel over to the other girl, who was trying unsuccessfully to clean her face with her muddy hands.

"How'd you fall down?" he asked as she began toweling her face and hair.

She looked up at him, her eyes wide. "I didn't *fall*. It was the pond! It's like something out of Stephen King. I just started walking out into it, and it pulled me in, knocked me over, and started to suck me down. I was lucky to get up again." She dropped the towel and threw her arms around him. "Thank you, thank you. You saved my life!"

It was then that Cordelia arrived. "I see you've met Jake." Jake disentangled himself from the mud-covered twin. "What are you two doing here? You're supposed to be on a scavenger hunt over by the barn!"

"It's too hot for a scavenger hunt," the muddy twin said.

"Besides," the other one added, "I never compete with Ginger. There's no point. She always wins. We saw the pond on the map you gave us and decided to swim instead."

This, Jake thought, was why they'd all been warned never to let the campers out of their sight.

"Our father is going to sue you for everything you've got!" the green twin said. "How come you

didn't warn us about this death pond?"

Cordelia smiled a bright and entirely unconvincing smile. "How come you didn't notice the sign in your bunk that says, No Swimming Without a Lifeguard Present?"

"Get me to a phone," said the blue twin. "Now! We're going home!"

"If you say so," Cordelia said, "but you have to come to the office to use the phone, and you're not setting foot in the office till you've had a shower. Besides, you're going to need some lunch. We hadn't expected to have campers here till dinnertime, but I make a mean peanut butter sandwich."

From the look on the girls' faces, Jake figured peanut butter sandwiches were not a staple of their diet. "Let's go, Winston," he said, picking up his socks and shoving his muddy feet into his sneakers.

The sound of Archie's pickup heralded the arrival of the floating dock as Cordelia shepherded the muddy twins back toward their bunk.

Chapter Eleven

1:55 P.M. Camper-arrival time minus five. E.D., standing on the Lodge porch, pinned her EXECUTIVE ASSISTANT name tag to her staff T-shirt, scanned her clipboard, and sighed with relief. In spite of the rocky start to this day, things seemed now to be under control. A long metal folding table had been put up in front of the two Zedediah Applewhite rocking chairs. REGISTRATION, said the paper taped to the front of it in large, plain block letters. E.D. had made that herself. Taped to the top of the table so it wouldn't blow away was a spreadsheet with the names

of the campers and their parents' names, addresses, phone numbers, and e-mail addresses, with boxes for checking off each of the campers as they arrived. She'd checked off Cinnamon and Ginger before she printed it. Four water bottles were lined up next to four canvas bags, and there was a plastic bin for collecting camper cell phones. On the far end of the table were the maps Cordelia had made.

Cordelia, E.D. thought, was a genius. Once the twins had recovered from the disaster at the pond, she had somehow managed to keep them occupied and away from the phone. Grandpa and Uncle Archie had put the new dock in place, tied to a pair of sweet gum trees and connected to solid ground by a wooden ramp. An hour ago her father had called from the airport to report that Samantha Peterman's flight had arrived on time, and she and Destiny were having lunch. "Destiny, of course, is talking her ears off," Randolph had said, "but she's doing her best to hide behind a book. It's a good thing Quincy Brown's plane gets in at two. Destiny has already filled up the drawing pad he brought along."

Her mother and Aunt Lucille had finished everything that could be done ahead of time for tonight's opening dinner and had gone off to change so they'd be ready to greet the campers as they arrived. Jake had finished the last-minute chores E.D. had given him. She herself had made and put out

cardboard signs along the drive with arrows pointing to Camp Registration, because Hal, whose job that was supposed to be, had closed himself in his old bedroom and was refusing to come out.

The screen door banged, and her mother emerged from the house. She was wearing the khaki shorts and shirt outfit she had bought years ago for a safari to research *Petunia Grantham on the Veldt*. On one of the many shirt pockets was pinned her name tag, SYBIL JAMESON, AUTHOR AND ASSOCIATE CAMP DIRECTOR. Her jaw was clenched with determination. Aunt Lucille came hurrying around the house now from Wisteria Cottage, dressed in a swirly skirt and flowered blouse, her curls falling loose and beginning to frizz. Her name tag said simply LUCILLE APPLEWHITE, POET. "This is so exciting!" The arrival of the evil twins did not seem to have dampened her enthusiasm. "Everything ready?" she asked brightly.

Before E.D. could answer, they heard, out beyond the bushes, a car turning into the driveway. Two o'clock, E.D. noted. Whoever this was, they were impeccably on time. Aunt Lucille and her mother took their seats behind the registration table. An ancient, battered Volkswagen bus came around the curve of the drive and pulled to a stop in front of the porch with a squeal of brakes. The driver's door opened, and a woman in cutoffs and a tank top, with a long brown braid reaching halfway down her back, jumped out.

E.D. had never seen anyone like her. Except for her face, every square inch of visible skin was covered with brilliantly colored tattoos. There were horses with flowing manes and tails ridden by figures that could have been humans or spirits, warriors or elves. There were dragons and flowers and strange, calligraphic symbols. The woman was a walking art gallery.

"Out, Harley!" the woman called. "I have to be in Asheville in time for setup."

This, E.D. realized, was Marlie Michaels, lead singer of Dragon's Breath and mother of Harley Schobert, age twelve. The other door opened then, and Harley slid down from the passenger seat. He had medium long, medium brown hair and a medium face on a medium body. He was wearing blue running shorts, a plain white T-shirt, and sneakers. In a crowd of kids—any kids—this boy, E.D. thought, would completely disappear. Marlie Michaels and Harley Schobert, mother and son. It was as if a starling egg had been slipped into a bird of paradise nest by mistake.

As Harley and his mother went up the porch steps to the registration table, E.D. heard another car on the driveway. This would be David Giacomo, she thought.

A dark red sedan pulled up behind the van. The woman who emerged from the driver's side—dark hair perfectly styled, wearing a yellow-and-white

sundress and white, strappy sandals—was staring at Marlie Michaels with an expression of horror. E.D. wondered whether she might be at that very moment changing her mind about leaving her son at *Eureka!* That was to be the last rational thought that went through E.D.'s mind that afternoon. Because just then David Giacomo stepped out of the car.

The photo he'd sent with his camp application had shown him to be good-looking. But this kid was not good-looking. This kid was—E.D. searched for a word that fit—*awesome*, that was it. Not the way her friend Melissa used it, for everything from a lipstick color to a hamburger, but for what the word really meant: "inspiring amazement and respect, combined with a feeling of personal powerlessness." That was it exactly. His longish, wavy, blue-black hair framed a face with a straight nose, high cheekbones, full lips, and large, wide-set eyes—eyes that were startlingly blue. She had seen a face like that somewhere before, but where?

David Giacomo was tall. He was slim. Ethereal. Absolutely awesome! There was a kind of glow around him—like an angel. Suddenly she knew where she had seen a face like this before: in the research for her spring semester paper on Renaissance art. David Giacomo was a Botticelli angel! E.D. felt like a little pile of iron filings, pulled inexorably toward a magnet.

He was fourteen. But he looked older. She reminded

herself to breathe. Then she hurried to the registration table, picked up a canvas bag and a water bottle, and took them to him. She was aware that the adults were talking, that David was answering a question. His voice was soft and smooth and resonant. She handed him the bag. As he took it, his long fingers brushed hers, and a tiny electrical shock traveled all the way down to her toes.

"E.D.! E.D.! Your phone!"

Her mother's voice penetrated her consciousness, and E.D. became aware that the cell phone in her shorts pocket was playing Reveille—her father's ring. "Excuse me," she said. "I should take this." A moment later she found herself behind the house, out of earshot, though she didn't remember walking away from the porch.

"Disaster!" her father yelled the moment she answered. She held the phone away from her ear. "Complete catastrophe! Quincy's plane has been delayed. Some nonsense about an equipment malfunction. Do they expect me to believe there is only one plane they could possibly send here from Atlanta?" With the image of David Giacomo filling her mind, E.D. found herself listening to her father's rant with surprising calm.

"The idiot agent I was talking to actually called security on me. They accused me of *shouting*, if you'd believe it. All I did was very calmly and entirely

rationally mention the possibility of a lawsuit. They threatened to kick me out of the airport. If Destiny hadn't started crying, they might have done it. They left one of the security guards to keep an eye on me. They say it'll be another three hours at least! Samantha's finished her book. And what am I going to do with Destiny? He's talking to the guard now. Asking questions. You know how Destiny can get on a person's nerves—the man has a gun, for heaven's sake."

"Take Destiny to the gift shop," E.D. said. "Buy him a new sketch pad. Maybe some new markers."

Before her father could say anything else, she told him a camper was arriving and she had to go. She flipped her phone shut. Her father was a grown-up, she thought. He could surely cope for a few more hours.

By the time she had hurried back around to the porch, the van had gone and her mother was deep in conversation with David's mother. David himself had disappeared, as had Harley. Her heart sank. "Where did he—they—go?" she asked Aunt Lucille, an odd quiver in her voice.

"Jake came and took them off to the boys' bunk. I'm going to go up and see if I can pry Hal out of his room."

"I'd better go make sure everything is okay over there," E.D. said.

The rest of the afternoon passed in a blur of images with David Giacomo in the center. There were two more frantic phone calls from the airport. Later, Cordelia, Ginger, and Cinnamon appeared with a bucket of homemade bubble mix and a handful of enormous wands they had made out of wire coat hangers, and challenged the boys to see who could make the biggest bubbles. David could, it turned out. *Of course*, E.D. thought. She remembered David's application. Zedediah had called him a "Renaissance man." David, apparently, could do anything.

At some point Cordelia organized a scavenger hunt with the rule that no one was allowed to go near the pond. "As if!" said the green twin. Cordelia had neglected, however, to warn the campers about the goats. So the scavenger hunt had been interrupted by a hysterical chase, first Wolfie chasing campers and then most of the Applewhites chasing Wolfie. David ran not only extremely fast, E.D. noticed, but with the grace of a dancer.

The campers were just bringing the last of their scavenger hunt finds to the Lodge porch when Randolph finally drove up in Sybil's station wagon.

Destiny bounded out of the car the instant it stopped. "Daddy almost gotted put in jail!" he shouted. "I was scared for a little bit, except the guard guy was really nice. He's got goatses at home, just like us, but

no dog and no parrot. And then Q came—his name's really Quincy, but he calls himself Q—and you know what he did?" Destiny didn't so much as take a breath before he answered his own question. "He gotted everybody dancing. Practically everybody in the whole airport!"

Randolph, Samantha Peterman, and Quincy Brown had gotten out of the car now as well. "Not so many," Quincy said, flashing a 500-watt smile. "The flight attendant just asked me to show what I did in Atlanta after they announced the delay."

"Destiny's almost right," Randolph said. "He even got that security guard dancing. Show them, Q."

The boy began stomping his feet on the gravel drive, slapping his hands on his legs, and clapping in an intricate pattern, slowly at first, then picking up speed.

"It's called Step!" Destiny said. "Isn't it great? I can do the hands and the feet both! He showed me while we was waiting for the suitcases to come!" He joined in now, stamping and slapping and clapping.

"In Atlanta, when they said they didn't have a plane for us, people started to get ugly," Quincy said when the routine was finished. "My grandfather says Step is good for cheering people up, so I started to do some. Pretty soon a couple of guys joined in. And then some more. People started coming to watch from whole different concourses! By the time they'd found us a

plane, there were old ladies clapping and stomping and a whole traveling baseball team using the trash cans for hand drums. The guys from the airline said they never saw people so happy about a delay in their lives! Somebody videoed it with his phone and said he's gonna post it online!"

As everyone else hurried over to greet the newcomers, E.D. found herself edging closer to David, who remained where he'd been during Q's performance, leaning elegantly against the porch railing, his arms crossed, a half smile on his face.

Chapter Twelve

At dinner, which was more than an hour late thanks to the plane delay, the boys all sat at one picnic table in the dining tent—except Hal, who took his food and sneaked off to his room—and the girls at another. Samantha brought a book with her and read steadily while she ate. Ginger, Jake noticed, kept her eyes fixed on him. Whenever he glanced that way, she broke into a toothy grin.

Destiny, at the boys' table, asked question after question, barely giving the guys time to answer before

he was on to the next. He wanted to know where Q had learned to do Step. How come he lived with his grandfather instead of his mother and father and whether they had a cottage like Zedediah's, or a parrot. How many floors there were in his apartment building. What it was like to live where you had to ride in an elevator to get home. Q just kept eating and answering till Destiny switched to Harley.

He wanted to know how come Harley was wearing a camera around his neck and was he going to take pictures of everything they did at camp and how come he didn't like taking pictures of people and why wasn't he eating any of Aunt Lucille's best-brownies-in-the-whole-world-ever.

When he started on David, David didn't answer. So Destiny just asked louder, till finally David told him to shut up and let him eat. This was surprising, Jake thought. People were almost never rude to Destiny. But Destiny was undaunted. "You don't gots to stop eating. It's not polite to *talk* with your mouth full, but it's okay to listen."

David was the only one at the boys' table who didn't find that funny.

The tour of Wit's End that was supposed to have happened before dinner had been postponed until afterward. If Jake had known Ginger was going to be at his heels the whole time, he would have excused himself and gone to hide out in his room, like Hal.

Every time he turned around, there she was, staring up at him. Twice he practically stepped on her.

It was almost nine, and Destiny had been sent, protesting, to bed, before they finally gathered everybody together at the campfire circle for the Opening Ceremony. The fire and marshmallow-toasting part of the plan had already been canceled because of heat and lack of time, and Zedediah had asked that all the welcoming speeches be cut as short as possible.

Again, as the campers went to find seats on the logs around the circle, the girls headed one way and the boys another. But as soon as Jake sat, Ginger scurried over and sat beside him—very, very close beside him. The night was hot enough, but she was like a little radiator. He could feel the sweat running down the middle of his back.

Zedediah spoke very briefly about the critical importance of creativity in human civilization and the intention for *Eureka!* to become a "true creative community—one for all and all for one." Randolph, however, took nearly half an hour to extol the virtues of theater—"the single art that includes all the rest." Jake wondered what his talk might have been like if he hadn't been asked to cut it short. Hal, on the other hand, was done in about ten seconds. He stood up, said he would be doing visual arts with an emphasis on painting, and sat down again.

Jake was after Hal. As he moved to get up, Ginger

grabbed for his hand. She pressed a folded piece of paper into his palm, closed his fingers over it, and let go. *Now what?* Jake thought. He stuck the paper in his pocket and went to the center of the circle. "I'm not much for speeches," he said, "but I'll be leading the singing workshop. Who here knows 'Doe a Deer,' from *The Sound of Music?*" When they raised their hands, he started the campers singing it. Unlike the Applewhites, the kids could carry a tune. Q sang every bit as well as he danced. David was good, too, but he sang louder than the others instead of trying to blend in with them. The only camper he couldn't tell anything about was Harley, who had sat bent over his camera through the whole thing and didn't sing at all. When the song was over, Jake went to the other side of the circle and sat next to Archie instead of where he'd been before.

By the time the campers were dismissed to their bunks to get ready for bed, it was 9:55, so Jake went to the Lodge, where a staff meeting was supposed to begin at ten. Nobody was in the living room when he got there. He pulled the paper Ginger had given him out of his pocket and sat down on the couch.

MY SAVIOR, JAKE SEMPLE

Nearly sucked to my doom
In the foul-smelling gloom,
I was crying, crying, crying,
Nearly dying, dying, dying!

But Jake came along
With his muscles so strong
And lifted me free,
Saving me, saving me!

Before camp could start
Jake had captured my heart.

It was printed in red marker and signed *Your FF,*
Ginger Boniface. There was an entire row of *x*'s and *o*'s
across the bottom. Jake groaned and stuffed it back
into his pocket. He had no tools for dealing with
something like this.

A few minutes later, Sybil came in to call Jake outside
to the dining tent. "There's been an insurrection!"

The campers, it turned out, had flatly rejected the
idea of roughing it. David, citing extreme sensitivity,
announced that if he and Quincy—David insisted on
using Q's full name—didn't get a fan in their room, he
would "die in the night from suffocation and heat
prostration." *Extreme sensitivity!* Jake thought. Sure.
David had made a fuss at dinner because there was no
vegetarian option. As much attention as Q got just
being his incredibly outgoing, incredibly positive self,
David was probably just trying to get somebody
besides E.D. to notice him. She'd been practically
drooling over the kid all day. Jake couldn't imagine
what she saw in him.

After that, of course, everybody demanded fans, including Hal and Cordelia. Jake and Archie were sent to the barn to see whether there were any fans left over from before air-conditioning. They located four, which were provided to the campers. Archie had to promise Hal and Cordelia that he would drive to town first thing in the morning to get two more.

Then there was the issue of whether individual reading lights could be kept on after lights-out, which Samantha Peterman insisted was absolutely necessary (*no*) and whether campers could listen to their personal music with earbuds after lights-out (*yes*—after Randolph, who maintained that it led to deafness and interfered with brain waves, had been argued down by Zedediah).

After that there was another uproar because the twins had discovered that the Wi-Fi in the Lodge didn't reach the cottages; not only did their phones not work, but they couldn't get online in their room. Cinnamon once again demanded a telephone to arrange to be taken home. Sybil, who by that time had lost whatever patience she'd been able to muster, informed her that only emergency phone calls could be made after ten and when Cinnamon claimed that this *was* an emergency, made up a rule on the spot that an emergency required a fever, severe bleeding, or vomiting.

Finally there was the question of whether, if they

kept the lights out, the campers could stay up talking and maybe hang out in the living rooms of the cottages (*most definitely not*). Whether the campers talked in their rooms or not (*quietly—in whispers— with no singing and no loud laughter*) was up to them, but they were to be in their beds at the stroke of ten with all lights out—except for this first night—and they were to stay there till wake-up call at 7:30 A.M.

Jake was nearly asleep on his feet by the time Randolph called the staff back to the Lodge for the staff meeting.

Chapter Thirteen

Everyone still had their official name tags on, E.D. noticed, when they were finally settled in the living room of the Lodge. The only staff members missing were Hal, Visual Artist/Counselor, and Cordelia, Dancer/Counselor, who were in the bunks watching over the hot, tired, and grumpy campers.

Randolph Applewhite, Camp Director, beamed around at the others. "All in all, an auspicious beginning. *Eureka!* is off to a brilliant start!" This was a stretch even for an Applewhite. E.D. had been

expecting something more like "What have we gotten ourselves into?"

"I would hardly call it brilliant," Sybil said. "Dinner was a catastrophe. The twins demanded whole wheat buns for their barbecue, and Harley doesn't like chocolate. What kind of kid doesn't like chocolate? David is a vegetarian and can't stand Kool-Aid, and—"

"You should have put a question on the application about food issues," Randolph said.

"We *did*!" E.D. said.

"David apparently only decided he was a vegetarian the day before yesterday! We've got to redo all the menus and go shopping again. Whole wheat buns? Whatever happened to kids who live on hot dogs, peanut butter, and chicken nuggets?"

Her mother had only agreed to share the job of cooking with Aunt Lucille, E.D. knew, because she'd been shamed into it by Randolph.

Jake Semple, Singing Coach, stifled a yawn. Even stifled, it was contagious. E.D. yawned and so did her grandfather. It was now well after eleven. Archie Applewhite, Sculptor, sitting on the couch with his head on Aunt Lucille's shoulder, appeared to have fallen asleep. Paulie stood on one foot on his perch, his beak tucked under his wing, Winston was snoring noisily at Jake's feet, and Destiny Applewhite, Camp Mascot, was surely doing the same in his bed upstairs. E.D. envied them.

"Things could have been worse," her father said now.

Her mother wasn't buying it. "Besides the food disaster," she said, "we've got a kid who threatens to go home every time something doesn't suit her—"

"Just don't let her get to a phone!"

"—and a mother who has already called four times to find out if her kid's okay."

"Which mother?" Lucille asked.

"Samantha's. Turns out the child has never been away from home overnight."

"That explains it! When the insurrection started, she came to me crying and begging me to let her call home."

"Bad idea!" Randolph said. "If we let the girl talk to her mother, they'll just stir each other up all the more. Next thing you know that child will be on a plane headed home. We are not going to lose a camper!"

"Never mind," Lucille said. "I gave her some breathing exercises and told her to give herself three days. By that time she'll be all caught up in camp activities. It's just homesickness. She'll be fine."

"And I explained to Mrs. Peterman the last time she called," Sybil said, "that we'd call *her* if there were any problems. We nearly lost a camper before he even registered. Mrs. Giacomo practically had a heart attack when she saw Marlie Michaels's tattoos. I had to do some fast talking, let me tell you! It's a good

93

thing *Harley* looked normal or David would have been back in Virginia by now."

Randolph slammed his hand down on the arm of the couch. "We aren't refunding deposits! No matter what. The income from this benighted idea is barely enough as it is."

Apparently her father had forgotten for the moment whose benighted idea it was, E.D. thought. At least he had come back from whatever rosy fantasy land he was inhabiting when the meeting started. If they were going to save Wit's End, they all had to gut this out no matter what it meant, but there was no point in pretending it was going to be easy.

"We need to talk about Community Service," E.D. said now. "Nobody mentioned it at the Opening Ceremony." She held up the stapled schedules she was planning to give the family tonight and hand out to the campers in the morning. "It's all here, and after seeing how they reacted to the idea of roughing it, I think when they find out about Community Service, we could have another insurrection on our hands."

During the weeks of planning for camp, E.D. had been the first to realize that all the usual chores that kept Wit's End livable would still need to be done. The jobs like laundry and cleaning, vacuuming and dusting had always been a source of considerable conflict in the family. No one liked doing them, and what they didn't like, they tended to avoid whenever possible.

From time to time Wit's End had, in fact, become very nearly *un*livable. That couldn't happen with people paying big money for their kids to be here.

Besides that, having six more people in residence and two more cottages lived in regularly meant that there would be even greater-than-usual need for most of these chores, so E.D. had come up with the idea of simply including them in the camp schedule. Each camper would be assigned a particular chore every day. "Calling this stuff Community Service should help support the whole 'all for one and one for all' thing," she'd said.

Lucille had agreed. "We will appeal to their higher natures." It had seemed a better idea at the time than it did now.

In her welcoming talk Lucille had mentioned that all beds were to be made each morning and the bunks straightened before her prebreakfast Welcome-the-Day Meditation and Yoga activity. There had been considerable groaning among the campers even at this. Community Service included plenty of worse jobs: cleaning bathrooms, setting up for meals, helping with dishes, weeding the vegetable garden, feeding the goats, cutting the grass.

"We should just spring their assignments on them every morning at breakfast," Sybil said. "That'll keep them off balance. These are intelligent and creative kids. Give them too much time, and they'll figure out

a way around actually doing anything."

"Off balance!" Randolph said then. "That's an excellent idea. We should spring the *whole schedule* on them a day at a time. It will encourage flexibility, one of the prime traits of the creative individual. Each camper will have to begin the day ready for anything."

E.D. thought of the effort and the time—days and days—she had put into creating the camp schedule for the whole eight weeks. The schedule, in its three-ring binder, was on top of a filing cabinet in the office. She had with her now the first week—three-and-a-half double-sided pages stapled together. They were neatly laid out, spreadsheet fashion, with workshops color coded for easy reference.

She had begun to think of the whole thing as a work of art, an absolutely practical work of art. The colors provided continuity for the whole eight weeks, even as daily schedules varied. Morning workshops and evening activities (*all required for all campers*) were in red, mealtimes in yellow, optional afternoon workshops in green, water activities in blue, and free time in purple. Staff members each had an icon—theater masks for Randolph, quill pen for Lucille, pencil for Sybil, musical note for Jake, ballet slippers for Cordelia, paintbrush for Hal, saw for Zedediah, and chisel for Archie. These icons, in the upper left corners of the color blocks, showed who was in charge of the activity.

Aunt Lucille reached over and patted E.D.'s hand. "Don't worry, sweetie, everybody knows what a great job you did with the schedule. The only thing that's changing here is when the campers see it."

Zedediah yawned again. "Everybody remember, it's only the first day." He looked at his watch. "Closing in on becoming the second. Staff meeting or no staff meeting, I'm going to bed. There's nothing more we can accomplish here tonight." With that, the old man pushed himself up from his chair and went over to Paulie's perch. "Bedtime, fella," he said, holding out his arm.

The parrot ruffled his feathers, stepped onto Zedediah's arm, and made his way up to his shoulder. "Night, night," the bird said. E.D. had a feeling, sometimes, that Paulie knew exactly what he was saying.

In the doorway, Zedediah turned back for a moment. "You did a fine job with the schedule, E.D. Give them just one day of it tomorrow, and we'll see what happens. We'll all have to take this a day at a time, you know. I have great faith that this family can accomplish whatever we set our minds to do—even if it *was* Randolph's idea. See you at breakfast."

"Oh, my God, breakfast!" Sybil said as Zedediah left. "*Breakfast!* I promised the twins stone-ground whole wheat bread by morning! And whatever will we do for lunch?"

Archie opened his eyes and stretched his arms over

his head. "I'm going to town for fans first thing. I'll stop at the grocery store while I'm there—just give me a list." He glanced around the room, saw that Zedediah was no longer there, and turned to Lucille. "I'm wiped. Let's go."

"All right, all right," Randolph said. "Meeting's over."

E.D. sighed. She couldn't go to bed till she'd printed out six copies of only the first day's schedule.

Chapter Fourteen

I t was only 7:45, and already the day was hot and muggy. After Destiny had been forbidden to go to Lucille's first Meditation and Yoga session, Jake had brought him to the goat pen. Jake had, of course, shut Wolfie and his food into the shed, because Destiny had been chased so often he had nightmares about brown-and-white monsters with huge lopsided horns.

Now Destiny was grumbling as he scooped feed into Hazel's plastic bucket. "I don't see how comes I don't get to do what the campers do," Destiny said.

"What's a mascot anyway? Doesn't mascots get to *do* anything?"

"You get to do things," Jake said. "You have a Community Service job every single day, just like everybody else. Today you and I both have goat duty."

"That's not a *camp* thing. We gots to do that all the time. I wanna do what Aunt Lucille's doing in the barn."

"It's just for campers."

"E.D.'s there, and she's not a camper."

"What can I tell you, kid? Life's not fair. Besides, it's meditation. You know you don't do meditation. You always talk the whole time."

"Sometimes I sing!"

"Right. Singing's good, but it's not meditation. Maybe, if you ask nicely and promise not to talk during it, Lucille will let you do the yoga part after today. They'll do that outside. It's the sun salutation."

"I *like* yoga," Destiny said. "I do downward-facing dog real good."

"You do. But you'd have to promise not to bark. *Listen*, Destiny—even if your aunt lets you do yoga with the campers, you're still not going to get to go to the workshops with them."

Hazel came over to get her breakfast, and Destiny patted her head. "Well, it's not fair. There's all these new kids here—I don't hardly ever get to see new kids—and nobody's letting me be with 'em!"

Jake sighed. Home schooling was a really good thing in some ways, but maybe not so much for a kid like Destiny. The more people there were for him to talk to, the happier he was, and the easier it was on everybody. "Tell you what. My workshop's about singing. If your parents say it's okay, you can come to that."

"Yay, Jake! I loves to sing. Singing makes my heart feel good."

Jake laughed. "Mine too." He ushered Destiny out of the goat pen, opened the door of the shed, sprinted across the pen, and slammed the gate behind him moments before Wolfie crashed into the fence. "Let's go back and see what's for breakfast."

"Maybe it's waffles! Waffles is the best of best."

As they came around the side of the Lodge, Jake heard a vehicle slowing down out on the road. "Archie must be back from town," he said to Destiny. "He went to get groceries."

Destiny stopped and listened. "Nope. That doesn't sound like the truck."

"Maybe he took your mom's car."

They could hear it turning into the driveway now, tires crunching on the gravel. After a moment it stopped, its engine idling.

"How comes he stopped?" Destiny asked. "Let's go see if he brung waffles for breakfast."

The car Jake and Destiny saw when they got

around the row of bushes wasn't Sybil's. It was a plain, black compact. As soon as the driver saw them, he threw the car into reverse, backed hurriedly onto the road, and roared away.

"Who was that?" Destiny asked. "Hardly nobody ever comes down that road."

Jake shrugged. "Or into the drive. Maybe he was lost."

"I coulda told him where he was. Mommy made me learn our address. Did you know our road doesn't even gots a name? Just a number."

"He was probably using the driveway to turn around."

"No, Jake. 'Cause when he went away I heard him goin' the same way he was already goin' before."

Destiny was right, Jake realized. He was one sharp kid.

"Look, look!" Destiny said, "Uncle Archie's truck's over by the tent. Let's go see if he brung waffles."

Chapter Fifteen

On the stage floor in the barn, Cordelia and the campers were sitting cross-legged— Samantha in full lotus position—in a circle around Lucille. Cinnamon was in blue again, Ginger in green. Q and David sat together, elbowing each other from time to time. Harley, a camera on a strap around his neck, was staring fixedly at something on the floor in front of him. E.D. had slipped in late and was standing in the shadows by the stage door, leaning against the rough barn siding. Hal must have skipped out again, she thought,

till she saw him in the back corner of the stage, his eyes already closed, probably pretending he was alone in a cave somewhere.

"Stillness is essential to the creative imagination," Lucille was saying now. "That's why we don't allow cell phones at *Eureka!* All the electronic technology we're surrounded with fractures our attention."

"Huh!" Cinnamon snorted.

Lucille went on as if she hadn't heard. "Meditation can mend that fractured consciousness. So now, if you are comfortable with it, close your eyes."

As far as E.D. could tell, most of the campers did that. Cinnamon, however, sat with her arms crossed in front of her, fingers tapping her upper arms, frowning into the shadows above the rows of theater seats.

"Become aware of the air moving in through your nostrils. Now, let it out again, with a gentle sigh, through your mouth." Lucille closed her eyes as well. "Try breathing that way for three minutes, keeping your attention on your breath. Feel the air moving in—out—in—out. Feel it. Listen to it. Let your mind go still."

Lucille had been trying to find a way to help E.D. meditate for years now. Sometimes, she said, instead of closing your eyes, you could still your mind by focusing your attention on something beautiful. A candle flame. A mandala. A lotus. E.D. focused her

attention on David, watching his shoulders and chest rise and fall with his breath. A thin shaft of sunlight shone between the boards of the barn wall and fell on his dark, wavy hair. E.D. began to imagine that light expanding until it surrounded him with a pale, golden aura. Little by little, the aura seemed to become real, growing around him with each breath. Stillness. E.D. smiled. She had achieved stillness!

Did angels have to breathe, she wondered suddenly. Did they have lungs? Botticelli, she knew, had painted his angels from human models, but did real angels have real bodies? Or weren't they real at all? Were they just figments of human imagination? David, of course, was no figment. . . .

A brilliant flash shattered the moment. Everybody's eyes were open now.

"Harley! No, no, no! There will be no cameras in morning meditation!" Lucille held her hand out. After a moment the boy took the strap off over his head and handed her his camera, muttering about the beautiful dead beetle he'd found.

"Can we be done?" Cinnamon asked. "My butt hurts."

"Maybe we could bring pillows next time," Samantha said.

"If you focus on your breath, you'll find that after a while you don't even notice the floor," Lucille said.

E.D. had tried this. It never really worked for her.

The floor was the floor. Apparently it hadn't worked for anyone else, either. The others had begun groaning and fidgeting now, so Lucille announced they could all get up and go outside. "Meditation takes practice. In fact, it *is* a practice. We'll start every morning this way"—Cinnamon sighed dramatically—"and you'll get the hang of it soon enough. Three minutes at first, then five, then ten; believe me, meditation will enhance your creativity and defuse stress. It will be a useful tool the rest of your life." She pushed herself up from the floor. "Everybody up! Let's go salute the glorious sun and get those bodies awake and energized and flexible. Balance, campers! Mind, body, spirit."

E.D. slipped out the door. If there was one thing she liked less than meditation, it was yoga. Her body was *not* flexible. Aunt Lucille—Cordelia too—could bend over at the waist and put their hands absolutely flat on the floor. E.D. had never gotten farther than her ankles. Even Jake did better at yoga than she did. She headed for the kitchen to get something to eat before she had to hand out the schedules in the dining tent.

Three hours later she was tromping through the woods in search of a missing camper. She should have realized that things had started off too well. There had been no rebellion at all about the first Community Service assignments. She had attributed that partly to assigning only easy chores this first day—no bathroom

106

cleaning—but mostly to the fact that it was Zedediah, with his white hair and mustache and that natural air of authority, who had explained the concept. Not even the Boniface girls had raised a complaint, though Cordelia had told her at breakfast that she'd had to teach them how to make their beds. "Can you believe they'd never done it before?"

After that, the first required workshop, Archie's Introduction to Natural Materials Sculpture, went well. E.D. attended, having decided that *Eureka!* needed a historian—someone to observe and take notes so there would be a record of what worked and what didn't, in case, against all sanity, they ever decided to do this again. As historian, of course, her iron-filing self would have an excuse to hang out around David-the-magnet. It made her heart beat faster, somehow, just to be in the same room with him. The second workshop had been Poetry. She hadn't been able to go to that one because Sybil needed her in the kitchen.

That was how she had missed the moment when things went wrong. Lucille had asked the campers to write a poem in their journals—a poem about the first feelings they'd had when they woke up that morning—and Cinnamon had said she needed to go back to Dogwood for a different pen. "I write better in color."

Lucille, of course, allowed her to go. Cinnamon had not returned. After ten minutes Lucille considered

sending Ginger after her sister, but Ginger was writing steadily and furiously in her journal and Lucille didn't want to interrupt. So she had simply continued her workshop, assuming that Cinnamon would show up at any moment. She did not.

Nor, when the workshop was over, was she found in Dogwood, in any of the bathrooms, at the pond, in the Lodge, or in any of the other cottages. E.D. had been sent to wake up her father, who was seldom functional till noon.

"Missing?" Uncharacteristically, he had leaped out of bed so fast that he had a dizzy spell and had to hold onto her shoulder for a moment. "A camper is missing? Don't tell the other campers," he said, running a hand through his sleep-tousled hair.

"They already know," E.D. said. "They were all in the workshop she didn't come back to."

"Then get the campers busy doing something and get everybody else out there searching. We have to find her! Now!" He grabbed for his jeans. "We simply cannot afford to lose a camper on the very first full day!"

As if we could afford to lose one ever, E.D. thought as she went back downstairs.

Zedediah gathered the campers in the dining tent to give the part of his Opening Ceremony talk he'd originally had to cut, while Cordelia, Hal, Jake, Destiny, and E.D. fanned out over Wit's End to search

108

for Cinnamon. Lucille and Sybil worked on lunch as if everything was completely normal, and Randolph insisted that Archie go back to town to buy walkie-talkies. "If Lucille had had a way to communicate with the rest of the staff, someone could have been sent to get the girl right away!" he said. "This must never happen again!" He had gone to the office, with coffee and a triple-chocolate brownie, "to man the command center," as he said.

E.D., thinking of Cinnamon's threat to go home, had headed into the woods that bordered the county road. The others had started their searches calling the girl's name, but E.D. didn't bother. This was not a kid who'd accidentally gotten lost and would be grateful to be found. It was altogether possible that Cinnamon had set out to hitchhike back to New Jersey. She might even now be riding in the back of some local farmer's pickup truck, heading north.

E.D. kept to the shade of the woods, peering out at the road over the patches of poison ivy and blackberry briars that grew thickly along the shoulder. She wiped the sweat from her face. Even here in the shade the humidity made the air feel almost too thick to breathe. Just ahead the woods ended and the meadow began, separated from the road by an old, sagging, barbed wire fence. It would be much worse to be out there in the direct sun. She stopped for a moment before heading out into the unsheltered

meadow. And heard the sound of someone crying.

"Cinnamon?" she called. "What's wrong?"

The sobbing stopped with a gulp and was replaced by loud snuffling, but no answer. E.D. pushed her way gingerly between a blackberry bush and a honeysuckle-draped shrub and found Cinnamon, kneeling on the shoulder of the road, next to the newly dead body of a possum. The girl looked up, her crimson face wet with tears. She wiped her cheeks, leaving streaks of dirt. Her feet, in her blue-sequined flip-flops, were filthy from walking in the dirt at the side of the road. Her cell phone lay on the ground by the corpse. For a moment neither of them spoke.

"Are you okay?" E.D. asked.

"What does it look like? Stupid road," Cinnamon said. "Doesn't anybody ever drive on it?"

E.D. looked at the dead possum. "Somebody did, obviously. Last night, probably. Possums freeze in headlights, you know. What were you doing out here?"

"Looking for some place my stupid phone would work. Or a ride to town. As if!"

"Let's go back. It's nearly time for lunch."

Cinnamon picked up her phone and pushed herself to her feet. "I thought maybe it was just pretending. 'Playing possum,' you know. But it's really, really dead." She wiped her nose with the back of her hand. "Stupid animal. Stupid, stupid, stupid animal!" Then she leaned down and touched its fur,

patting it gently, as if it were still alive. "You'd think it could cross a completely deserted road without getting itself killed!"

All the way back to the house, Cinnamon muttered about the stupid road, the stupid possum, and her stupid phone.

Chapter Sixteen

So far, on this first full day, camp was a whole lot like babysitting Destiny, Jake thought as the two of them walked toward the pond in their bathing suits with towels around their necks. Jake was carrying the life jacket Destiny would wear when they went swimming.

"Does all the campers have to go in the water?" Destiny asked.

"Yes. They have to take a swim test before they can have free swim."

"Betcha they won't all! The green twin says she

isn't going in the water ever again. She says the Death Pond tried to pull her in and just about drownded her. She says if you hadn't saved her, she'd be dead now and you're a superhero."

Jake sighed. Ginger had sat next to him at lunch— the only girl at the boys' table—and had given him another poem. She had brought him a handful of Queen Anne's lace. And she stared at him all the time. The girl had become some kind of stalker. "She wasn't *drowning*. She just got stuck in the mud, like Winston does sometimes. The dock's there now, so she won't have to go anywhere near the mud."

"Mommy says the twins are 'dentical. Isn't that s'posed to mean they're just exactly alike?"

"Pretty much. These two are, for sure. If they didn't wear different colors, we couldn't tell which was which."

"That's silly. Except for how they look, they're not the same at all. Cimma—Cim—the blue twin's sad and the green twin isn't. The blue twin's really, really sad."

"Seems to me she's *mad* most of the time."

Destiny shook his head solemnly. "Nope. Sad." He started humming "Twinkle, Twinkle," and stopped suddenly. "Did you know possums gots fingerprints, Jake?"

"What?"

"Fingerprints. Possums got beautiful, star-shaped paws and fingerprints just like us. And beautiful fur,

too. The blue twin says they just get a bad rap 'cause of their tails. That's what the blue twin says. She's just like Aunt Lucille about aminals—she talks to 'em."

"What possum? Destiny, what are you talking about?"

"The blue twin and the possum that got killded on the road. She wants to make a funeral for it. She really, really wants to. Can she do that? It would make her feel better."

"How do you know all this?"

"She was crying on the porch of Dogwood Cottage during rest time."

"Where was Cordelia?"

"With everybody else learning walkie-talkies."

"Cinnamon should have been in her room. The campers are supposed to have their feet on their bunks for rest time."

Destiny shook his head. "She didn't want her sister to see her crying. But I saw her. So I went to see what was the matter. The possum was the matter."

Amazing, Jake thought. He would have to tell Lucille about the possum funeral. Maybe Harley, who had so far had only dead bugs to photograph, could take pictures of the deceased. And the funeral too, for that matter.

They had reached the pond now, where the campers, in swimsuits, were all lined up on the dock. Archie was out on the diving platform, a whistle on a lanyard

around his neck. Q and David were jostling each other, threatening to throw each other off, while the others did their best to stay out of their way.

Dragonflies buzzed purposefully back and forth across the water, changing direction suddenly, occasionally having what appeared to be a dogfight near the reeds on the far side of the pond. Hal and Cordelia, looking even more stunning than usual in her swimsuit, were stationed on the ramp, cutting off the only route of escape should a camper decide not to participate. Ginger, at the back of the line, had her arms folded across her chest and held her head in an unmistakable attitude of defiance, but clearly the only way she could avoid going into the water would be to jump off the dock sideways and brave the muck.

Archie blew the whistle. "Okay, we'll do this one at a time," he called to them. "Q, you'll dive—or jump—in, swim over here and touch the platform, then swim back to the ladder and climb out. As soon as he's up on the dock, Samantha, you dive in and do the same thing. And so on. When everybody has swum from the dock to the platform and back, we'll have free swim. Got that?"

"When do I gets to go in?" Destiny asked Jake. "I'm hot!"

"Me, too. But not till free swim. You have to put on your life jacket first."

"*They* don't gots life jackets," Destiny said.

"They know how to swim."

"I do too! Paddle and kick. Paddle and kick!"

"Okay, Q," Archie called. "When I whistle, you go."

Q crouched as if for a racing dive, and when Archie blew the whistle again, he launched himself into the water.

"See, Jake? Paddle with your arms and kick with your feet," Destiny said. "I can do that!"

One after the other, the campers dived in, swam to the platform, returned, and took their places at the end of the line until only Ginger was left, standing next to the ladder, her arms still folded. Harley had already climbed out of the water, and the rest of the campers were standing behind her on the dock, waiting to be allowed to go in again. Destiny wasn't the only one who wanted to get into the water.

Archie whistled. Ginger didn't move. "Come ahead," he called.

Jake could feel the sun getting hotter and hotter on his shoulders.

"I wanna swim!" Destiny said. He kicked off his flip-flops and picked up his life jacket. "I *said*, I wanna swim!"

Jake buckled him into his jacket. "Just wait. As soon as Ginger goes, everybody can swim."

"She's not going," Destiny protested. "I told you she wouldn't. You go, Jake. She'll get in if you do, I betcha."

Jake shook his head. "Let Archie handle it."

Destiny suddenly ran toward the dock, pointing into the sky. "Look, look, look!" he shouted at the top of his lungs. While everybody was looking up to where a turkey vulture was circling over the pond, its wings in a steady V, Destiny pushed past Hal and Cordelia and the campers, grabbed Ginger by the arm, and launched himself off the end of the dock, dragging her, shrieking, with him. Jake rushed after him and reached the end of the dock as Ginger and Destiny came up through the cannonball splash, water streaming down their faces. "Paddle and kick!" Destiny hollered as Ginger sputtered and began to tread water. "Paddle and kick! Like me. You can do it!"

And so, of course, she could. While Destiny bobbed cheerfully up and down in his life jacket, smacking the water with both hands and repeating "paddle and kick, paddle and kick," she swam to the platform, touched it, and swam back to the dock.

"I'll get you for this," she said to Destiny as she grabbed hold of the ladder. Then she saw Jake and broke into a smile. She reached up for his hand, so he pulled her up. "Thanks," she said, her face radiant with stalker passion.

Jake groaned.

From the diving platform, Archie's whistle shrilled again. "Free swim!" he called. "When I call 'Buddy check,' grab hands with your buddy and raise them so

I can see!" The campers cheered and flung themselves back into the pond.

"I guess we're buddies," Jake called to Destiny. He held his nose and jumped. The water was wonderfully cool and surprisingly clear. As he came back up, he could see Destiny's feet kicking sporadically beneath the red cylinder of his life jacket. The moment Jake's head broke the surface of the water, Ginger Boniface did a cannonball off the dock that swamped him and Destiny both.

Chapter Seventeen

It was a few minutes after noon on *Eureka!* Day
Three, and everyone except Hal (and Randolph,
who probably wasn't up yet) had gathered in the
dining tent for announcements. E.D. had chosen
to sit with Aunt Lucille, Uncle Archie, and her
grandfather. As usual the boys and Ginger were at one
table and the girls and Destiny, who sat next to
Cinnamon, were at another. Watching Q and David,
E.D. couldn't help but think of all the nature
documentaries where lion cubs or wolf pups or young
hyenas were constantly wrestling and chewing on

each other. The two of them were at each other every minute.

Obviously, David—however powerful his aura—was *not* an angel. But knowing that did nothing to change the effect he had on her. It was possible it made that effect even stronger. As good as David was at everything, even E.D. was beginning to see that Q was better. She thought about David's application, and how full it was of obvious successes. He was used to being the best. Suddenly, he wasn't. He must feel the way she did last fall when Jake had found the great spangled fritillary—the very last butterfly for her Butterfly Project—the one she'd been looking for for weeks. She'd been furious at him. Hurt and furious!

Jake, as a staff member, ought to at least try to stop the roughhousing, she thought now. But he didn't. In fact, he tended to participate. If somebody punched him, he invariably punched back. What had the family been thinking of to make their resident juvenile delinquent a member of the staff?

Sybil rang the temple gong Lucille had donated for the purpose of getting everyone's attention. She had to do it twice more before it got quiet. "You may be glad to know that from now on all meals will be served buffet style." After several food insurrections, she and Lucille had given up trying to invent menus that would please everybody. "There will be a variety

of foods laid out in the kitchen, and you can choose whatever you like—"

"Or whatever you don't hate," David said. David, exercising what leadership he could, had started most of the insurrections.

"In any case," Sybil went on, "your choices will be entirely up to you. As you see on the schedule E.D. gave you this morning, the Required Workshop this afternoon is once again Poetry, which will be held at the pond, because today's subject will be Images of Nature."

"Do we need to bring our journals?" Ginger asked.

"Of course. And something to write with."

David raised his hand.

"Yes? Do you have a question?"

"On Monday Zedediah said individual passion is the source of all creativity."

"Yes—"

"Well, see—I don't have a passion for poetry. I'm pretty good at it, but it definitely isn't a passion."

Q nodded. "It's not exactly my favorite, either. . . ."

"It's *my* passion," Ginger said. "I *love* poetry!"

"I hate it!" Cinnamon said. "It's Ginger's thing. I don't do it, and I'm not *going* to do it!"

Samantha looked up from the fantasy novel she was reading. "If Cinnamon won't, I won't, either. My passion, besides reading, is art. Painting—and sculpture." She went back to her book.

E.D. thought of all the hours, all the days, she'd spent figuring out the best way to schedule the workshops. *Nodes of chaos,* E.D. thought. That's what these kids were. *Nodes of chaos!* E.D. loathed chaos.

"I think poetry's actually pretty stupid, if you want to know the truth," David said. "Hardly anybody reads it. And you can't make any money at it!"

Lucille rose from her seat, her face drained of color, a hand at her throat. She looked, E.D. thought, as if someone had suggested using poison on her garden or weed killer in the yard.

"It's nothing against you!" Q said hurriedly. "*Your* poetry's great!"

E.D. waited for David to agree. He didn't. His aura, she thought with a pang, was fading fast.

Instead, David said, "Of all the things I'm good at, it's just singing and dancing and acting that I have a total passion for. You *can* get to be rich and famous doing those things, if you're good enough! I don't think there should *be* required workshops. If you really believe what Zedediah says, we should get to follow our passions."

There was a moment of silence. *Nodes of chaos,* E.D. thought again.

Harley, who had been taking a picture of something on the ground next to his feet and seemed not to have been aware of what the others were saying, looked up then as if the silence had suddenly registered with

him. "Instead of poetry," he said in a small and tentative voice, "I'd rather have a workshop in photography, if that would be all right."

Lucille, tears glistening in her eyes, sat back down, and Archie patted her hand comfortingly.

Zedediah stood then. "Let me get this straight," he said. "There is only one camper who wishes to continue focusing on the art of writing poetry, is that correct?"

Everybody nodded.

"It's my most favorite thing in all the world!" Ginger said.

What happened next was something E.D. should have expected the moment Zedediah had first used the word *passion*. She wanted to leap up from her seat and insist on keeping the schedule the way it was. There was such a thing as exploration, as learning. Such a thing as discipline! People ought to be required to do things whether they had a passion for them or not! But she knew she was the only Applewhite who thought that way.

So she sat there, unable to do anything about it, as the whole camp schedule came crashing down around her. Zedediah asked the campers to take some time after lunch to rank the workshops in the order that most interested them. It would be like the lunch buffet, E.D. thought. They would not be required to attend any workshop they didn't want to attend.

Lucille, somewhat recovered, agreed then and there to work with Harley on photography.

"Flexibility," Zedediah said before sending everyone in to get their lunch, "is *also* essential to the creative life!"

All well and good, E.D. thought, but Grandpa didn't have to *schedule* flexibility!

After lunch when the campers had gone off to put their feet on their bunks and create their lists of priorities, E.D., whose Community Service was kitchen cleanup, mentioned to her aunt her thought about the value of exposing the campers to a few things they didn't choose for themselves. "Don't you think that would be good for them?"

Lucille, who had been wiping the counters, straightened up and shook out her cloth. "Nonsense. It would thwart the very essence of who they are. We are not about thwarting essence!"

On her way out of the kitchen, E.D. nearly collided with her father, who had never made it to lunch at all. His hair had not yet been combed, and he looked even more stressed and preoccupied than normal. In one hand he held the usual collection of Applewhite mail: assorted catalogs and advertising circulars, and a few bills. In the other he clutched a crumpled piece of paper.

"What's the matter?" E.D. asked.

"Hmmm? What?" He looked at her abstractedly for

a moment and then made a visible effort to collect himself. "Oh, nothing. Nothing important. Nothing at all."

Right, E.D. thought as she headed for the office. *Nothing.* That was because he hadn't been there to see chaos take over *Eureka!* Whatever was stressing her father, she couldn't think about it now. She had to come up with something to do with five campers this afternoon instead of poetry.

Chapter Eighteen

It was a good thing, Jake thought, that E.D. had been sent out with a folding chair, a lantern, and her walkie-talkie to sit between the boys' bunk and the girls' to listen for possible disturbances so Hal and Cordelia could come to the staff meeting. She'd been freaking all afternoon about the destruction of her precious camp schedule, and the stress level was high enough in the room already. Winston, always upset by intense emotions, had gone from one person to another at first, wagging his tail, trying to comfort everybody. But he'd given up and gone to

hide out in the hall. Jake knew how he felt.

So far no one had done anything in this meeting except complain. It hadn't occurred to the family, when they'd planned to have the campers do all the things that gave *them* joy, that the campers were likely to be as different from one another as the Applewhites. The camper priority lists had been something of a shock. Randolph's theater workshop was the only one that all six wanted to take. Jake's singing workshop was next, with five, and then Cordelia's, with four. Even Lucille had lost her usual glow of rosy optimism. "I'd been so looking forward to sharing the joys of poetry with six children. Now there's only one!"

"At least you've got one," Archie said. "Hal and I have to *share* Samantha Peterman."

"The good thing is, that means I only have half a person," Hal pointed out, "or a person only half the time. The bad thing is, she wants to do murals! She says a piece of canvas is too small to hold her vision!"

"It isn't just that I only have one," Lucille said. "It could be wonderful to have only a single budding poet to concentrate on. It could be an opportunity to help shape a whole life's work. But this afternoon I shared with her some of the very best of contemporary American poetry—to show her how magnificent, how transcendent, a poem can be—and she was *impervious*. She listens. She nods. But what does she write? *Verse!*"

Lucille shuddered as she said the word. "All her poems rhyme. They gallop. Da-da-da-da-da-da-da-*dum!* Da-da-da-da-da-*dum*!"

"It would appear," Zedediah observed, "that she understands rhythm, at least."

Cordelia moaned. "Don't mention that word! While Lucille was doing Poetry, I had Dance. Thanks to all the talk about passion, Q decided the workshop ought to be all about Step! He was like a freight train. He took over entirely. Step. All rhythm. No music. Think about that—dance with *no music*! All foot stomping and hand clapping."

"You have to admit, he's really, really good at it," Hal said.

"Of course he's good at it! He's good at everything! He'd be good at any kind of dance—*including the kind I want to teach*! And then there's David. David brought tap shoes today! I ask you—tap shoes? The two of them were absolutely competing with each other. My workshop has turned into some kind of a reality show. Q teaches the girls a Step routine, so then David insists on getting them to do shuffle, ball, change, which Q does as well as he does, by the way—better, really. I felt like I was caught in a war zone. I couldn't get either of the boys to so much as try a grand jeté or a glissade, and they won't lay a hand on the barre. David called it a crutch! Ginger and Cinnamon have both had ballet, but Cinnamon

says she 'prefers modern dance.' What am I going to do? I'd planned that contemporary *Swan Lake* for the end-of-camp show. I'd already started on the choreography!"

Sybil had been curled up in her easy chair chewing on a pencil. Now she spoke. "Cinnamon is the only camper who chose fiction. I talked to her about it at dinnertime, and she tells me Destiny wants her to write a children's book. I have no *idea* how to write a children's book. Plot I can teach. How to slip in clues I can teach. How to create an interesting ongoing character. But Cinnamon wants her main character to be a possum! A *beautiful* possum! She wants it to be a *picture* book so Destiny can do the drawings for it. The absolutely only thing I know about picture books is that they're thirty-two pages long."

"Give Cinnamon some Petunia Granthams to read," Zedediah said. "I should think plot, at least, would be pretty much the same from a Petunia Grantham mystery to a picture book. Except shorter. And without the murder."

Randolph had gotten up and was now pacing around the edge of the room like a tiger in a cage. "Nonessentials!" he said suddenly. "Niggling quibbles! Every one of you is capable of handling a talented kid—even a roomful of them. When you find out what they do best, you just let them do it. Push them a little to do it even more, even better."

Lucille snorted. "I'm a poet! I refuse to encourage Ginger to write *verse*."

Jake had been thinking about the poems Ginger had forced on him. The last few had reminded him a little of country and Western love songs. He raised a tentative hand. "What if you didn't think of her stuff as *poetry*? What if you thought of it as song lyrics? Lyrics pretty much always rhyme."

"Song lyrics." Lucille pondered this for a moment. "Not poetry at all." She nodded. "Pure genius, Jake. Now all we need to do is find somebody she can work with to compose the music! Cordelia? You compose."

"No way," Cordelia said. "I don't do *songs*."

Jake thought about Cordelia's music for her one-woman ballet, *The Death of Ophelia*. All discordant chords and no hint of melody. She had that right!

"What did I tell you?" Randolph said. "Even Jake knows how to do this. Every one of these kids has talent. A good director with talented actors needs to give them their heads, let them experiment, trust them to find their way. The most he does is nudge them in a useful direction. Just be good *directors*. Figure out what they're doing well and support it."

"That should be easy to do with Harley," Lucille said, "if I can get him to take pictures of something besides corpses. He showed me some of his work—he has a fabulous eye for composition and design."

"Workshops aren't problems," Randolph said. "We need to focus on the *problems*!"

"Like what?" Sybil asked.

Randolph turned on Hal and Cordelia. "I looked into the boys' and girls' cottages this afternoon. It looks like tornadoes have been rampaging through there. Clothes, books, papers—*mess*—everywhere! We wouldn't keep the goats in a mess like that."

Cordelia laughed. "If we did, Wolfie would gobble it all up!"

"This isn't funny. This whole place is a disaster. We're only three days in, and already the bathrooms in the cottages are absolutely filthy. The grass is knee-deep—who knows what vermin could be multiplying in there? The green twin claims—"

"Ginger, dear," Sybil put in.

"Whatever! She claims there's a mouse living in their bedroom. And there are ants in the kitchen!"

"I've asked the ants to leave," Lucille said. "They've let me know they're just passing through. They'll be gone by the end of the week."

"Get some ant traps next time you're in town!" Randolph told Archie.

"Don't you dare," Lucille said.

"Nothing at Wit's End is the least bit worse than normal, Randolph," Sybil said testily.

"Normal isn't good enough! This isn't just where we live anymore; it's a camp! A public facility!"

"The kids don't care," Cordelia said. "Well, except Ginger doesn't like mouse pee and poop in her dresser drawers."

"*Well, I care!*"

"Good heavens, why?" Sybil asked.

Zedediah spoke then. "Have E.D. put bathroom cleaning and grass mowing on the Community Service schedule tomorrow. That's not so difficult. Find a live trap for the mouse. Now that I don't have anyone to do workshops for, I'm going back to turning out furniture and making money, you'll all be glad to know. Anybody else have anything worth talking about?"

"I do," Jake said. "I'm a little nervous about my singing workshop. I've got everybody except Harley—"

"That seems very strange, don't you think?" Lucille said. "The son of a pair of singers with a band so successful their concerts are all sold out six months in advance—"

"I think it's just a cult following," Hal put in.

"The point is, his parents are professional singers, and he absolutely refuses to sing."

"Could be that's the reason," Zedediah said. He glanced meaningfully at Archie. "It can be a challenge, competing with a parent."

"Anyway," Jake went on, "Q and David are both great singers, which would be good except that I don't know how to help either one of them get any better. David keeps reminding me that he's had a private,

professional coach, and Q has his grandfather, who taught him enough to win all those talent shows. All I did when I taught Destiny to sing was to get him singing with me. I don't have a clue what to do with these guys."

"If you want to learn to play chess," Zedediah said, "the best way is to play with somebody better than you are."

"But isn't a teacher supposed to be better than the people he's teaching? I'm definitely not better!"

Zedediah smoothed his mustache. "This isn't a school. And even if it was, a good teacher is always learning. You're doing a workshop. Think about that word. You're all of you working together. Find out what each of them does best, and make sure everybody else learns from *that*. Make it a collaboration."

"Between David and Q?"

Zedediah laughed. "So think of your job as using their competitive drive to spur them all on to better things. For them, and for you, too. Be as competitive as they are, at least in terms of getting better. Cordelia, same thing. Now, if no one else has anything substantial, I assume we can adjourn. I have a rocking chair order to start on tomorrow."

"Somebody make sure E.D. gets the message about what needs to go on Community Service!" Randolph said. "Hal and Cordelia, it's your responsibility to keep those bunks neat and clean."

"That's why we get the big bucks," Hal said bitterly.

"Very funny. Archie—*ant traps!* And mouse poison. First thing tomorrow!"

Jake saw Archie jump as Lucille pinched his leg. There would be no ant traps or mouse poison, he knew.

"Meeting adjourned!"

Chapter Nineteen

E.D. sat alone on the end of the dock, her bare feet in the water, listening to the frogs and katydids calling from all around her. The water felt good. So far she had refused to actually swim in the pond. The idea of living things under and around her that she couldn't see— things that might have teeth or slime or jaws like a snapping turtle—was just too horrible. It was a muggy day as usual, but cloudy, so even though it was late morning, the sun wasn't beating down on her. She kicked her feet, watching the circles the

splashes made spread across the surface of the pond.

In spite of the coming of chaos, everybody seemed to be surviving. If anything, Lucille was even happier than usual. With fewer workshops, she had expanded her morning meditation, and the kids actually seemed to be liking it. E.D. suspected some of them were using it to get a little extra sleep—nobody was really doing the lights-out-at-ten thing. But Samantha had told Cordelia that meditation was changing her life. "I used to stress about everything, and now I just breathe!" Yoga, too, had expanded—instead of the sun salutation, it had become a whole forty-minute session. Lucille had flung herself into research on song lyrics and had become practically obsessed about helping Harley to expand his photographic range. "Turns out what he likes about dead things is that they never move, so he can absolutely control the image he gets. We're working on that issue."

Archie and Hal had both come up with projects for Samantha, Cordelia had decided that Step and tap might both be able to be worked into modern dance somehow, and though Jake wasn't talking much about his singing workshop, he'd found a bunch of karaoke music, and Destiny's repertoire had suddenly expanded. Now, whenever he wasn't talking, he was singing. Sybil had decided to learn everything she could about children's books. She'd come back from the library in town with shopping

bags full of them and was reading her way through the lot.

Everybody except E.D. herself was loving the theater workshop. She'd joined it as a way to be close to David—even without his aura, the magnet thing was still at work. Cordelia claimed it was hormones and perfectly normal.

The trouble was, Randolph wouldn't let anybody, not even the camp historian, hang out just to observe. E.D. had to do scenes like everybody else. It was easy enough to memorize the words, but she did *not* like having to actually get up onstage and say them. She was painfully aware of how bad she was compared with the other kids. For one thing, she could never figure out what to do with her hands!

Her father knew Jake and the campers loved his workshop. He knew they were doing well, and he could see they were learning stuff all the time. So he should have been as happy as anybody. Instead, he seemed to be getting more and more uptight as the days went by, fussing about things he'd never so much as noticed before, like the time somebody forgot to put the lid on a trash can and a raccoon got into it and strewed trash all over the yard. He'd completely freaked about that—and even picked up some of the mess himself.

And then there was the Fourth of July celebration, when they'd gathered all the campers down by the

pond. All the kids were given sparklers, and Archie and Zedediah had set off bottle rockets. Randolph had come tearing down from the house shouting about fireworks being illegal in the state of North Carolina. This had never bothered him before. They'd had fireworks every year since they'd moved to Wit's End, and—

E.D. looked up. Something had moved in her peripheral vision. Something in the woods on the other side of the pond. *Yes*. There it was again. Something—*someone*—was moving among the trees. She reached for the walkie-talkie on her belt and realized she'd left it on the desk back in the office. No, no, no! If this was a camper sneaking away, she'd be in trouble. "Keep these with you at all times," her father had told everyone the day he'd handed them out.

She scrambled up, shoved her feet into her sneakers, and hurried back to shore. As she started around the cattails that lined the edge of the pond toward where she'd seen the movement, a man stepped out of the woods. Instinctively, she crouched down and peered between the reeds. The man was wearing a suit, a white shirt, and a tie, and was carrying a clipboard. He stood for a moment gazing across the pond, jotted something down on the clipboard, and then slipped back among the trees.

He hadn't seen her, apparently. Never once in the whole four years they'd lived here had a stranger

turned up on their property, much less a stranger in a suit with a clipboard. *Weird.* Who would go wandering around the countryside dressed like that?

Follow him, a voice in her head told her. *Go tell somebody,* another voice answered. *If you go back to the office now, he'll get away,* the first voice said. *You need to find out what he's doing.* E.D. stood up. The man was no longer visible. She hurried around the pond and ducked in among the trees. Once in the woods, it was hard to move quietly—hard for that matter, with the bushes and vines and fallen branches, to move at all. She stopped to tie her sneakers, and realized that the man was having the same trouble with the underbrush as she was and was making at least as much noise. If she moved slowly and carefully enough, she could follow him by ear without him hearing her.

Five minutes later she realized she had moved *too* slowly and carefully. She couldn't hear him anymore. And of course she couldn't see him. Too many trees, too many vines and bushes. She'd lost him!

Chapter Twenty

A mosquito landed on Jake's arm and he swatted it. He was sitting in his sanctuary atop a vine-shrouded boulder in the woods, having slipped away while Ginger was busy talking to Lucille. It was the only place in the whole of Wit's End that he was safe from her. Nobody knew of this place where he always came when he felt the need to be alone. Not even Destiny had ever found him here. But somebody was very close right now, moving noisily through the woods in his direction. He parted a curtain of leaves and saw

E.D., her back to him, peering anxiously this way and that, apparently looking for something.

"What are you doing?" he asked.

She jumped and spun around. It took her a moment to see him. He should have kept quiet, he realized. She might have gone on past.

"*Shhh*!" she said, and whispered, "Did you see him?"

"See who?" Jake whispered back.

"The man in the suit."

Jake shook his head. "Nobody came by here."

"Rats," E.D. said in her regular voice. "I really did lose him. What are you doing up there?"

Jake sighed. "It's my secret hideaway. At least it *was*."

"Where's Winston?"

"I closed him in my room. I can't bring him out here with me—you never know when he's going to bark at something."

"If he'd been here with you, he would have scared the guy off."

"Yeah, and brought my stalker right to me. She knows that if she finds Winston, she'll probably find me. And she has a free period now."

"Ginger?"

"Of course Ginger. She's like a burr. Or a leech."

"I think it's cute."

"You wouldn't think it was cute if you were the one she was stalking! Lucille's been doing the songwriting

workshop in Wisteria Cottage, so Ginger's taken to leaving stuff for me on my bed! Flowers, cookies, songs—all of them dedicated to me—notes on lavender paper. She thinks it's my favorite color because of my room." Jake sighed, and then realized what E.D. had said. "A man in a suit? In the woods?"

"Suit and tie! He was skulking around by the pond with a clipboard taking notes. It's weird."

"Yeah. Seriously weird." Jake remembered the black car he and Destiny had seen. "Like that car."

"What car?"

"A plain black car. It started up the driveway one morning. First day of camp, I think it was. Destiny and I thought it was Archie, back from getting groceries in Traybridge, but when we went to see, the guy backed up and drove away. Fast."

"Why didn't you tell anybody?"

"What's to tell?"

"Was he wearing a suit and tie?"

"I didn't get a look at the driver. I barely saw the car before it took off."

E.D. shook her head. "I don't like it. Something's going on, and I want to know what. A guy in a suit skulking around with a clipboard, a car that takes off the moment somebody sees it, and the strange way Dad's been acting."

"What do you mean strange?"

"Like how he reacted to the way Q cut the grass."

Jake laughed. "That was pretty funny. Q after Q after Q all over the place. Kind of like crop circles!"

"Yeah, but that's exactly the kind of stunt Dad should have *admired*. The kind of thing he might have done himself when he was a kid. Instead, he hollered and fussed and made Q cut all the rest so it would look like a plain, ordinary lawn. When did Dad ever care about a lawn? And another thing: he's started going out to the mailbox to collect the mail—*getting up way before noon to do it.*"

That, Jake thought, *was* strange. "Maybe he's expecting a check and wants to be sure nobody else gets it." He stretched and climbed down off his boulder. "Don't tell anybody about my hiding place, okay?"

E.D. looked around her. "Tell anybody? I couldn't find it again if I tried."

"We should go back. It's nearly lunchtime." Jake watched E.D. start back the way she'd come. "Wrong way," he said. He grinned. Could be, he thought, he'd found a crack in E.D.'s organized perfection.

"Right!" she said. "Of course."

Jake led the way back toward the Lodge. Apparently he hadn't lost his sanctuary.

That night Jake sat in the dark barn wondering where E.D. was. She'd never missed a theater workshop before. Maybe she'd finally decided David wasn't worth the humiliation of getting up onstage and going

143

through a scene like some kind of robot. Jake thought it was strange that somebody who could come up with a completely bogus story in two seconds on the phone—like she'd done with Mrs. Montrose when she told her the camp was full—could be so incredibly stiff and awkward onstage speaking memorized lines. It was good that she didn't know the kinds of things David said about her behind her back. If he ever said them to her, Jake intended to deck him.

The stage lights and the houselights had been turned off in the barn. Outside, the sun had fallen below the tree line, but it would still be light for a while yet. Inside, it was hard to make out where Randolph Applewhite was sitting, a slightly darker shadow among the shadows of the rows of empty theater seats.

Randolph's voice came now from the darkness in front of them. "Tonight we're going to play a theater game called Harbor. Half of you will be on one side of the stage and half on the other. I've placed chairs in a line stage left and chairs in a line stage right. Those chairs are docks, and the stage is the harbor. You'll be boats heading from a dock on one side of the harbor to a dock on the other side. The object is to get safely to your new dock without sinking anyone else or getting sunk."

"How will we keep from crashing into each other?" Harley asked.

"That's the whole point of the game. Each of you will decide what sort of boat you are and what sort of

noise that boat would make. As you cross the harbor, you'll make your sound so that the other boats will know where you are, and at the same time you have to listen for everybody else."

"Who wins?" David asked.

"Trust him to ask," Q whispered to Jake.

"Nobody *wins*," Randolph said. "This is theater, not sports. Either you all win or you all lose. The successful working of a harbor requires that boats move around without running into one another. The whole point is to get safely to an empty dock on the other side of the harbor. If there's a collision the game starts over again. But—*listen up; this is important!*—no matter how often you have to start over, there is to be *no talking*. No talking during a round, no talking in between. No sounds except the boats. Understood?"

"Understood," they all answered.

"Okay then. Everybody up. No more talking as of *now.*"

Jake scrambled to his feet as everybody else was doing, cracking elbows with Q in the process.

Randolph's voice came from the theater seats. It had grown even darker now so that it was no longer possible to see him at all. "Pick a side, find a chair, and sit down. Be thinking about the kind of boat you want to be and what sound it would make. When I say Go, the game will begin."

Jake began moving like a sleepwalker, his hands in

front of him, aware of the sounds of movement around him: of chairs scraping on the stage floor, of grunts and yelps as people bumped into one another. Someone brushed past his hands, but he managed not to run into anyone, and he found a chair by knocking into it. He sat.

"Go!" came the command. Jake stayed sitting for a moment as the others rose around him, beginning to make their boat sounds, before he decided to be a sailboat, making a whispery, blowing sound between his lips meant to be the sound of his hull slipping smoothly through the water. He rose and began moving slowly, straining to see the movement of the others he could feel and hear around him. He was surprised how unsettling it was not to be able to rely on his eyes. And how hard it was to make sense of all the boat noises. Next to him was a puttering engine sound, ahead of him on the other side of the stage a loud foghorn sound of a very large ship. That would be Q. *"Splish, splish, splish"* came from his left—a rowboat maybe? *"Vroooooommm! Vroooooommm!"* ahead and to the right. David. And then, inevitably, Jake thought, the sound of people colliding. Groans rose from all sides of the stage.

"End of round one," Randolph called.

"Don't be so loud," someone said. "I can't hear anybody else."

"Not my fault—"

"No talking! Take your places again." A pale light glowed from the seats as Randolph switched on a flashlight briefly. "Not great. That was only forty-five seconds. You've been used to working as individuals. But plays are not just assemblies of individuals. This game is designed to create an *ensemble*. I assume you all know what that means. Theater is a collaborative art. You need to rely on yourselves, of course, but also on one another. When we begin again, remember to listen to the others and assert yourself at the same time. Listen. Share the space. Cooperate. And remember the goal."

The second round lasted very little longer than the first. Jake had been sunk by *Vroooooommm!*, who had been too loud and moving too fast to hear the sound Jake was making or even the *Putt, putt, putt* Jake had been trying to avoid. David had been making so much noise, he must have been expecting everyone just to get out of his way.

In the third round everyone was temporarily blinded by a sudden flash of light. "Everybody freeze!" Randolph shouted. He wouldn't have needed to tell them, Jake thought. They were all dead in the water. Randolph came to the stage with his flashlight and took Harley's camera from him.

"I needed to see where I was!" Harley said. "I was afraid I'd fall off the stage."

"So change docks with somebody at the back. Who's

willing to come to the front?" In the light of the flashlight, Harley and Samantha changed places, and they began again.

Not being able to talk through what had happened in each round, everyone had to figure out for themselves how to do it better. "Can we change what boats we are?" Jake risked asking when he'd been hit again and everyone was stopped. His whispery sound was apparently too hard to hear among all the other boats.

"Do you get to change roles halfway through a play?" Randolph asked.

It took an unbelievable fourteen rounds before they finally found their way to the docks on the opposite sides of the stage without any collisions. Everybody cheered, and Randolph turned the lights back on, which blinded them all over again.

"Remember this!" Randolph said. "*Ensemble!* And just for the heck of it, see if you can get back to your bunks now without your flashlights."

"Will we be doing scenes again tomorrow?" David asked.

"Tomorrow we work with improvisation."

As the campers headed out of the barn, the spotlights that illuminated the barn's parking area were turned out. Jake was always surprised at how dark night in the country was. The light in the windows of the Lodge did little more than show the

direction they needed to go. One by one the boat sounds started up around him, though it wasn't really hard to see each other. David's *Vroooooommm!* and Q's foghorn were in front of Jake, the two boys crashing into each other as they went. *Both boats,* Jake thought, *should be at the bottom of the harbor by now.* A moment later Ginger *splish, splish*ed into him.

Chapter Twenty-one

.D. hurried down the dark hallway, her spiral notebook clutched to her chest, and stood for a moment at the closed door of her parents' bedroom. Before *Eureka!* started they had always left the door open, but her mother insisted on keeping all the bedroom doors closed now in case any campers happened to go upstairs. She didn't want the campers to know that nobody (except E.D. of course) ever made their bed in the Applewhite household. E.D. took a deep breath. With the door closed like this, going into her parents' room felt like spying. *You* are

spying, she reminded herself. *That's the whole point.* She wanted to find out what was going on with her father. In the Petunia Grantham mysteries, Petunia was always finding critical information by digging through people's trash. There had been nothing useful anywhere else. This was E.D.'s last resort.

She opened the door and slipped inside, shutting it quickly behind her. Her father was in the barn doing the theater workshop. It was the counselors' night off (Cordelia had insisted they get one a week), so she had dragged Hal to town to see a movie. Everybody else was over at Zedediah's watching television. E.D. turned on the overhead light.

There was one wastebasket in her parents' room, and it was nearly full. Perfect. Her father's hysteria about housekeeping had apparently not carried over to his own bedroom. She upended the contents onto the rug. There were plenty of crumpled tissues, a sock with a hole in the toe, some catalogs that should have been put in the recycle box, and several crumpled envelopes and balled-up sheets of white paper. *Petunia Grantham strikes again!* she thought. Gingerly, she fished these out of the pile.

None of the envelopes had been mailed. There were no stamps, no return addresses, not even the address of Wit's End. On each envelope was the name Randolph Applewhite, spelled out in letters that had been cut from magazines or newspapers

and pasted in place, like ransom notes from a kidnapper. It gave the envelopes a threatening air.

She smoothed out one and slipped it into her spiral notebook. The others she put back with the rest of the trash. Then she picked up one of the balled-up sheets of paper and carefully straightened it out. It had been printed on what looked like an ink-jet printer. There was not much on it, but what there was sent a shiver up her spine.

15A NCAC 18A.1004 PERMITS

No person shall operate a summer camp within the State of North Carolina who does not possess a valid permit from the Department.

It had to have been copied from an official document. Department of what? She thought back to the months of preparation for *Eureka!*, trying to remember whether anyone had ever mentioned having to have a permit or having to deal with the state.

Hurriedly, she opened another crumpled sheet.

15A NCAC 18A.1001 DEFINITIONS

"Summer Camp" includes those camp establishments which provide food or lodging accommodations for groups of children or adults engaged in organized recreational or educational programs.

She wondered how many children constituted a group.

"Department" shall mean the Secretary of the Department of Environment and Natural Resources or his authorized representative. "Sanitarian" shall mean a person authorized to represent the Department on the local or state level in making inspections pursuant to state laws and regulations.

State laws and regulations. What kinds of laws and regulations? She pulled open another wad of paper.

15A NCAC 18A.1005 PUBLIC DISPLAY OF GRADE CARD

Inspections of summer camps shall be made in accordance with this Section at least once during each season's operation. Upon completion of an inspection, the sanitarian shall remove the existing grade card, issue a grade card, and post the new grade card in a conspicuous place where it may be readily observed by the public upon entering the facility.

There was no official grade card posted where it could be observed by the public—or anywhere else. She spread the last page out on top of the others.

15A NCAC 18A.1008 GRADING

The sanitation grading of all summer camps shall be based on a system of scoring wherein all summer camps receiving a score of at least 90 percent shall be awarded Grade A; all summer camps receiving a score of at least 80 percent and less than 90 percent shall be awarded Grade B; all summer camps receiving a score of at least 70 percent and less than 80 percent shall be awarded Grade C; and no summer camp receiving a score of less than 70 percent, or Grade C, shall operate.

Official language was stupidly repetitious and obvious, E.D. thought. Were they writing for five-year-olds? But then she looked again at the last part. Without a grade of at least C, *no summer camp shall operate.* Did that mean the state could shut them down?

Were these messages warnings or threats? *Threats.* Why else the cut-and-pasted letters on the envelope? And why was her father keeping these messages a secret? He was engaging in a classic cover-up, E.D. thought with a sinking feeling in her stomach. She had once done a research paper on political cover-ups. She knew where they led. Nowhere good.

She also knew it was illegal to put anything other than actual mail into somebody's mailbox. So whoever was doing it must be waiting till after the mail had been delivered. Who could it be?

E.D. flashed, suddenly, on the first morning of camp. The phone call from Mrs. Montrose about the rejection of Priscilla. "Tell your father he hasn't heard the last of this." These messages were exactly the sort of thing Mrs. Montrose would do. But was she just threatening, or had she actually turned them in to the state?

The man in the suit. The plain black car Jake had seen. Mrs. Montrose *must* have turned them in. They were being watched by "the department"!

E.D. folded the smoothed-out pages and put them in her spiral notebook. She gathered up the rest of the trash and put it back in the wastebasket. She knew something nobody else except her father knew. Something he didn't want the rest of the family to know. The question was, What should she do about it?

Chapter Twenty-two

Staff meetings had gotten very short and less full of complaint. Except for Randolph. He was on a rampage now about food storage, going on and on about whether eggs and milk were being kept at sufficiently low temperatures to prevent spoilage. And whether the lunch buffet allowed tuna or chicken or egg salad to be at room temperature long enough to risk salmonella or botulism.

"Has any one of us ever gotten salmonella or botulism?" Lucille asked when Randolph took a

breath. She didn't need to wait for an answer. "Well, there you are. We are actually feeding the campers considerably better and more carefully than we have ever fed the family!"

"Give us a peanut!" Paulie screamed from his perch, then burst into hysterical laughter.

It really was uncanny, Jake thought, how often Paulie managed to connect with what was being said.

"Let's get on with it," Zedediah said. "Anybody have anything important to report?"

Hal nodded. "Samantha's planning to do her mural on the side of the barn! The barn needs painting anyway. She wants to do all nature images—with maybe a few elves or fairies."

"And we have our first interworkshop cross-fertilization," Lucille said. "Harley's started taking pictures of things that aren't dead: leaves, flowers, the pond. As long as they don't move. He's taking pictures to give Samantha some ideas. He'll make a photo-montage, and she'll paint a version of it on the side of the barn. She wants it to be like a gigantic patchwork quilt, end-to-end and ground-to-roof."

Randolph began muttering about the danger of allowing a camper on a ladder.

"We're putting up a scaffold," Archie said.

"I have news as well!" Sybil said. She looked around the room, beaming with satisfaction. *"I have begun a new book."*

"Raising Petunia Grantham from the dead, are you?" Archie asked.

"Not quite. I've begun writing a children's book. The heroine is Petunia Possum."

"Isn't that the name of Cinnamon's picture book?" Randolph asked. "Do you mean you're *plagiarizing* a camper?"

"It isn't plagiarism. It's cross-fertilization. I thought about what Zedediah said about working together. So Cinnamon and I have created a character. She's putting the character into a picture book with illustrations by Destiny; I'm putting her into a mystery book for older children. Cinnamon's been hanging around the goat pen to get to know Wolfie. He's going to be her villain."

"Isn't it beneath you to write a children's book?" Randolph said.

"I've been doing research. The main difference between literature for children and literature for adults is the age—or in this case the species—of the protagonist. With a bit of luck—you know perfectly well I've always had uncommonly good luck—children's books can make a *fortune*. Consider Harry Potter. An absolute fortune!"

At that moment Hal's walkie-talkie chirped. "Mayday, Mayday," E.D.'s voice called. "Q and David are throwing each others' clothes out the window of the cottage."

Hal went pale. "I can't," he said. "I can barely deal with them when they *aren't* fighting."

"I'll go," Zedediah said, holding his hand out for Hal's walkie-talkie. "On my way," he said into it. He turned back at the door. "Meeting's over anyway, right?"

Randolph nodded abstractedly. "A fortune," he muttered as everyone else in the room stood up to leave. "An absolute fortune. . . ."

Jake sat on a log at the fire circle where E.D. had brought him when she'd materialized out of the darkness as he and Winston left the staff meeting. Lightning bugs were blinking on and off around them. She was sitting next to him, the messages she had found in her father's wastebasket spread on the ground in the light from her flashlight. "I'm going to watch the mailbox and see who's leaving these things. But it may be too late. Remember how upset Mrs. Montrose was when we rejected Priscilla? I'm pretty sure she's behind this. Bet you anything she's already reported us to the state."

Jake nodded. "It's just the kind of thing that woman would do." Winston whuffed at a firefly. "You think the state could shut *Eureka!* down?"

"Looks like it! And if we get shut down, the families won't have to pay for the rest of camp. We'll lose Wit's End! I keep thinking about that hovel in New Jersey."

"Your mother says she's about to make a fortune writing a children's book, and Zedediah's working—"

"It's a lot more than the money now, though. Everybody's gotten committed to *Eureka!* If the state shuts the camp down it will be a *failure.* A massive—*public*—failure! Do you have any idea what it would be like for the whole family to fail at something? All at once? Bad enough if one single person gets a negative review. You should have been here the time the Petunia Grantham mysteries were called 'literary potato chips' in the *New York Times*! Or when some stuffy art critic said Uncle Archie's Furniture of the Absurd was not only absurd but 'ill-conceived and badly executed.' Notice that I can quote these things! Ask any one of them if they've ever had bad press, and they'll be able to repeat word for word every negative thing anybody ever said about them! Applewhites do not handle failure well. To have *Eureka!* shut down would be—would be—I'm not sure we'd ever recover."

Jake sighed. "I get it."

"The point is, *What are we going to do?*"

Jake shrugged. "What *can* we do? And how come your father's keeping all this a secret?"

"That's easy. *Eureka!* was his idea. If it fails, he'll get all the blame. Uncle Archie and Grandpa will take him apart for not going to the state in the first place. At least it explains why he's been so obsessed about

stuff like mice and garbage. I was beginning to fear for his sanity."

"Does he know about the guy in the suit?"

"I don't think so."

"You should tell him. Maybe he could just call the department of whatever it is and ask what he needs to do to make everything legal."

"This is Randolph Applewhite we're talking about. The director. Directors think they rule the world. My father doesn't knuckle under. *Rules are made to be broken*. That's practically a family slogan."

Somewhere in the woods an owl hooted—twice, then twice more. "In that case we need to take it to the whole family," Jake said. "We did a theater game about the power of ensemble—where everybody wins or everybody loses. If it works for these kids, it'll work for anybody. *All for one and one for all!*"

Chapter Twenty-three

It was 9:43 A.M. and E.D was crouched in the bushes between the house and the road, watching the mailbox. Almost always the mail was in their box by ten, and it wasn't there yet. A seriously annoying sharp twig was sticking her in the back of the neck, and occasionally one of the big, black ants that were charging purposefully around among the leaves would get sidetracked and end up crawling up her arm or—worse—down her shirt. So far none of them had bitten her at least.

She had peeked in on her father before she came

outside. He'd been asleep, tangled in the sheet as if he'd been fighting to free himself from some dream monster. An alarm clock, an item seldom used in the Applewhite family by anybody except E.D., had been standing on his bedside table, close to his head. That was how he'd been getting up in time to be at the mailbox by about ten thirty—the crack of dawn in his world. She had crept in and turned off the alarm.

As she was brushing away another ant, she heard an approaching vehicle. She peered between the leaves. It was the mail truck, coming fast down the empty road and angling toward their mailbox. It pulled to a stop with a screech of brakes, its hazard lights blinking. An arm reached out and opened the box. The arm withdrew into the truck, then reappeared with a batch of mail, flung it into the very back of the mailbox, and slammed the door shut. With a squeal of tires on hot pavement, the truck headed on down the road.

E.D. waited. Nothing. Nothing. She watched the heat waves wrinkling the air above the empty road. An ant began crawling up her bare leg. She stomped her foot to dislodge it. A yellow jacket buzzed past her head. A crow called from the field across the road. If this was what it was like to be a detective on stakeout, Petunia Grantham could have it! Jake had a workshop this morning or she'd have taken him up on his offer to do the stakeout. She was glad it was all happening

after Jake instead of before, she thought. It meant she had an ally. Now, instead of driving her crazy, his combination of creativity and good sense was a comfort.

Finally, she heard the sound of a distant car coming from the direction the mail truck had gone. It was a black car. A plain black compact car.

The car veered out of its lane and across the road, heading toward the mailbox directly into what would have been oncoming traffic, if there had been any, which, of course, there was not. As the car slowed, the window went down. A bare, hairy arm reached out, slipped an envelope into the mailbox, and disappeared again. The window went up as the car lurched forward, veered back into its own lane, and sped away.

E.D. waited another long minute and then hurried to the mailbox. The envelope looked just like the others—RANDOLPH APPLEWHITE was spelled out in pasted-on letters. She ripped it open and pulled out the page inside.

15A NCAC 18A.1012 RECREATIONAL WATERS
A natural or artificial body of water may be approved by the Department for recreational purposes based upon the results of inspections, bacteriological examinations of the water, and sanitary surveys.

She stuffed the page and envelope into her pocket and headed for the dance studio, where Jake would be preparing for his singing workshop.

When she got there, Winston, who had been asleep on an old beach towel in the corner, came wagging over to greet her. She reached down to rub his ears. Jake was setting out the folding chairs for his workshop. "Another message came," she told him.

"Did you see who brought it?"

"Only his arm. But it was the car you saw the first day of camp. Plain and black." She gave him the sheet of paper and waited while he read it.

"*May* be approved? So they could refuse to approve the pond for swimming." Jake shook his head. "Do you suppose that guy took some water for testing?"

"He'd have had to step in the muck to get close enough to collect a sample."

"He could've gone out on the dock to get it."

"I was on the dock when he showed up at the pond. He came from the woods on the other side. All he did was look at it for a while and take some notes. We should tell everybody tonight at the staff meeting."

Jake shook his head. "If we tell them all at once, they'll gang up on your father."

Jake was right, of course.

"And once they gang up, he'll naturally have to fight back. Hard to get an ensemble going after that."

"So what do we do instead?"

"Tell them one at a time. Ask everybody just to think about it for a while and not to talk to anybody else. In that harbor game everybody had to keep quiet. It keeps people from arguing, and that makes them have to think."

"I saw Aunt Lucille and Harley over by the woodshop as I was coming here," E.D. said. "I think it would be good to tell her first."

"Okay. And I could tell Archie after my workshop. We'll just tell them not to talk about it yet."

When E.D. got to the woodshop, Lucille and Harley were outside taking pictures of what looked like a huge tangle of honeysuckle and wisteria vines stretched between two upright branches maybe four feet tall that were set into buckets of sand. The sweet smell of the honeysuckle blossoms filled the air. They didn't notice E.D. at first.

"Don't focus too long or too hard," Lucille was telling Harley. "Just keep clicking and changing your angle the tiniest bit each time. You never know what angle of light or what perspective will make the difference between a snapshot and a work of photographic art. The more images you get, the better your chances."

"But I want to know ahead of time exactly what I'm getting," Harley said. "I want to control how it turns out. . . ."

"I know. But you need to leave room for the magic," Lucille said. "Craft is about control. Art requires magic."

"Excuse me," E.D. said, "but can I talk to you for a minute, Aunt Lucille? In private?"

Harley clicked his camera shutter, moved a little, and clicked again.

"Sure," Lucille said. "What do you think of Samantha's sculpture? It's her first project for Archie's workshop. She calls it an Elf Net."

E.D. seldom understood Uncle Archie's work, but the Elf Net was pretty. And interesting. She could almost imagine elves making it—to catch birds maybe, or unwary people tramping around in their world. "But won't the honeysuckle blossoms die?"

"That's why Samantha wants me to take pictures of it now," Harley said. "She thinks that way it can be two different pieces of art. One when the net's alive and one when it's just a skeleton."

"That ought to be right up your alley," E.D. said.

"The live one won't last," Lucille said, "but the pictures will. There will still be a three-dimensional sculpture after the vines die, but Harley's work captures and keeps images of the original."

"Dead things don't seem quite so dead," Harley said, "when you've still got pictures of them."

"You keep working here," Lucille told Harley. "Go on changing perspectives. I'll just talk to E.D. for a

minute or two." E.D. and Lucille moved around to the other side of the woodshop. "What's up?" Lucille asked.

E.D. explained about the messages in the mailbox.

"Just like Randolph to keep it a secret," Lucille said. "Archie'll never let him hear the last of this."

"That's why Jake thinks it would be better for everybody just to think about it for a while before we get together—maybe there doesn't have to be a fight. Dad doesn't even know all of it." E.D. told Lucille about the man in the suit.

"You think he's a state inspector?" Lucille asked.

"What else? If we don't pass inspection, they'll close us down."

"There must be something we can do."

Harley's voice startled both of them. "Distract and delay."

E.D. and Lucille turned. He had come around the woodshop and heard at least the last part of the conversation.

"What do you mean?" Lucille asked him.

"It's the state you're talking about, right?" Harley asked. "That means bureaucracy and red tape. Nothing ever works fast. If the guy's an inspector, he has to finish the inspection and make his report before anybody can do *anything*. And it's never just one person who can make a decision. One guy has to call another, and that guy has to get somebody else

to sign something. It can take just about forever."

"How do you know this?" Lucille asked.

Harley shrugged. "My parents deal with bureaucrats all the time when they're setting up their concerts. Permits for this, permits for that. They say the best way to handle any problem you have with a bureaucracy is *distraction and delay.*"

Chapter Twenty-four

"Are we going to do some *solo* work today, O Great Emperor of Singing?" David said as he came into the dance studio. "I don't see how all this 'sing-along' stuff is worth my time. It's not like I'm planning to join a *chorus*."

Jake turned from the table where the music system was set up. Q had come in behind David and was heading for a chair. "Q? You have any thoughts about that?"

"Sure! One, harmony. Can't learn harmony by

singing alone all the time. Two, you ever been in a musical?"

David sniffed. "Sure. We did *Guys and Dolls* at school last year."

"Then you've already sung with a chorus! Musicals are ensembles just like the rest of theater. You can't just be like those dudes on television, showing off their style all the time."

David turned a chair around and straddled it. "Nothing wrong with the 'dudes on television'! My vocal coach says—"

Jake broke in. "We can do solos today if everybody wants to."

Samantha had come in and taken a seat. "I do a terrific 'Over the Rainbow.' Do we have the music for it?"

Cinnamon stuck her head in the door. "Anybody know where Destiny is? He usually meets me at the dining tent, but he wasn't there."

"Last I saw him was breakfast," Q said.

"He was with your sister after yoga," David said.

"*She's* not here either!" Jake realized he ought to have noticed this a whole lot sooner. Ginger was always the first person to show up for his workshop. Most of the time she brought him a present of some kind. Or a snack for Winston.

Jake picked up his walkie-talkie. "Anybody know where Destiny is? Or Ginger?"

After a moment Cordelia responded. "Not in Dogwood Cottage."

"Not in the art studio," Hal answered.

"They're not by the woodshop, either," E.D. reported.

"Better send a search party," Archie said through a crackle of static.

Jake had just begun to consider whether he should go ahead with the workshop and let the rest of the staff look for Ginger and Destiny when he heard Destiny's voice in the distance. He was singing a song he'd learned at the last workshop when they were doing the music from *West Side Story.* After a moment Ginger's voice joined in, both of them singing at the top of their lungs about how pretty they felt as they came steadily closer.

"Ta-dah!" Ginger said as she came bursting in through the door. In one hand she carried her canvas bag. In the other she held Lucille's hair clippers, which she waved triumphantly in the air. Both sides of her head were shaved, a little patchily, all the way to the scalp. Down the center of her skull ran a raggedy-looking strip of carroty frizz.

Destiny followed her in and Jake groaned. Now, for sure, he thought, Sybil was going to kill him. All that was left of Destiny's thick white-blond hair was a narrow stripe of buzz cut. "My Mohawk gotted a little short," he said. "Ginger's hand slipped. But she says it's okay cuz it'll grow right back."

Chapter Twenty-five

The good thing about Destiny and Ginger having new and grotesquely bad haircuts, E.D. thought, was that it distracted her family from the power of the government of North Carolina to swoop in and destroy their lives. Everybody knew about it now, but as far as she knew, nobody had started in on her father yet.

She had come into the camp office thinking of going online to see if she could check whether the warning messages were official state regulations or counterfeits. It had come to her suddenly that Mrs.

Montrose might have invented the whole thing just to freak out the man who had traumatized her daughter. There might be no such department and no such rules. But Harley was already at the computer when she came in, uploading the photographs from his camera. Even now they were flashing on the screen for a split second, one after another.

She would figure out tomorrow's schedule instead and get online later. She settled at the desk and spread copies of the previous day's schedules out so that she could see who had done which Community Service chores. She could just imagine the cry that would go up if she accidentally assigned anyone to bathroom cleaning two days in a row. It was bad enough when Q noticed that David had not yet had to clean bathrooms a single time. Nobody had bought her protest that it had been an oversight. She would give David the job tomorrow and prove that she hadn't been playing favorites.

"No!" Harley said now from the computer. *"No!"*

"What?" she asked.

"There's something wrong with this computer."

"It's old!" she said. She was used to the machine's sudden fits and sulks. She got up and went over to see if there was anything she could do. "Is the cursor being slow again?"

The photo on the screen was one Harley must have taken in the theater workshop she'd missed.

The campers were scattered around the stage in various awkward poses.

"Look! Just look! Right above their heads."

E.D. looked more closely. In the air above the campers' heads she could see four perfectly circular splotches of different sizes and slightly different colors. Like pale balls of colored light. "What are those?" she asked.

"I don't know what they are. I've never seen anything like them. There must be something wrong with the computer."

She touched one on the screen. Nothing.

"They aren't on the monitor," Harley said, "they're *in the picture*!"

"Maybe they're waterdrops. Could some water have gotten into your camera somehow? Or onto the lens?"

"No way."

"What happens if you zoom in on them?"

Harley zoomed in on the largest splotch. There was a kind of pattern in the middle of it, like one of Aunt Lucille's meditation mandalas. It had a bluish fringe around the edge that reminded E.D. of the way children draw points around the sun to show that it's shining. Whatever this was, it was a part of the photo, all right. The more he zoomed in, the fuzzier and more pixilated it got, but there was no way to tell what it was. He zoomed in on the others,

one at a time. The two smaller ones were just plain white and hazy, with no patterns in the middle; both of the larger ones—a pinkish one and one with a tinge of gold—had the mandalas and the bluish fringe. They were quite pretty really.

"It *could* be the camera," she said. "A light leak or something."

Harley shook his head. "I've been taking pictures with this camera for a year, and I haven't ever had this happen before."

"Did you notice it on the camera screen right after you took the picture?"

Harley shook his head again. "The screen's too small to see something like this. Anyway, it was dark. That's why I took it in the first place. I wasn't even trying to take a picture; I just needed the light from the flash."

"Check out the other pictures."

He closed that photo and clicked on another of the thumbnails on the screen. This one was a dead dragonfly caught in a spiderweb. It had been taken on the front porch of the Lodge. There were no splotches in this picture.

"There," Harley said. "I told you it wasn't the camera."

"It isn't the computer, either, then. Try another."

Harley clicked on another thumbnail. "No! No, no, no!" he said as the photo filled the screen.

This was one of the photos he'd taken of Samantha's Elf Net. It took E.D. a minute to see what he was pointing at. A large bluish-pinkish sphere seemed to be floating a little above it, faint against the silvery siding of the woodshop. It was considerably bigger than the ones in the other picture.

"That wasn't there when I took the picture!"

He clicked then on the photo he'd taken in the dining tent at lunch when everybody was going ballistic over Destiny's and Ginger's hair. Destiny and Ginger were standing together, grinning into the camera. There were clusters of balls of light around their heads—all with mandala centers. There were also two misty white ones down near Ginger's green-sequined flip-flops and a small, very bright thing that was more of a cylinder than a ball. It looked as if it had been caught moving—a line of white stretched out behind a bright circle in the front.

"I gather you didn't see anything like those when you took that picture, either."

"You were there! There was *nothing*!"

E.D. found herself literally scratching her head. "Did you take them all with a flash?"

Harley shrugged. "The first one. And this one. I guess the Elf Net one could be one I used the flash for. Lucille wanted me to try different kinds of lighting."

"So maybe the flash lit up dust particles in the air.

You know how you can see dust in the air when sunlight comes through a window? Dust you can't see otherwise?"

Harley pointed at the one that seemed to be moving. "How fast can a speck of dust move? Do you have any idea how fast dust would have to be going to make that long a streak in the split second of a flash?"

"Pretty fast."

"Yeah. Pretty darn fast!"

"Aunt Lucille ought to see this," E.D. said. She unclipped her walkie-talkie and called her. "Can you come to the office?"

"Tell her 9-1-1," Harley said.

"It isn't an emergency," E.D. said. "The photos aren't going anywhere." He pointed at the screen where he had called up the second photo he'd taken in the dining tent at lunch. The picture was filled with balls of light. It looked like a swarm, all sizes and intensities, so thick they almost obliterated the images of Destiny and Ginger. *What were those things?*

"9-1-1!" Harley repeated.

"9-1-1!" E.D. added. "Lucille to the office, please, 9-1-1." She looked at the last photo again. "The dining tent could be very dusty," she said. But these balls of light just didn't look like dust. And if they were, how come they weren't in the picture he'd taken in the same place just a moment before?

By the time Lucille arrived, pink and breathless, a first aid kit in her hand, with Archie and Zedediah behind her, Harley had the theater workshop photo on the screen again.

"Who's hurt?" she asked.

Harley didn't answer. He just pointed to the balls of light in the photo.

"Ooooooh, Harley!" Lucille exclaimed, dropping the first aid kit on the floor and hurrying to peer at the computer screen. "Orbs! You've caught *orbs*! I've never had them. Not once!"

"What are orbs?" Harley asked.

"Dust," Zedediah said. "An optical anomaly. The barn's a dusty place."

"So says the skeptic," Lucille said. "Nobody knows for sure. I've got a book about orbs, and I think the author's right. I think they're spirits. *Friendly spirits!*"

"Dust particles," Zedediah said. "Causing a flare in the flash."

"Could be water molecules," Archie said. "Humid as it is here, it could be water molecules catching the flash."

"For artists, the two of you are sadly lacking in imagination. I think they're *conscious beings from other dimensions*. Like the nature spirits that help me garden." Lucille smiled hugely. "I love that they've showed up at *Eureka!* The book's author says they're drawn to light and joy. It means we're doing

something right! Are there any in your other photos?"

Harley began showing the other pictures, and E.D. decided to take the schedules up to her room and work on them there. She was not fond of things she couldn't understand. Even less fond of things nobody could understand.

Chapter Twenty-six

BRINGING LIGHT

I long to go out fishing
On a midnight sea of stars,
To net one constellation
And catch the fire of Mars.
I'd bring them gently back to Earth
And offer them to you
To chase the shadows from your heart
Whenever you are blue—
To chase the shadows from your heart

And light your world anew.

You'd feel their crystal brilliance
And know that they were there
Forever when the nights seemed dark
And your heart was full of care.

Forever when the nights grow dark
May you remember me
And feel the light I wished to bring
From a far-off midnight sea.

Your BFF, Ginger

Jake, on his way to the theater workshop, read the page he'd found stuck into his camp bag after dinner. And read it again.

"What are you reading?" Harley, with two cameras around his neck instead of one, had come up behind him.

"Something Ginger wrote."

"Pretty radical, that girl! Can you imagine what her parents'll say when she gets home without hair? Is that the lyrics for another song?"

Jake nodded. "Working with Lucille is really making a difference."

Harley laughed. "In more ways than one. She says she found the hair clippers in the bathroom at

Wisteria when she was there for Poetry and smuggled them out in her bag. Can I see what she wrote?"

Jake gave the page to Harley, who read it as they walked. When he'd finished reading, Harley stopped. Jake went on a few steps and then looked back. Harley was staring off into the middle distance. "What?" Harley didn't answer. He didn't even seem to have heard. "Earth to Harley, Earth to Harley!"

Harley shook himself a bit, as if he really had come back from some other place. "This is weird. I'm hearing music in my head."

"Like when you get a song stuck in your mind?"

"No. Nothing I ever heard before." He read the page again. *"I think it's the tune for Ginger's song.* Like it was just there in my head waiting for the words. Wow! Would it be okay if I kept this for a while?"

Jake shrugged. "I don't see why not. She's been wanting to find a composer. Maybe you're it."

Footsteps came thundering down the path behind them, and David pushed his way between them. "He's what? What's this?" He snatched the paper from Harley's hand.

Jake snatched it back. "None of your business."

"Touchy, touchy!" David looked at Harley. "How come the extra camera?"

Harley shrugged. "It's an experiment. Lucille wants me to take pictures of the workshop tonight with both cameras to see which one works better."

"Photographing people now, huh? What'd you do, run out of corpses?"

David went on ahead, and Jake gave Ginger's lyrics back to Harley. "Everybody's favorite camper," he said when he thought David was out of earshot.

"And God's gift to the theater," Harley said.

"Yeah, well, we'll see how he does with improv," Jake said. "He won't have anybody else's words to rely on."

Harley folded the paper and slipped it into his pocket. "Improv's sorta scary."

Q joined them. "It's my favorite thing of all! Except dancing."

Inside, Randolph told them to find seats. But there were only five chairs on the stage. Cinnamon and Ginger got there first, Samantha and E.D. joined them, and David and Q had a brief shoving match to see who would get the last chair. David won and stuck his foot out to trip Q. Q jumped nimbly over it.

"The people in the chairs will do the first exercise," Randolph said. "Jake, Q, and Harley, come sit down here in the house."

"Lucille asked me to take some pictures," Harley said. "Would that be okay?"

Randolph thought for a moment. "We'll make it part of the exercise. Okay, listen up! This is improvisation. That means you invent it all—words, actions, interactions—as you go along. We'll do an exercise

about *emotion*. The setup is a party. Samantha, you'll be the host. The others will be the guests. Here's how it works. The stage is your living room, and wherever you choose to see it, there's a front door. The doorbell rings—I'll say *ding dong*—and you go to answer it. Whoever is at the door comes in expressing an emotion as vividly as possible."

"Do you want us to talk?" David asked.

"Sometimes words help, sometimes they don't—it's up to you. So the first person—that'll be you, Cinnamon—comes in with an emotion; and Samantha, as the host, you need to pick up the emotion, whatever it is. The two of you will then create a scene using that emotion. Then the doorbell will ring again and a second guest—that'll be you, Ginger—will come in. You also come in expressing a vivid emotion, but a different one. The other two 'catch it' from you, and you all create a scene with this second emotion. The doorbell rings, and so it goes. Each new person brings a new emotion, and the others pick it up and run with it. After Ginger it's David, after David it's E.D. Got that?"

Everyone on the chairs nodded. "Now one more twist," Randolph said. "Harley, you'll take some pictures during the party; and when the flash goes, everybody will revert to the previous emotion until the next flash. So—let's say there's been anger and then grief. When the flash goes, whoever's at the

party has to go immediately from grief back to anger. Give them a little time with that, Harley, then take another picture. At that flash, everybody goes back to grief. Don't take too many, Harley, and don't take them too fast. Give the scenes a chance to develop before you switch them."

Jake was glad he wasn't in the first group. It was fun watching. When the doorbell rang and Samantha opened the imaginary door, Cinnamon stormed in, swearing like Paulie about some fool who'd cut her off in traffic.

It took Samantha a moment to catch the emotion, but then she yelled, "That creep! I hate when that happens! Some fool did that to me just the other day, and I crashed right into his bumper."

"Serves him right!" Cinnamon said. "And I was going to bring a cake for the party, but the stupid bakery got the order wrong. . . ." The two girls ranted on till Randolph interrupted with *"Ding dong."*

Ginger came in laughing. She said nothing, just laughed steadily harder till she was nearly hysterical. Jake found himself chuckling even though she hadn't explained what she was laughing about. She never did use words—just kept on laughing until the others were laughing with her. By then the laughter was real. Everybody—both onstage and off—was laughing when Harley's flash went off. Ginger immediately stopped laughing and shouted at Harley for taking a picture

when she wasn't ready. The others joined in, Cinnamon once more cursing like Paulie on a roll.

David brought fear in with him, claiming to be running from a clutch of zombies. That gave everybody a chance to scream and shriek and run around.

When it was E.D.'s turn, though, she came in looking as if she'd just lost her last friend in the world. "My dog!" she wailed. "Someone just ran over my dog! I got him as a puppy from the pound. The poor little thing had been beaten half to death. He was so little and so scared he couldn't even eat. I had to feed him by hand, a bite at a time. That was five years ago, and he's been with me practically every minute ever since. He slept on my feet every night. And now he's gone! He's gone! What'll I do?"

Amazing, Jake thought. What had happened to E.D. the robot? He had a sudden, horrible image of Winston lying in the road. It was as if a sharp stone were lodged in his throat as he thought of Winston never again throwing himself onto his chest as he lay in bed.

Cinnamon had actually started to cry now. "Just like the possum," she choked out the words. "The beautiful possum, dead in the road! Murdered!"

Harley's timing was perfect, Jake thought. Just as Cinnamon hollered *murdered*, he took a picture and everyone had to go back to fear.

⏴⏴⏴⏵⏵⏵

After the workshop, as they all headed back to the cottages, David kept shouting about the zombies coming out of the woods till everybody was screaming and running from the imaginary horrors chasing them. Archie came out with a flashlight to see what catastrophe was going on, and Lucille and Sybil decreed there should be a campfire with s'mores to get them focused on something cheerier before bedtime. As the campers went to find sticks for toasting marshmallows, there were several more zombie scares and at least two sightings of vampires. It was amazing, Jake thought, how scary running in the dark could be. The more you ran, especially if someone was screaming nearby, the more certain you were that something was chasing you. At one point E.D. jumped out at him from behind a tree brandishing a marshmallow stick, and he practically jumped out of his skin.

"Scared you!"

"Startled me is all," he said.

Q appeared and pointed over Jake's shoulder with a look of horror on his face. *"Aaaaah!"* he screamed.

When both Jake and E.D. turned to look, Q yelled "Gotcha!" and ran off.

"That improv thing was really fun, wasn't it?" E.D. said.

Jake nodded. "And you think you aren't creative!"

E.D. shrugged. "Maybe I'm just a really good liar!"

"Maybe that's one definition of creative."

"Jake, Jake!" Ginger came running up with two marshmallow sticks. She gave him one of them, and E.D. went off to get a marshmallow. "Did you read my new lyrics yet? Did you? Did you?"

"I did. I think they're really good. And guess what—Harley thinks he has the music for them. Could be he's the composer you're looking for."

Ginger ran a hand through her raggedy Mohawk. "Lyrics by Ginger Boniface, music by Harley Schobert?"

"Sounds good to me."

"Maybe his parents would record it!" She handed him the other marshmallow stick. "Where is he?"

"Out there somewhere chasing werewolves," Jake said, pointing off into the woods.

Without another word, Jake's pet stalker took off to find Harley.

Chapter Twenty-seven

The staff meeting where everybody finally talked about her father's failure to get the state's approval for the creation of *Eureka!*—and his subsequent cover-up— had not been quite as bad as E.D. had expected. Jake's idea to have everybody think for a while first might have worked.

In spite of the shouting and recriminations and character assassination with which the discussion had begun, the family had come around surprisingly fast to a somewhat grudging willingness to face the crisis

together. Lucille had decided that the orbs that were showing up in Harley's photographs were benevolent spirits who had come specifically to support their work, so she kept reminding everyone that there were cosmic forces on their side and there was absolutely nothing to worry about. She also shared Harley's idea about distraction and delay.

Once they'd quit criticizing Randolph for not setting things up properly with the state in the first place, no one in the family turned out to be any more willing than he was to accept North Carolina's right to interfere with or regulate what they were doing. They quickly settled on thwarting that interference any way they could. "We need to keep this whole thing quiet, though," Randolph said. "We don't want the campers' parents to get wind of it."

"But we have to tell the campers," E.D. had insisted. "Otherwise, it's still a cover-up. And cover-ups are always a bad idea. If we really believe in a creative community, we have to tell them what's up."

Lucille agreed. "We have an opportunity here to model a creative, collaborative approach to handling a crisis. We must share all this with the campers first thing tomorrow morning and then listen to what they come up with. I guarantee you they'll have ideas. After all, who's better at distraction and delay than kids? Creativity. Individuality. Cooperation. Isn't that the whole point of the camp?"

Even Randolph had agreed to this, on the condition that Lucille would do the talking and he didn't have to be there.

"I'll tell them about it after yoga, when everyone's fresh and energized," Lucille promised. "You'll see—their ideas will at least be worth listening to."

So E.D. had gone to yoga and struggled her way through it, hoping David wasn't watching as she kept tipping out of tree pose and had to bend her knees to touch the ground after waterfall. It wasn't until the final pose, when Jake, Destiny, and Winston came around the corner of the barn, that she realized she could have just shown up at the end to hear what Lucille would say and how the campers would take it. Winston flopped down in the shade of a sweet gum tree and lay with his head on his paws, watching. Jake and Destiny did the corpse posture (the only one E.D. did really well) with everyone else at the end, Destiny talking all the time about how fun it was to lie down and play dead when all the time you knew you were going to sit up afterward instead of getting "buried under the dirt with flowers on you."

When Lucille had rung the chimes to bring them back to sitting position, she announced that she had something to tell them and she wanted all of them, including Destiny, to just listen. They did.

"The state can make an unannounced inspection," Lucille said, wrapping up the story. "E.D. saw a man

by the pond taking notes, but there's much more to a state inspection than that. So we're pretty sure he'll be back."

"If we fail the inspection, will they shut down the camp?" Q asked.

"Shut it down?" Destiny burst into tears. "No, no, no! I'm not finished the Petunia Possum drawings. And Cimmamon doesn't got all the words done, either."

"Archie and Hal just got the scaffolding up for my mural!" Samantha said, pointing to the side of the barn where a platform was rigged with ropes and pulleys. "I haven't even started it!"

"Harley's doing music for my lyrics!" Ginger said. "I want to have one of our songs in the end-of-camp show! If they shut us down, there won't *be* a show!"

"There *has* to be a show!" David said. "My mom's hiring a videographer to make a DVD. It's supposed to be my professional audition piece!"

"And Cordelia and I have been working on a way to combine Step with ballet," Q said. "We're going to revolutionize the world of dance!"

"Take it easy, everybody," Lucille said. "Breathe! We may be on the state's radar screen, but nothing has really happened yet. Tell them about distraction and delay, Harley."

When Harley had explained that they couldn't fail an inspection that hadn't been completed, E.D. told

them that what they needed to do was think of ways to keep the inspector from getting it done. "He was probably just taking preliminary notes. An inspection includes collecting a water sample from the pond for testing, and I'm sure he hasn't done that yet. We need to keep it that way."

"So what do we do if he shows up at the pond to get some water?" Cinnamon asked. "Shoot him and sink his body in the muck?"

"Now there's an idea!" David said.

"That's what would happen in a Petunia Grantham mystery!" Cinnamon pointed out.

"This is *not* a Petunia Grantham mystery," Lucille said.

"Maybe we could keep him from getting to the pond in the first place," Q said. "How about we string trip wires across the trails and through the woods?"

"Oh sure, trip wires!" David said. "*That'll* stop an agent of the state."

E.D. sighed. She was beginning to wish her hormones would go back to wherever they came from. She suspected that Botticelli must have had nicer models for his angels.

"We could weave Elf Nets across the trails," Samantha said.

"*Elf* Nets?" David scoffed. "What the heck are Elf Nets?"

"Nets made out of vines and strung between trees.

Like the sculpture I made in Archie's workshop."

"She used honeysuckle and wisteria vines," E.D. said, "but if we wore gloves—and shirts with long sleeves—while we worked, we could use barbed wire vine and maybe even poison ivy, too. Nobody would dare try to get through a net like that. We could block every single trail in from the road. Maybe it wouldn't stop him completely, but it would sure slow him down."

"What if he comes through the meadow instead of the woods?" Ginger said.

"We could let Wolfie out of the goat pen," Destiny put in. "That would scare him away. Wolfie scares everybody."

"If he's sneaking around, how will we even know when he comes back?" Q asked. "He could show up anytime and anyplace. We need some kind of watch system."

"Winston! Winston!" Destiny said. "He always barks at strangers." Hearing his name, the dog looked up and thumped his tail. "See? Winston wants to be a watch system."

Jake nodded. "He could do it, but he'd have to see or hear or smell the guy. I guess he and I could take a walk around Wit's End a couple of times a day."

"Me, too! Me, too! I wants to go along!"

"We could all take turns," Q said. "We could walk the perimeter every hour or two. The dog could use the exercise."

"We could put 'walk the dog' on the Community Service list," David said. "That would be a heck of a lot better than cleaning bathrooms!"

Aside from vetoing murder, Aunt Lucille let the kids go on spinning out methods for distraction and delay without comment. She was listening in a way that E.D. recognized. The Applewhites believed in individual initiative and independence. She had a feeling the adults were going to let the kids do whatever they could think of short of murder and mayhem. She remembered a term from a program she had seen on television: *plausible deniability*. This way, if things went wrong somehow, the adults could all say they hadn't known about any of it. It was just a bunch of kids goofing around behind their backs. What the kids needed to do was make sure things didn't go wrong.

Chapter Twenty-eight

"Jake, Jake!" Harley's voice came over the walkie-talkie. "Code red! Winston's barking his head off."

This was it, Jake thought, his stomach starting to knot. It was July 11, four days since they'd started planning, and the man in the suit hadn't been spotted once. They'd developed Plans A through F to distract and delay the inspector no matter where or when he showed up, and the adults were letting them use the walkie-talkies to keep in touch. All the kids—including Hal and

Cordelia—had spent their mornings, wearing gardening gloves and sweating in long-sleeved shirts and jeans, building Elf Nets across the woods trails. They'd finished the last one just this morning. The rest of the time, except for the perimeter dog walks, camp had gone on as usual, E.D. coming up with daily schedules that managed to fit the workshops into the afternoons, with theater, as usual, taking up the evenings. Nobody expected an inspector to come after dinner.

Jake had been hoping the inspector wouldn't come back. The truth was, he'd had enough run-ins with state government to last the rest of his life. Rhode Island had banned him from public school and put him in foster care. He wasn't looking forward to trouble with North Carolina. At least this time, he reminded himself, it wasn't Jake Semple alone against a whole state. He figured he was pretty much an innocent bystander.

"Did you hear me, Jake? Code red!"

"Roger," Jake said. "Where are you?"

"Meadow. Not far from the goat pen."

"Ten-four. Meadow's Plan C. Can you see him?"

"Guy in a suit. Heading in from the road."

"Has he seen you?"

"Don't know. He can't miss the barking!"

"Okay. Stay out of sight if you can. But don't lose him. I'll get the others on it."

Jake wished there were enough walkie-talkies for everybody to have one, but Randolph had vetoed buying more. In the afternoons the campers tended to be scattered all over camp. He'd been printing out song lyrics in the office when Harley called in. Now he looked at the Wit's End map on the wall and checked the afternoon schedule. This was the first after-lunch session of the day, which meant Ginger was in Wisteria Cottage with Lucille.

Samantha was at work on the scaffolding at the barn. Harley had finished his photomontage. Samantha had laid out the patchwork pattern on the barn wall and should be painting her mural now. Cordelia, Q, and David were in the dance studio, probably arguing, as usual, over the best way to create a fusion of Step, tap, and ballet. And Cinnamon—*perfect!*—Cinnamon was at the goat pen already, where she was supposedly trying to tame Wolfie so the Petunia Possum picture book could have a happy ending. The inspector's route and timing couldn't be better for Plan C. He thumbed the walkie-talkie to transmit. "Cinnamon! Did you hear? He's somewhere near you."

There was a brief crackle of static. Then "Roger that. I've spotted the target. Ten-four. Waiting for him to get closer."

The only person Jake couldn't locate on the schedule was E.D. But she had a walkie-talkie with her. He hoped she had it turned on. "E.D. Where are you?"

"Dance studio."

The dance studio. David was there. Was she still hung up on that jerk? "Mobilizing Plan C. Blue already in place. Step One about to begin."

"I heard. Cordelia, David, and Q on their way. I'm heading for Wisteria to change Green Twin to Blue and deploy. Cinnamon!"

"Yep?"

"Got your scarf with you?"

"Yep."

Destiny was going to be terribly disappointed to have missed this, Jake thought. He'd wanted to be part of what he called "destruction and delay." He'd been carrying an empty single-portion cereal box around with him, calling it his "walkie-talker." But Sybil had taken him with her to the library in town to get more kids' books for her market research. "I'm a nil-ustrator," he'd told Jake importantly as he climbed into the car after lunch with a backpack to fill with picture books. "I gots to do research too."

Jake hurried out of the office and ran toward the goat pen. Step One for Plan C was the release of Wolfie, and he didn't want to miss it. After that, of course, though everybody had a job to do, they had to be flexible and creative. Once Wolfie was loose, there was no way to predict how things would unfold.

As he got closer, he could hear barking and

shouting. He arrived at the goat pen out of breath and sweating. Cinnamon was standing by the open gate. Hazel was next to her, nibbling contemplatively at the hem of Cinnamon's shorts. All the action was in the meadow. Harley was shouting at Winston, who was chasing Wolfie, who was chasing a man in a dark suit, who was dodging around among the waist-high weeds and grass and thistles, flapping a clipboard behind him and hollering for someone to "Call him off, call him off!"

"Run for the woods!" Harley shouted at the man now. "It's your only hope!"

Dodging and weaving, the man began angling toward the trees on the other side of the meadow, Wolfie closing on him fast. The man caught sight of the beginning of a trail and headed for it, putting on a final burst of speed, apparently thinking, from Harley's warning, that Wolfie would stop once he got in under the trees. Wolfie, of course, would not stop. But the man would, Jake knew. Not more than ten yards into the woods an Elf Net was strung securely across the trail.

Sure enough, there was a scream just about the time Wolfie headed in among the trees and then another—louder and more bloodcurdling—as Wolfie apparently caught up to the inspector, who was surely caught in, or at least stopped by, the Elf Net. It occurred to Jake that injuring a representative of

the government was probably not a good idea. But he need not have worried. Cinnamon put two fingers in her mouth and whistled a whistle that could have been heard in the next county. A moment later Wolfie appeared at the edge of the meadow, a narrow strip of dark fabric caught on his twisted horn.

"Stay where you are, mister!" Harley shouted toward the woods, "while we catch the goat. Don't come out till we say it's okay!" It wasn't an instruction the man was likely to ignore. Cinnamon, with Hazel at her heels, hurried across the meadow to meet Wolfie.

Jake could hardly believe his eyes as he watched Wolfie fall in next to Hazel and the two goats trot docilely after Cinnamon straight back into the pen. Too bad Lucille wasn't here to see, he thought. Cinnamon, the goat-whisperer, slipped into the shed and returned with a coffee can full of feed, which she poured on the ground. As the goats began to eat, she went out of the pen and closed the gate. By that time Ginger had arrived, dressed now in blue, a matching scarf securely covering her Mohawk haircut. Cinnamon whipped an identical scarf out of her pocket and tied it on over her red curls. The two girls now looked exactly alike. Destiny could probably tell them apart, Jake thought, but nobody else could.

He pushed the transmitter button on his walkie-

talkie. "Samantha. Blue and Blue deployed."

"Roger. I'll be ready if he comes this way."

What happened next would depend on the twins. Cinnamon would go down the trail and ask the inspector where he wanted to go. Then she'd offer to take him on a shortcut through the woods. After that she and Ginger would take turns disappearing and popping up in unexpected places. When he'd seen Cinnamon disappear behind a tangle of bushes and vines in one direction, Ginger was to pop up in the opposite direction and ask why he was going that way. By the time he got out of the woods, they figured he'd be doubting his sanity. Depending on the route they were able to pick out, which was something they hadn't been able to plan, they might lead him to the barn, where Samantha could accidentally spill a can of paint down on him from the scaffolding, or back to the meadow, where Q and David would be ready to open the gate and turn Wolfie loose again.

When they'd planned it originally, they weren't sure how David and Q would get Wolfie back once he was free, but now it was clear they'd only need Cinnamon to come and whistle for him. *How did she do that?* Jake wondered.

There wasn't anything more for Jake to do now except wait either to see the man emerge into the meadow again or to hear from Samantha that she'd

dumped paint on his head. Distraction and delay. So far, so good. If he were the guy stuck in the Elf Net, Jake thought, he wouldn't be any too eager to come back to Wit's End—ever.

Chapter Twenty-nine

E.D. missed the whole of Plan C. When she'd arrived at Wisteria Cottage, Ginger and Lucille had been poring over a book of folk songs, comparing verses and choruses and talking about the uses of repetition in songwriting. "Code red!" she shouted as she went in. "The inspector's back—in the meadow! Plan C has started already. You need to change clothes, Ginger, and get out there as fast as you can."

"It's okay, go!" Lucille said. Ginger turned and ran for Dogwood Cottage. "Plan C?"

"Plausible deniability," E.D. said. "You don't want to know."

"Nobody will get hurt, right?"

"That'll pretty much depend on Wolfie," E.D. said as she headed for the door. She wanted to get back in time to see the action.

"Wait!" Lucille said. "I want you to look at something."

"But I have to go—"

"Do you play a central role in Plan C?"

"No—but—"

"Okay, then. This'll only take a minute." Lucille pulled E.D. over to Archie's laptop on the kitchen table. She didn't let go of her arm as she brought a photograph up on the screen. "I'm thinking of starting a blog about all this. Something wonderful is happening. I've already written three poems. It's not just Harley's camera. Look here!"

That was how E.D. missed what happened in the meadow. Lucille insisted on showing her all the evidence that orbs couldn't be accounted for by the camera flash lighting up dust particles or moisture in the air. Lucille and Harley had been conducting experiments. They'd stirred up dust in the storage rooms of the barn and taken pictures. Those photos had some orblike blobs, but they all were fuzzy and indistinct. None of them had the interior mandala patterns, and none of them had blue fringes. They'd run the shower in Wisteria's bathroom until the room was full of mist, and none of

the photos they'd taken had orbs in them at all. There were even two photos with colored orbs that had been taken outside without a flash. *Incontrovertible evidence,* Lucille called these photographs.

"But the best thing of all," she announced with triumph, "is that you can *call* them! At least I can. Harley refused to try."

"Well, thanks for showing me these," E.D. said. "But I really should get back—"

"Just a few more! Look here."

E.D. sighed. "I don't see any orbs."

Lucille nodded. "Exactly! There weren't any. So I closed my eyes, went into a meditative state, and asked them to show up and let us take their picture. And they came! I'm afraid Harley's a little freaked by it all. He's considering giving up photography altogether."

By the time E.D. finally managed to get away, she found Jake and the campers at the goat pen, congratulating themselves on their success and complaining about the things that hadn't worked the way they'd expected.

It turned out that Ginger and Cinnamon had gotten themselves just as lost in the woods as the inspector until Ginger finally stumbled onto the road by accident. As soon as the man had seen pavement, he took off running, or at least limping very fast, to find his car. "I think Wolfie must have hurt the man's leg a

little when he tore his pants," Ginger said.

"So we didn't get to sic Wolfie on him again," David said. "Too bad! I don't think he even drew blood the first time."

"And Samantha didn't get to dump her paint," Jake added.

"I'm just as glad," Samantha said. "I'd finally managed to get the colors right, and I didn't want to waste the paint. Besides, I got four whole patches of the barn quilt finished. You all need to come see it!"

"Archie's gone to the pond. He's giving us an extra optional swim," Q said. "Cordelia went to get Hal and change into her suit." The others agreed they were more than ready for a swim.

E.D. had still not convinced herself that the pond was okay for swimming, so while the others went to change into their suits, she headed back to the air-conditioned office. She'd been thinking about Aunt Lucille and Harley looking for evidence about orbs, and realized there was still no evidence that the messages that had continued to appear in the mailbox were real. She'd never actually gotten around to checking. If the whole thing was really Mrs. Montrose trying to get revenge on her father, it could be that the woman had exaggerated the danger. Maybe the state couldn't actually shut them down at all. The thing to do was go online and check out the North Carolina Department of Environment and Natural Resources.

Before they harassed a state inspector again, it would be a good idea to know for sure how much was riding on his report.

Fifteen minutes later, E.D. had found the regulations. They had not been exaggerated. Not only were they word for word what the messages had said, there were pages and pages more. On the department's home page she had also found the phone number for customer relations, and that gave her an idea. If she pretended to be someone reporting violations, she might be able to find out exactly what the state could and would do about them. And maybe, even more important, how much time it would take them to do it.

E.D. picked up the phone and put it down again. Calling a government office was scary. Then she remembered the improv exercise. As bad as she was at acting, she was really pretty good at improvising. *I can do this!* she thought. She would pretend to be somebody like Mrs. Montrose. She would call in to report violations at some anonymous camp and just see what happened. She took a deep breath, picked up the phone, and dialed the customer service number.

When a friendly voice answered, E.D. lowered her voice, doing her best to sound like her mother. "I'd like to talk to whoever is in charge of regulating camps in North Carolina," she said.

"Resident camps?" the friendly voice asked.

"Yes—resident camps."

"That would be Joseph Gant. He is out of the office at the moment, but I can connect you with his assistant, Daryl Gaffney. One moment. I'll put you through."

It was working, E.D. thought. The woman hadn't acted as if she was talking to a kid. "This is Daryl Gaffney, how may I help you?"

"Mr. Gaffney," E.D. said in her best Sybil voice, "I have some questions about possible rule violations at a summer camp."

"What sorts of violations?"

"There are several. Vermin infestation, for instance." She thought about Paulie in the kitchen while Aunt Lucille and her mother fixed meals. That was absolutely against the sanitary regulations. "Live animals in the kitchen during meal preparation. Unsanitary conditions in living quarters. I think your department should send an inspector to investigate this facility immediately."

There was a slight pause before Mr. Gaffney responded. "I missed your name, Ms. . . ."

"My name is . . . Sybil . . ." E.D. looked wildly around the office for a possible last name. A dictionary was leaning against the printer. "Sybil Webster."

"Well, Ms. Webster, our department does not actually conduct those inspections. They are done by the county health department in the county where the camp is located. Such inspections are, of course,

done *for* the state, which issues the camp permits, but not *by* the state. How large a camp is this?"

"Sixteen acres," E.D. said.

There was a muffled chuckle on the other end of the line. "I'm sorry, ma'am—I meant how many campers are served by the facility?"

"Six."

"Six? You mean six *hundred*? On sixteen acres?"

"No. I mean six. Six campers."

Now there was no question that Mr. Gaffney was doing his best to suppress a laugh. He wasn't quite succeeding. "I'm very sorry, Ms. Webster, but as you may know, the state of North Carolina, like most states, works under considerable budgetary restraint. We are snowed under with regulations—there's the ban on smoking in public restaurants and bars, for instance—a nightmare, that one! There simply isn't the staff to enforce them all. We do our best, but you really have no idea how many regulations we and the county health departments have to deal with! We are stretched very, very thin! *Six campers!* Has anyone become ill at this camp? Has anyone—*died*?"

"Certainly not!"

"Then, Ms. Webster, I suggest you begin by taking up the issue with the camp management. Ask them to clean up their act, as it were. Ask them to call in exterminators. And get the animals out of the kitchen. If you could see the load of casework we deal with at

our end, you'd understand that a situation of this—this— Is there such a word as *minitude*? The opposite, I mean to say, of *magnitude*? Well, I mean, I just have to tell you that a camp of that size is not going to readily make its way to the top of our workload. Or that of the particular county's health department, for that matter." Daryl Gaffney was openly chuckling now. "Is there—is there anything else I can help you with?"

"No, thank you," E.D. said. "I appreciate you taking the time to speak to me."

"Think nothing of it," Mr. Gaffney said. "You've been a breath of fresh air in a very dull day. *Six campers!*"

He was laughing outright when E.D. hung up. The regulations were real. But if the state—or the county health department—didn't have the staff to enforce them, *who was the man in the suit?*

Chapter Thirty

Destiny hadn't gotten back from the library in time to swim, so Jake had been free to swim with the campers. He'd taken Winston along, and the dog was so exhausted that once he'd gotten a drink from the pond edge, he dragged his muddy body back, flopped down in the shade, and went instantly to sleep.

Not once during the whole of optional swim did Jake catch Ginger staring at him with that look of adoration. As relieved as he was, Jake had to admit to

himself that he was almost sorry. Nobody in his life had ever looked at him that way before. He pretty much doubted it would ever happen again.

With Archie overseeing the water activities, they staged individual races, most of which Q won; relay races with endless arguments over who should be on which team and whether the fastest swimmers on a team should go first or last; a diving contest, which David won with a forward front flip that Jake could hardly believe could be done without a diving board; and finally a game of Marco Polo that went badly wrong when Samantha, Cinnamon, and Ginger accused David of cheating. The argument over that got so heated that Archie kicked everybody out of the pond fifteen minutes early.

The twins said everybody should go see Samantha's mural; David stormed off to the boys' cottage by himself; and the others, except for Hal, who reluctantly went to keep an eye on David, gathered their sandals and towels and set off toward the barn.

As Jake started after them, Harley hung back. "Can I talk to you?" he said. "Privately?"

"Sure! What's up?"

"Well. Um." Harley fiddled with the towel around his neck. "You know how I told you I don't sing?"

"Yeah."

"See, the thing is—I sort of do. I mean, I really do—I *can*—but I don't. I mean I haven't." He rubbed his

nose. "I've spent my whole life on the road with my folks, going from concert to concert. I was 'bus schooled,' is how my mom puts it. There were never any other kids in my life—just my parents and the band and their fans. I didn't get much chance to be a kid."

Jake nodded. As different as his life had been from Harley's, he sort of knew how that was.

"So I decided when I was still pretty little that the way to be *me* was to not be *them*. I learned to play the guitar way back before I figured out the 'me' thing, but I don't carry one around with me or anything. Since I didn't want to sing, I was gonna be a painter till I found out I wasn't any good at it, and then I decided to do photography instead."

"But you *can* sing?"

"Oh, yeah. I can. So what I wanted to ask is, Is it too late to join your workshop?"

Jake laughed. "As long as you don't expect much from me as a singing coach. We just all sort of figure stuff out together."

"It's not so much for the singing part. You know the music that came into my head for Ginger's lyrics? Well, I was thinking she and I might be able to sing a duet at the end-of-camp show. I mean, if we have an end-of-camp show. If the state doesn't shut us down or anything. Trouble is, I didn't bring my guitar—"

"Archie has one," Jake said.

"I didn't know he plays the guitar."

"He doesn't. He bought it a long time ago when he was going around the world on a tramp steamer. Thought he'd learn to play and use it to impress girls." Jake chuckled. "He learned a few chords; but since he doesn't sing, the whole thing just never worked out. He's still got it though. It's in a closet in Wisteria Cottage. I'm pretty sure he'd lend it to you."

Archie had just swum across the pond from the diving platform and was climbing onto the dock. "Go ask him," Jake said. "We could definitely use somebody in the workshop who can play live music for us! Are you any good?"

Harley nodded. "The bass guitarist told me I was a prodigy."

"Be careful of that word," Jake said. "Go ask!"

After they'd all checked out Samantha's mural, which was really big, really original, a little strange, and—everybody agreed—really good, Jake, with Winston tagging behind, went back to Wisteria Cottage to shower and change. When he got there, Archie had dug out his guitar and dusted off the case.

"It's about time this old thing got some use!" he said. "So Harley's a guitar prodigy, huh? Lucille's right. This group just gets more and more interesting. Have you seen Samantha's mural?"

Jake nodded. "It seems pretty good to me. I don't

know that much about art—"

"One thing's for sure: when it's done, we're going to have ourselves the most unusual barn in the state! If the government doesn't close us down, I'm thinking we could sell tickets to the end-of-camp show. Would you take this to Harley?"

E.D. was heading up the steps of Wisteria Cottage when Jake and Winston came out later. "We have to talk," E.D. said, waving at the rocking chairs on the porch. "Sit!" Winston sat. So did Jake. From the look on E.D.'s face, there was just no point in arguing.

"So, if this guy isn't a state inspector," Jake said when she finished telling him about her call to the department, "who *is* he?"

"That's what *I* want to know!"

"We should tell your folks. No sense letting them go on worrying that the state could come swooping down on us any minute."

E.D. didn't answer at first. She just stared off into the trees for a while. Then she smiled in a way that looked to Jake more conspiratorial than cheery. "I'm thinking it wouldn't hurt to let them go on worrying awhile. After all, they're the grown-ups here—the talented, creative, famous grown-ups! And not one of them thought to check with the state before they put everybody to the trouble of creating the camp! And bringing in the campers! Now that *I* know we

aren't in danger, I don't mind at all that they still think we are. Serves Dad right when you come right down to it. All I want is to find out who this guy really is."

"After what happened to him today, you expect him to come back?"

E.D. shrugged. "Let's see if the messages keep turning up in the mailbox. If so, it means the charade continues. So we go on keeping watch. Then—if he comes back—instead of chasing him off, we need to catch him and get the whole story."

Jake looked at Winston, who was asleep again, snoring noisily. "Winston's practically worn to the bone tromping around the whole of Wit's End four times a day. He's so exhausted that a butterfly actually landed on his head this afternoon and he didn't do a thing."

"It's about time he figured out he's never going to catch one. Winston's not worn to the bone; he's just lost a little weight. That dog's in better shape than he's been since he was a puppy."

Jake thought about what had changed since E.D. had found the threatening messages and caught sight of the guy in the suit. When they'd thought there was a threat to the camp, everybody had started pulling together. Even David and Q had begun cooperating, at least occasionally. The threat really had turned them—adults and kids alike—into an ensemble, all focused on the same thing. "Okay.

So what do we do instead of distraction and delay?"

"I don't know yet."

"Harley's joining my singing workshop, so if you bring Hal and Cordelia to the next one, we can tell everybody together."

Chapter Thirty-one

For almost a week the messages went on showing up with the mail, and E.D. took guilty delight in watching her father prowl around Wit's End obsessing over mess and looking for signs of vermin infestation. He was the only one who still seemed to be taking the threat seriously. When the results of Plan C had been reported at a staff meeting, Zedediah said they might as well just go on taking things a day at a time. "We haven't heard directly from the state, after all. I doubt that we'll see the man again. It's hard to imagine that

a little operation like ours will seem worth risking life and limb over."

Lucille insisted there was no need to worry in any case since they were so clearly under the protection of cosmic forces. She had taken to keeping her camera with her all the time and taking sudden flash photographs without warning. "We are positively surrounded by orbs!"

Then, very early on the morning of July 17, when all the campers were at yoga, Sybil was in the kitchen getting breakfast, and E.D. was putting up the daily schedule in the dining tent, the plain black car came up the drive and pulled to a stop by the front porch with a squeal of brakes. The man, this time wearing a light blue suit, emerged from the car with his clipboard in hand and leaned on the horn.

E.D. flipped on her walkie-talkie. She hoped Jake was awake and that wherever he was, he had his walkie-talkie with him. "Jake! Jake, are you on? 9-1-1. Repeat. 9-1-1. Come to the Lodge. Right now!"

At the sound of the horn, Paulie, in the kitchen, had begun screaming like someone being attacked by an ax murderer. The horn, beeping over and over, had apparently sent him into a frenzy. Sybil hurried to the door and came out on the porch, wiping her hands on her apron. "May I help you?"

"I'm from the Department of Environment and Natural Resources!" the man shouted over the sound

of Paulie's screams. "Who's in charge here?"

"Well I suppose I am at the moment," Sybil said. "I'm the associate director."

He waggled an official-looking name tag at her. "I'm Thomas Timmons, and I've come to inspect this camp." He looked at his clipboard. "*Eureka!* Is that the name? Strange name for a camp."

"Inspect the camp?" Sybil said as if she'd never heard of such a thing. "We've had no call about an inspection!"

"Of course you haven't had a call. This is an unannounced inspection, as per Section 15A of the North Carolina Administrative Code. What is there about the term 'unannounced' you don't understand?"

Paulie's screams subsided, and he began instead a series of his most colorful curses.

"Am I correct in assuming that someone at this camp is swearing at an agent of the government? I will not be sworn at!" Brandishing his clipboard, the man stormed up the steps of the porch, and Sybil retreated until she was backed up against the screen door.

"That's just Paulie," she said. "My father-in-law's parrot."

"Parrot?" The man pulled a pen from his jacket pocket and jotted something on the clipboard. "A live bird on the premises. Clear danger of psittacosis. I hope this bird does not reside in the kitchen. That

would be a serious violation of regulations!"

Sybil's face drained of color. "Reside? Well, no! Paulie *resides* in Maple Cottage. He was just brought over this morning to be—"

"This is to be a full inspection: food preparation area, lodging facilities, sanitation and bathing facilities, drinking water, vermin control, recreational waters. All of it. The future of this camp will depend on the results. I wish to begin with food preparation. Take me to your kitchen!"

"What is that infernal racket?" Randolph's voice could be heard now amid Paulie's gradually diminishing shrieks and curses. "Doesn't anyone down there know what time it is? It is barely past dawn!"

At that moment Winston came around the house barking his terrorist protection bark. Jake hurried after him, walkie-talkie in hand. Destiny, still in his pajamas, followed.

"Someone put up that dog!" the man yelled over the tumult. "It is against the law for an unrestrained animal to be present during an official inspection."

"Jake!" Sybil said. "Take Winston somewhere else, would you please?"

"Is that the *bad man*, Mommy?" Destiny demanded. "The *destruction and delay* man?"

"Hush, Destiny. Of course not," Sybil said.

"Come on, Winston!" E.D. called. "You too, Destiny."

If they were to put the plan they had come up with into effect, she had to let the others know what was going on. "Let's go watch the campers do yoga!"

"Oooh, goodie! Can I do it, too? I'm really, really good at yoga," Destiny told the man as E.D. grabbed his hand and tried to aim him toward the barn, "but they never lets me do it. They say I'm too loud. Am I too loud, do you think?"

By this time Randolph, in undershorts and T-shirt, had come to the door, smoothing his tangled hair. "What's all this? Who are you?"

"Thomas Timmons, from the Department of Environment and Natural Resources!" the man repeated, glancing over his shoulder from time to time at Winston, who was now growling menacingly and uttering the occasional *woof* as he followed E.D.

"Then I suggest you go look after the environment. Get out there and protect some of our natural resources and quit intruding on the affairs of the citizens of this state whose taxes are responsible for keeping you employed."

The man waved his clipboard again. "I *demand* to be taken to your kitchen. Immediately!"

Jake hurried to the porch steps. "Excuse me, sir," he said. "But the campers haven't had breakfast yet, so the kitchen is very busy at the moment. I'd be happy to take you to see the lodging facilities, and we can come back to the kitchen when the campers are

eating. The food preparation area won't go anywhere while we're gone, I promise you."

"I want you to know that I'm calling your superiors!" Randolph blustered through the screen door now. "It's a crime to send anyone here before normal work hours. *Eureka!* is not open to the public until ten o'clock, I'll have you know!"

"Randolph! Go upstairs and get dressed," Sybil was saying as E.D. pulled Destiny away.

Chapter Thirty-two

wo can play at this game, Jake thought as he led the still-blustering Thomas Timmons, or whatever his name really was, on as roundabout a route as he could manage past the far side of the Lodge toward the boys' and girls' cottages. He began explaining *Eureka!* as if he really believed the man was an inspector from the state.

"This used to be a motor lodge," he told him, "so the campers stay in self-contained cottages. Each one houses three campers and a counselor and has a full kitchen and a full bath. Even though the cottages aren't air-conditioned, we like to think *Eureka!*

provides exceptionally luxurious accommodations."

"The department doesn't care about luxury," the man said, scratching the back of his neck with one hand. His frown got even more ferocious. "What we care about is the health and well-being of the campers. What we care about is sanitation. Sanitation and *safety*!"

Jake hoped this guy's intimidating attitude was all an act. If the plan they'd figured out—the plan he hoped E.D. was getting organized right now—was going to work, the man pretty much had to be a good guy at heart.

When they'd gathered to figure out what to do, David had suggested replacing distraction and delay with "capture and torture."

Q had accused him of watching too much television, but Cinnamon pointed out that the capture part was right. "We need to catch him instead of chasing him off. But how?"

Destiny had started jumping up and down. "I know how, I know how! We can dig a Heffalump trap. Like Pooh and Piglet. We can dig a *pit* where he'll fall in and he won't be able to get out."

Everyone had laughed at this at first. But it was Destiny's Heffalump trap that finally led them to their plan. Of course, they had thought the man would sneak into Wit's End the way he had before. They hadn't expected him to make a frontal assault. But

now that he had, they would just have to make the best of it. *Creativity and flexibility,* Jake thought. *Like Zedediah said.* Jake figured his job was to stall for time and give the man a false sense of confidence. Thomas Timmons needed to believe they were buying his act.

The two of them had arrived at the boys' cottage now, and Jake led the man onto the porch. "You'll be interested in the Community Service aspect of the *Eureka!* program. We've involved every person at the camp, staff and campers alike, in making sure that everything is kept clean and in order." With that he opened the door so that the man could go inside. *It's a good thing this isn't real!* Jake thought. Nothing about what greeted them as they entered was clean and in order.

Because Hal needed a room of his own, Harley had been sleeping on a foldout couch in the living room. Not only was the couch-bed not made, but the tangle of bedclothes was strewn with pages of music, some of it printed, some handwritten, and Archie's guitar lay on top of it all. The guitar case was open on the kitchen table, and empty soda bottles and glasses littered the counter. The mess was clearly not Harley's alone. There were clothes, dirty socks, smelly sneakers, and wet towels strewn on the floor, along with a pair of men's ballet slippers and one tap shoe. A flowerpot filled with sand supported a dead branch

festooned with tangles of equally dead honeysuckle where someone had been practicing weaving Elf Nets.

Thomas Timmons whipped out his pen and began making marks on the sheets of paper clipped to his board, clicking his tongue and shaking his head. Jake bit his lip to keep from laughing and led the way down the hall to Hal's room, and David and Q's, both of which made the living room look neat by comparison. He had decided to save the bathroom for last.

Chapter Thirty-three

When E.D., Winston, and Destiny approached the parking area in the shadow of the barn, the barefoot campers and Cordelia were in a semicircle around Lucille doing tree pose. Lucille, Cordelia, and Samantha were each standing perfectly balanced on one leg, the other foot flat against the inside of the knee and their hands entwined above their heads, gazing raptly skyward. Nobody else had managed to look up. Most of them were teetering on one leg and waving their arms and

hands in the air to try to maintain balance.

"Aunt Lucille, Aunt Lucille!" E.D. shouted. It was as if the sound knocked them all over. Even Lucille tipped sideways and stepped out of the pose. "There's a state inspector demanding to see the kitchen!"

"What? An inspector? Now? Good heavens, not the kitchen!"

"Jake took him off to the bunks first, but Mom needs help!"

"Cordelia!" Lucille said, pushing her feet into her flip-flops and snatching up her water bottle. "Can you finish the yoga session? Just do one sun salutation, I think." She was off even before Cordelia could answer, running toward the Lodge.

"This is it," E.D. told the others when she was sure her aunt was out of earshot. "He drove right up to the Lodge and identified himself as the state inspector. Has a fake ID and everything. Mom's freaking, Dad's furious. They have no idea, of course, that he isn't what he says he is. Jake's stalling him—letting him do his inspector act at the bunks. We have time to get ready, but we have to hurry. Have you got your camera, Harley?"

Harley grabbed it and held it up.

"Good. Destiny? Do you remember what you're supposed to do?"

"I'm the honeypot!" Destiny said. "For the bottom of the pit. 'Cept I gotta yell and yell."

"Where's your life jacket?"

"We left it by the dock," Ginger said, "so it would be there when we needed it."

"I'll go get Wolfie," Cinnamon said.

"Be sure to keep him out of sight—and leave him on his rope till we see if we need him. Destiny could be enough."

"Yeah, yeah, I know. We don't want to chase the guy away again."

E.D. checked her watch. "I don't know how long it'll take for him to inspect the cottages. . . ."

"If Dogwood's as bad as ours, it'll take a while," Q said.

"It's pretty bad," Cordelia said. "I'll run over and lead him through it—pretend I'm afraid of what he's going to report. This is going to be fun."

"There are still mouse turds in our room," Ginger said. "Act as if you're trying to hide them so he'll be sure to notice."

As Cordelia started away, E.D. called to her. "Tell Jake to beep my walkie-talkie when you're done at the cottages. You can say you'll take the guy to the pond before he goes back to inspect the kitchen. I'll meet you all on your way there."

"Ten-four!"

"Everybody remember what you're supposed to do?" E.D. asked.

"Gee, no, we're all idiots," David said.

That, E.D. thought, was enough. Hormones or no

hormones, she was finished with David! What had she *ever* seen in him? "Let's go!"

"I gots to get my swimming suit!" Destiny said.

"No time for that. You can go in your pajamas," E.D. told him.

"Head 'em up, move 'em out," Q shouted.

"All for one and one for all," Harley called as they started toward the pond.

Chapter Thirty-four

O nce Cordelia arrived it got harder and harder for Jake to keep a straight face. She came tearing up the path and stood in front of the door of Dogwood Cottage with her arms folded across her chest. "You can't come in here," she told the man. "We're not ready."

"That is the point of an unannounced inspection," the man said. His voice, Jake thought, had softened suddenly. Cordelia, in her yoga outfit, her hair curling damply around her face, was looking particularly gorgeous. "We need to see conditions as they really

are, not as they've been fixed up to impress us."

Cordelia, with a great show of reluctance, moved aside and let him open the door.

Jake hadn't been inside the girls' cottage since the first night of camp. Except that here it was Cordelia who slept on the foldout couch, the scene inside was much more like the boys' cottage than he would have guessed. If anything, it was worse, mostly because the girls seemed to have a lot more clothes. Blue and green shirts and shorts, sneakers and sandals, jeans and T-shirts and bathing suits were draped on furniture and lay in piles on the floor, along with a surprising number of Cordelia's skirts and blouses. In the midst of the clothes were Samantha's books—piled, strewn, and stacked everywhere.

"Normally, it's much neater than this," Cordelia said, blushing slightly as she slipped some underwear under a blouse.

Thomas Timmons nodded. He seemed to be paying as much attention to Cordelia as to the mess he was inspecting. Alternating between jotting notes on the pages of his clipboard and using his pen to scratch his neck, he muttered "dreadful," "appalling," and "disgusting" under his breath. As he started down the hall, Cordelia whispered to Jake E.D.'s message about letting her know when they were finished here.

In the twins' room, Cordelia kept putting herself between Thomas Timmons and what he was trying to inspect as if she wanted to keep him from seeing something. Finally, he actually put out a hand and moved her, surprisingly gently, out of the way.

"Vermin!" he said triumphantly, pointing at the scattering of mouse droppings all along the baseboards and the small pile in the corner. "This cabin is infested with mice!"

"We're planning to get a cat!" Cordelia said, and Jake had to clamp a hand over his mouth and leave the room entirely.

When the man had taken more notes in the bathroom, which wasn't so much dirty, Jake thought, as incredibly cluttered with tubes and bottles and jars and various zippered bags, combs, and brushes covering every square inch of horizontal surface, they went out onto the porch and Jake pressed the key on his walkie-talkie that would let E.D. know they were coming. Cordelia asked what else the man needed to inspect.

"Everything, of course!" he said. "Except, perhaps the woods. I don't need to go hiking all over the whole sixteen acres."

"Shall we take you to see the goat pen?" she asked innocently.

"I think not," he said quickly. He made a show of flipping through the forms on his clipboard. "There

is nothing in here about goat facilities."

"Okay, then," Cordelia said, starting down the path toward the pond. "We might as well take you to the pond. It's where we swim. Quite nice. Lovely clear water."

"I'll be the judge of that," the man said, following closely behind her.

"After that we'll take you back to the Lodge so you can inspect the kitchen," Jake said, trailing along after them. "The campers should be gathering in the dining tent very soon for breakfast. This is a creativity camp. Tell him about our workshops, Cordelia. And the end-of-camp show we're planning."

"End-of-camp show? I hope you haven't spent a lot of energy on that!" the man said. "It's highly likely, given what I've seen so far, that the department will decide to close this camp down."

Cordelia yelped. "Close it down? Why? When? How?"

As the man talked, citing violation after violation, Cordelia led him on toward the pond until E.D. came hurtling up the path and crashed into them. She was out of breath, her face red and terrified.

"Oh, thank God. Come quick!" she yelled. "Destiny's fallen into the pond, and something's got him! I think it's a snapping turtle! The biggest one I've ever seen." She looked up at Thomas Timmons, clearly distraught. "Oh, please, please come and help us save

my little brother! Snapping turtles can bite through a grown man's leg. What'll it do to a five-year-old? I tried to reach him, but I couldn't! Maybe you can! But hurry! Oh, please! Hurry, hurry, hurry!"

She turned around and tore off down the path. The man ran after her, and Jake and Cordelia closed in behind. No doubt about it, Jake thought, E.D. was really good at improvisation! He almost believed her himself.

As they got closer to the pond, they could hear Destiny shrieking at the top of his lungs. "Oww! Owwwww! It gots my foot. It hurts! Help, help, help! Somebody help! Oooowwww!"

Winston was standing belly-deep in the pond, barking.

Ginger and Samantha were running back and forth along the edge of the pond screaming about the monster that had hold of Destiny. "It's huge!"

"Even with his life jacket, it could pull him under!"

"He'll drown!"

"Or maybe bleed to death!"

"Oh, help, help, help!"

Out just a little way beyond the end of the dock, Destiny was splashing frantically and continuing to yell.

E.D. ran out to the end of the dock, crouched down, and reached toward Destiny. "You need to get closer," she shouted to him.

"I can't! Oooowwww! He gots me. I can't!"

Thomas Timmons threw down his clipboard, ran onto the dock, and moved E.D. out of his way. Then he knelt and stretched one arm toward Destiny, who went on screaming and splashing, still well out of reach. E.D. scuttled back off the dock as David and Q came running from the woods with the dock ropes they'd untied from the trees. Jake snatched away the ramp that led onto the dock while Cordelia, E.D., and the other two girls began shoving it out into the water. Harley came from the woods with his camera and started clicking one picture after another.

At the front of the dock Thomas Timmons, still focused entirely on the screaming and splashing in front of him, had taken off his suit jacket and was waving it at Destiny. "Here, here! Try to grab on to my jacket. If you can get it, I can pull you over."

As the dock floated steadily toward him, Destiny, still yelling and splashing, managed to paddle steadily backward. The others had stopped pushing now, but Jake and Cordelia, up to their knees in muck, gave one last tremendous shove. Thomas Timmons, having finally reached Destiny's hand, dropped his suit jacket on the dock behind him and pulled Destiny around to the ladder as the dock floated completely away from the shore.

Destiny stopped yelling and climbed the ladder

as the man got to his feet. "Thanks, oh thanks! The monster thingie letted me go!" he said. Then he pointed back toward the edge of the pond. "But we can't get back to the land anymore."

It wasn't until then that Thomas Timmons discovered he'd been caught in a Heffalump trap.

Chapter Thirty-five

Getting the man out of the Heffalump trap turned out to be considerably more difficult than getting him into it. As the dock floated away, it had dragged the ropes into the water, where they'd sunk immediately muck-ward, so there was no way to pull it back in. Destiny, not the least bit bothered by muck, jumped off the dock and paddled his way back till he could stand up and slog his way to solid ground, where a dripping Winston met him, wagging with relief, and shook pond water all over him.

"My idea worked! Did you see how good it worked?" Destiny burbled to E.D. as he unbuckled his muddy life jacket. "I was a very good honeypot. Don't you think I was a good honeypot?"

The man called out that he had no intention of ruining his suit by swimming to shore. So Cordelia hurried off to find Archie and Zedediah, who brought down a coil of rope. Jake swam one end of it out to the dock, and the others pulled it back in.

The impostor, still pretending to be an agent of the state, announced as he stepped off the dock onto the shore that the state could shut them down immediately on the basis of the pond alone. But when he noticed Harley taking pictures, he went suddenly silent and allowed himself to be escorted back to the dining tent, glancing over his shoulder every few steps at Winston, who was trotting along behind him, alternately growling and whuffling all the way. Sybil, Lucille, and Randolph met the procession, and Paulie, who'd been moved out of the kitchen and into the tent, greeted them all with his usual cascade of curses and then demanded a peanut.

It wasn't until Lucille and Sybil had seated him at a picnic table and Harley announced he was going to the office to upload the photographs he'd taken of the "rescue" at the pond that Thomas Timmons broke down and admitted that he was neither Thomas Timmons nor an agent of the state.

Randolph threatened to call the police on the spot.

"No one's had breakfast yet," Sybil protested. "It's never good to make important decisions on an empty stomach!"

"There's no decision to be made!" Randolph said. "This person has perpetrated a fraud! I guarantee you there's a law about impersonating a government employee and terrorizing innocent citizens! He is a criminal, and it's our *duty* to turn him over to the authorities!"

"He's not *going* anywhere, Randolph," Zedediah said. "Breakfast first, authorities later. I for one would like to hear the young man's story before we send him off to jail."

Lucille smiled beatifically. "Think of it this way, Randolph. Terror can be an excellent motivator. Just go inside and look at the kitchen. It's absolutely sparkling. I don't think the refrigerator has *ever* been so clean!"

"And now we know why," Sybil added. "Cleaning a refrigerator is an appalling job!"

So it was decided that everyone who needed to would shower and change and gather back in the dining tent for breakfast, while Lucille and Harley printed out the pictures Harley had taken—pictures, Randolph reminded the impostor, that would serve as evidence of fraud in a court of law.

When breakfast was over, the interrogation of the prisoner began.

"My name is Jonathon Sandler," he said, surrendering his fake ID badge. "I live in Traybridge. I'm an actor."

"An actor?" Randolph scoffed. "There's no work for an actor in Traybridge!"

"You're telling me! That's why I went to New York right out of college. I tried my luck there for three years and only managed to get two roles in all that time—both of them off-off-Broadway. No money. I survived as a bookkeeping temp."

Zedediah, who had been sitting next to Destiny watching him draw possums on a sketch pad, looked up. "Were you any good at it?"

"I got a couple of pretty good reviews—"

"I meant at bookkeeping!"

"Oh. Everybody I did temp work for wanted to hire me full-time. But I wanted to stay free to take whatever acting job came along. A lot of good that did me. I finally just gave up and came home. I figured even if Traybridge Little Theatre didn't pay, I could at least get onstage there. When I went to audition, Mrs. Montrose offered me this job instead."

Randolph erupted in fury. "This *job*? It isn't an acting job; it's a criminal conspiracy! Call the police *now*! We can get that wretched woman on conspiracy to defraud! I knew all along she had to be behind this."

Jonathon Sandler, scratching his neck, grinned sheepishly. "She offered to pay really well!"

When the whole story came out, it was pretty much

what E.D. had suspected. When Mrs. Montrose couldn't get the state interested in *Eureka!*, she'd decided to get revenge on the Applewhites as best she could.

"It was to be a kind of terrorist action at first," Sandler explained. "The intention was to inflict psychological trauma. So she had me deliver all those messages about the state regulations day after day. Then I was supposed to let myself get seen skulking around. She didn't warn me about the goat! I wouldn't have come back after that horrible day, but the goat tore the suit. It was from the costume shop at the Little Theatre, and she told me she'd take the cost of it out of my pay. I had to come back to earn the rest of it or I'd have ended up in debt!"

"She intended to inflict psychological trauma?" Randolph said. "When the case comes to trial, she'll discover that it didn't work. Applewhites are made of stronger stuff!"

Right, E.D. thought, remembering the look on her father's face the morning she'd seen him with one of Mrs. Montrose's threatening messages crumpled in his hand.

"After the inspection she was planning to forge a 'cease and desist' order from the state—and send it by mail from Raleigh. She thought you'd shut yourselves down to avoid prosecution."

"Never!" Randolph insisted. "We would have fought the state to the last breath!"

E.D. explained the policy of distraction and delay then, and told Jonathon Sandler she was sorry Wolfie had ruined the suit.

Cordelia, who was sitting across the table from him, said, "I hope he didn't hurt you!"

Sandler smiled at her and shook his head. "He scared the devil out of me, though. The worst part wasn't the goat." He scratched at his neck. "It's the poison ivy I got in the woods. It started on my neck, and it's spread all down my back!" Cordelia patted his other hand comfortingly.

Destiny looked up from his drawing pad. "Tell 'em about the Heffalump trap, E.D.!"

She explained about her call to the department. "So we knew you couldn't be a real inspector."

"You *knew*?" Randolph said. "You knew and didn't tell your family? How sharper than a serpent's tooth . . ."

David pointed a finger at Sandler. "I suggested capture and torture. You're lucky everybody else here is such a wimp."

"Then I had a Pooh and Piglet idea!" Destiny crowed. "The dock was a Heffalump trap, and I was the honeypot! And it worked! We caught you!"

"Yeah. You caught me." Sandler breathed a long, shuddery sigh. "And now I'll never get the rest of my pay. I'm back to being a starving artist!"

"You're going to jail—that's what's going to happen

to you! Don't think for one minute that we won't bring the full force of the law down on your head. And on the head of that vengeful, sadistic woman!" Randolph turned to Lucille. "You printed out those pictures, didn't you? They'll be all the evidence we need."

Lucille held up Harley's photographs. "They're evidence, all right. But we're not going to turn them over to the authorities."

"What do you mean? Of course we are!" Randolph said.

"There is a Higher Authority involved here, Randolph," she said. "Take a look." She spread the photos on the table. In almost every one of them, orbs could be seen clustered around Jonathon Sandler's head. "There. You see? Orbs! Benevolent spirits, drawn to light and joy. They would not be in these photographs if this young man had come here with malicious intent. He is here for some higher purpose—a higher purpose than Mrs. Montrose could ever have imagined."

"And what," Randolph asked with acid in his voice, "might that purpose be exactly?"

"It will emerge in time," Lucille said blithely. "You may be sure of that."

"It may have emerged already," Zedediah said. "Zedediah Applewhite Handmade Wood Furniture is in serious need of a bookkeeper. I've been working overtime, and I can't keep up with the books. For that

matter, this whole family would benefit from having somebody around who knows how to keep track of money."

"Now *there's* a good idea!" Sybil said.

"I do have a degree in accounting," Jonathon said. "Of course, I really prefer acting. . . ."

"It's possible," Sybil said, "that there will be a place for you in one of Randolph's productions from time to time."

"Are you *kidding*?" Randolph said. "After all he's done . . ."

"Well, the least you could do is let him audition, dear," Sybil said. "As well as he played the part of Thomas Timmons, he could turn out to be a real asset!"

Jonathon Sandler was smiling. E.D. noticed that Cordelia hadn't moved her hand from his since she'd patted it.

Sandler looked up at Randolph. "It would be an honor to be in a Randolph Applewhite production," he said.

"There now! All's well that ends well," Lucille said. "The whole point of *Eureka!* is to nourish creativity in these children, and look how creative they've been. Look how brilliantly they worked together to save the camp."

"It was never actually in danger," Randolph pointed out.

Zedediah stood up and swept his arm around the dining tent where the breakfast dishes were drawing flies and yellow jackets. "Who has KP for Community Service? The day is getting away from us. We still have a camp to run, after all!"

Chapter Thirty-six

"It seems to me," Zedediah said at that night's staff meeting, "that camp, like education, involves an adventurous quest. Kids learn not so much from what they're *taught* as from what they *do*."

"Not just kids," Sybil said. "The more I work on my children's book, the better I get! *Petunia Possum, P.I.* It's going to be a stunner."

"Don't forget magic," Lucille added. "The orbs are with us!"

"Orbs!" Paulie muttered sleepily from his perch. "Orbs, orbs, orbs."

Zedediah rubbed his hands together. "All right, then. You all have another month to encourage these kids to do what they do best—"

"Not *just* what they do best!" E.D. protested.

Jake nodded. "If that's all they do, how will they ever find out the rest of who they are?"

Hal, who almost never spoke up at a staff meeting, cleared his throat. "Like me being a counselor. Doing the hard stuff's what makes it an adventure."

"Focus, focus, focus!" Randolph said. "If we aren't going to prosecute Mrs. Montrose, it's time to get serious about an end-of-camp event that will show her and the whole of Traybridge, North Carolina, what real talent and creativity can do! Theater, dance, music, art. I say we sell tickets and rub her nose in our success!"

"We already have a theme," Lucille said. "The barn's becoming a patchwork quilt. We could make it a whole day of family activities and call it the Patchwork Summer Festival of the Arts. Just imagine it: strolling singers—"

"—storytelling for kids," Sybil added.

"Face painting!" Cordelia said. "And Q can teach people Step!"

Hal nodded. "Art gallery in the barn . . ."

Lucille clapped her hands. "Perfect! A gallery of sculpture and photographs. We can have a whole section just for orbs. We'll have to have food, of course.

Barbecue, hot dogs, fried green tomatoes. I'll see if I can get my guru, Govindaswami, to come and do a booth with Indian food. . . ."

"If Cinnamon has really tamed Wolfie, we could have a petting zoo!" Sybil said.

"And most important," Randolph said, "a show to cap it all off. We'll call it *A Patchwork Evening of Scenes and Improv.*"

"Don't forget New Fusion Movement—that's what we've decided to call it—ballet, Step, tap, and modern dance," Cordelia put in. "Jonathon told me he studied dance the whole time he was in New York. He could be in it too!"

"Sybil and I will start organizing the publicity tomorrow!" Lucille said. "It'll be a sellout."

Jake looked at E.D.; E.D. looked at Jake. Both of them sighed.

Archie, who had offered to watch the campers during the staff meeting, had built a campfire and gathered them all for a marshmallow roast to celebrate *Eureka!*'s reprieve from the state. He sent Samantha to the Lodge to invite the staff to join them after the meeting.

Jake and E.D. stood together, leaning on the porch rail, after the others had gone out to the campfire circle. Winston had settled next to them, chin on his paws.

"They're off again, aren't they?" Jake asked.

E.D. looked up at Jake's face, lit by the full moon. When had he gotten so much taller, she wondered. And why hadn't she noticed? His Mohawk had begun to tip over, softening his old delinquent look. The ring in his eyebrow glittered in the moonlight. "There's nothing like the passion of the Applewhites," she said.

"You ought to know," Jake said. "You *are* one." He grinned. "That was some act you put on today."

Jake thought back to the first time he'd seen her—not even a whole year ago. She'd had scabby elbows and knees then, chopped-off hair, and a body like a ten-year-old boy. And she had clearly hated him. The feeling, he remembered, had been mutual.

The sound of Archie's guitar floated up to them from the campfire. After a moment Harley and Ginger began to sing Ginger's latest song. "Moonlight on the water, mockingbird in the trees, come and join the laughter caught on the evening breeze. . . ." An owl hooted from the woods.

They could never say later whether E.D. had kissed Jake or Jake had kissed E.D., but Winston's tail thumped on the porch floor. Even the dog knew how much had changed.